Governing from Below

Throughout the world, more and more of policy making and the politics that shape it take place in the urban regions where most people live. This book, drawing on eleven case studies of similar but disparate urban regions in France, Germany and the United States from the 1960s into the 1990s, documents the growth of urban governance and develops a pioneering analysis of its causes and consequences. This analysis traces the origins of urban governance to the expansion as well as the devolution of policy making, to mobilization around local business and institutional interests in high-tech and service activities and to the growth and incorporation of local social movements. Although nation-states shape the possibilities for this urban governance, they operate increasingly as infrastructures for local initiatives rather than through dictates from above. Where urban governance has succeeded best in combining environmental quality and social inclusion with local prosperity, local officials have built not only on supportive infrastructures from higher levels but on regimes in the local economy and civil society and on favorable positions in the global economy.

Jefferey M. Sellers is Assistant Professor of Political Science at the University of Southern California. Professor Sellers has taught comparative public policy and comparative politics at Yale University, Boston University, Humboldt University in Berlin and the University of Southern California. His numerous fellowships include the Berlin Program of the Social Science Research Council and the Free University of Berlin and the James Bryant Conant Fellowship in German and European Studies at the Center for European Studies at Harvard University. His articles have appeared in such journals as the *Politische Vierteljahresheft*, the *Law and Society Review*, the *European Journal of Political Research*, *Ethnic and Racial Studies*, the *Journal of Urban Affairs*, and the *Yale Law Journal*.

Cambridge Studies in Comparative Politics

General Editor

Margaret Levi   *University of Washington, Seattle*

Associate Editors

Robert H. Bates   *Harvard University*
Peter Hall   *Harvard University*
Stephen Hanson   *University of Washington, Seattle*
Peter Lange   *Duke University*
Helen Milner   *Columbia University*
Frances Rosenbluth   *Yale University*
Susan Stokes   *University of Chicago*
Sidney Tarrow   *Cornell University*

Other Books in the Series

Stefano Bartolini, *The Political Mobilization of the European Left, 1860–1980: The Class Cleavage*
Carles Boix, *Political Parties, Growth and Equality: Conservative and Social Democratic Economic Strategies in the World Economy*
Catherine Boone, *Merchant Capital and the Roots of State Power in Senegal, 1930–1985*
Michael Bratton and Nicolas van de Walle, *Democratic Experiments in Africa: Regime Transitions in Comparative Perspective*
Valerie Bunce, *Leaving Socialism and Leaving the State: The End of Yugoslavia, the Soviet Union and Czechoslovakia*
Ruth Berins Collier, *Paths Toward Democracy: The Working Class and Elites in Western Europe and South America*
Donatella della Porta, *Social Movements, Political Violence, and the State*
Gerald Easter, *Reconstructing the State: Personal Networks and Elite Identity*
Roberto Franzosi, *The Puzzle of Strikes: Class and State Strategies in Postwar Italy*
Geoffrey Garrett, *Partisan Politics in the Global Economy*
Miriam Golden, *Heroic Defeats: The Politics of Job Loss*
Merilee Serrill Grindle, *Changing the State*
Frances Hagopian, *Traditional Politics and Regime Change in Brazil*
J. Rogers Hollingsworth and Robert Boyer, eds., *Contemporary Capitalism: The Embeddedness of Institutions*
Ellen Immergut, *Health Politics: Interests and Institutions in Western Europe*

Continues on page following Index

Governing from Below

URBAN REGIONS AND THE GLOBAL ECONOMY

JEFFEREY M. SELLERS

University of Southern California

CAMBRIDGE
UNIVERSITY PRESS

PUBLISHED BY THE PRESS SYNDICATE OF THE UNIVERSITY OF CAMBRIDGE
The Pitt Building, Trumpington Street, Cambridge, United Kingdom

CAMBRIDGE UNIVERSITY PRESS
The Edinburgh Building, Cambridge CB2 2RU, UK
40 West 20th Street, New York, NY 10011-4211, USA
477 Williamstown Road, Port Melbourne, VIC 3207, Australia
Ruiz de Alarcón 13, 28014 Madrid, Spain
Dock House, The Waterfront, Cape Town 8001, South Africa

http://www.cambridge.org

First published 2002

Printed in the United Kingdom at the University Press, Cambridge

Typeface Janson Text 10/13 pt.   *System* QuarkXPress [BTS]

A catalog record for this book is available from the British Library.

Library of Congress Cataloging in Publication Data
Sellers, Jefferey M.
    Governing from below : urban regions and the global economy / Jefferey M. Sellers.
        p.   cm. – (Cambridge studies in comparative politics)
    Includes bibliographical references and index.
    ISBN 0-521-65153-0 – ISBN 0-521-65707-5 (pbk.)
    1. Metropolitan government.   2. Urban economics.   3. Regional economics.   4. Globalization.
5. Metropolitan areas – United States – Case studies.   6. Metropolitan areas – France – Case
studies.   7. Metropolitan areas – Germany – Case studies.   I. Title.   II. Series.
JS241 .S45 2001
    330.9173′2 – dc21   2001022306

ISBN   0 521 65153 0   hardback
ISBN   0 521 65707 5   paperback

For one investigating the regime – what each sort is and what its quality – virtually the first investigation [is] to see what the city actually is.

Aristotle, *The Politics* (Carnes Lord, trans.)

I do not see how we can do what needs to be done until an integral part of our culture and habits of thought is a vision of the potentiality of the city as a major civilizing force; a unit of human proportions in a world grown giant, demonic, incomprehensible; an optimal site for democracy; an education in the arts and habits of democratic life; an association in which citizens can learn that collective benefits from cooperation and peaceful conflict are so great that rational self-interest must act as a restraint on self-destructive egoism; an opportunity to engage in creating a new kind of community the shape of which no expert can foresee and to which every citizen can contribute.

Robert Dahl, *After the Revolution?*

Contents

Acknowledgments

The origins of this research go back to my first attempts to understand the French state in the late 1970s. Having arrived in France for a semester to follow the national elections of 1978, I found myself confronted constantly with aspects of policies and politics in daily life that neither the national press coverage nor the existing comparative literature on French politics addressed. To develop an international comparative project to reach those matters has required years of additional work and thought. At Yale Law School I learned much of what I know about law, lawyers and political power in the United States. The initial project that led to this book took the form of a dissertation in the Political Science Department at Yale. Rogers Smith first convinced me that work like this could be done as political science, and he has served as a constant source of advice and encouragement ever since. My dissertation, an intensive comparison of local politics and society in Freiburg, Montpellier and New Haven, drew heavily on the legendary intellectual and personal generosity of my advisor, Juan Linz. Herbert Kitschelt, who gave me an opportunity to spend several additional years in Europe, played an indispensable role in the expansion and reconception of my research. Since my return to the States, Charles Maier and Abby Collins of the Harvard Center for European Studies, Alan Altshuler of the Taubman Center for State and Local Government at Harvard, David Cameron of the Yale Political Science Department and Terry Clark at the University of Chicago have provided me with crucial support during the process of writing and rewriting.

Many others have contributed to the gestation and development of this project. In addition to those who provided feedback at numerous faculty workshops and paper sessions, I would like to thank Erhard Blankenburg, Louise Davidson-Schmich, Tom Ertmann, Susan Fainstein, Mary Graham, Carol Hager, Cynthia Horan, Arn Howitt, Patrick Le Galès, Hartmut Häussermann, Vincent Hoffmann-Martinot, David Luberoff, David Mayhew, Karen Mossberger, Paul Pierson, Stephanie Pincetl, Douglas Rae, Susan Rose-Ackerman, Alberta Sbragia, James Scott, Clarence Stone, Ezra Suleiman, Todd Swanstrom and Hal Wolman. Enrico Schaar, Matthias Maier, Tom Hogen-Esch, Philipp Karch and Jeff Whitten furnished indispensable research assistance. Further thanks must go to the local officials, professionals and activists I interviewed in the cities themselves and to official statistical offices at all levels in all three countries. Carrie St. John of Chicago CartoGraphics prepared the European city maps and directed preparation of the American ones, and Jody Battles assisted in the preparations for publication. At Cambridge University Press, I would like to thank Alex Holzman, Lewis Bateman and Camilla Knapp for ushering the manuscript along and Susan Greenberg for enhancing the style in numerous places. The German Academic Exchange Service, the Council of European Studies at Columbia University, the Social Science Research Council Berlin Program in German and European Studies at the Free University of Berlin, the Yale Graduate School, the Humboldt University in Berlin, the James Bryant Conant Fellowship of the Center for European Studies at Harvard and the James F. Zumberge Research and Innovation Fund at the University of Southern California furnished financial backing at various stages. Parts of the material from the Madison and Freiburg case studies are reprinted from Jefferey M. Sellers, "Translocal Orders and Urban Environmentalism," in Keith Hoggart and Terry Clark (editors), *Citizen Responsive Government* (New York: JAI, 2000) (pp. 117–148) with permission from Elsevier Science.

My brothers and their families have given different varieties of advice, understanding and comfort. My parents have provided long-distance support of all kinds. Laura has brought not only patience but also her own unique blend of contributions to bear toward realizing this project.

1

Places in the Global Economy

Across the advanced industrial world and beyond, a far-reaching transformation is under way. For decades now, the five-hundred-year-old system of political authority that emerged with the system of European states has been giving way to a new order. Even as policy makers, the media and much of political science remain transfixed by Washington, Paris, London and Bonn, or Brussels or Frankfurt, more and more of the politics that matters most for the lives of citizens is shifting elsewhere. To secure some of the most important goals of advanced industrial society, presidents, prime ministers and elite bureaucrats look increasingly to regional economies, to private markets, to urban partnerships, to citizen activism. Efforts to promote prosperity, to protect the environment and to further equity for the disadvantaged increasingly rely on activities at the regional and local levels. This new reality requires a new realization of the role that localities and regions play in wider political economies and renewed attention to the metropolitan areas where people live. In these places lie principal sources not only of environmental and social successes but also of economic rigidities in Germany; of the mixed successes of recent policy making in France; and of persistent inequities, as well as recurrent dynamism, in policy making in the United States. In developed countries, and more starkly in the developing world, efforts to govern urban regions confront parallel dilemmas between prosperity, equity and the quality of life.

To account for a global transformation of this order requires a search for equally far-reaching causes. For many in the social sciences and public life, the explanation lies in an emerging global economy of transnational finance, mobile firms, information flows and consumer culture. The specter of a creeping dictatorship of imperatives in the

(a) Germany

(b) France

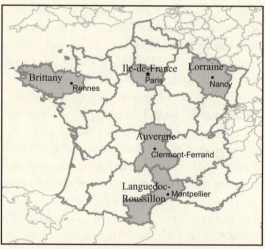

Figure 1   Locations of the City Regions and Intermediate Governments

service of business elites has haunted such accounts.[1] Yet this "global local-ization" ultimately stretches far beyond the domain of economic decision

[1] See, e.g., the discussion in Suzanne Berger and Ronald Dore (eds.), *National Diversity and Global Capitalism* (Ithaca: Cornell University Press, 1996); Robert Boyer and Daniel Drache (eds.), *States Against Markets* (London: Routledge, 1996). For applications to cities, see Saskia Sassen, *Cities in a World Economy* (Thousand Oaks, CA: Pine Forge Press, 1994); Peter Marcuse and Ronald van Kempen (eds.), *Globalizing Cities: A New Spatial Order?* (London: Blackwell, 2000). Journalistic examples include Thomas Friedman, *The Lexus and*

(c) United States

Figure 1   (*continued*)

making.[2] Much of the expansion of local initiatives has taken place in set-tings with little expectation of attracting new corporate headquarters. The sources often trace more to actors and interests within urban political economies than to pressures from without. The sheer diversity of the paths that similar urban regions in different advanced industrial countries have followed suggests how much conditions and choices within urban regions matter.

Take a western German city like Freiburg, an educational and admin-istrative center in the Black Forest mostly rebuilt on the ruins of World War II. The spotless Old Town, packed with modern department stores, bookstores and specialty shops, maintains much of the human scale of a medieval urban center. On Saturdays or in the evenings, throngs of foreign

---

the Olive Tree (New York: Farrar, Straus, Giroux, 1999); William Greider, *One World, Ready or Not* (New York: Touchstone Books, 1997).

[2] Speaking of a similar process, but retaining an economistic focus, Eri Swyngedouw uses the term "glocalisation." See "The Mammon Quest: 'Glocalisation,' Interspatial Compe-tition and the Monetary Order: The Construction of New Scales," in Mick Dunford and Grigoris Kafkalas (eds.), *Cities and Regions in the New Europe* (London: Belhaven Press, 1992), pp. 39–67.

tourists, daytime shoppers, university students and political activists converge on this central area. Outward from it, and beyond the central-city boundary, unmitigated urban sprawl is hard to find. At regular intervals throughout the urban region, a highly developed system of trolleys and buses takes riders past clusters of housing, cafés, bakeries, coffee shops and small grocery stores. Extensive forests and preserved farmland occupy the spaces in between. Social class distinctions continue to mark privileged neighborhoods around the edges of the Black Forest and have increasingly spread to outlying villages like Günsterstal and Merzhausen. But the most disadvantaged citizens rarely reside by themselves. Even industrial zones like Brühl, where the highest proportions of foreigners and unemployed residents concentrate, retain the same local shops, restaurants and bakeries as other areas of the city. Another German city of similar size will generally conform to these patterns. Even smaller, less bustling Old Towns contain many of the same stores and offices. Even in those cities that have done away with trolley systems, the convenience of buses, bicycle routes and pedestrian walkways makes it practical to commute without a car. The pockets of unemployment and ethnic minorities that have emerged in some German cities seldom add up to citywide patterns of spatial exclusion.

Among the similar-sized urban centers of provincial France, greater variety predominates. Even more than their German counterparts, the downtowns of the most fortunate French cities present showcases of prosperity. With crowds of tourists, café goers and strollers at all hours, a refurbished central square like the Place de la Comédie in Montpellier or the Place Sainte Anne in Rennes is a place to see others and to be seen. New quarters of modern malls, hotels, convention centers and fast-food restaurants surround medieval Old Towns, which have been refurbished as boutiques and offices. But in Clermont-Ferrand, as in the many other French cities that have recently suffered stagnation or decline, the twentieth century still only occasionally intrudes on the ancient facades and quieter rhythms of the old center. Outside the downtowns, the divergences deepen. Around Rennes, the regular alternations between villages and farmland contrast with the sprawl to the east and south of Montpellier, the east of Clermont-Ferrand or the south of Nancy. Disadvantaged residents also live in markedly different relations to more privileged citizens. In some urban regions, like Rennes and Clermont-Ferrand, North Africans and other minorities and the poor seldom reside separately from the rest of the population. But in cities from Paris and Lyon to Nancy and Montpellier, as the downtowns have emerged as bastions of residence for professionals and executives, desolate, high-rise estates of public housing have absorbed growing concentrations of disadvantaged groups.

In comparison with these European urban regions, the diverse urban landscapes of the United States generally share basic commonalities. European visitors often observe that urban regions like New Haven are not cities at all. Whether in fast-growing cities like those of the Sun Belt or in the declining manufacturing centers of the Northeast, downtowns share the same modest public amenities, the same jumble of architectural styles, the same emphasis on roadways over pedestrian areas, the same lack of public transit and the same ramshackle parking lots and deserted blocks. Occasionally, cities like Madison or Portland have maintained an urban center to compare with European Old Towns. In Madison, on the isthmus between Lake Mendota and Lake Monona, offices, universities and residences have helped sustain malls or other commercial centers. But beyond the central areas of most American cities, the roadways, neighborhoods, parks and commercial strips follow the predictably random pattern of urban sprawl. Shopping, offices and commercial activities concentrate in separate zones from housing and other activities. Yet even in Madison, where a drive beyond the city limits still encounters woods or prairies, only a small portion of development within those limits concentrates around the center. As in most U.S. cities, spatial demarcations along ethnic, racial and socioeconomic lines have long pervaded the entire urban region. Madison has its neighborhoods of immense tracts and large houses, its subdivisions of middle- and working-class whites and its concentrations of minorities and the poor.

All politics is local. Coined by the late U.S. House Speaker, Tip O'Neill, the expression grew originally out of the legislative politics of a peculiarly American federalism. Yet throughout the contemporary developed world, a portion of the politics that matters has always centered in the neighborhoods and urban regions where people live, work and play. Expanding local activities of this sort have produced and accentuated these divergences in urban landscapes. Rather than simply reflect mobilization from the top down in either politics or markets, local businesses, institutions, activists, consumers and voters have themselves caused much of the difference. Within states this localization has outstripped what traditional notions of formal devolution from above can encompass and has come about through the expansion as well as the contraction of policy making from above. Within the economy, local coalitions have often done more to spur integration into widening systems of production, marketing, networks and service provision than have global actors like international firms.

This chapter sets out a framework for analysis of these developments. The next section outlines the considerations that any such analysis must take into account and the issues of policy my analysis will consider. I conclude with an overview of the research design for this study.

The Global, the National and the Local: A Framework and Alternative Models

To analyze the role of local actors and conditions in the pathways of urban regions requires a conceptual framework that also takes into account other influences. Within an urban region, the actions and institutions that comprise *urban governance*, or local efforts to shape local society, need to be separated out from local social and spatial conditions. These local influences can be fully understood only in light of the governments, policies, institutions and organized interests embedded at higher levels of the state, and translocal markets and economic actors.

The simplest and in a sense the most elegant accounts of localized governance have analyzed it as a matter of bargaining and institution building among the property owners or other stakeholders who seek to cooperate in a given setting.[3] In urban political economy, however, patterns of inequality, power and conflict define who can govern urban regions at all. Perhaps the most pervasive question in this field concerns the very possibility of localized governance in such settings. Both neoclassical and neomarxist accounts of urban political economy have frequently insisted on the decisive influence of external capital or markets on policy making within city regions.[4] The growing body of international comparative work on urban political economies, focused mostly on the biggest metropoles of advanced industrial societies, has developed a set of propositions about economic globalization that mirror much of these earlier accounts.

[3] See, e.g., Elinor Ostrom, *Governing the Commons* (New York: Cambridge University Press, 1990); Robert Ellickson, *Order Without Law* (Cambridge, MA: Harvard University Press, 1992).

[4] See, e.g., Manuel Castells, *The Urban Question* (London: Edward Arnold, 1977); David Harvey, *The Urban Experience* (Oxford: Basil Blackwell, 1989); Paul Peterson, *City Limits* (Chicago: University of Chicago Press, 1981).

Places in the Global Economy

In what might be called a theory of global urban dualization,[5] this analysis has centered around urban concentrations of financial capital, corporate headquarters and related producer services. From these settings, the theory holds that mobile, externally oriented economic elites have grown to dominate both the world economy and the political economy of urban regions. Under the sway of this influence, local development and related policies serve the interests of the very rich in technologically advanced offices, penthouse apartments, luxury hotels and expensive restaurants and protect the occupants of these privileged sites from unwanted intrusions. At the same time, as skilled blue-collar work in these same cities gives way to jobs that employ unskilled, largely immigrant labor or to unemployment that causes poverty, urban economies suffer from increasing spatial and social polarization. Local choices in favor of global elites preempt social, environmental and other measures to address the needs of disadvantaged groups and wider publics. Although initial accounts of global economic dualism pointed to a small number of "global cities" at the peak of urban hierarchies as the sites of the transformation, other analyses point to similar processes in other large cities and beyond.[6]

Even though much of the literature on this subject has built upon cross-national urban comparisons, it has so far neglected to confront the most direct and obvious challenge to this view of global transformation. Long before political science emerged as a professionalized discipline, the study of comparative politics demonstrated the difference that nation-states make for what goes on within them. In recent analyses of economic, social and even environmental outcomes, the analytic tools and concepts of a "new institutionalism" now fortify these traditional contentions that nations in fact matter.[7] Neoinstitutionalist work leaves little doubt that

---

[5] Work in this vein includes Robert Reich, *The Work of Nations* (New York: Random House, 1991); Sassen, *World Economy*; John Friedmann, "The World City Hypothesis," *Development and Change 17* (1986): 69–84; H. V. Savitch, "The Emergence of Global Cities," *Urban Affairs Review 31*(1) (1995): 137–142. For a similar characterization, see James W. White, "Old Wine, Cracked Bottles: Paris, Tokyo and the Global City Thesis," *Urban Affairs Review 33*(4) (1998): 492–521.

[6] See, e.g., Marcuse and van Kempen, *Globalizing Cities*; Kenneth A. Gould, Allan Schnaiberg and Adam S. Weinberg, *Local Environmental Struggles* (Cambridge: Cambridge University Press, 1996).

[7] Paul J. DiMaggio and Walter W. Powell (eds.), *The New Institutionalism in Organizational Analysis* (Chicago: University of Chicago Press, 1991), pp. 41–62; Peter Hall and Rosemary Taylor, "Political Science and the Three New Institutionalisms," James G. March and Johan P. Olsen, *Rediscovering Institutions Political Studies 44*(5) (1996): 936–957;

institutional arrangements at national scales help make collective action possible, determine much of the thrust of that action, shape the linkages between elites and the remainder of societies and often resist pressures for subservience to the demands of mobile firms and capital.

Of course, cross-national comparative analysis of institutions at the national level alone remains ill-suited to account for the political trajectories of urban regions. In part, this necessity results from purely methodological considerations. Since varying local social and economic conditions may affect the realization of urban policy, holding these conditions equal through selection of subnational cases enables an analysis to better single out the differences that nation-states themselves make.[8] At the same time, compelling substantive reasons arise from the lasting challenge that studies of urban power, such as Dahl's *Who Governs?*,[9] have presented to elitist accounts of the way national political institutions and economies operate. Mayor Richard Lee of Dahl's New Haven rarely comes across as in thrall to the federal department heads and congressmen higher up in the hierarchy of formal state authorities. Rather, his entrepreneurship is what makes urban renewal work. His initiatives in search of resources take him to the grant programs of the federal and state governments, to the political ties of the national party systems and to the networks of informal contacts that linked Yale University alumni and benefactors. Within the city of New Haven and its suburbs he cultivates lateral connections among a local political coalition, local businesses and neighborhood groups. Even as national urban programs proved indispensable to many of Mayor Lee's efforts, Dahl and his students have sustained a convincing case that the mayor and his executive-centered coalition were crucial to bringing those programs to New Haven.

As a touchstone of the U.S. academic literature on urban politics, the endeavors of Mayor Lee have come to exemplify the specific activities that

---

(New York: Free Press, 1989); Sven Steinmo, Kathleen Thelen and Frank Longstreth, *Structuring Politics* (New York: Cambridge University Press, 1992).

[8] Phillip Gregg, "Units and Levels of Analysis: A Problem [of] Policy Analysis in Federal Systems," *Publius* (1974): 59–108; Arendt Lipjhart, "The Comparative Method," *American Political Science Review* 65(3) (1973): 682–693; Adam Przeworski and Henry Teune, *The Logic of Comparative Social Inquiry* (New York: Wiley-Interscience, 1970); Juan J. Linz and Amando de Miguel, "Within-Nation Differences and Comparisons: The Eight Spains," in Richard L. Merritt and Rokkan Stein (eds.), *Comparing Nations: The Use of Quantitative Data in Cross-National Research* (New Haven: Yale University Press, 1966), pp. 267–319.

[9] Robert Dahl, *Who Governs? Democracy and Power in an American City* (New Haven: Yale University Press, 1961).

I will call urban governance. I use this term to single out the actions and institutions within an urban region that regulate or impose conditions for its political economy. In light of the growing number of uses to which the term has been put,[10] it is important to distinguish clearly what urban governance is and is not. It often includes or even relies on governmental participation, but it could just as well depend on business and labor groups, parapublic companies or neighborhood associations alone. It could rely on either informal coordination or formal organization and on initiatives from below in the state or in private organizations as well as on decisions handed down from above. Activities of this sort within the urban region comprise part of this governance; what occurs outside does not. Although a local territorial official or a local office of a national firm can participate directly in urban governance, a ministry official or an international corporate executive with no personal connection to the city cannot. Although the control, regulation and transformation that define this governance revolve mainly around the specialized initiatives of elites and activists, these are not the only relevant local actors. The citizen who votes and the consumer who buys a home also exercise more limited choices within the range of alternatives offered them. At the same time, their anticipated choices also figure in the calculations of developers, political officials and activists.

To understand how this governance varies among countries necessitates a kind of *multilevel* comparison that has all too rarely been attempted. Either urban governance itself or the wider institutions and other practices within which those actions nest can have the more decisive effect on policy. Only comparison that considers influences from various levels, and that takes into account other local influences beyond urban governance itself, can furnish a full assessment of which influences are most important. The existing literature identifies several general categories of influences to be taken into account.

First, as the preceding has already suggested, *translocal markets and market actors* need to be assigned a crucial place. Analyses focused on the largest metropoles have developed a broad account of how the far-reaching economic changes of recent decades in advanced capitalist countries have also transformed the political economies of cities. But the ultimate implications

---

[10] For a discussion, see the essays in Jon Pierre (ed.), *Governance* (Oxford: Oxford University Press, 1999).

of these changes extend beyond the economic domains that have preoccupied these analyses and far beyond the cities generally recognized as
"global" or "world cities."

Several types of changes linked to the emerging global economy entail
especially important implications for the urban regions of advanced industrial society. First, technological innovation has helped make growing
mobility possible among firms, people, information and capital. Although
the international dimension of these flows most easily accords with
the term "globalization," mobility among places within countries or
even within city regions themselves belongs to the same global shift.[11]
Most analyses of this emerging political economy have focused on
the increasing global reach of financial networks and the consolidation
of firms and markets. But consumers also now face more global (if not
always more varied) choices among products and services. City residents
commute more. Tourists travel more. Second, especially in advanced
industrial societies, technology and innovation have increasingly determined the possibilities for prosperity.[12] Since the human capital that
grows out of education and high levels of skill comprises an essential
element in research, development and applications of technology, this
element has also emerged as an increasingly crucial prerequisite for the
economies of nations as well as urban regions. With these transformations
in the most developed countries, globalizing firms have found it increasingly efficient to shift manufacturing production to sites with lower wages
and other costs in the developing world. As a result of both processes,
advanced industrial countries have become service economies.

The thesis of global urban dualization looks to these developments to
explain urban transformations.[13] Focused on the biggest cities, and above
all on centers of international finance like London, New York and Tokyo,
this theory points to how communication, coordination and travel have
strengthened global networks among business, financial and professional
elites. Since this group dominates the politics and service industries of the
city, postindustrial reconstruction centers around elite demands for ser-

---

[11] For the broadest, most ambitious account of these developments, see Manuel Castells, *The
Information Age*, 3 vols. (Malden, MA: Blackwell, 1997).

[12] Reich, *The Work of Nations*; Susan E. Clarke and Gary Gaile, *The Work of Cities*
(Minneapolis: University of Minnesota Press, 1998).

[13] See Marcuse and van Kempen, *Globalizing Cities*; Sassen, *World Economy*; Janet L. Abu-
Lughod, *New York, Chicago, Los Angeles: America's Global Cities* (Minneapolis: University of
Minnesota Press, 1999).

vices, infrastructure and amenities in urban economies. Even the concentrations of immigrants and minorities in these centers grow partly out of the need for cheap labor to be employed in these activities. Alongside social polarization, increasing spatial polarization separates out elite enclaves and poor ghettos.

Accounts like that of Gould, Schnaiberg, and Weinberg suggest that much of this model can be extended throughout the economies of developed countries.[14] Indeed, only the unproven assumption that financial and business elites in the biggest cities have accumulated growing control over the rest of the global economy limits the applicability to these metropoles. Such an assumption not only flies in the face of substantial evidence of decentralization in business organization,[15] but neglects two fundamental economic transformations that also have major implications for urban regions. First, technology and applied innovation have proven at least as pivotal for developed economies as systems of finance.[16] The activities that serve these ends extend far beyond the summits of corporate and professional hierarchies. The institutions and companies that pursue research and development have increasingly emerged as crucial. Organizations like hospitals and universities, as well as milieux of other private professionals and firms, serve the critical function of applying innovation. Systems of education prepare future workers and citizens to participate in these activities.[17]

Second, as national job statistics in advanced industrial societies attest, a diverse array of services has replaced manufacturing production as the main source of employment (Figure 1.1). Rooted partly in the growth of disposable wealth among large portions of the population, these activities extend far beyond matters of technological innovation. As a proportion of business activities, such sectors as hotels and restaurants have often grown as fast as financial and business services. Among social and personal

---

[14] Gould, Schnaiberg and Weinberg, *Local Environmental Struggles*; see also the essays in Marcuse and van Kempen, *Globalizing Cities*.

[15] Following the logic of transaction costs analysis (see, e.g., Oliver Williamson, *The Economic Institutions of Capitalism* [New York: Free Press, 1985]), much of the case for global integration in the literature on business management rests on the growing possibilities for more decentralized, diffuse forms of organization. See Elizabeth Moss Kanter, *World Class* (New York: Simon and Schuster, 1995), pp. 46–48.

[16] See Robert J. Barro and Xavier Sala-i-Martin, *Economic Growth* (New York: McGraw-Hill, 1995); Gene M. Grossman and Elhanan Helpman, *Innovation and Growth in the Global Economy* (Cambridge, MA: MIT Press, 1991).

[17] Clarke and Gaile, *The Work of Cities*.

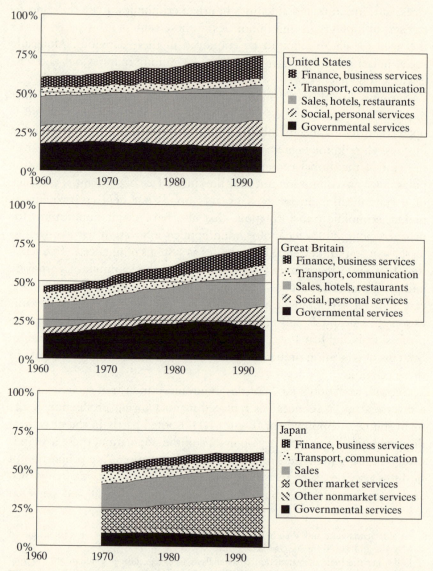

Figure 1.1 The Rise of Services to Predominance in Advanced Industrial Economies, 1960–1995 (Proportion of Total Employment in Service Industries) *Source*: OECD, *International Sectoral Data Base, 1960–1995*, Disk files.

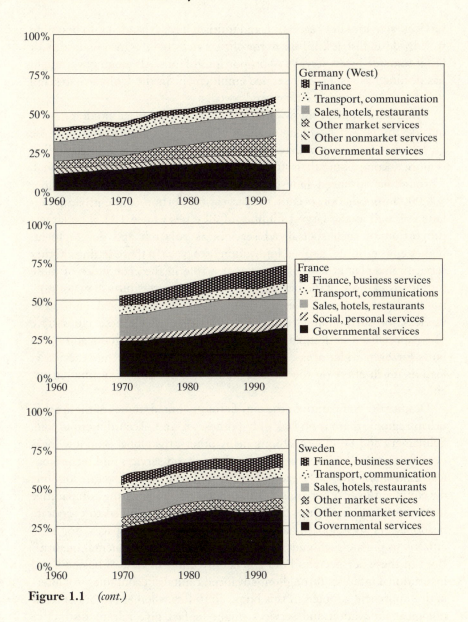

Figure 1.1 *(cont.)*

services, activities like recreation and tourism have expanded into booming worldwide industries. Often nonprofit services have grown as fast as or faster than for-profit services as proportions of jobs. Although government has declined as a source of service employment in the United States and Britain, it has grown in France and Sweden.

Since both applied innovation and services take place predominantly outside the largest cities, an analysis of how the transformations in the global economy relate to urban political economies requires research that is more encompassing than studies of these settings have so far attempted. Throughout advanced industrial societies, urban service centers under 500,000 in population occupy the largest proportion of the urban population as well as the largest number of all cities (Table 1.1). The largest proportion of such specialized services as research and development, higher education and applied innovation take place in these settings. Other services also play at least as prominent a role in the economies of these settings as in those of the biggest cities. Service centers furnish major portions of governmental, health, administrative, recreational and other services for surrounding regions. At the same time, these cities have often specialized as destinations for tourists, convention goers and opera buffs for even wider areas. Global economic shifts have thus exerted at least as much effect on the parallel settings of this sort as on the biggest cities.

Despite the comparative absence of cross-national studies of these other urban regions, there is no lack of hypotheses to test. According to Gould, Schnaiberg and Weinberg, among many others, the global economy locks even those urban political economies that rely on services and technological innovation into a "treadmill of production" that fosters economic development over other ends.[18] Still others, emphasizing the comparative insulation of these settings from economic pressures linked to corporate headquarters and global finance, have pointed to "free spaces" for local citizens to pursue such ends as social justice and environmental quality.[19] Both of these perspectives hold a generally uniform view of business and institutional interests throughout advanced capitalist economies. An alternative approach, adopted in this book, considers whether sectors of technological innovation and services might in fact give rise to distinctive

---

[18] Gould, Schnaiberg and Weinberg, *Local Environmental Struggles*.

[19] Sarah M. Evans and Harry C. Boyte, *Free Spaces: The Sources of Democratic Change in America* (New York: Harper and Row, 1986).

Table 1.1 *Metropolitan Centers, Service Centers and Other Urban Centers in the Urban Systems of Advanced Industrial Countries, 1980s–1990s*

	Metropolitan Centers (Over 500,000)		Mid-sized Urban Service Centers (50,000–500,000 and over 50 percent of employed in tertiary occupations)		Mid-sized Urban Centers of Manufacturing and Other Activities (50,000–500,000 and under 50 percent employed in tertiary occupations)	
	All Cities (%) (number)	National Urban Population (%)	All Cities (%) (number)	National Urban Population (%)	All Cities (%) (number)	National Urban Population (%)
Germany (1987)	7.2 (11)	37.6	70.4 (107)	51.4	15.8 (24)	11.0
France* (1990)	5.0 (2)	33.1	75.0 (30)	55.2	20.0 (8)	11.6
United States (1990)	5.5 (24)	38.9	77.3 (338)	52.4	17.4 (76)	9.4
Japan (1989)	5.3 (23)	29.7	70.3 (300)	58.0	26.9 (115)	12.4
Sweden (1986)	2.9 (1)	16.7	82.9 (29)	74.6	17.1 (6)	8.7

* French data only for cities with populations over 100,000.

Source: Fiscal Austerity and Urban Innovation Project data.

economic interests within these urban political economies.[20] The local and regional economic interests in a service center, for instance, should have more reason to follow a logic of serving and maintaining consumer demands than one of producing goods. To survive and prosper in inter-local markets for services, high-tech activities, local firms and institutions should have to attract higher-status workers, well-to-do consumers and mobile clienteles. These collective interests at the core of an urban political economy can furnish economic rationales for the pursuit of other aims besides economic development.

Even recent analyses of the biggest cities have pointed to less uniform, more ambiguous influence from the emerging global economy on urban regions than earlier, simpler models of globalization suggested.[21] Closer examination of urban contexts beyond metropolitan centers will ultimately generate new insights into the local significance of global economic transformations in the biggest cities.

Governmental and political influences encompass a range of policies and institutions usually imbedded at higher levels of government. Alongside familiar classifications of territorial structures like federalism and unitary government at higher levels of states, more recently established typologies of local government and politics furnish part of the basis for understanding how these influences vary. A full analysis requires attention to the state-society relations of urban regions and to lateral relations among municipalities.

Recent comparative classifications of local government and politics in advanced industrial societies have retained a traditional focus on formal governmental institutions.[22] These analyses have set out largely similar

---

[20] For a rare analysis of economic sectoral influences on urban governance, see Cynthia Horan, "Beyond Governing Coalitions: Analyzing Urban Regimes in the 1990s," *Journal of Urban Affairs 13*(2) (1991): 119–135.

[21] See the arguments in White, "Old Wine," 1998 and the qualifications in Marcuse and von Kempen, *Globalizing Cities*.

[22] Robert J. Bennett, "European Local Government Systems," in Robert J. Bennett (ed.), *Local Government in the New Europe* (London: Belhaven Press, 1993); Arthur Gunlicks, *Local Government in the Federal Republic of Germany* (Durham: Duke University Press, 1986); Edward Page and Michael J. Goldsmith (eds.), *Central and Local Government Relations: A Comparative Analysis of West European Unitary States* (London: Sage, 1987); Mike Goldsmith, "Autonomy and City Limits," in David Judge, Gerry Stoker and Harold Wolman (eds.), *Theories of Urban Politics* (London: Sage, 1995), pp. 228–252; J. J. Hesse and L. J. Sharpe, "Conclusions," in J. J. Hesse (ed.), *Local Government and Urban Affairs in International Perspective* (Baden-Baden: Nomos, 1991), pp. 603–621.

Table 1.2 *National Infrastructures of Local Government and Politics: The Three Main Systems*

	Northern Europe	Southern Europe	(Anglo-)American
Administration	*(Local)*	*(Supralocal)*	*(Local)*
Governmental organization, finance	Standardized but decentralized	Centralized (prefectoral system)	Decentralized, unstandardized
Legal supply	Extensive local authorities	Administrative regulation	Limited, functional authority
Politics	*(Supralocal)*	*(Local)*	*(Local)*
Supralocal representation of municipal interests	Weak	Strong	Moderate
Political parties, organized interests	Strong	Moderate	Weak

typologies of the principal cross-national variations in local governmental organization, public finance and political representation. Derived from cumulative histories, each type rests on distinctive, interrelated logics of political representation on the one hand and policy making on the other. In northern European areas like Scandinavia and the Germanic countries, systems of law and administration assign local governments a major role in the implementation of national programs (Table 1.2). At the same time national systems of rules, finance and public administration standardize much of what local officials can do and how they can do it. As strong national political parties and highly organized national economic interests dominate policy making, the system of central-local relations allows representatives of municipalities little opportunity for influence.

In the southern European countries where Napoleonic reforms introduced the prefectoral system, as well as in Japan and those parts of eastern Europe and Latin America that adopted similar systems, territorial officials at the local level have traditionally administered rules. Conversely, municipal officials have lacked much of the legal authority or independent administrative capacity of their northern European counterparts. At the same time, mayors and other local territorial representatives have wielded greater influence over policy making at higher levels as well as implementation of those policies. Political parties and organized interests have remained weaker at the local level and have less dominated intergovernmental representation of local interests.

Hesse and Sharpe assign the United States along with most other former English colonies to a third category. Although legal authorizations and sometimes local finance often limit local authority in these settings, processes of policy making and administration also assign much of what the state undertakes to local discretion. In many U.S. states, this choice extends to forms of local government. Supralocal rules impose less standardization on these decisions from above than in northern Europe. In the presence of weaker political parties and less hierarchically organized economic interests, representatives of cities have often asserted interests in policy at various supralocal levels.[23] Much of local politics remains subject to purely local decisions.

Such typologies cannot be subsumed into the distinct tradition of analyses based on state structures at higher levels. Vertical organizational integration of this last sort, embodied largely in differences between centralized, unitary structures and decentralized, federal ones, often coexists with more than one type of local government and politics. The northern European infrastructure pertains as much to a federal state like Germany as to centralized, unitary ones like Sweden and Austria. The southern European infrastructure has persisted in more decentralized countries like Italy and Spain as well as in the centralized France of the Gaullist state. Only occasionally, as in the United States, do the organizational patterns of the infrastructure for local government and politics mirror patterns at higher levels. At both levels, the globalization of corporate and financial activity and the global diffusion of ideas about such policies as privatization threaten inroads into national divergences.

Neither divergences nor any such convergence can be fully understood without analyses that take account of national institutional influences beyond government and politics. In part, as this book will show, this necessity stems from the importance of lateral relations among municipal governments. At the same time that cooperation among localities plays a direct role in efforts to address such problems as urban sprawl and social segre-

---

[23] On this specific point, which plays less of a role in their typology than in that of Page and Goldsmith, see Stephen Erie, *Rainbow's End* (Berkeley: University of California Press, 1988); Nancy Burns and Gerald Gamm, "Creatures of the State," *Urban Affairs Review 33* (1997): 59–97.

gation,[24] work on fiscal federalism highlights direct correspondences between the territorial allocation of governmental functions and finance and the dynamics of interlocal markets.[25]

A generation of scholarly work on the organization and incorporation of economic interests like business, labor and farmers into governance at multiple levels also points to the significance of formalized or corporatist systems of economic-interest representation in places like Sweden, Germany and Austria. Rarely have the influences of these systems on urban political economies been compared with that of less-organized or pluralist systems such as the United States. Yet at the higher levels of aggregation, of which urban regions comprise a dominant part, such institutions appear to have influenced not just social equity but environmental policy and economic dynamism.[26]

Besides organized interests, the potentially relevant local and translocal influences extend to regulatory instruments, parapublic organization and other means that tie local officials to the urban economy and local business to officials. Beyond the domain of business and institutional interests alone, procedural mechanisms, public subsidies and market encouragements have also contributed to the growing but diverse role of neighborhood, social and environmental movements in urban political economies.

Closer attention to these areas will ultimately point to the role that urban political economies play in national patterns of governance and the need to reconceptualize the difference that nation-states make for the governance of urban regions. As policy initiatives from above have dictated less and less of the actual governance pursued from below, national infrastructures for government and politics within urban regions have grown

---

[24] See Gregg, "Units and Levels of Analysis," George Frederickson, "The Repositioning of American Public Administration," *PS: Political Science and Politics 32*(4) (1999): 701–711.

[25] See, e.g., Paul Peterson, *The Price of Federalism* (Washington, DC: Brookings, 1995); David Wildasn (ed.), *Fiscal Aspects of Evolving Federations* (Cambridge: Cambridge University Press, 1997).

[26] See, e.g., Geoffrey Garrett, *Partisan Politics and the Global Economy* (New York: Cambridge University Press 1998); Lyle Scruggs, "Institutions and Environmental Performance in Seventeen Western Democracies," *British Journal of Political Science 29* (1999): 11–31; David R. Cameron, "Politics, Public Policy, and Distributional Inequality: A Comparative Analysis," in Grant Reeher and Ian Shapiro (eds.), *Essays in Honor of Robert Dahl* (New Haven: Yale University Press, 1989), pp. 219–259; David Soskice, "Innovation Strategies of Companies: A Comparative Institutional Approach of Some Cross-Country Differences," in Wolfgang Zapf and Meinolf Dierkes (eds.), *Institutionenvergleich und Institutionendynamik* (Berlin: Edition Sigma, 1994), pp. 271–289.

19

in significance for local outcomes. Only research that encompasses state-society relations within and among cities as well as government and politics can furnish the proper basis to analyze these infrastructures. As this book will ultimately demonstrate, these wider relations also follow distinctive patterns.

No sharp line delineates the translocal influences of governments, firms and markets on cities from the strictly *internal components of an urban political economy*. Yet even a model of urban political economy that denies the importance of agency within city regions must take account of the geography and the socioeconomic structures particular to an urban region.

Geographers emphasize the *spatial structures* of an urban political economy.[27] Like the policies and institutions of the wider state, the natural and built environments fix conditions that politics and markets can rarely avoid and must often draw upon. Transportation arteries, residential and business construction, property rights to specific land and corridors of new development all embody elements of spatial structure. Though often linked to national urban traditions,[28] these spatial influences are fundamentally local. Although U.S. cities generally lack the medieval built inheritances of European Old Towns, for instance, older, preserved urban cores exist in the United States as well as in Europe. Distinct types of spatial arrangements also grow out of the economic history of a city region. Manufacturing from the industrial age, for instance, leaves factories to be converted or torn down and pollution to be remedied. Specialized service centers that escaped the industrial revolution can derive advantages from the lack of such legacies.

The *social structures* of everyday life among households, workers and citizens also help to determine the character of an urban political economy. Occupational status and ethnic formations define much of the identities

[27] See, e.g., Kevin Cox, "Governance, Urban Regime Analysis, and the Politics of Local Economic Development," in Mickey Lauria (ed.), *Reconstructing Urban Regime Theory* (Thousand Oaks, CA: Sage, 1997), pp. 99–121; Michael Dear, *The Postmodern Urban Condition* (Oxford: Blackwell, 2000).
[28] Arnaldo Bagnasco and Patrick Le Galès, "Les villes européennes comme société et comme acteur," in Arnaldo Bagnasco and Patrick Le Galès (eds.), *Villes en Europe* (Paris: La Découverte, 1997), pp. 7–46; Norman I. Fainstein and Susan S. Fainstein, "Restructuring the American City: A Comparative Perspective," in Norman I. Fainstein and Susan S. Fainstein (eds.), *Urban Policy Under Capitalism* (Berverly Hills, CA: Sage, 1982), pp. 161–190.

and resources available to be mobilized in urban politics. Partly reflective of national variations, these social structures also differ domestically among urban regions. The greater predominance of services in the United States, for instance, has generated more of both higher-status and lower-status service jobs than in many European countries.[29] Yet both major metropoles and specialized service centers with larger proportions of these workers exist in all advanced industrial countries. Regardless of the national context, professional and managerial workers and students play a larger role in both the electoral and market constituencies of these urban centers. In centers of traditional manufacturing, the industrial working class retains a similarly disproportionate presence. Ethnic and racial groupings make up a further element of urban social structure. Deepening division within metropoles between higher-status white elites and the growing populations of impoverished immigrants and minorities figures prominently in accounts of global urban dualization. The growing numbers of isolated, disadvantaged immigrant minorities in Europe have increasingly prompted comparisons with U.S. minorities like African Americans.[30]

Since the earliest debates about community power in the United States of the 1950s, the relation of urban governance to these other influences has posed a persistent question. A consistent strain of analysis, reflected in contemporary accounts of global urban dualization, has minimized the importance of urban governance for the fate of city regions.[31] A contrasting strain, exemplified in Dahl's study of Mayor Lee asserts that urban governance in fact matters. Constructed from the categories of influences just surveyed, two alternative models of urban political economy will serve to frame the issue more precisely.

---

[29] Gosta Esping-Andersen, *Changing Classes* (London: Sage, 1993); Wallace Clement and John Myles, *Relations of Ruling* (Montreal: McGill-Queen's University Press, 1994).

[30] W. J. Wilson, *When Work Disappears: The World of the New Urban Poor* (New York: Knopf, 1996); Ronald van Kempen and Peter Marcuse, "A New Spatial Order in Cities?" *American Behavioral Scientist* 41(3) (1997): 285–298; Loïc J. D. Wacquant, "Urban Outcasts: Stigma and Division in the Black American Ghetto and the French Urban Periphery," *International Journal of Urban and Regional Research* 17(3) (1993): 366–383.

[31] Paul Kantor, *The Dependent City Revisited: The Political Economy of Urban Development and Social Policy* (Boulder: Westview Press, 1995); Peterson, *City Limits*; Fainstein and Fainstein, "New Haven: The Limits of the Local State," in Susan S. Fainstein, Norman I. Fainstein, Richard C. Hill, Dennis Judd and Michael P. Smith (eds.), *Restructuring the City*, 2nd ed. (New York: Longman, 1986), pp. 27–79.

Begin with the null hypothesis, or what can be called a Hierarchical Model. This model emphasizes the effects from translocal politics and policy on the one hand and the global economy on the other (Figure 1.2). The outcomes from policies and markets depend on the spatial and social structures of an urban region and on how translocal political and economic forces respond to and transform those structures. In a model where the global economy alone dominated, the global would determine the local. Regardless of the national or regional context, service centers would give rise to one set of results, manufacturing centers to another. A more complex version would recognize national institutions, policies and organized interests as a source of qualifications to global forces but would still ascribe no effective agency to local efforts. Even cross-national comparative studies focused on local outcomes have sometimes presumed that the policies and politics that matter for local outcomes only do so at the more aggregated scales of higher-level governments.[32] Under either version of the Hierarchical Model, local agency corresponds at best to the random "noise" of an error term in a regression. Actors within an urban region face no other realistic choices than what translocal forces offer them. Not only the global city–dual city hypotheses, but much of earlier structuralist and public choice analyses of urban political economy would concur with some version of this model.

A model centered around urban governance challenges this view of local agency. Here the collective action among the politicians, administrators, voters, businesses, movements and activists within a metropolitan area contributes to outcomes in systematic ways. Even the property owners who come together to regulate common property interests in a neighborhood or the upper-middle-class home owners who converge on a gentrifying neighborhood take part to some degree in this governance.[33] In its more encompassing forms, urban governance relies on electoral coalitions and governing alliances with businesses and others in the community to surmount the institutional and social fragmentation that often pervades city regions. Governing coalitions that manage to institutionalize their

---

[32] This appears to be the implication in Margaret Weir, "Poverty, Social Rights and the Politics of Place," in Paul Pierson and Stefan Leibfried (eds.), *European Social Policy* (Washington: The Brookings Institution, 1996), pp. 329–354. The analysis of Paul Kantor, H. V. Savitch and Serena Vicari Haddock, "The Political Economy of Urban Regimes," *Urban Affairs Review 32* (January 1997): 348–377, suggests a similar dual determinism.

[33] Elinor Ostrom, *Governing the Commons* (Cambridge: Cambridge University Press, 1990); Neil Smith, *The New Urban Frontier* (London: Routledge, 1996).

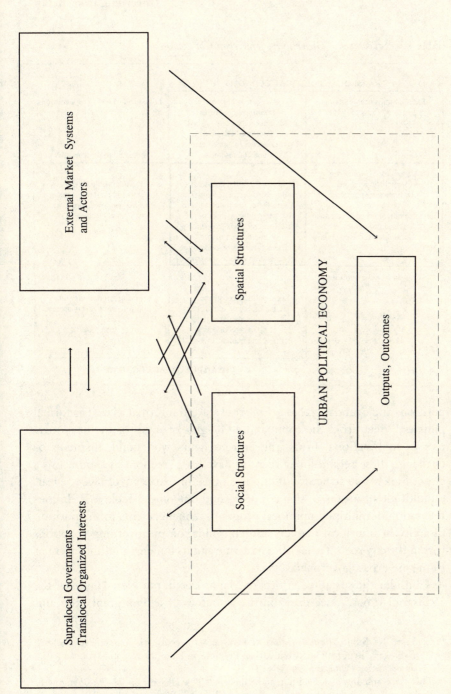

Figure 1.2 A Hierarchical Model of Urban Political Economy

Table 1.3. *Structures of Opportunity for Urban Governance*

TRANSLOCAL POLITICAL ECONOMY

(External translocal relations)	(Asymmetrical influences) Multilocational firms Markets among city regions Translocal clienteles Production networks and markets Financial resources	**Translocal Market Opportunities**
		Local Spatial Structures
(Asymmetrical influences) Clientelistic relations Discretionary policies Financial resources Infrastructure of urban governance Translocal parties Translocal interest organization	Local governmental autonomy (in policy, finance, implementation) Metro firms, institutions, plants Metropolitan markets Interlocal relations (cooperative and competitive) Electoral coalition-building Incorporation of local movements	Settlement patterns Natural and built environment Jurisdictions within metro area Spatial "lock-ins"
Translocal policy/politics		
Local Social Structures	Local political constituencies (ethnic, racial, socioeconomic) Local market clienteles (ethnic, racial, socioeconomic) Political and market "lock-ins"	(Portions of everyday life uninvolved in governance)

URBAN POLITICAL ECONOMY

positions and agendas create *urban regimes* from informal as well as formal policies.[34] Seen from the commanding heights of states or the headquarters of multinational firms, the entrepreneurs who build, maintain or challenge these regimes may seem to have little freedom of action. But a closer look at the structure of opportunities for urban governance reveals a multitude of means to shape outputs and outcomes (Table 1.3). Implementation of multiple supralocal programs, enhancements to the position of a city in translocal markets and consolidation of governing coalitions within the city region itself offer a regime and its builders multiple avenues to pursue urban governance.

Consider the sustained efforts of Mayor Lee in the New Haven of the 1950s and 1960s.[35] Lee drew on the resources of federal grant programs

[34] Clarence N. Stone, *Regime Politics* (Lawrence: University of Kansas Press, 1989); Gerry Stoker, "Regime Theory and Urban Politics," in Judge, Stoker and Wolman (eds.), *Theories of Urban Politics*, pp. 54–71.

[35] This paragraph draws on Fainstein and Fainstein, "New Haven," pp. 27–79; Raymond E. Wolfinger, *The Politics of Progress* (Englewood Cliffs, NJ: Prentice-Hall, 1974).

obtained from above and on powers in the city government derived from the state-sanctioned city charter. He relied on translocal connections with prominent businessmen to bring such projects as the Chapel Square Mall to the downtown. Within the city's political economy itself, the process of demolition and new construction helped "lock in" the mayor's agendas.[36] Initial investments in downtown clearance rendered completion of renewal an inescapable need; once construction on the downtown stretches of Interstate 91 had begun, it became more efficient to complete them than to leave the sites unfinished. At the same time Lee "locked in" political and economic commitments to his development strategy among downtown businesses. Opportunities to participate in new construction contracts or to carry out projects of their own secured support from individual firms. Yale University and downtown banks gained a chance for reconstruction of their surroundings. In the efforts of the city under the Model Cities program, representatives of minority communities gained influence in the local political and administrative process.

These activities amount more to *mediating* influences than to fully independent ones[37] (Figure 1.3). The agency in urban governance not only is difficult to separate out from other institutions and contextual influences but often depends on them. Mayor Lee, for instance, depended heavily on federal programs to build a local governing coalition. Regimes built around the strong attractions of a city in translocal markets for new offices or high-tech companies depend in similar ways on outside forces. But even the necessity of these translocal influences need not make urban governance any less important. Over time, as a result of the repeated efforts of Mayor Lee, a regime of arrangements for governance emerged within the central city around his electoral and governing coalitions.

Even a Hierarchical Model can ill afford to neglect the local structural conditions that can alter the significance of translocal influences. But over much of the history of urban political economy, the opposition between this kind of model and the Model of Urban Governance has dominated theoretical discussion. For the biggest cities, if not for others, theories

---

[36] On the process of "lock ins," see Brian W. Arthur, *Increasing Returns and Path Dependence in the Economy* (Ann Arbor: University of Michigan Press, 1994); Anthony Woodlief, "The Path-Dependent City," *Urban Affairs Review 33*(3) (1998): 405–437.

[37] For a similar point about urban regimes, see Clarence N. Stone, "Urban Regime Analysis: Theory, Service Provision and Cross-National Consideration," paper prepared for Joint Sessions of the European Consortium for Political Research, Bern, Switzerland, 1997.

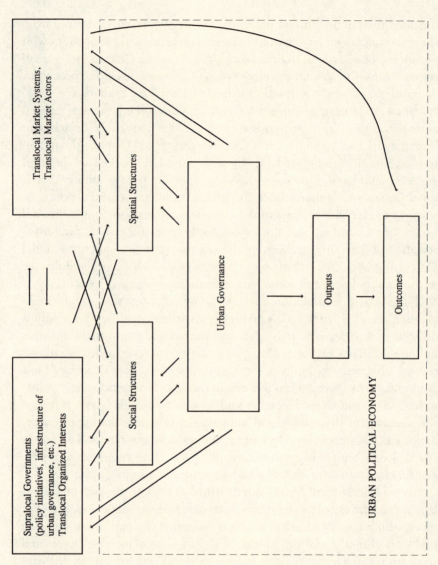

Figure 1.3 Urban Governance in a Model of Urban Political Economy

Translocal Market Systems, Translocal Market Actors

Supralocal Governments (policy initiatives, infrastructure of urban governance, etc.) Translocal Organized Interests

Spatial Structures

Social Structures

Urban Governance

Outputs

Outcomes

URBAN POLITICAL ECONOMY

of global urban dualization assert that the emerging global economy has finally resolved this question. Although the global cities at the peak of urban hierarchies have assumed the role of "command centers" for the world economy, this "control" takes the form of global business domination.

An International Comparative Analysis of Urban Governance

In a field as new as comparative urban governance, and for a type of urban setting beyond the most frequently analyzed cities, the task of research lies as much in generating as in testing hypotheses. Hypotheses from comparative studies of the biggest cities provide at best a starting point. Closer analysis of service and high-technology centers will prompt further hypotheses about how national institutional infrastructures, translocal markets and social and spatial structure affect propensities in urban governance. My inquiry will center around case studies of three distinct policy domains in eleven cities: Clermont-Ferrand, Montpellier, Nancy and Rennes in France; Bielefeld, Freiburg, Göttingen and Münster in Germany; and Durham, Madison and New Haven in the United States. Although my analysis draws on both more comprehensive samples of cities and more intensive studies of single cities, it steers a course between either of these traditional approaches.

To assess how much of a difference urban governance has made requires an analysis of its role in more than one type of policy domain. This analysis will scrutinize efforts to *promote growth*, to *protect environmental quality* and to *remedy inequities*. Although my account will focus on policy decisions about the use of urban land, the analysis encompasses more general policy strategies in all three domains. Theories of social ecology highlight these domains as critical objectives of policy making.[38] Insofar as actors in urban regions contribute to these policies, urban governance must also assume part of the responsibility for addressing more general dilemmas of advanced industrial society.

Long a primary objective for local policy makers in the United States, economic growth has emerged in recent decades as an important aim in

---

[38] Thomas Jahn, "Urban Ecology – Perspectives of Social-Ecological Urban Research," *Capitalism, Nature, Socialism* 7(2) (1996): 95–101; Alain Liepietz, *Green Hopes*, trans. Malcolm Slater (Cambridge: Polity Press, 1995).

many European cities.[39] U.S. analysts in particular have increasingly recognized urban political economies as crucial components of national economic-development strategies.[40] Efforts to market cities as business sites, local initiatives to provide training and business support and local public-private cooperation to spur innovation and development now take place regularly on both continents. Spatial policy making has reflected these emphases with publicly sponsored projects, public-private partnerships, public infrastructure and incentives for new development.[41] Even social policies devoted to education, health services, urban renewal and public housing have often derived part of their justification from the prospective stimulus they give to local growth.

Gould, Schnaiberg and Weinberg portray this gathering impetus toward developmental policies at multiple levels as part of a uniform threat to the environment from a global "treadmill of production." But at the same time, environmental policies and movements have proliferated at local as well as supralocal levels. Throughout most Western cities, environmental measures increasingly provide for regulation of pollution, historical and environmental preservation, maintenance of urban spatial contours, limits on auto traffic and amenities from forest and other open space. In domains related to land use, where the conflicts with economic development policies have often been most direct, local environmental measures have been especially abundant. Regulations constitute only the most obvious instance of environmental control. Nondecisions, refusals to provide infrastructural services and indirect measures like development impact fees often serve analogous purposes.[42] Such amenities as public parks, bicycle paths, pedestrian zones and public transit require not only protection but also initiatives that change patterns of land use.

---

[39] On U.S. cities, see, e.g., David Imbroscio, *Reconstructing City Politics* (Thousand Oaks, CA: Sage, 1997); John R. Logan, Rachel Bridges Whaley and Kyle Crowder, "The Character and Consequences of Growth Regimes," *Urban Affairs Review* 32(5) (1997): 603–630. On European trends, see Patrick Le Galès, *Politique Urbaine et Développement Local* (Paris: L'Harmattan, 1993); Michael Keating, "The Politics of Economic Development," *Urban Affairs Quarterly* 28(3) (1993): 373–396; Alan Harding, Jon Dawson, Richard Evans and Michael Parkinson, *European Cities Towards 2000* (New York: St. Martin's, 1994).

[40] Alberta Sbragia, *Debt Wish: Entrepreneurial Cities, U.S. Federalism, and Economic Development* (Pittsburgh: University of Pittsburgh, 1996).

[41] See, e.g., Peterson, *City Limits*; Fainstein and Fainstein, "New Haven," pp. 27–79; Harding, *European Cities*.

[42] Alan A. Altshuler and José Gómez-Ibáñez, *Regulation for Revenue* (Washington: Brookings Institution, 1993).

The objective of social equity stands in potential conflict with both developmental and environmental policies. Unlike the economic expansion of the earlier manufacturing ages, growth in high-technology and service sectors has generally brought about more polarized employment structures or rising unemployment.[43] Often local environmental goods, as "luxury" goods, serve the interests of elites disproportionately.[44] Similar to the structuralist and public choice accounts of urban political economy on which it draws, the hypothesis of urban dualization depicts the pressures of the global economy as an irresistible impetus toward inequality. But local elites and activists can still employ public provision of housing and services for working-class and lower-income people, protect jobs and living conditions for these residents, redirect of the profits from land development through the state and secure greater environmental goods and fewer environmental bads for ethnic minorities and the poor.[45] In many European cities practices of this sort have long been in place, often institutionalized at supralocal as well as local levels.[46] U.S. planners have also occasionally sought in recent years to generate growth in depressed areas, to counter patterns of land use that have excluded disadvantaged groups and to further equity in other ways.[47]

If urban governance proves significant for policy outputs, then aspects of the wider dilemmas among these policies are being resolved at least partly within urban political economies. For cities as for countries, a similar question pertains. To what degree, and under what circumstances, does the global economy make it possible to pursue all three ends at once? Comparative analysis can furnish the beginnings of an answer to this question.

My analysis will concentrate on several midsize cities of 100,000 to 300,000 (in urban regions from 200,000 to 600,000) where specialized

[43] Sheldon Danziger and Peter Gottschalk, *America Unequal* (Cambridge, MA: Harvard University Press, 1995); William J. Baumol, "Macroeconomics of Unbalanced Growth: The Anatomy of Urban Crisis," *American Economic Review 57* (1967): 416–426.

[44] J. Martinez-Allier, "The Environment as a Luxury Good or 'Too Poor to be Green'?" *Économie Appliquée 48*(2) (1995): 215–230; Jefferey M. Sellers, "Public Goods and the Politics of Segregation," *Journal of Urban Affairs 21*(2) (1999): 237–262.

[45] Susan S. Fainstein, *The City Builders* (Oxford: Blackwell, 1993).

[46] See George Steinmetz, *Regulating the Social* (Princeton: Princeton University Press, 1993); Patrick Dunleavy, *The Politics of Mass Housing in Britain*, (Oxford: Clarendon Press, 1981).

[47] For examples of this trend, see Imbroscio, *Reconstructing City Politics*; Phillip Nyden and Wim Wiewel, *Challenging Uneven Development* (New Brunswick, NJ: Rutgers University Press, 1991); Dennis Keating and Norman Krumholz, *Rebuilding Urban Neighborhoods* (Thousand Oaks, CA: Sage, 1992).

educational, health, and administrative services had grown by 1990 into one of the primary components of the urban economy. Although cross-national comparisons of cities in advanced industrial countries have focused mostly on metropoles, these midsize settings exemplify postindustrial transformations at least as much. Historical precedents for these service centers trace back to the origins of universities and states. But only in the middle and late twentieth century have mass education, technical advances and expanded governmental administration grown into the dominant economic presence in a wide range of metropolitan areas. As Figure 1.4 shows, the preponderance of services in such settings stood out from the wider patterns of national economies as early as the 1960s. By the 1990s, as manufacturing and agriculture shrank into ever smaller domestic economic sectors, the predominance of services in the German, French and U.S. national economies had grown to resemble the pattern in these cities. As in global metropoles like Hamburg, Paris and New York, services had attained even more dominant positions in the midsize cities of this study. Moreover, the services common to both types of cities comprised more pervasive components of advanced industrial economies than the elite financial and business services that made the biggest urban economies "global." As Figure 1.1 has already suggested, expanding financial centers and corporate headquarters constitute only a small proportion of overall service growth.

Size and these postindustrial elements made the eleven cities I chose similar enough to be closely comparable. At the same time, in selecting these settings from comprehensive samples of cities in each country, I looked to basic dimensions of variation that the analysis would test.

The sample encompassed principal international variants in institutions related to urban governance. Germany, France and the United States embody each of the three main types that typologies of local government have emphasized. At the same time these nation-states captured a large range of the variations among advanced industrial countries in state forms and state-society relations. France has long provided a textbook example of a unitary, centralized state. Both Germany and the United States are federal, largely decentralized states. German arrangements qualify decentralization with standardized practices, but American institutions generally do not. In Germany, moreover, corporatist interest aggregation, strong political parties and accompanying state policies and institutions correspond closely to an "organized" model of capitalism.[48] In the United States a contrasting neoliberal model dominates beliefs and institutions. French practices stand between these two models and include additional statist components. Different institutional elements often entailed contradictory implications for local politics and policy. Domestic variations among cities provided a way of testing the significance of separate elements.

Regional variations, for instance, enabled me to consider how the variety of political institutions and policies among the American states and the German Länder affected local processes and outcomes. Connecticut exemplifies the divide in much of the Northeastern United States between urban machine politics and the town meeting traditions of suburbia. Wisconsin was one of the centers of Progressive reformism in the Midwest. North Carolina presents a version of reform institutions found in much of the Sun Belt. Within western Germany, Rhineland-Westphalia reflects the Social Democratic dominance, activist government and more nearly parliamentary municipal institutions of the north. Baden-Württemberg manifests the stronger conservatism, less activist government and stronger mayoral powers of South Germany. Lower Saxony features a stronger separation of powers in local government and has alternated between Social Democratic and Christian Democratic rule.

The sample also encompassed some of the most important international variations among urban and regional economies. The service centers selected in each country differed among each other along similar lines. As Figure 1.4 shows, at least one in each national sample had developed from manufacturing centers into service centers or had acquired specialized services while maintaining a manufacturing base. In the early 1960s the urban economies of Bielefeld, Clermont-Ferrand and New Haven remained more manufacturing centers than service centers. In each case the proportion of local employment in the productive sector stood well above the national average. Even into the 1990s the concentrations of manufacturing employment in Bielefeld and Clermont-Ferrand exceeded national averages. Although none of these cities could lay claim to the status of a full-fledged metropole, several with greater size and more central positions within wider spatial economies had assumed more metropolitan functions. The contrasts between such places as Madison, Montpellier,

---

[48] David Soskice, "Innovation Strategies of Companies," pp. 271–289; Maurice Albert, *Capitalisme Contre Capitalisme* (Paris: Seuil, 1991).

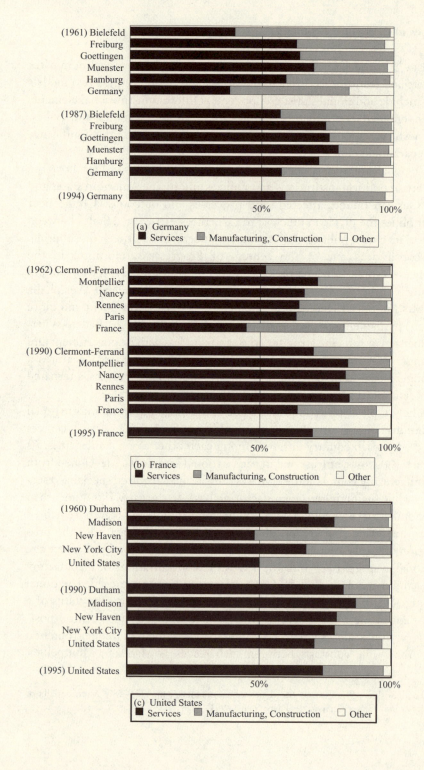

(a) Germany
- ■ Services
- ▨ Manufacturing, Construction
- □ Other

(b) France
- ■ Services
- ▨ Manufacturing, Construction
- □ Other

(c) United States
- ■ Services
- ▨ Manufacturing, Construction
- □ Other

Rennes and Freiburg and smaller, less prominent centers like Göttingen provided a partial indicator of the difference those functions made. The regional variations among the cities also captured principal variations in the wider dynamic of economic geography within each country. Nancy, Bielefeld, Münster and New Haven each stood in a declining industrial region. Since the 1960s, the regions surrounding Freiburg, Montpellier and Durham have emerged as boom areas.

Differences in the social and spatial structure of cities comprised a further source of national and within-nation contrasts. Authors who compare U.S. and European cities have stressed how the built legacies of medieval Old Towns, the historical constraints of city walls and the historically smaller proportions of ethnic minorities in European cities have laid different structural foundations for urban politics.[49] My choice of cities provided what amounted to a partial control for these conditions. With Madison I selected one of the most European of U.S. cities in each of these respects. The original, planned downtown district, the centralized early settlement and the small numbers of African Americans and Hispanic

---

[49] Eric H. Monkkonen, *America Becomes Urban* (Berkeley: University of California Press, 1988); Bagnasco and Le Galès, "Les villes européennes."

Figure 1.4   *(facing page)* Service Centers in Comparison with National Political Economies, 1960–1995
Note: French and U.S. city data and German figures for Göttingen measure proportions of employed residents within city limits at the time of the census. Other German city data measure proportions of employed adult residents within the area of the 1987 boundaries, and French city boundaries remained the same. German data and French city data from 1961/2 also include unemployed residents, generally a small group at the time. French and U.S. sectoral categorizations shifted slightly between the 1960 and subsequent censuses.
Sources: (French cities) unpublished INSEE data; (French national statistics) INSEE, *Annuaire Statistique de la France 1965*, pp. 73–75; INSEE, *Annuaire Statistique de la France 1996*, pp. 63–64; U.S. Census Bureau, *Statistical Abstract of the United States 1997*, p. 846; (German cities) *Land* and city statistical offices; (German national statistics) Statistisches Bundesamt, *Statistisches Jahrbuch für die Bundesrepublik Deutschland 1964*, p. 148; Statistisches Bundesamt, *Statistisches Jahrbuch für die Bundesrepublik Deutschland 1989*, p. 94; Statistisches Bundesamt, *Statistisches Jahrbuch für die Bundesrepublik Deutschland 1996*, p. 110; (U.S. cities) U.S. Census Bureau, *Standard Metropolitan Statistical Area (SMSA) Reports, 1960, 1990*; (U.S. national statistics) U.S. Census Bureau, *Statistical Abstract of the United States 1963*, p. 228; U.S. Census Bureau, *Statistical Abstract of the United States 1994–1995*, p. 870; U.S. Census Bureau, *Statistical Abstract of the United States 1997*, p. 846.

Americans in Madison furnished conditions and ethnic homogeneity analogous to those in German cities of similar size. Compared with the more typical U.S. conditions of a city like New Haven as well as with European settings, this case will help to address whether institutions and urban governance or social and structural conditions caused wider similarities and differences in processes and outcomes. Especially among the French cities, but also between French and German ones, variations in the centralization of urban settlement will provide additional bases for testing how patterns of settlement shape interests, mobilization and policies.

From the wide variety of urban contexts in advanced industrial societies, this design thus singled out a single, similar type of city. Controlled variations among these otherwise similar cases furnished one way to highlight and clarify the influences within and upon urban political economies. Extensive interviews, statistics, documents and other materials enabled me to supplement this analysis of variations with detailed analysis of each case as well as with findings about wider patterns.[50] The resulting account will furnish both an international overview of urban governance in one of the most pervasive types of urban regions among developed countries and more general hypotheses for future research to test.

The Plan of This Book

The analysis of this book starts from a comparison of the ultimate outcomes from policies and markets in the eleven service centers. Whatever the national or regional context, the growth, environmental quality and

---

[50] The analysis of this book draws in part on 242 standardized interviews with local elites and activists concerned with spatial policy in Freiburg, Montpellier, and New Haven. Conducted in 1990 and 1991, with a mostly precoded questionnaire, the interviews provided more precise cross-national data to address questions about norms, cognitions and institutions. Assembled through a snowballing method, the respondents included parallel proportions of respondents from the most critical roles in civil society as well as from officialdom concerned with policy making about land use. Respondents also included a mix of people holding various political ideologies, suburban and urban residents and age cohorts (Jefferey M. Sellers, "Grounds of Democracy: Public Authority and the Politics of Metropolitan Land in Three Societies" (Ph.D. diss., Yale University, 1994), Appendices. Subsequent interviews included 5 to 10 prominent actors in planning and politics in the other urban regions selected. In each case, I supplemented the interviews with extensive secondary, documentary and statistical research, including analysis of at least one central city budget from the years 1992–1995.

socioeconomic polarization in these settings set them apart in different ways from both global metropoles and longtime manufacturing centers. At the same time, in all three categories of outcomes, this assessment finds variations according to both region and nation. The German urban regions grew less overall, and at more similar rates. Especially in the central cities, growth in the U.S. and French urban regions differed more widely. At the same time the German settings maintained higher levels of environmental amenities and the least spatial polarization between privileged and disadvantaged neighborhoods. Only occasionally did either environmental goods or spatial integration in the French cities approach these German results. In the U.S. cities, environmental outcomes varied, but class and ethnic polarization among neighborhoods persisted and in some respects grew.

The remainder of the book probes the sources of these variations in outcomes. Chapter 3 considers policies of supralocal governments. Despite repeated influences from these policies in all three policy domains, close analysis demonstrates the growing role of urban political economies in these same policies. Cumulative legal authorizations and the spread of localized environmental and economic policies have contributed to this convergent trend. National infrastructures for urban governance have usually shaped these supralocal initiatives more decisively than have the territorial organization of states at higher levels. Thus supralocal policy making in federal Germany fostered more equivalent local efforts among disparate cities and diverse regions than in centralized, unitary France or the federal United States.

The next chapters turn the lens on governance within the eleven urban regions. Chapter 4 sketches the local electoral formations and agendas that have emerged to accommodate the three domains of policy in various ways. These local coalitions and their agendas go well beyond implementation of policy handed down from above and account for much of what national policies cannot explain. Here and in Chapter 5, I analyze how the protagonists of urban governance have drawn on infrastructures of political parties, metropolitan cooperation, local government, public-private relations and interest representation to bring about local, national and global variations in policy. Especially in service centers, translocal firms, institutions and market incentives have furnished part of the impetus for local economies and official actions. But urban governing coalitions, in tandem with supralocal policies, have helped to fashion both markets and networks. Especially in environmental domains, neighborhood and social movements have increasingly contributed to local choices. Their influence depends both on neighborhood interests and civic association within communities and on incorporation into wider governing coalitions. The concluding chapter recasts my findings to propose new typologies for analysis of urban political economies and reconsiders the implications of urban governance for national political economies.

2

Postindustrial Transformation and the Service City

As services, consumption and technology have grown to predominance in advanced industrial societies, a distinctive type of city has emerged. Far more than the market towns of medieval and early modern Europe, it operates as a node in vast networks of translocal markets, organizations, communications and distribution. In place of the smokestacks and tenements that dominated the skyline of nineteenth- and early-twentieth-century manufacturing cities, office towers, university campuses, business parks and shopping facilities now mark these metropolitan landscapes. In earlier urban service centers professionals, administrators and students seldom made up more than a small fraction of the total population. In contemporary service centers these groups often comprise the biggest single segment of local workforces, electorates and markets. Many such cities have sprung from localities where the industrial revolution left few traces. Others stem from the postindustrial metamorphoses of an urban economy long dominated by traditional manufacturing. Whatever its starting point, however, the transformation of urban service centers in advanced industrial societies has departed in crucial ways from parallel changes occurring in the biggest urban centers. Within as well as among France, Germany and the United States the variety of outcomes from this transformation manifests the significance of local conditions and local choices.

The extent and character of local growth, the evolution of environmental conditions and the degree of social and territorial polarization in the eleven urban regions provide indispensable data for understanding the consequences of policy. To lay the groundwork for subsequent analysis, this chapter considers these manifestations of policies and market strategies. As the U.S. and European literature on policy implementation has long made clear, mapping "backward" from these results reveals essential information that more conventional "forward" mapping from elite decisions leaves obscure. Urban governance often adds dimensions, strategic considerations and even aims that go beyond or contradict what policy makers at the heights of national states have sought. Even within the state's hierarchies, mapping policy backward from results enables an analysis to take into account "reciprocity in the relationship between superiors and subordinates in organizations; the connection between hierarchical control and increased complexity; discretion as an adaptive device; and bargaining as a precondition for local effects."[1] Without comparative review of local outcomes, it would be difficult as a matter of evidence to separate out the outcomes within urban regions from those at wider scales. To judge these outcomes in relation to each other as well as to those in global cities, the patterns within service centers must be distinguished from and related to transnational, national and regional tendencies. Backward mapping of this sort also hardly dispenses with the need to consider elite decisions as influences on policy. Correspondences within an urban political economy and the surrounding region or nation may ultimately point to elite choices as a cause. But only by comparing the local results from policy can what forward mapping shows be fully comprehended.

This "bottom-up" perspective starts from evidence of the consequences from governance at all levels. Variations that defy explanation in terms of translocal influences at wider scales suggest that urban governance, or at least local structural conditions, have played an important role in policy and its consequences. Proof that one urban region among several had controlled sprawl more completely, or that one had mobilized more around growth, would require closer examination of how policies and markets had produced a result. Unexplained variations among local political economies should nonetheless cast doubt on explanations due to global, national or regional causes.

Equivalent outcomes suggest consistent influences. Yet even this consistency could come about through repeated local choices and interlocal dynamics rather than through the choices of policy makers or firms at more encompassing scales of governance. The point remains as valid for the promotion of economic expansion as it does for the provision of environmental quality or for the maintenance of equality among neighborhoods. Regardless of global forces or even international exchanges, local,

---

[1] Richard Elmore, "Backward Mapping: Implementation Research and Policy Decisions," *Political Science Quarterly 94*(4) (1980): 601, 611–612.

regional and national efforts within countries could have brought about results like the emergence of high technology and service provision. Similarly, not global financial and corporate elites, but local choices, conditions and markets could have caused the polarization and business concentrations of the largest cities.

Similarities among cities within a single national society often prompt comparative urban analysts to speak of an "American," a "European, or even a "German" city.[2] But nation-specific tendencies of this sort seldom make for uniform contrasts. What divergences do occur rarely come about solely or even mostly through the initiative of national states, organizations or policies. Parallel local efforts to control urban sprawl, promote development or limit socioeconomic segregation could stem from similar physical legacies of urban development as a result of parallel histories, or could spread through diffusion to urban regimes throughout a society. Similarly, tendencies within the region that encompasses an urban region, such as a U.S. state or a German *Land*, could owe more to the markets and politics within that urban region than to any efforts beyond the suburban frontier.

Common trends at the global, national or regional scale may suggest that wider forces are at work, but they do not explain the role of local and translocal influences in those forces. Local variations in economic, environmental and distributive outcomes furnish initial indications of the importance of individual urban political economies. My analysis of these outcomes will begin with economic growth, then turn to environmental quality and distributive equity.

Centers of Growth

In the advanced economies of the industrialized world, growth derives increasingly from the added value that services bring. In important ways, growth in midsize urban regions reflects the implications of this fact for cities more than do patterns in the largest or "global" urban economies. Though they are tied more closely than are the biggest urban economies

[2] Pietro S. Nivola, *Laws of the Landscape* (Washington: Brookings Institution, 1999); Arnaldo Bagnasco and Patrick Le Galès, "Les villes européennes comme société et comme acteur," in Arnaldo Bagnarco and Patick Le Galès (eds.), *Villes en Europe* (Paris: La Découverte, 1997), pp. 7–46; Eric H. Monkkonen, *America Becomes Urban* (Berkeley: University of California Press, 1988); Kenneth Jackson, *Crabgrass Frontier* (New York: Oxford University Press, 1985).

to regional and national economic trends, midsize service centers share an analogous dependence on postindustrial economic sectors. Despite a general expansion in these midsize urban regions, the central cities usually led the surrounding regions in relative prosperity and rates of growth.

Local growth can take the form either of expanding workforces or of increasing wealth. Alongside the nation-specific determinants of growth that have preoccupied analysts of "national capitalisms,"[3] taking individual cities and regions as units of analysis demonstrates the role of influences at other scales. Formerly peripheral regions like the American Sun Belt, the south of France and southern Germany have attracted stronger growth, as regions of older manufacturing have suffered relative declines. Growth in service centers needs to be assessed in relation to these regional patterns as well as national economies. On the one hand, the local patterns may reflect national or regional influences that extend beyond these urban regions. On the other, an urban region that departs in some manner from the growth or decline of the surrounding region demonstrates partial independence from the regional pattern.[4]

---

[3] Wolfgang Streeck and Phillip C. Schmitter (eds.), *Private Interest Government: Beyond Market and State* (London: Sage Publications, 1985); Roger J. Hollingsworth and Robert Boyer (eds.), *Contemporary Capitalism* (Cambridge: Cambridge University Press, 1997). Standard economic models that specify determinants of growth have also pointed to national societal differences like birth rates (Robert Barro and Xavier Sala-i-Martin, *Economic Growth* [New York: McGraw-Hill, 1995], Ch. 1).

[4] A word about the definitions of "urban region" is in order. Because the three countries did not define metropolitan areas in the same way, I had to devise definitions that not only were as parallel as possible but also corresponded to the wider designations that the planners had used.

In one of the U.S. metropolitan areas, the Standard Metropolitan Statistical Area (SMSA) designations for Durham, Madison and New Haven produced results too divergent to use. In general, these designations defined boundaries by the larger units of counties rather than by towns (see U.S. Bureau of the Census, *1990 SMSA Reports*, pp. A8–A9). In the monocentric metropolitan area of Madison, I found no alternative designations besides Dane County. In both other settings, the Census Bureau had changed the definition between censuses, and the telephone service areas differed from the census designations. The five-county Raleigh-Durham SMSA included outlying counties that would have been considered predominantly rural in Europe. But the larger city of Raleigh was 20 miles away as well as outside the phone service area. Since the polycentric pattern of settlement also extended westward the 26 miles to Burlington as well as eastward to Raleigh, I decided to incorporate the polycentric character of the SMSA as a variable rather than a parameter and to focus on the region counted as an SMSA up to 1970 (Durham and its periphery in Orange County). As in Madison, this definition corresponded to the phone service area. For New Haven, the definition corresponded more closely to the 1990 SMSA. However, I excluded Meriden, a city of 60,000 population halfway between New Haven and

Postindustrial Transformation and the Service City

Since the 1960s, midsize urban regions specializing in services have generally expanded. Although the residential population reflects demographic trends as well as economic ones, this figure offers the most reliable indicator available for both the central cities and their surroundings (Figure 2.1). In every census and in every city region, local residents have increased. Montpellier, Rennes, Freiburg, Durham and Madison have expanded rapidly. Moreover, even as the central cities of Clermont-Ferrand, Nancy, Bielefeld, Münster and New Haven declined, the metropolitan populations in these settings followed the more general trend. Despite the worsening prospects of such settings, a visitor to the downtown during the 1980s or early 1990s could scarcely fail to notice an array of construction projects designed to capitalize on wider metropolitan trends. Thus even as the central city population in Münster shrank, expansion in the urban region accelerated.

The growth of these urban regions stood out not only from the national and regional settings but also from the more modest expansion of the most global urban regions (Figure 2.2). Over much of the period since 1960, the central cores of New York, Paris and Hamburg lost

Hartford, and included Milford, a nearby town within the metropolitan planning organization and telephone service area, as well as Cheshire, an outlying suburb also within the telephone service area.

For the German metropolitan areas, I employed two definitions depending on the purpose of the statistics. For statistical as well as for planning purposes, the comparatively extensive jurisdictions of the surrounding *Landkreise* (counties) have been taken as metropolitan boundaries. Although this set of towns made particular sense for assessments of efforts to channel development, it encompassed larger entities with bigger populations than most of the U.S. or French metropolitan areas. For a more cross-nationally comparable measure of the peripheral population and its growth, I obtained the only statistically derived designations available for German cities from a private firm, BIK Aschpurwis + Behrens. The formula employed by the firm yielded a narrow definition of urban regions – in Münster and Bielefeld, essentially the handful of local jurisdictions in the first ring around the central city. For Chapter 2 and most other purposes I have employed the *Landkreis* statistics.

French statistics also generally lacked categories that corresponded strictly to U.S. metropolitan areas. The urban units (*unités urbaines*) essentially identified those communes with built-up or urban areas (INSEE, *Composition communale des zones de peuplement industriel ou urbain: Population et délimitation* [Paris, 1992], p. 3), and the zones of industry and urban population proved too broad. In two of the settings an intermediate category provided alternatives. Territorial officials of the state in Montpellier had assembled data on a total of 63 communes designated as "Greater Montpellier," with less than half the number in the zone of industry and urban population. The planning region around Clermont-Ferrand encompassed 72 communes. In the other two French settings, using distance as well as patterns of periurban growth, I constructed roughly comparable regions. Around Rennes, the area included a band of adjacent surrounding communes beyond the 32 in the district of Rennes.

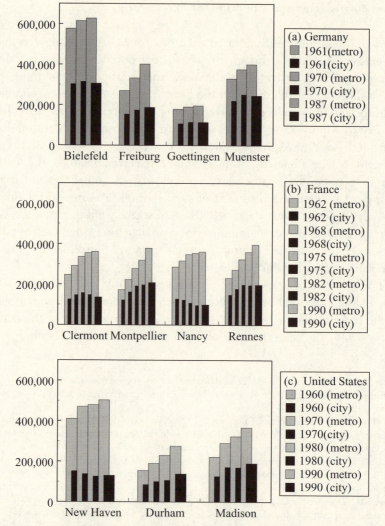

Figure 2.1 Increases in Metropolitan and City Population, 1960–1990
Sources: National Censuses. For determination of Metro Areas, see Chapter 2, note 4.

Figure 2.2 (*facing page*) Annual Growth in Service Center Populations in Comparison with National, Regional and Global City Averages, 1960s–1990s
*For Hamburg, where no consistent metropolitan boundaries exist, the surrounding state of Lower Saxony corresponds to the region. For Paris, in the absence of wider regional boundaries, the region of Ile-de-France corresponds to the metropolitan area. For New York City, New York County is here taken as the city and all five counties as the metro area.
Note: U.S. data reflect changing boundaries of Durham and Madison; all other data for constant boundaries defined by latest full census.
Sources: (U.S.: national and states) U.S. Bureau of the Census, *Statistical Abstract of the United States 1962*, pp. 10–11; id., *1990 Census of Population, Social and Economic Characteristics: United States* (1993); (U.S.: metropolitan areas and cities); id.,

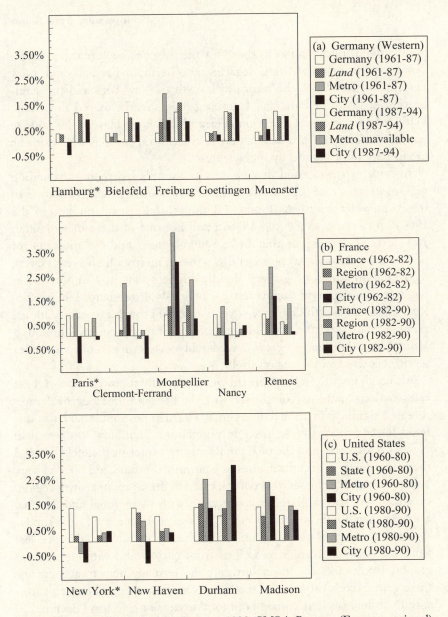

1960 Metropolitan Area, State Reports, 1990 SMSA Reports; (France: national)
INSEE, *Annuaire Statistique de la France 1991–1992*, p. 50; id., *Annuaire Statistique
de la France 1965*, p. 32; (French regions) *Statistiques et Indicateurs des Régions
Françaises* (1992); id., *Recensement au 1/20 de 1962*, Regional Reports (1964);
(France: metropolitan areas and cities) id., *Recensement Général de la population
de 1982: Données communales comparées 1975–1982*, Departmental Reports;
id., *Recensement Général de la population de 1990: Évolutions démographiques
1975–1982–1990*, Departmental Reports; (Germany: national and *Land*) Statistisches Bundesamt, *Statistisches Jahrbuch für die Bundesrepublik Deutschland 1996*, p.
49; (Germany: cities) Deutscher Städtetag, *Statistisches Jahrbuch Deutscher Gemeinden 1994*, pp. 28–30; and *Land* statistical publications and computer files.

population at rates similar to those for the losses in such midsize service centers with manufacturing legacies as Clermont-Ferrand and New Haven.[5] In the 1980s, the return of growth to New York and the stabilization of losses in Paris and Hamburg only slightly altered this trend. With the exceptions of Clermont-Ferrand and New Haven, the midsize service centers grew proportionately in the central cities as well as in the urban regions at manifestly higher rates.

In both expansion and decline, service centers led their surrounding regions in ways that suggest the centrality of midsize urban economies to trends at wider scales. As Figure 2.2 shows, the growth rates from the 1960s up to the early or mid-1980s in all but one of these metropolitan areas exceeded those of the surrounding region. For the most recent period even the one exception to this pattern, metropolitan New Haven, recovered to levels of growth slightly higher than in Connecticut at large. In one region in each country – Baden-Württemberg, Languedoc-Roussillon and North Carolina – overall rates of growth exceeded national averages. The service centers located in each of these regions – Freiburg, Montpellier, Durham – grew considerably faster than both the other service centers and the region itself.

Although growth in the German cities generally followed each of these cross-national patterns, comparison with the French and U.S. growth rates reveals a significant national divergence. German postindustrial cities suffered fewer proportionate losses in population. Hamburg lost less than New York or Paris, and the old manufacturing center of Bielefeld escaped the major declines of central cities in Clermont-Ferrand and New Haven. Yet even Freiburg, the service center located in the German growth region, expanded less spectacularly in comparison with its regional and national averages than did those French and U.S. cities that benefitted from similar regional contexts. Rates of expansion in the German cities diverged less from the national average as well as from each other. Although demographic factors like the lower birthrate in Germany help to account for these lower levels of growth,[6] the lesser variation suggests other nation-specific influences that curbed both local expansion and local decline.

---

[5] Saskia Sassen, *Cities in a World Economy* (Thousand Oaks, CA: Pine Forge Press, 1994), p. 41; Paul Kantor, H. V. Savitch and Serena Vicari Haddock, "The Political Economy of Urban Regimes," *Urban Affairs Review 32* (January 1997): 348–377.

[6] In 1998, the German birthrate of 10 per 1,000 population compared to rates of 13 in France and 14 in the United States (U.S. Department of Commerce, *Statistical Abstract of the United States* [Washington, 1999], pp. 8, 84).

Postindustrial Transformation and the Service City

The more fragmentary available indicators of local wealth furnish the means to assess how much these movements in population corresponded to economic growth. Rising incomes could signal growing prosperity in a shrinking population. In the largest or global cities, where the population remained comparatively stable or even declined, this is precisely what occurred. Sassen and other proponents of the global urban dualization thesis hold that higher-level economic activities now center increasingly in such settings.[7] As data derived from somewhat different sources of income in each country show,[8] the accumulation of wealth in the urban core of New York City did indeed go well beyond any demographic effect (Figure 2.3). If the average for New York as a whole rose from 1.15 times to 1.19 times the national average, the level in Manhattan jumped from 1.67 to 1.94 times that average. Even the parallel rise of Connecticut to the highest per capita income of any U.S. state largely reflects the wealth of the New York suburbs. Although Paris has long contained disproportionate wealth, the elevated taxable income there as well as the disproportionate increase in higher-status workers (see Figure 2.6) are consistent with Sassen's more detailed account of a parallel process in France. A more limited version of the same process was also under way in Hamburg prior to the last national census in 1987. Over the preceding two decades, higher-status workers had flocked more to this city than to its German counterparts (see Figure 2.6). Even though average salaries in Hamburg had risen slightly less than the national average by that time, they remained much higher there than elsewhere and had increased around two times more rapidly than in the other German cities.[9]

---

[7] Saskia Sassen, *The Global City: New York, London, Tokyo* (Princeton: Princeton University Press, 1991); Sassen, *Cities in a World Economy*.

[8] The German data in Figure 2.3 include only salaries. Since this measure excludes investment earnings as well as the earnings of, say, the proprietor of a business, it fails to reflect the full income of wealthier workers. The French figures, taken partly from a survey of households and partly from tax statistics, measure taxable income by consumption unit or *foyer* rather than by person. Since this basis treats some two-income couples as single units, it probably exaggerates income in urban areas, where such households comprise larger proportions of the total.

[9] Since the German averages in Figure 2.3 include salaries but not investment and other earnings, they fail to reflect as much of the accumulation of wealth that took place in Hamburg and the financial center Frankfurt. In Hamburg the average fell from 1.20 times the national average in 1970 to 1.15 times the average in 1987. In Frankfurt the same figure dropped from 1.32 to 1.27 the national average. In the three service centers with figures, however, the declines ranged from .10 to .18 times the national average.

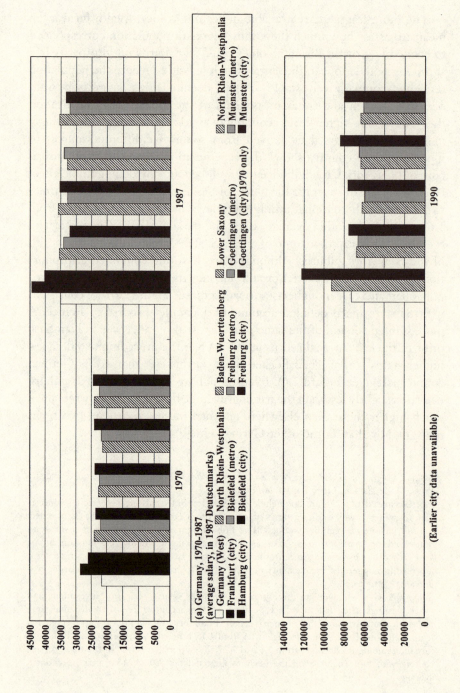

(a) Germany, 1970–1987
(average salary, in 1987 Deutschmarks)

Germany (West)
North Rhein-Westphalia
Frankfurt (city)
Bielefeld (metro)
Hamburg (city)
Bielefeld (city)

Baden-Wuerttemberg
Freiburg (metro)
Freiburg (city)

Lower Saxony
Goettingen (metro)
Goettingen (city)(1970 only)

North Rhein-Westphalia
Muenster (metro)
Muenster (city)

1970

1987

1990

(Earlier city data unavailable)

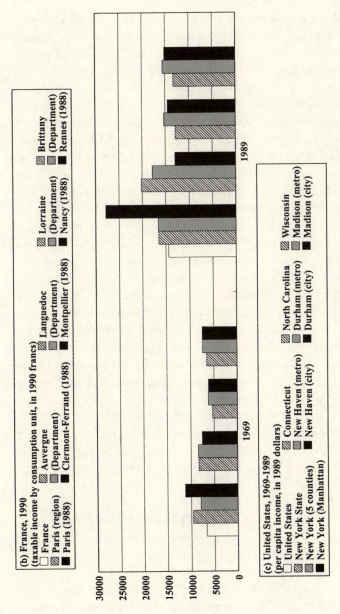

Figure 2.3 Growth in National, Regional and Local Average Income, 1970–1990
Sources: (Germany) Statistisches Bundesamt, *Arbeitstättenzäblung 1970*; id., *Arbeitstättenzäblung von 25.5.1987: Unternehmen und Arbeitstätten,* Fachserie 2, Heft 1; (France) INSEE, *Les Salaires en 1990,* unpublished city data from id., *Communoscope 1988*; (United States) U.S. Census Bureau, *Census of Population and Housing 1970, 1990: Economic and Social Characteristics of the Population,* State and National Reports.

Although midsize service centers also grew in wealth as well as in population, average income growth in these settings highlighted the distinctiveness of the biggest cities. Average wealth increased less dramatically in these smaller urban settings, and the trends retained obvious links to wider regional trends. In the growing service centers of the United States, and most likely in the parallel cities of France, incomes within the metropolitan areas advanced slightly beyond the rate of growth in regional averages, but not dramatically so.[10] In all three countries, the legacy of local manufacturing and ongoing industrial decline brought lower income in relation to regional averages. In Bielefeld and New Haven, average urban income declined in relation to both regional and metropolitan averages. Since 1980, if not before, the parallel exodus from Clermont-Ferrand has probably induced a comparable decline. Even where a massive influx of people probably included less well-off residents in search of work, the example of Durham suggests that service centers could gain more than their share of comparatively prosperous newcomers. Local income in that urban region still rose in relation to the North Carolina average. As the last section will show, occupational data on the shifts in Montpellier suggest a similar local benefit from rapid regional growth there. In the U.S., the separate data for the city region and central city in Figure 2.3(c) manifest a distinctive suburbanization of wealth. By 1970 in New Haven and by 1990 in Durham and Madison, per capita income in the metropolitan area exceeded that of the central city.

As was true for rates of population growth, rates of income growth in the German urban regions differed less from one region to another or from the national average than they did in the United States or France. From 1970 to 1987 in Germany, average salaries in even the global cities of Frankfurt and Hamburg had increased less, proportionately, than the national average had (Figure 2.3(c)). In Germany, unlike the clear trend in the midsize U.S. service centers and the most likely trend in the parallel French settings, faster growth in population than in the surrounding region brought comparatively lower average wages. In comparison with Germany at large as well as with the surrounding regions, average salaries dropped still more over the 1970s and 1980s in midservice centers than they did in the biggest cities. Even were nonsalary income to be removed

---

[10] In metropolitan Durham the average rose from 1.17 to 1.19 times the national average, in Madison from 1.13 to 1.17 times that average.

from the French and U.S. figures to enhance comparability, a similar fall seems unlikely. Both Freiburg and Münster, the central cities that gained the most population, retained higher salaries than those in their respective urban regions. But as each central city grew, the average salary there fell from above the metropolitan level in 1970 to below that level in 1987.[11]

As data on employment by economic sectors confirms, relative and often absolute declines in jobs linked to manufacturing or primary production underlay the shifts in population and income (Figure 2.4). Such firms as the Michelin Tire Company in Clermont-Ferrand, the Winchester gun manufacturer in New Haven and the machine tool companies of Bielefeld had all reduced their workforces through improvements in efficiency and had shifted production from these cities to overseas. Even those cities that had acquired additional manufacturing jobs since the 1960s – Rennes, Montpellier, Durham and Madison – relied on services for disproportionate numbers of new jobs. In these places too the proportion of jobs in manufacturing shrank.

As in the growth of the most prosperous settings, the central cities also led sectoral declines at both metropolitan and wider regional scales. In the three global cities, as in Bielefeld, Clermont-Ferrand and New Haven, the disappearance of jobs in primary and secondary sectors accounted for much of the losses in population. In Nancy too, where earlier urban industry and subsequent regional mining had collapsed, the losses of employment in the city come mainly in these sectors. Especially in New Haven, but also elsewhere, these declines of primary and secondary production within the central city exceeded regional rates. At the same time, regional shifts away from these sectors as proportions of all jobs often exceeded declines in the cities.

The German cities' more limited, more consistent proportionate losses in these sectors help to account for the greater uniformity and stability of trends in their populations and incomes. A distinctive German variant of national capitalism, based on exported manufacturing goods, offers one reason for the lesser proportionate decline of manufacturing in these

[11] Unlike in the statistics on population growth, the 1970 figures here are unadjusted for the narrower central city boundaries that preceded the territorial consolidation of the early 1970s in both of these metropolitan areas. The change in boundaries appears to have made little difference in relation to wider *Land* averages. If it did, the central city average should have also declined in relation to the metropolitan area. But each central city continued to exceed the metropolitan figures by similar amounts in 1987 as in 1970.

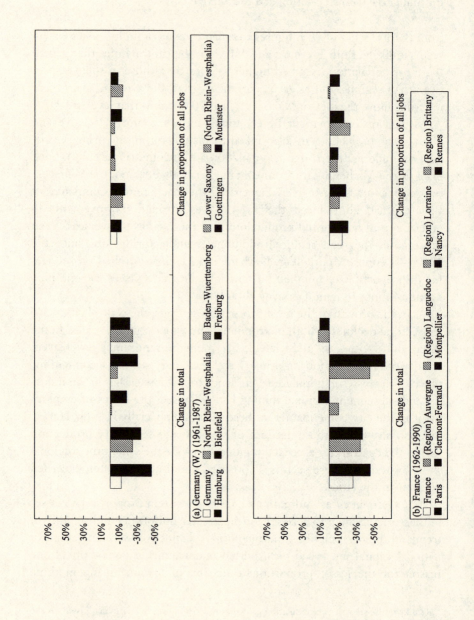

Change in proportion of all jobs

Change in total

(a) Germany (W.) (1961-1987)
☐ Germany   ▨ Baden-Wuerttemberg   ▨ Lower Saxony   ▨ (North Rhein-Westphalia)
▨ North Rhein-Westphalia   ■ Freiburg   ■ Goettingen   ■ Muenster
■ Bielefeld   ■ Hamburg

Change in proportion of all jobs

Change in total

(b) France (1962-1990)
☐ France   ▨ (Region) Languedoc   ▨ (Region) Lorraine   ▨ (Region) Brittany
▨ (Region) Auvergne   ■ Montpellier   ■ Nancy   ■ Rennes
■ Paris   ■ Clermont-Ferrand

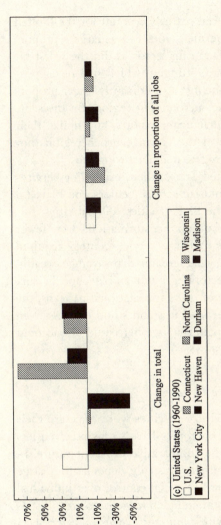

Figure 2.4 Declines in National, Regional and Local Jobs in Mining, Manufacturing and Related Production, 1960s–1990s

Note: U.S. data reflect changing boundaries of Durham and Madison; all other data for constant boundaries defined by latest census. German data at all levels from 1961 and French figures for 1962 from national and regional levels include small numbers of unemployed, not more than 3 percent of the total active population for any division. German 1961 data also do not include military service, while all others do. Job categorizations vary slightly between countries.

Sources: (U.S.: national and states) U.S. Bureau of the Census, *1960 Census of Population Supplementary Reports*, PC(S1)-17 (May 16, 1962); id., *Statistical Abstract of the United States 1962*, pp. 10–11; id., *1990 Census of Population, Social and Economic Characteristics: United States* (1993); (U.S. cities) U.S. Bureau of the Census, id., *1960 Metropolitan Area Reports, 1990 SMSA Reports*; (France: national) INSEE, *Annuaire Statistique de la France 1991–1992*, p. 56; id., *Annuaire Statistique de la France 1964*, p. 64; (French regions) *Statistiques et Indicateurs des Régions Françaises* (1992); id., *Recensement au 1/20 de 1962*, Regional Reports (1964); (French cities) unpublished census data obtained from INSEE; (Germany: national) Statistisches Bundesamt, *Statistisches Jahrbuch für die Bundesrepublik Deutschland 1963*, p. 141; id., *Statistisches Jahrbuch für die Bundesrepublik Deutschland 1989*, p. 94; (German cities) Land statistical offices.

cities.[12] Yet export dependence alone can scarcely account for the limited subnational variation. None of the German cities lost as large a proportion of its total jobs from the manufacturing sector as did the worst-hit U.S. and French settings. Except for Göttingen, which had never possessed a large manufacturing base, none lost a significantly larger proportion of jobs in this sector than in the surrounding region. By the same token, despite the emphasis on manufacturing exports, and unlike their U.S. and French counterparts, none of the German urban regions nor their surrounding regions gained aggregate manufacturing jobs.

Throughout Europe and the United States, then, expanding services both contributed to the growth of midsize service centers and played a role in the accumulating wealth of the biggest cities. Global cities, following broadly similar trajectories of urban transformation, drew fewer but wealthier people to urban cores. Midsize service centers acquired larger numbers of people with somewhat greater-than-average wealth. These service centers usually led sectoral growth and decline in surrounding regions. Within the bounds of these transnational patterns, the German service centers grew less, declined less and stood out less from surrounding regions. But even these patterns together could not account for the full variety of local trajectories.

Environmental Outcomes in Service Centers

Among the first things that a casual visitor to cities will notice are their environmental differences. But these outcomes have so far received less attention than other factors have in the comparative urban literature. In an urban setting, environmental governance usually depends to a large degree on governmental or other means of social control over individual behavior.[13] Control of this sort relates in complex ways to growth: Just as the physical development associated with economic expansion can place a burden on the environment of an urban region, an attractive environment can enhance a region's economic prospects. Global cities present problems of growth management, pollution control and energy usage of a different order from the difficulties in midsize service centers. In domains like land

---

[12] E.g., Maurice Albert, *Capitalisme contre capitalisme* (Paris: Seuil, 1991); Wolfgang Streeck, "German Capitalism: Does It Exist? Can It Survive?" in Colin Crouch and Wolfgang Streeck (eds.), *Modern Capitalism or Modern Capitalisms?* (Paris: La Découverte, 1995).

[13] Thomas Rudel, *The Politics of American Land Use Policy* (Cambridge: Cambridge University Press, 1989).

preservation, however, large urban regions in Europe, such as Paris, often manifest significantly better environmental outcomes than do global centers in the United States, such as New York.[14] Among midsize settings, wide national and regional variations also mark environmental outcomes. The divergences relate closely to social and market preferences for environmental protection. Such preferences often grow in salience in the presence of attractive natural attributes like forests, mountains and coastlines.[15] Cultural and geographic influences of this sort are as much a part of political economies within urban regions as they are a part of political and economic processes at wider scales. This section examines first a range of protections accorded land and other components of the environment within the central cities and then the results of growth management in the urban regions beyond.

Within the central cities, data about the environment permits the most comprehensive comparisons. A largely quantitative index constructed to measure consequences from a range of environmental policies demonstrated differences among cities both within and between countries. In general, centers with declining manufacturing encountered environmental outcomes that were worse than those of service centers. Other variations in rates of regional or local growth made less systematic difference for these outcomes. Almost uniformly, the German cities attained higher levels of outcomes than their French or U.S. counterparts.

Based on a Boolean approach, the index combined parallel quantitative indicators for eight categories of environmental outcomes (Table 2.1).[16] Indicators for maintenance of forest, maintenance of agriculture, historic preservation and pedestrian zones reflected formal or informal constraints on the conversion of land for development. Parks and street-related amenities as well as bicycle paths and mass transit measured collective investments in the quality of the built environment. At the same time, mass transit, bicycle paths and pedestrian zones as well as protection of outlying land fostered more ecologically sensitive alternatives to automobile traffic. Specific indicators unavoidably mirrored spatial differences beyond

---

[14] H. V. Savitch, *Post-Industrial Cities* (Princeton: Princeton University Press, 1988).

[15] For discussion of regional variations in the United States, see Terry Nichols Clark and Edward G. Goetz, "The Antigrowth Machine: Can City Governments Control, Limit or Manage Growth?" in T. N. Clark (ed.), *Urban Innovation* (London: Sage, 1994), pp. 105–145; Samuel Hays, *Beauty, Health and Permanence: Environmental Politics in the United States, 1955–1985* (Cambridge: Cambridge University Press, 1987).

[16] Charles Ragin, *The Comparative Method* (Berkeley: University of California Press, 1987).

the influence of contemporary policies or markets, such as the physical and cultural legacies of medieval Old Towns in Europe. But multiple indicators, by helping smooth over idiosyncracies in particular domains, highlighted more general propensities in environmental control.

Several systematic patterns emerged from this compilation. Among the service centers of each country, the cities emerging from an industrial past invariably secured lower levels of environmental goods. Compared with at least one of the other places in the same country, Bielefeld as well as Clermont-Ferrand and New Haven resembled each other. In each, pedestrian zones have remained smaller or nonexistent; farmland has disappeared faster or earlier; historical preservation and parks have remained more limited; city funds have supported the upkeep of streets less; and bicycle paths have remained less extensive. Physical legacies like the undeveloped brownfields that mark each of these cities can scarcely account for such extensive contrasts with the other cities. A full accounting will have to look more specifically to local politics and markets.

In the German cities, where growth had taken the most similar paths, environmental outcomes also followed a distinctive national pattern. Environmental amenities in Bielefeld might approximate the level in specific French and U.S. cities, but the average for the entire set of German cities stood distinctly higher than the averages for the cities in either other country. In comparison with their counterparts in France and the United States, the German cities had generally established bigger pedestrian zones, protected forests and farmland better, provided more support for parks, spent more on streets and built more bike paths. Urbanists who have focused on New York and Paris have been quick to take the systematic planning of the French capital as revelatory of a national propensity,[17] but provincial French service centers differed nearly as much as their American counterparts in environmental outcomes. Although the French cities averaged somewhat higher than the U.S. settings, the total score in Madison exceeded the levels in both Nancy and Clermont-Ferrand. This overall Franco-American contrast reflected different emphases among the categories. The medieval Old Towns of France maintained more extensive preservation, and French mass transit extended further. But the American cities, benefitting from larger jurisdictions, had preserved more forest as well as more parkland within the city.

---

[17] See, e.g., James B. White, "Old Wine, Cracked Bottles: Paris, Tokyo and the Global City Thesis," *Urban Affairs Review* (1998); Savitch, *Post-Industrial Cities*.

Table 2.1 *Public Provision of Environmental Amenities in Central Cities, 1980s–1990s*
(0 = None, 1 = Low, 2 = Intermediate, 3 = High)

	Pedestrian Zones	Maintenance of Forest	Maintenance of Agricultural Land	Historic Preservation	Parks (Extent, Expenditure)	Streets (Lighting, Cleaning, Upkeep)	Bicycle Paths	Mass Transit	Sum of Scores (0–24)
Germany									
Bielefeld	1	3	2	2	2	2	2	2	16
Göttingen	2	3	2	3	3	2	2	2	19
Münster	2	3	2	3	3	3	3	2	21
Freiburg	3	3	3	3	3	3	3	3	24
France									
Clermont-Ferrand	1	1	1	2	1	1	0	2	9
Nancy	1	1	1	3	1	2	1	2	12
Montpellier	2	1	2	3	2	2	1	2	15
Rennes	1	2	1	3	3	3	2	2	17
United States									
New Haven	0	2	0	1	2	1	1	1	8
Durham	0	2	1	1	3	1	1	1	10
Madison	1	2	2	2	3	2	2	1	15

Note: Adjusted predicted levels repeat the totals from the right-hand column of Table 2.1, adjusted from a 10-point to a 24-point scale.

Indexes based on the following measures:

Category	3	2	1	0
Pedestrian zones (early 1990s)	5,000 or more m	2,000 to 5,000 m	2,000 or fewer m	Insignificant amount of streets
Maintenance of forest (late 1970s–early 1990s)[a]	Decline of less than 3%	Decline of 3 to 10%[b]	Decline of 10% or more, or a total of up to 10% of all land	No forest
Maintenance of agricultural land (late 1970s–early 1990s)[a]	Decline of less than 3%	Decline of 3 to 10%	Decline of 10% or more, or a total of up to 10% of all land	No farmland
Historic preservation (early 1990s)	Partly qualitative ratings based on extent of historic districts (France, U.S.), number of protected buildings (Germany, U.S.), degree of protection (based on interpretation of legislation and implementation)			
Parks (early 1990s)	Land area exceeded 10 cm^2 per person, or annual expenditures exceeded $65 per person	Land area from 1 to 10 cm^2 per person, and annual expenditures under $65 per person	Land area less than 1 cm^2 per person, but greater than zero	No parks
Streets (municipal expenditures on lighting, cleaning, upkeep of streets in early 1990s budgets)	Over $175 per person	$100 to $175 per person	Under $100 per person	None
Bicycle paths (early 1990s)	Over 100 km of off-street paths	20 to 100 km of off-street paths	1 to 20 km of off-street bicycle paths	Insignificant off-street bike paths
Mass transit (early 1990s)	Partly qualitative ratings based on existence of subway or trolley alongside bus service, on extent of service and on available statistics on proportionate usage.			

Notes to Table 2.1. (*continued*)

[a] Among the U.S. cities parallel land use data enabled a similar calculation only for Madison. For Durham and New Haven I estimated losses on the basis of maps and other data.

[b] In Rennes, an increase in the proportion of forest in the early 1990s justified a rating of 2 despite an overall level of 10 percent or less.

Sources: Forest. District of Rennes, *Schéma Directeur* (1994), p. 31b; other French cities from INSEE *Communoscope* computer files; Bielefeld, Münster, from *Land* statistical office computer files; Freiburg, *Erläuterungsbericht zum Flächennutzungsplan* (1980), p. 51, Freiburg, *Jahresheft 1987* (1988), p. 66; Niedersächsisches Landesamt für Statistik, *Nutzungsarten der Bodenflächen* (1980, 1991, 1993); Durham City-County Planning Department, *Durham County Open Space Corridor System* (1993), p. 1; computer files, Dane County Planning Commission; South Central Regional Council of Governments, *Growth and Change: Issues for the 1990s* (North Haven, 1988), p. 26. *Agricultural land.* INSEE *Communoscope* computer files on French cities; Bielefeld, Münster, from *Land* statistical office computer files; Freiburg, *Erläuterungsbericht*, p. 50, (1988), *Jahresheft 1987*, p. 66; Niedersächsisches Landesamt, *Nutzungsarten der Bodenflächen* (1980, 1991, 1993); U.S. cities from same sources as for forests. *Pedestrian zones.* Estimates from city zone maps in Michelin Tire Company, *Michelin Deutschland 1980, 1994; Michelin France 1981, 1994.* Others estimated from city maps. *Parks (expenditures).* 1990s budget figures. *Parks (extent).* Montpellier, *Plan d'occupation des sols: Rapport de présentation* (1985), p. 28; Nancy, *Plan d'occupation des sols: Rapport de présentation* (1995), pp. 243–247; ADUAN, *Atlas de l'agglomération nancéienne* (1994), p. 20; Rennes, *Plan d'occupation des sols: Rapport de présentation* (1976), p. 45; id., *L'Activité municipale 1993*, p. 29; Bielefeld, Münster, from *Land* statistical office computer files; Freiburg: *Jahresheft*, p. 2; Niedersächsisches Landesamt, *Nutzungsarten der Bodenflächen* (1980, 1991, 1993); Durham City-County Planning Department, *Open Space* (1989), p. 9; computer files, Dane County Planning Commission; for other cities estimates from local maps. *Streets (expenditures).* 1990s budget figures. *Bicycle paths.* ADUAN, *Atlas*, p. 51, Map 15; District of Rennes, *Notre espace 2010* (1993); R. Tressel, "Verkehrsverhalten von Studenten," in Amt für Statistik und Einwohnerwesen Freiburg, *Stadtverkehr wohin?* (Freiburg, 1990), pp. 56–57; Freiburg, *Jahresheft*, p. 71; W. Theine et al., *Verkehrliches Leitbild Göttingen* (Hannover, 1994), p. 24; Münster, *Statistischer Jahresbericht 1992*, p. 123; id., *Verkehrsbericht Münster* (1993), p. 4; Durham City-County Planning Department, *Durham Urban Trails and Greenways Master Plan* (1988); Madison, *Community Profile* (1995), p. 47; others estimated from maps. *Mass transit.* Clermont-Ferrand, *Clermont-Ferrand en chiffres 1994* (1994), p. 94; SIEPAC, *Schéma Directeur* (1994), p. 79; Montpellier, *Montpellier Déplacements* (1990), p. 6; ADUAN, *Atlas*, p. 26; District of Rennes, *Schéma Directeur*, pp. 16B–17B; Christian Presch, "... denn sie wissen nicht was sie tun," in Hartmut Hein (ed.), *Ausgerechnet Bielefeld* (Münster: Westfälisches Dampfboot, 1991), p. 164; Tressel, ibid.; Freiburg, *Jahresheft*, p. 71; Theine et al., *Verkehrliches Leitbild*, p. 30; Detlef Hatje, "Einpendler und Auspendler in Göttingen 1987," *Göttinger Statistik: Vierteljahresbericht* (1990), p. 11; Münster, *Statistischer Jahresbericht 1992*, p. 146; Münster, *Verkehrsbericht*, pp. 6–7; U.S. Bureau of the Census, *1990 SMSA Reports.*

Clearly neither industrial legacies nor nation-specific tendencies can account for all variation among these cities. Even with the manufacturing centers left out, the indexes diverge by five points within each country. Neither the rapid growth nor the central-city decline relates systematically to these outcomes. Beyond the processes that produced the systematic differences, closer scrutiny will reveal localized variations at work.

A similar puzzle emerges from environmental outcomes in the wider metropolitan settings. Some of the most obvious, measurable results of this sort center on the protection of forest, open space and agricultural land from urban sprawl or on the spread of low-density development outward beyond the urban fringe. The German city regions, like their central cities, manifested the most control over this process. But comparable evidence of control also emerged from French and U.S. settings.

Over the fifty years since the end of the Second World War, as each of these service centers has grown, settlement has expanded outward. The resulting problem of control over expansion in the urban periphery confronts city regions throughout the advanced industrial world.[18] Yet a drive through any of these urban regions offers a view of recognizable national patterns for urban settlement. Outside the German cities, small towns and villages dot the countryside at regular intervals. New housing, most often in multifamily units, clusters in or near village centers with a full array of similar food stores, bakeries, butcher shops, bars and coffee shops. In France, dense concentrations of development in the central area give way quickly to a more haphazard pattern of strip developments, business parks, super- and hypermarket complexes and dusty, declining village centers. These chaotic "pavilion zones" often line the main roads out from the urban center. In the United States, the typical suburban sprawl of subdivisions, malls and small office centers usually follows the main freeways throughout the metropolitan area. The origins of such patterns often trace far back into the early histories of settlement, whether to the nineteenth century in Madison or to the medieval configurations of agrarian and market towns in Europe.

Changing gradients of population density offer a parallel, quantitative indicator that can be used to compare the degree of sprawl in these patterns. Employed by economists over the last several decades, this measure

---

[18] Peter Hall and Dennis Hay, *Growth Centres in the European Urban System* (London: Heinemann Educational, 1980).

of the dispersal of settlement derives from a regression of population density against distance for the census tracts of a metropolitan area. To take into account the exponential decline in density with distance from the central, densest locations, the equation for the density gradient takes the natural logs of both terms.[19] Throughout the United States and Western Europe, density gradients have declined in recent decades.[20] In U.S. metropolitan areas, average gradients by the 1980s hovered around .20. Overall, the metropolitan areas of Durham, Madison and New Haven averaged around this level as well (Table 2.2). In Germany, especially around Bielefeld and Münster, settlement in villages scattered at intervals across the countryside kept gradients lower despite strong concentrations in the city center. In France, the centralized traditional patterns had maintained density gradients at generally high levels into the 1970s.

Whatever these original patterns, the preservation of forests and open spaces and the prevention of sprawl outside the center posed parallel problems. As the last section showed, metropolitan populations expanded consistently regardless of whether the central city grew. Even more consistently than environmental outcomes in the central cities, control over dispersal in the German settings exceeded that elsewhere (Table 2.2). The growing, increasingly dense population of a metropolitan area like Freiburg might have been expected to move farther out from the center than in the other German urban regions. But even in this region, despite steady growth into the 1980s, the rate of dispersal persisted at the uniformly low levels of the other German settings. Around Münster as well, where overall density rose at a faster pace, the rate of spread outward remained the lowest among the German urban regions. Rates of declining gradients varied among these settings by only four ten thousands of a point.

Rates of spread varied among both the French and the U.S. settings by six or seven times as much. The contrast between effective control over growth around Paris and unregulated development around New York

---

[19] The density gradient derives from an ordinary least-squares regression that employs the natural log of the density for census tracts to estimate:

$$D^*(x) = D_0^* - > x + u,$$

where $D(x)$ is the gross population density at distance x from the city center, D_0 is density at distance zero, $>$ is the density gradient, u is a random normal error term and $*$ indicates the natural log.

[20] M. Macauley, "Estimation and Recent Behavior of Urban Population and Employment Density Gradients," *Journal of Urban Economics 18* (1985): 251–260.

Table 2.2 *Overall Density and Density Gradients, 1970–1990*

	Overall Density		Density Gradient		
	Persons/km^2	Increase in persons/ km^2 (per year)	Gradient	R^2	Change in Gradient (per year)
Germany (1970–1987)	[1987]		[1987]		
Freiburg	230	1.26	0.190	0.86	−0.0005
Münster	231	0.81	0.124	0.80	−0.0002
Bielefeld	390	0.35	0.098	0.89	−0.0006
Göttingen	219	0.04	0.174	0.75	−0.0003
France (1975–1990)	[1990]		[1990]		
Montpellier	191	3.36	0.399	0.74	−0.0047
Rennes	322	3.93	0.219	0.94	−0.0018
Clermont-Ferrand	417	2.21	0.268	0.74	−0.0025
Nancy	504	1.22	0.313	0.81	−0.0017
United States (1970–1990)	[1990]		[1990]		
Durham	154	2.38	0.180	0.75	−0.0048
Madison	118	1.26	0.250	0.95	−0.0009
New Haven	548	1.75	0.188	0.79	−0.0017

Sources: (Germany) Local statistics offices; (France) INSEE, *Évolutions démographiques 1975–1982–1990*, Departmental volumes; (United States) U.S. Bureau of the Census, *1970, 1990 SMSA Reports*.

scarcely begins to encompass the variety of outcomes around the service centers of France and the United States. In the fastest growing urban regions of both countries, Montpellier and Durham, urban sprawl advanced much more rapidly than it did elsewhere. Despite considerable growth, the region around Madison had curtailed sprawl up to 1990 more effectively than either its French or its U.S. counterparts. Dispersal there and in Rennes, another metropolitan area with more modest growth, ranged below that of metropolitan areas that grew less. In both cities, as Chapter 3 will confirm, development since 1970 had moved away from agricultural and forest land. Although an exodus from the declining central cities of New Haven, Nancy and Clermont-Ferrand into the surrounding metropolitan areas could account for the greater difficulties there, so could the comparative absence of effective control over dispersal.

As determinants of environmental results in both the central cities and the urban regions at large, it is important to single out local causes from those at other levels. Especially in the United States and France, regional and national data on land use demonstrate the role of urban political economies in the most successful instances of urban environmental provision. Even where the local results fail to stand out from wider propensities, as in the consistent environmental performance of the German settings, the local political economies crystallize the national tendencies.

As the U.S. and French urban regions with the best environmental outcomes demonstrate, local success can stand out at wider regional scales. Madison had attained a significantly higher score in the index of outcomes than the other U.S. settings, and the urban region had generally controlled development the most effectively. Rennes ranked highest among the French cities for its parks, natural preservation, street maintenance and bicycle paths, and had one of the lowest rates of population dispersal. In the areas surrounding both of these urban regions, however, environmental outcomes differed little from the growth regions surrounding the less successful settings of Montpellier and Durham. Despite somewhat more moderate growth than in North Carolina, Wisconsin had lost farmland over the 1980s and early 1990s at a rate much faster than either of the other two states (Table 2.3). If the state lost forest land at a less rapid rate, it continued to do so at more than the national average, and from a smaller proportionate base. Similarly, Brittany lost utilized agricultural land at nearly a third of a percentage point a year. This comparatively high rate resembled that at which similar land disappeared in the region of Languedoc-Roussillon around Montpellier. As farmers deserted their farms in both regions, Brittany gained forested land at only a slightly higher rate. It would be difficult to argue that either Wisconsin or Brittany possess environmental characteristics that foster stronger environmentalist preferences than in North Carolina or Languedoc. Comparatively low population densities and high levels of either forests or farmland predominated in all of these regions. The better environmental outcomes in both Madison and Rennes owe more to differences within the urban regions themselves than to contrasts at higher scales.

At the national scale, the more consistent environmental successes of the German cities again suggest wider processes at work. As Table 2.3 indicates, a national population density roughly half again as high as in all but one of the regions in these other countries could easily have fostered social

Table 2.3 *Population Density and Retention of Forest and Agricultural Land at Regional and National Scales, 1970s–1990s*

	Population Density (per km^2)	Percent Land in Forest	Annual Gain/Loss (percent)	Percent Land in Agriculture	Annual Loss (percent)
Germany (W.)	(1987)	(1993)	(1985–1993)	(1993)	(1985–1993)
(National)	245	30.0	+.05	53.5	−.21
North Rhine-Westphalia (Bielefeld, Münster)	490	24.7	+.01	52.6	−.24
Baden-Württemberg (Freiburg)	259	37.6	+.14	48.1	−.25
Lower Saxony (Göttingen)	150	20.8	+.01	62.7	−.19
France	(1990)	(1989)	(1979–1989)	(1990, utilized)	(1980–1990)
(National)	104	27.2	+.09	56.2	−.23
Auvergne (Clermont-Ferrand)	51	27.5	+.07	61.5	−.14
Languedoc-Roussillon (Montpellier)	77	29.2	+.03	41.5	−.34
Lorraine (Nancy)	98	36.9	+.02	41.5	−.14
Bretagne (Rennes)	103	11.9	+.06	50.2	−.30
United States	(1990)	(1992, rural)	(1987–1992)	(1992, rural)	(1987–1992)
(National)	27	20.4	+0.0	19.7	−.42
North Carolina (Durham)	53	47.4	−.32	17.7	−.20
Wisconsin (Madison)	35	37.3	−.02	30.1	−.48
Connecticut (New Haven)	262	54.8	−.22	7.1	−.06

Sources: (Germany) Statistisches Bundesamt, *Bevölkerungsstruktur und Wirtschaftskraft der Bundesländer 1989*, Table 5.4.2; Statistisches Bundesamt, *Statistisches Jahrbuch 1997*, p. 18; (France) INSEE, *Statistiques et indicateurs des régions françaises 1992*, pp. III 20; INSEE, *Statistiques et indicateurs des régions françaises 1995*, pp. III 12, III 20; (United States) *Statistical Abstract of the United States 1993*, p. 220; *Statistical Abstract of the United States 1997*, p. 229.

and market preferences in favor of national policy. Historically if not recently, as Jackson has argued,[21] higher land costs and greater threats of depletion in European settings like Germany undoubtedly contributed to the emergence of stricter controls. Functional imperatives of this sort, however, fail to explain the stronger growth management even in urban regions with lower densities that in greater New Haven or greater Nancy (Table 2.2), or the effectiveness of forest and farmland preservation at regional and national scales in France (Table 2.3). Surveys point to generally stronger values in support of environmental policy among German mass publics than those in the United States or France.[22] But mass values diffused on a national scale, like global values, amount to preferences within local as well as national political economies. Repeated actions in local markets or local political processes express those values. Local conditions, and the framing of markets and policies within urban regions, can cultivate or discourage them. In the environmental field, many of the most prominent national and regional movements in support of those values rely on service centers like the ones in this study to maintain activists and organizations. The comparative success of environmental policies and movements at a national scale in Germany can be understood only in light of the place that environmentalism increasingly occupies in urban political economies across the country.

Only for Germany do the consistently favorable local environmental outcomes point clearly to the need for such a national explanation. Alongside similar, more limited patterns of growth, the German service centers furnished higher levels of environmental amenities in the center and stemmed sprawl more throughout the metropolitan area. In Germany as in France and the United States, longtime service centers achieved generally better environmental outcomes than places with strong legacies of manufacturing. But among the central cities of all these service centers and in France and the United States among the surrounding urban regions, the variety of urban environmental outcomes highlighted the importance of local conditions and choices.

[21] Jackson, *Crabgrass Frontier*, Ch. 10.
[22] In a 1988 survey, 25 percent more German than French respondents identified the environment as an "immediate and urgent" problem. In 1993, 9 percent more did (Jefferey M. Sellers, "Grounds of Democracy: Public Authority and the Politics of Metropolitan Land in Three Societies" [Ph.D. diss., Yale University, 1994], p. 364 n. 4).

Polarized Jobs and Polarized Places

Studies that take national political economies as units, as well as analyses of the largest cities, generally point to rising inequality in jobs and earnings as a consequence of postindustrial growth.[23] Beyond the overall employment and earnings structure of each country this polarization has two dimensions within urban regions. First, as the hypothesis of global urban dualization postulates, local structures of employment and income may not just reflect polarized regional and national patterns, but may aggravate or alleviate them. Second, as U.S. observers in particular have emphasized, polarization in the spatial structure of metropolitan areas can exacerbate the disadvantages that result from inequalities in employment and income. Wealthier, more privileged groups can enhance their privileges by keeping to themselves. Segregation confronts disadvantaged groups like ethnic minorities and poor people with added difficulties like crime and delinquency within their neighborhoods and often with less access to jobs, amenities and services. In somewhat different ways, midsize service centers and the biggest cities manifest both types of local polarization. Like the other outcomes, these global patterns vary widely among cities as well as among countries.

As the economies of advanced industrial countries have depended increasingly on technological innovation and service provision, new socioeconomic inequalities have emerged. The departing sector of traditional manufacturing has given way to new disparities between higher- and lower-status service jobs, and in Europe to higher unemployment. In urban centers of innovation and services, these disparities often surpass the tendencies in regional and national economies. Divergent categories of jobs in national censuses cannot disguise the common tendency toward greater inequality (Figure 2.5). But in midsize service centers the

---

[23] See, e.g., Torben Iversen and Ann Wren, "Equality, Employment and Budgetary Restraint: The Trilemma of the Service Economy," *World Politics* 50(4) (1998): 507–546; W. J. Wilson, *When Work Disappears: The World of the New Urban Poor* (New York: Knopf, 1996); Sheldon Danziger and Peter Gottschalk, *America Unequal* (Cambridge, MA: Harvard University Press, 1995); Sassen, *The Global City*; Robert Reich, *The Work of Nations* (New York: Knopf, 1991).

Figure 2.5 (*facing page*) Changes in Central City Occupational Structure as a Result of Service Economies

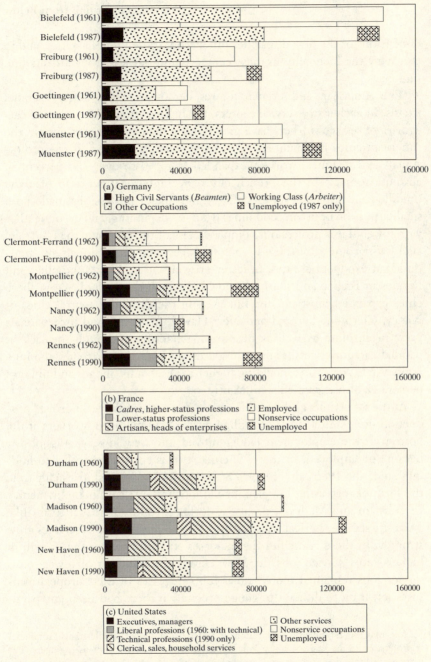

(a) Germany
- ■ High Civil Servants (*Beamten*)
- ⊡ Other Occupations
- □ Working Class (*Arbeiter*)
- ▨ Unemployed (1987 only)

(b) France
- ■ *Cadres*, higher-status professions
- ▨ Lower-status professions
- ▧ Artisans, heads of enterprises
- ⊡ Employed
- □ Nonservice occupations
- ▨ Unemployed

(c) United States
- ■ Executives, managers
- ▨ Liberal professions (1960: with technical)
- ▧ Technical professions (1990 only)
- ▨ Clerical, sales, household services
- ⊡ Other services
- □ Nonservice occupations
- ▨ Unemployed

Sources: (Germany: workplaces) *Arbeitstättenzählungen* data 1970, 1987 from *Land* and local statistics offices; (France: workers at place of residence) INSEE, *Recensement général de la population de 1962: Résultats du sondage au 1/20*, Departmental Reports (1964); unpublished data from 1990 census; (U.S.: employed residents at place of residence) U.S. Bureau of the Census, *1960 Census of Population and Housing: Economic and Social Characteristics of the Population*, State Reports; id., *1990 Census SMSA Reports*.

dimensions of the new disparities differ from those in global cities, and in Germany the inequality in these centers stand out less from surrounding regions.

The American and French figures demonstrate the largely parallel trends. In each set of service centers, the highest-status, best-earning categories of service workers have grown more than any other group. In the American cities the numbers of managers and executives, liberal professionals and technical workers expanded from 40 to over 300 percent in absolute terms.[24] In the French cities the higher-status group of *cadres* (middle- and higher-level executives) and liberal professions made up a smaller portion of urban economies from the beginning, and even together with lower-status professions comprised less of the economy than did parallel U.S. groups. But these French managers and professionals also multiplied at exponential rates. In faster-growing places like Montpellier and Rennes in France and Durham and Madison in the United States, these elites expanded most rapidly. But even in the declining central cities of Nancy, Clermont-Ferrand and New Haven, managers and professionals grew in absolute as well as proportionate terms. Although the lack of parallel categories in Germany obscures any such wider trends, the lone higher-status category, including higher civil servants, judges and military personnel, also expanded significantly.

At the same time, as the traditional working-class jobs on "Fordist" production lines shifted to more skilled work or disappeared, workers at the bottom of the employment ladder moved into new lower-status jobs or became unemployed. In the U.S. cities, consistent with established findings since the 1980s about the U.S. "job machine," this shift usually took the form of increasing low-pay menial jobs rather than unemployment.[25] In Durham and Madison, despite a decline in older personal forms like domestic service, clerical, sales, household and miscellaneous services grew strongly. In these two cities the increases still fell short of the growth in higher-status service jobs. In New Haven the numbers of lower-status service jobs remained more stable. Job categories of the European censuses left it more difficult to gauge precisely if there had been any paral-

---

[24] Note that the 1960 census publications included a number of middle-status "technical" professions in the same category with higher-status professionals such as engineers. The figure includes these professions separately in 1990.

[25] Danziger and Gottschalk, *America Unequal*; Joel I. Nelson and Jon Lorence, "Employment in Service Activities and Inequality in Metropolitan Areas," *Urban Affairs Quarterly* 21(1) (1985): 106–125.

lel increases in jobs. Among the other occupations in Germany, the category of *Angestellten* encompassed higher-level executives as well as secretaries and telephone operators. The French term *employé* excluded the *cadres* and technical professions but included a range of office and service workers. Except in Montpellier, where the entire local economy virtually doubled, these additional categories in both countries grew more modestly than did parallel jobs in the U.S. cities. As local jobs failed to expand, unemployment increased. Already in 1990 the level in Montpellier had reached 14 percent. By the mid-1990s, rates in the German cities would also move above one-tenth of the workforce.

In all three types of national political economies, then, similar trends toward polarized employment accompanied the growth of service centers. This common tendency reflects the wider disparities that emerged as services and technological innovation moved to the forefront of advanced industrial economies. Variations in those disparities manifested wider contrasts between European and American varieties of market economies. At the same time, the urban political economies of service centers often accentuated wider disparities. In no country did these settings attract the more extreme polarities of global cities. But growth in the French and U.S. service centers usually aggravated local inequalities in employment and income, while in the German service centers it generally did not.

Comparison of service centers with both global cities and wider regional and national patterns brings out these trends (Figure 2.6). Since many more of the most privileged residents in the U.S. settings lived outside the central cities, my comparison of these processes took metropolitan as well as central-city figures in those settings into account. With this qualification, the changes at the top and the bottom of the occupational ladder in the settings in the United States and France largely resembled each other (Figure 2.6). In both countries, the service centers attracted or generated significantly larger proportionate increases in higher-status occupations than the wider region did. This component of growth lagged behind in each country's declining center of manufacturing, Clermont-Ferrand and New Haven. Although Durham and Madison enjoyed more dramatic increases in these categories than did their French counterparts, this result differed little from the broader U.S. pattern. In both countries, the number of lower-status jobs in the service centers either grew less than in the surrounding region or simply shrank. In the U.S. cities, as upper-status occupations grew more, lower-status occupations fell as a proportion of the economy. But especially in Durham and

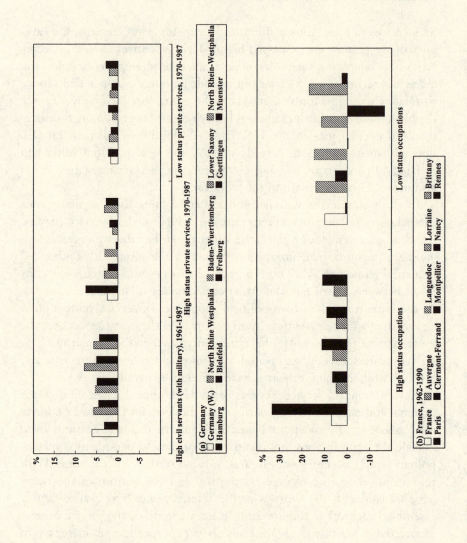

High civil servants (with military), 1961–1987

High status private services, 1970–1987

Low status private services, 1970–1987

(a) Germany

Germany (W.)	North Rhine Westphalia	Baden-Wuerttemberg	Lower Saxony	North Rhein-Westphalia
Hamburg	Bielefeld	Freiburg	Goettingen	Muenster

High status occupations

Low status occupations

(b) France, 1962–1990

France	Auvergne	Languedoc	Lorraine	Brittany
Paris	Clermont-Ferrand	Montpellier	Nancy	Rennes

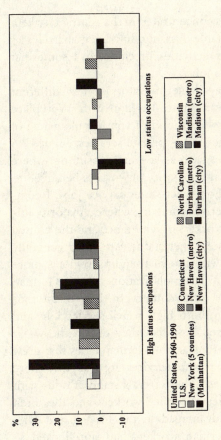

%

High status occupations

Low status occupations

United States, 1960–1990	□ Connecticut	▨ North Carolina	■ Wisconsin
□ U.S.	▨ New Haven (metro)	▨ Durham (metro)	▨ Madison (metro)
■ New York (5 counties)	■ New Haven (city)	■ Durham (city)	■ Madison (city)
■ (Manhattan)			

Figure 2.6 Changes in High- and Low-Status Service Jobs as Percentage of All Jobs, 1960–1990

Note: For definitions of occupations, see notes 24 through 26 and accompanying text in Chapter 2.

Sources: (Germany: civil servants) *Land* and local statistical offices; (types of service activities, by workplaces) Statistisches Bundesamt, *Arbeitstättenzählung 1970; Arbeitstättenzählung von 25.5.1987: Unternehmen und Arbeitstätten*, Fachserie 2, Heft; (France: workers at place of residence) INSEE, *Recensement général de la population de 1962: Résultats du sondage au 1/20*, Departmental Reports (1964); unpublished data from 1990 census; (U.S.: employed residents at place of residence) U.S. Census Bureau, *1960 Census of Population and Housing: Economic and Social Characteristics of the Population*, State Reports; *1990 Census of Population and Housing: Economic and Social Characteristics of the Population*, State Reports; id., *1990 SMSA Reports*.

New Haven, the lower status workers concentrated in the central city kept the proportion of this group either stable or rising. In Nancy, sharp losses in manufacturing jobs and in other activities precipitated a somewhat anomalous fall in lower-status service jobs.

For Germany, the most parallel available indicators suggest different implications for local polarization from service-based growth. Workplace statistics for types of businesses provided the most comparable gauge of this process. As an indicator of higher-status private services, Figure 2.6 utilizes employees in business services such as law and consulting, where national cross-tabulations showed that a majority of workers belonged to the higher occupational categories. For lower-status service jobs, I compared cleaning and a miscellaneous service category, where a majority utilized skilled or unskilled blue-collar workers. As in France and the United States, both types of jobs grew. The higher-status categories generally increased more. But in comparison with the surrounding regions, more modest overall growth also brought less polarization to the German service centers than to those in either other country. In three of the four cities, the exception being Göttingen, both higher civil service jobs and higher-status private services increased less than they did in the wider regions. Moreover, in Freiburg and Münster, the German cities that grew most in population, the lower-status private services grew slightly more than they did in the surrounding *Land*. These trends stand at odds with the growing concentrations of privileged service workers and the often lower proportions of the most disadvantaged in the French and U.S. service centers. Since privileged German workers had not flocked to service centers as much as had their French and American counterparts, both local disparities and average incomes remained comparatively low in relation to surrounding regions.

Despite the more limited urban inequality in Germany, the polarization that the thesis of global urban dualization posits has generally accompanied the growth of midsize service centers. This dualization pales by comparison, however, with parallel processes in the biggest cities of all three countries. As Figure 2.6 makes clear, a sharp influx of elite business activities and other higher-status service work accompanied the overall decline in jobs in downtown Paris and Manhattan. The proportionate shift toward workers in this group nearly doubled the magnitude of the strongest shift in midsize service centers in the United States and reached three times the level of the other cities in France. Even in Germany, higher-status private service employment grew by several times as much in Hamburg as it did in any of the midsize cities. However much these new concentrations consolidated what Sassen and others term "control functions" over the rest of the economy in the biggest cities,[26] global cities magnified the pronounced shift of midsize service centers. At the same time, lower-status service occupations grew about as modestly as in the midsize service centers of each country. In Europe, unemployed workers reinforced the growing disparities in the occupational structure.

As Figure 2.7 shows, these processes gave rise to different patterns of social and economic stratification in midsize service centers from those in the biggest cities. Both Paris and Manhattan had accumulated significantly larger proportions of the local workforce in high-paying professional and managerial occupations; parallel occupational categories for Germany would probably have demonstrated a more modest but similar concentration in Hamburg. In many of the midsize centers devoted to innovation and services, however, concentrations of highly educated workers fostered a distinctive pattern of stratification based more on education than on occupation. Not only the universities but also the governmental networks and professional services in the economies of these settings depended on the cognitive skills and credentialing systems that higher education provided. Only in Bielefeld, Clemont-Ferrand and New Haven, where services replaced declining manufacturing, did the concentration of educated workers remain limited by comparison with that in the surrounding area. Compared even with Manhattan or Hamburg, the other service centers had attracted larger proportions of workers with college degrees. As it does in other respects, this polarization appears less dramatic in the German urban regions.[27] Spatial segregation of elite residences often enhanced the advantages of these privileged groups. Within as well as between the

---

[26] See Sassen, *The Global City*; Sassen, *Cities in a World Economy*. Even before the age of the internet, other writers portrayed globalization as a process of global corporate decentralization rather than as the centralization that new control functions would require. See Rosabeth Kanter, *World Class* (New York: Simon and Schuster, 1995).

[27] Figure 2.7 also reflects how the much larger proportions of both higher-status jobs and higher educational degrees in the U.S. cities follow the wider pattern in American society. Terry N. Clark, "Is There Really a New Political Culture: Evidence from Major Historical Developments of Recent Decades," in Terry Nichols Clark and Vincent Hoffmann-Martinot (eds.), *The New Political Culture* (Boulder, CO: Westview Press, 1998), pp. 75–92; Gosta Esping-Andersen, *Changing Classes* (London: Sage Publications, 1993). Although the category for Germany encompasses other tracks to postsecondary degrees through more technically oriented schools, two-thirds or more of those in this category had university educations.

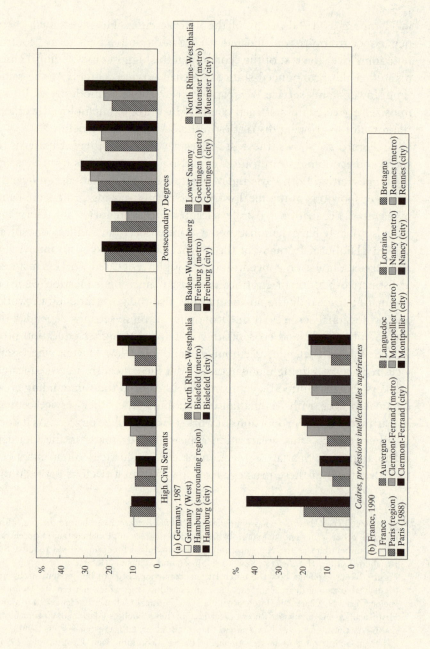

High Civil Servants

Postsecondary Degrees

(a) Germany, 1987

Germany (West)	North Rhine-Westphalia	Baden-Wuerttemberg
Hamburg (surrounding region)	Bielefeld (metro)	Freiburg (metro)
Hamburg (city)	Bielefeld (city)	Freiburg (city)

Lower Saxony	North Rhine-Westphalia	
Goettingen (metro)	Muenster (metro)	
Goettingen (city)	Muenster (city)	

Cadres, professions intellectuelles supérieures

(b) France, 1990

France	Auvergne	Languedoc
Paris (region)	Clermont-Ferrand (metro)	Montpellier (metro)
Paris (1988)	Clermont-Ferrand (city)	Montpellier (city)

Lorraine	Bretagne	
Nancy (metro)	Rennes (metro)	
Nancy (city)	Rennes (city)	

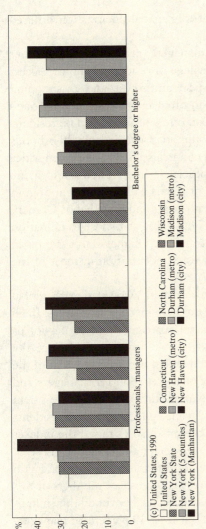

Figure 2.7 Concentrations of Higher-Status Workers in Service Centers

Note: German higher civil servants include *Beamten*, judges and military as proportion of employed adults. Postsecondary degrees include those with professional degrees from *Berufsschulen* and *Fach-schulen* as well as *Fachhochschulen* and *Hochschulen*, as proportion of population from 15 to 64 not still in school. French figures for *cadres*, *professions intellectuelles supérieures* as proportion of employed adults. U.S. figures for professional and managerial workers as proportion of employed adults, and for those over 25 with 4-year bachelor's or higher degree.

Sources: (Germany) 1987 Census data from Statistisches Bundesamt, *Bevölkerung und Erwerbstätigkeit*, Fachserie 1, Heft 4; and from *Land* and local statistics publications or computer files; (France) INSEE, *Recensement de la population de 1990, France métropolitaine et régions*; and computer files; (United States) U.S. Census Bureau, *1990 Census of Population and Housing: Economic and Social Characteristics; id., 1990 SMSA Reports*.

three countries, however, the extent of this spatial polarization differed greatly.

Their higher incomes usually gave managers, professionals and other highly educated workers the further privilege of residential choice. Access to environmental goods such as open space and forest land, to shopping and sometimes to services like education often hinged as much on one's residence in the right neighborhood as on one's occupation. The residential segregation of these privileged groups in privileged neighborhoods varied among metropolitan areas within countries as well as between wider national contexts. In every city, local officials I interviewed could name comparatively exclusive neighborhoods or towns with little prompting: in Bielefeld, the Teutobürger Forest; in Rennes, around the Thabor Garden; in Madison, the town of Shorewood Hills. But statistical examination revealed much more systematic concentrations of higher-status groups in the U.S. metropolitan areas and much less concentration in most of the German cities.

The general pattern that analysts have often associated with global urban dualization predominated among the U.S. metropolitan areas. In all three metropolitan areas, highly educated managers and professionals dominated the new peripheral settlements that had expanded since the 1960s. These privileged groups comprised such a pervasive element of the local population that the standard index of segregation for managers and professionals, the dissimilarity index, remained at modest levels of less than 30 (Table 2.4). In Durham and New Haven, college-educated residents concentrated in neighborhoods around the universities raised the indexes for that category into the 40s.[28] These rates generally exceeded those of the European settings. But the most striking contrast with Europe lay in the degree that segregation had combined with the sheer numbers of this group to enable them to dominate in whichever neighborhood they inhabited. In all three U.S. metropolitan areas, at least 39 percent of managerial and professional workers lived in census tracts where 40 percent or more of working residents belonged to their own higher-status category. Within the city limits of Durham and Madison, over half of these workers lived in such places. Even with the statistical disparities that limited

---

[28] By 1990 in Durham, the dissimilarity index for those with a bachelors or higher degree reached 41.27 for the city and 43.70 for the metropolitan area. In Madison, the index stood at 34.67 for the city and 35.10 for the metropolitan area. In New Haven, the index reached 47.70 within the city but 31.38 for the metropolitan area.

Table 2.4 *Concentrations of Highest-Status Residents by Neighborhoods*

	United States (Executives, Managers, Professionals, 1990)						France (Cadres, Professions Intellectuelles Supérieures, 1990)				Germany (Degree from *Hochschule* or *Fachhochschule*, 1987)			
	Durham	(Metro Area)	Madison	(Metro Area)	New Haven	(Metro Area)	Clermont	Montpellier	Nancy	Rennes	Bielefeld	Freiburg	Göttingen	Münster
Total group in neighborhoods, by proportions of neighborhood residents in that group (%)														
50+	29.35	32.11	34.43	22.98	23.53	11.60	0.00	0.00	0.00	0.00	0.00	0.00	0.00	0.00
40–49	25.77	24.76	21.36	16.38	12.37	27.99	0.00	0.00	0.00	0.00	0.50	0.00	15.49	0.00
30–39	18.20	19.56	12.38	21.20	25.24	26.99	19.76	7.76	28.73	37.31	0.00	0.00	20.08	0.00
20–29	15.78	14.91	22.98	30.92	28.30	27.44	13.31	51.87	44.54	25.15	11.13	54.01	2.51	40.31
10–19	10.13	8.27	8.84	8.51	10.56	5.98	42.71	36.63	23.76	34.83	34.03	37.66	50.25	58.53
0–9	0.78	0.39	0.00	0.01	0.00	0.00	24.23	3.74	2.97	2.71	54.34	8.33	11.66	1.16
Index of Dissimilarity*	29.58	28.52	25.41	24.44	31.00	22.52	26.82	19.42	18.35	27.34	19.78	20.16	21.45	12.51
Index of Absolute Centralization*	0.03	0.49	0.20	0.75	0.30	0.33	—	—	—	—	0.56 (city), 0.37 (metro)	0.55 (city), 0.69 (metro)	0.57 (city), 0.66 (metro)	0.59 (city), 0.45 (metro)
Highest-status residents (%)	34.05	35.07	35.31	32.51	30.00	32.51	12.61	20.14	22.31	17.40	7.88	17.18	18.61	14.22

* For explanation of indexes, see Douglas S. Massey and Nancy A. Denton, "The Dimensions of Residential Segregation," *Social Forces* 67(2) (1988): 281–315.

Note: U.S. percentages indicate those in executive, administrative, managerial and professional specialty occupations as proportion of employed residents. French percentages denote managerial workers and executives (*cadres*) and higher-status professions (*professions intellectuelles supérieures*) as proportion of employed residents. German percentages give those with postsecondary educational degrees (i.e., from *Hochschulen* or *Fachhochschulen*) as proportion of the resident population over 25.

Sources: (United States) U.S. Census Bureau, *1990 SMSA Reports*; (France) Institut National de la Statistique et des Études Économiques, computer files; (Germany) city statistical offices.

comparison with the most parallel European categories taken into account, the privileged groups in Europe could hardly have dominated their neighborhoods so much.

In ways familiar to students of U.S. cities, elite neighborhoods there accumulated systematic privileges. In all three cities, the local public schools with the best reputations were located in such neighborhoods: the Chapel Hill school system, the west side schools of Madison, the suburban schools outside New Haven. Private amenities in these areas often provided higher levels of environmental quality as well as greater chances for recreation than elsewhere. Country clubs, neighborhood associations and even the large lots of individual home owners often assured ample protection of land and forest in addition to places for leisure. Increasingly, exclusive private residential associations or restrictive covenants in individual contracts perpetuated many of these amenities.[29]

Madison presented a partial exception to this general pattern. Within its metropolitan area, the settlement of managers and professionals as well as of residents in general had remained somewhat more centralized than around Durham or New Haven. The index of centralization for this group stood even higher than in German metropolitan areas (Table 2.4). In the Isthmus neighborhood of downtown Madison, residential concentrations of managers and professionals had persisted to a degree unknown except in the university neighborhoods of Durham and New Haven. But even more than managers and professionals in either of the other cities, those of this midwestern city lived in neighborhoods where they predominated. Within the city limits of Madison, the settlement of managerial and professional residents remained dispersed.

The critical mass necessary for a number of exclusive neighborhoods had emerged in the European settings as well, despite the smaller numbers of higher-status workers. But as both the segregation indexes and the neighborhood percentages of these groups reflected, the European elites lived in less exclusive residential patterns. Even in the French metropolitan areas, as other residents fled to the exurban frontiers, higher-status groups had not followed their U.S. counterparts in the flight from central neighborhoods. And only in specific instances did the European elites concentrate to a significant degree in areas at even a limited remove from the

---

[29] Evan McKenzie, *Privatopia: Homeowner Associations and the Rise of Residential Private Government* (New Haven: Yale University Press, 1994); Edward J. Blakely and Mary Snyder, *Fortress America* (Washington: Brookings Institution, 1999).

downtown. In Nancy and Rennes, sizeable proportions had maintained residences in exclusive neighborhoods in and around the preserved Old Towns. In the eastern villa quarters of Göttingen, sandwiched between the Old Town and the Göttingen Forest, professors and researchers had settled in a similar enclave. But even these areas near the city center remained less exclusive than did their U.S. counterparts, and they usually preserved less exclusive access to neighborhood amenities and other services.

As the segregation indexes as well as the percentages of Table 2.4 indicate, the German cities had generally maintained the least segregated settlement patterns for these higher-status groups. In the U.S. metropolitan areas, managers and professionals lived most consistently in their own neighborhoods and generally received the most exclusive benefits from segregated patterns of residence. In all three countries, however, aspects of the patterns in individual cities diverged from those of other cities.

At the opposite end of the spectrum of wealth and social status, spatial segregation had a contrary meaning. Even the most prosperous service centers also retained portions of the most disadvantaged citizens in advanced industrial society. For these residents, separation from the remainder of society could not only directly frustrate their equal access to basic goods like a healthy environment or good schools and jobs. Spatial isolation could also reinforce the difficulties they encountered in joining the wider society.[30] In the U.S. cities, regardless of the size of local minorities, spatial segregation confronted a large part of the worst-off groups with compounded disadvantage. The residential patterns of German cities reinforced less spatial isolation. In the French cities, a variety of results prevailed.

Much like the biggest cities, albeit on a smaller scale, midsize service centers harbored relative concentrations of the most disadvantaged. With a few exceptions, unemployment rates in these settings exceeded those of the surrounding region (Figure 2.8).[31] The most prominent groups of

---

[30] For parallel U.S. and French overviews of these processes, see Douglas S. Massey and Nancy A. Denton, *American Apartheid* (Cambridge, MA: Harvard University Press, 1993); Jean-Claude Boyer, *Les banlieues en France: Territoires et sociétés* (Paris: Armand Colin, 2000).

[31] In Bielefeld and Münster, the decline of the neighboring Ruhr Valley in the *Land* of North Rhine-Westphalia accounted for a somewhat better performance in relation to the region. Similar regional declines in such industrial areas as Milwaukee in Wisconsin explain a similar anomaly in Madison.

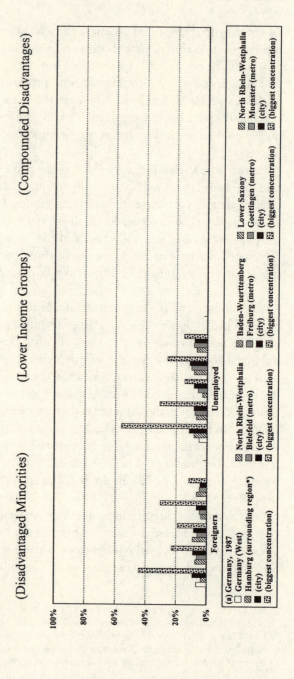

(Disadvantaged Minorities)   (Lower Income Groups)   (Compounded Disadvantages)

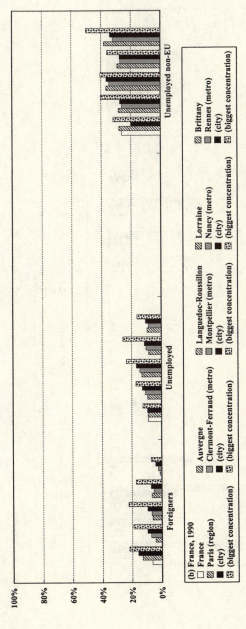

Figure 2.8 Concentrations of Disadvantage Compared with Regional and National Averages, 1990
*Results for Lower Saxony.

Note: Biggest concentrations in the European settings report results for census districts in central cities with highest proportions in category; these districts usually differ by categories. The most depressed areas in the U.S. settings correspond to a census tract or tracts with highest average proportions of all groups. Unemployment is measured as percentage of adult workforce, all other proportions in relation to total population. Parisian employment data for foreigners in workforce outside EU and unreported. In other French cities, data for foreigners from outside EU only.

Sources: (Germany) Statistisches Bundesamt, *Bevölkerung und Erwerbstätigkeit: Volkszählung vom 25. Mai 1987*, Fachserie 1, Hefte 1, 4; *Land* and local statistics publications; (France) INSEE, *Recensement de la population de 1990, France métropolitaine et régions, Résultats du sondage au vingtième*; (Paris) id., *Logements-population-emploi, Évolutions 1975–1982–1990*, and unpublished data from INSEE; (United States) U.S. Census Bureau, *1990 Census: Economic and Social Characteristics, State Reports*; id., *1990 SMSA Reports*.

79

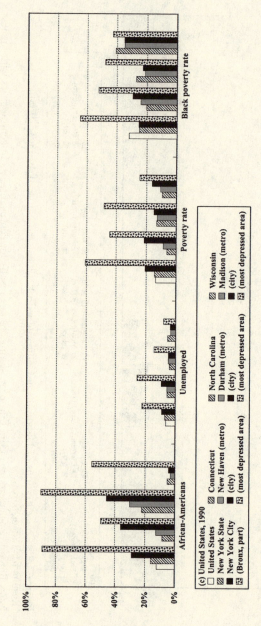

Figure 2.8 *(continued)*

disadvantaged ethnic minorities – foreigners in France and Germany, African Americans and Hispanic Americans in the United States – also usually clustered in these urban centers.[32] Even at the end of the 1980s, the levels of unemployment in these European settings exceeded those in the U.S. service centers. In the 1990s, as national rates in Germany as well as France rose above ten percent, this contrast would grow. As the high poverty rates for the U.S. settings indicate, many of the jobs that reduced U.S. unemployment rolls paid badly and provided few benefits. For this reason, the poverty rate supplemented unemployment as an indicator of disadvantage there. Further indicators, in France of unemployed workers from outside the European Union and in the United States of African American poverty, demonstrated compounded difficulties from ethnic disadvantage and joblessness.[33] In all three countries, individual neighborhoods registered concentrations of at least 20 percent of residents with some form of these disadvantages.

In parts of both New Haven and Durham, as in the most deprived neighborhoods of metropolises like New York, compounded ethnoracial and economic disadvantage took perhaps the most pronounced form. As they did in areas like the South Bronx, economic and social marginality predominated throughout much of downtown Durham and New Haven. African Americans made up half or more of the population in the Hill and Newhallville neighborhoods just to the west of the downtown and the Yale campus in New Haven, while Hispanics comprised much of the remainder. In Durham, long a center of the black middle class, African Americans constituted the vast majority in most downtown neighborhoods. By the 1990s, thirty years and more after urban renewal, both the Hill in New Haven and South Central in Durham had slipped into deepening poverty and urban decay.

Segregation indexes furnish more comprehensive indicators of the growing residential exclusion of the poor as well as the persistent

---

[32] The foreigners in the European contexts might appear to be simply immigrants and therefore to differ from long-standing ethnic minorities in the United States. But by 1990 large proportions of French North Africans and German Turks had in fact resided in these two countries for three generations or more without citizenship.

[33] Parallel indicators were usually unavailable for the German settings even at the city level. Those foreigners who remain in Germany have generally registered higher unemployment than native Germans but lower levels than French immigrants from outside the EU (Jefferey M. Sellers, "Norms in the Politics of Housing for Minorities: Evidence from a French, a German and a U.S. Metropolitan Area," *Ethnic and Racial Studies 19*[3] [1996]: 585–607).

segregation of the most disadvantaged minorities (Table 2.5). If the dissimilarity indexes for blacks fell short of the 80s or 90s that Massey and Denton found in the biggest U.S. metropolitan areas, the levels still approached or exceeded the limit of 60 that these authors took as one criterion of "hypersegregation." Increasingly, segregation along economic lines accompanied generally persistent residential separation by race.[34] Even as the poverty rates in Madison and Durham had fallen slightly over this period, while increasing in New Haven, the concentration of poverty had grown in all three settings. In 1970, metropolitan dissimilarity indexes for persons below the poverty line in the three cities had ranged between 23 and 38; by 1990, the same indexes had climbed from 11 to 20 points and exceeded 42 in each place. As the statistics for the most distressed places in Figure 2.8 suggest, poor minorities stood at the center of the most disadvantaged neighborhoods.

As we shall see, worse schools, fewer shopping opportunities and lower environmental quality followed these concentrations. Analyses of U.S. inner cities emphasize the social and political pathologies that this separation cultivates.[35] A third to 45 percent of the families in the worst-affected areas – from five to seven times the proportion in the metropolitan area – lived below the official poverty line. Female-headed single-parent families resided four times more frequently in these places than in the wider metropolitan area.

The unusually favorable social and economic conditions of Madison might have been expected to alter these outcomes. The overall proportions of minorities, unemployed workers and single-parent families there remained significantly smaller than even in the other U.S. service centers. In contrast with most other U.S. cities, in Madison African Americans made up less of the population than did all but the smallest urban populations of foreigners in Europe. Since these disadvantaged groups remained too small to dominate entire portions of the city, one might expect less spatial concentration of these groups. Instead, the segregative tendencies here had produced the most intense concentration of metropolitan disadvantage that I found. In part of South Madison, a band of

---

[34] In metropolitan Durham, the index of dissimilarity for African Americans had fallen almost 9 points from 63.22 since 1970. But in metropolitan New Haven the index had remained virtually identical, and in Madison it had climbed around 6 points from 51.86.

[35] Massey and Denton, *American Apartheid*; Cathy Cohen and Michael Dawson, "African-American Political Mobilization and Neighborhood Poverty," *American Political Science Review* 87(2) (1993): 286–302.

Table 2.5 *Residential Segregation of Disadvantaged Groups (Index of Residential Dissimilarity)*

	Mean Population of Districts	Disadvantaged Minorities (%)	Disadvantaged Minorities		Lower-Income Groups		Mean
Germany (1987)		(Foreigners)	Foreigners		Unemployed		
Bielefeld	3,321	8.8	29.14		11.98		20.56
Freiburg	4,581	8.4	18.99		13.01		16.00
Göttingen	1,856	7.1	34.33		16.02		25.18
Münster	5,471	4.4	24.74		11.14		17.94
AVERAGE			26.80		13.04		19.92
France (1990)		(Foreigners)	Foreigners	From Outside EU	Unemployed		
Clermont-Ferrand	9,717	10.2	23.22	33.26	11.45		22.64
Montpellier	10,396	9.6	54.76	53.31	59.53		55.87
Nancy	8,529	7.2	53.25	51.91	55.92		53.69
Rennes	11,617	4.3	30.93	33.80	10.96		25.23
AVERAGE			40.54	43.07	34.46		39.36
United States (1990)		(African Americans)	African Americans		Unemployed	Below poverty line	
Durham city	992	47.4	59.31		36.05	48.82	48.06
(Metro area)	(1,307)	(30.8)	(57.24)		(33.41)	(45.18)	(45.28)
Madison city	1,431	4.2	48.68		31.14	49.80	43.21
(Metro area)	(1,385)	(2.9)	(51.44)		(39.44)	(53.61)	(48.16)
New Haven	1,004	36.1	58.28		32.42	40.38	43.69
(Metro area)	(1,112)	(13.6)	(68.02)		(29.18)	(49.28)	(48.83)
AVERAGE			55.42		33.20	46.33	44.99
(METROPOLITAN AVERAGE)			(58.90)		(34.01)	(49.36)	(47.42)

Note: See p. 59, note 19 for formula. Unemployed are measured in all three countries as proportion of active civilian population. Disadvantaged minorities and U.S. poverty rates are measured as proportion of resident population. Note that different levels of aggregation limit but do not eliminate the cross-national comparability of these figures. Partly as a result of more dense settlement in particular neighborhoods, the units averaged somewhat larger in Germany and much larger in France than in the United States. In the United States the calculations derive from block groups, a somewhat smaller level of aggregation than United States census tracts or German census districts. For the central cities in the United States, several of these block groups include areas beyond but adjacent to the municipal jurisdiction.

Sources: (United States) U.S. Census Bureau, STF files; (France) Institut National de la Statistique et des Études Économiques computer files; (Germany) local statistical offices.

neighborhoods between Lake Monona and the Beltline Highway, blacks made up nearly ten times more of the population than they did in the larger metropolitan area. Well over half of the black families here remained below the poverty line. Thirty-nine percent of all unemployed blacks and black families below the poverty line in the entire metropolitan area lived within these 1.1 square miles. White workers below the poverty line also concentrated heavily in this area.

More limited neighborhood statistics offer a less precise picture of the comparable concentrations in German cities. But what is available affirms the more limited residential segregation in Germany that other comparisons with the United States have generally found.[36] If unemployment in the German service centers already tended somewhat higher than in the U.S. counterparts, three of the four German cities had kept neighborhood levels to no more than twice the overall city average for any census district. In Hamburg, despite more integrated patterns overall than in U.S. cities, segregated pockets of foreigners and the unemployed emerged increasingly over the 1980s and 1990s.[37] Although in Freiburg and Bielefeld foreigners comprised a proportion of the urban population comparable to that in the larger metropolis, the strongest concentrations of foreigners by neighborhoods in these cities remained lower. Overall, even the neighborhood closest to a departure from this pattern – a small area of older housing called Schildesche Bauernschaft in downtown Bielefeld – proved an exception. In Bielefeld as in Freiburg and Münster, the dissimilarity indexes demonstrated consistently stronger integration than they did in any of the U.S. settings (Table 2.5). Only in Göttingen did any of the indexes exceed 30. In comparison with the worst-off U.S. areas, moreover, German residential disadvantage was less cumulative. Where more foreigners lived, more working-age residents would usually be employed; where the lowest overall proportion of workers worked, the proportion of foreigners would remain somewhat lower.

[36] Peter Marcuse and Ronald van Kempen (eds.), *Globalizing Cities: A New Spatial Order?* (London: Blackwell, 2000); John O'Loughlin and Jürgen Friedrichs, *Social Polarisation in Post-Industrial Metropolises* (Berlin: Walter de Gruyter and Co., 1996); Elizabeth D. Huttman, Wim Blauw and Juliet Saltman, *Urban Housing Segregation of Minorities in Western Europe and the United States* (Durham: Duke University Press, 1991); Ceri Peach, Vaughan Robinson and Susan Smith (eds.), *Ethnic Segregation in Cities* (London: Croom Helm, 1981).

[37] See Jens Dangschat, "Warum ziehen sich Gegensätze nicht an?" in Wilhelm Heitmeyer, Rainer Dollase and Otto Backes (eds.), *Die Krise der Städte* (Frankfurt: Suhrkamp, 1998), pp. 21–96.

French local statistics broke down city neighborhoods less minutely than in the German figures. Still, the concentrations that these figures revealed sometimes approached levels in the U.S. cities. The largest proportions of both foreigners and the unemployed lived in districts of large-scale public housing, such as La Paillade in Montpellier, Haut du Lièvre in Nancy and Cleunay in Rennes.[38] As statistics unavailable for German neighborhoods showed, people from outside the European Union, or EU, made up the largest proportion of the foreign population and a highly disproportionate portion of the unemployed. These minorities faced the greatest disadvantages in employment markets of any group in these settings.[39] Even before unemployment in France at large had reached the levels of the mid-1990s, urban unemployment for non-European Union foreigners stood at between a fourth and a third of all workers. These averages surpassed those for U.S. blacks in the worst inner-city neighborhoods. Non-Europeans clearly faced obstacles beyond housing markets; however, rates of joblessness among this group in the most underprivileged neighborhoods stood out less than rates for impoverished African Americans from the rest of the city. Foreigners had located in the most disadvantaged areas at from two to just over three times their average proportion in the metropolitan population. In the worst-off neighborhoods in three of the four cities, unemployed residents had congregated at under two times the metropolitan rate. As in Germany, unemployment and foreigners usually concentrated at the highest rates in different census districts.

In Nancy and Montpellier, as the dissimilarity indexes of Table 2.5 confirm, the stronger and more cumulative spatial concentrations in isolated peripheral public housing had compounded these disadvantages. Conditions for housing the disadvantaged there followed a pattern more familiar from the outlying suburbs of bigger French cities like Paris and Lyon.[40] Elite groups dominated residence in an increasingly gentrified old city. At the same time, the immense housing estates of Haut du Lièvre and La Paillade contained larger proportions of both minorities and the unemployed than any single district in the other French settings. A study by the local planning agency in Nancy pointed to even more extreme concentrations in the public housing projects of a few municipalities just beyond the

---

[38] This may also be an artifact of the wider territorial breakdowns in French settings.

[39] On the difficulties of these groups, see M. Tribalat, *De l'immigration á l'assimilation* (Paris: INED-La Découverte, 1996).

[40] Boyer, *Les banlieues en France*; J. Brun and C. Rhein (eds.), *La Ségrégation dans la ville* (Paris: L'Harmattan, 1994).

central city.[41] Within that metropolitan area, the segregation of these groups probably approximated that of poor African Americans in the U.S. cities. But exurban rather than inner-city isolation reinforced social distance from the rest of the population.

Like the other outcomes, spatial inequalities at the highest and lowest ends of metropolitan social and economic hierarchies corresponded at best only partly to national boundaries or regional characteristics. In midsize service centers as in the biggest cities, the inequalities among people and places generally confirmed the local polarization linked to global urban dualization. But the disparities in these smaller settings depended more on educational background and less on stark income differences than in the global cities. Not just in the wider patterns of employment that national capitalisms perpetuated but in local departures from these wider patterns and in local spatial polarization, both the midsize cities and the global cities have followed a wide range of trajectories. In the German settings, alongside less dramatic occupational polarization than in the wider national and regional economies, spatial inequalities remained the most muted. Just as consistently, the U.S. cities had evolved and maintained strikingly parallel systems of spatial inequalities to compound aggravated social disparities. In France, despite a growing social polarization like that of the U.S. settings, local spatial polarization varied the most with the local settings.

Conclusion: Toward Analysis of the Causes

The service centers of this study comprise a distinct type of urban region that has proliferated in advanced industrial countries. This type reflects the increasing predominance of services in these countries and relations between national economies and the wider global economy. As services and innovation have furnished more and more of the impetus behind economic expansion in advanced economies, these settings have emerged as centers of growth. Where the surrounding region has grown, expansion has concentrated in these metropolitan areas. Where local and regional legacies of manufacturing have depressed this growth, the urban centers have borne more of the burden of postindustrial transformation to services. Urban regions have often led the way in provision of urban environmental amenities and in control over sprawl in outlying areas. They

---

[41] Agence de Développement et d'Urbanisme de l'Agglomération Nancienne, *Observatoire du Parc H.L.M. de l'Agglomération Nancéienne au 1er Janvier 1994* (Nancy, 1995).

have absorbed more than equal shares of the highly educated, well-paid workers who increasingly dominate the service economy, and of students preparing to move into such positions. At the same time, their persistent and often growing populations of marginal service employees, unemployed workers, and disadvantaged ethnic and racial minorities have frequently faced spatial as well as social polarization.

In most of these respects, midsize service centers follow trends apparent from the largest metropolitan areas. But propositions derived solely from the biggest cities would give a misleading view of these smaller places. The urban cores of cities like New York, Paris and Hamburg have often lost residents as wealth in these cores has increased. Midsize service centers, however, have mostly gained population and have grown more in educational and occupational status than in average wealth. Global cities follow economic trajectories that are increasingly delinked from national patterns. Service centers stand at the nexus between national or international economic forces and surrounding regions. The biggest places have evolved the most polarized job structures and often the highest levels of economic and ethnic segregation. Service centers retain social and spatial disparities in education and occupational status despite less dramatic inequalities in wealth. Especially in service centers with fewer legacies from manufacturing, smaller size has also often enabled more extensive environmental amenities in the center and more effective control over sprawl in outlying areas.

As side-by-side comparison of the outcomes demonstrates (Table 2.6), the developmental, environmental and distributive outcomes in these service centers have varied widely. In the postindustrial settings of Bielefeld, Clermont-Ferrand and New Haven, prominent local legacies from manufacturing within the central city fostered similar difficulties for local outcomes. Service growth remained more modest than in the other service centers of each country, and only in Bielefeld did it offset the losses in manufacturing. Environmental outcomes within the central city also fell comparatively short in each case.

Characteristics of the surrounding regions corresponded in more contingent ways to differences in local outcomes. Although the central-city economy of Nancy was already predominantly postindustrial by 1962, the surrounding industrial and mining region in decline appears to have had consequences for local growth analogous to the local manufacturing decline of, say, Clermont-Ferrand. But Münster had grown for much of the period since 1960 despite its location next to the massive, declining

Table 2.6 *Outcomes of Policies, Politics and Markets: A Summary*

	Growth in Metro Area / Central City	Urban Environmental Amenities / Control of Exurban Development	Limits on Privileged Enclaves / Spatial Concentrations of Disadvantage (No Positive Ratings)
France			
Clermont-Ferrand (I)	+/–	–/–	0/–
Montpellier (G)	++/++	+/––	0/––
Nancy (IR)	+/–	+/0	–/––
Rennes	++/+	+/0	–/–
Germany			
Bielefeld (I)	0/0	+/++	0/–
Freiburg (G)	+/+	++/++	0/0
Göttingen	0/0	++/++	–/–
Münster (IR)	+/0	++/++	0/0
United States			
Durham (G)	++/++	0/––	––/––
Madison	++/+	+/+	––/––
New Haven (I)	+/–	–/0	––/––

Key: ++ = Strongly positive outcomes; + = Net positive outcomes; 0 = Mixed outcomes; – = Net negative outcomes; –– = Strongly negative outcomes.
(I) = Sites of declining manufacturing; (IR) = Surrounded by region of declining manufacturing; (G) = Growth region.

mining and industrial complex of the Ruhr Valley. Unlike Nancy, the German city had also maintained among the highest levels of environmental amenities. In the fastest growing, surrounding regions of all three countries, Durham, Freiburg and Montpellier had each expanded at rates well beyond those of either the wider region or the other service centers. But in Durham and Montpellier, this expansion corresponded to greater segregation and somewhat lower levels of environmental amenities than in less dramatically growing regions within each country. In Freiburg, the urban region had maintained comparatively integrated settlement patterns and the strongest environmental ratings of all.

Nation-specific tendencies have emerged most clearly as patterns of within-nation variations. For these patterns the degree of consistency matters as much as which aspects of urban outcomes are more or less consistent. In each category of outcomes, the German service centers resemble each other and even the most global of German cities more than do similar urban regions in either France or the United States. Some aspect of the German national context, whether supralocal or local, must have brought about this consistency. The service centers there have both grown less dramatically and avoided sharp postindustrial decline more effectively than French and U.S. counterparts. Even the most industrial of these German cities have attained levels of urban environmental goods beyond the levels of most French and U.S. service centers, and all have controlled urban sprawl outside the center. At the same time, they have limited or reduced socioeconomic disparities and curtailed spatial segregation more consistently. In both France and the United States, local outcomes generally varied more. Contingencies rooted in urban regions and their wider subnational surroundings made a more manifest difference in local growth, environmental quality and local social equity. Only in the consistent urban segregation of the United States did outcomes in these countries approach the relative uniformity of the German settings.

The similar trajectories of service- and technology-based growth, enhanced environmental protections and rising inequalities make it difficult to dismiss the presence of global influences and trends in these urban regions. But the outcomes of Table 2.6 also vary in too many ways for global causes to explain. The commonalities of limited growth, environmental amenities and relative integration in the German cities furnish the most powerful among several indications that national influences have been at work. But to collapse the divergent variations within countries into types like "the German," "the American" and "the French" city would also be more misleading than helpful. Alongside variations due to regional growth, regional decline and interlocal markets, these local environmental, economic and social outcomes differ in ways that depend on the local political economy itself. Only an analysis that maps policies and market decisions forward from each of these levels – from the heights of the European Union, national states and transnational firms down to the influence of neighborhood movements – can fully assess these influences.

3

The Real World of Decentralization

Policy and its consequences pervade outcomes within cities. Whether through initiatives and incentives on behalf of urban economic development, political control in support of environmental protection or reinforcements of as well as constraints on spatial advantages and disadvantages, governments at higher levels have affected outcomes in all three domains. Yet mapping even these measures forward from above demonstrates how important the local influence on them has been. Politicians, businesspeople, activists and electorates within metropolitan settings often play as crucial a role as national, regional and supranational policy elites. Higher-level governments may finance vast expansions in physical infrastructure, education and research, but local initiatives often decide which places receive these assets. Higher-level governments may legislate protections on land, but local decisions determine what land is in fact protected. Higher-level officials may allocate funds for new public housing, but local choices can decide whether that housing will create ghettos. In all of these areas, and in urban regions across the advanced industrial world, localized decision making has proliferated even as policy making at higher levels has in many respects expanded.

What has become known as regulation theory has analyzed these actions as essentially the consequence of capitalist interests in economic production. Yet not only interests besides those of business but also institutional logics inherent in government and policy give shape to these policies. Beyond formal devolution from above, the localization of policy has also grown directly out of expanding state activity. The more that national, intermediate and transnational governments have tried to shape urban political economies, the more that governing from above has depended on governance from below. New policy aims closely linked to the conditions

90

of places, like environmental protections and market-oriented economic development strategies, reinforce this reliance on local decision making. With the rise of localized policy has come a new importance for the structures of policies and institutions that impose the rules of the game for local decision making. In political science, the traditional distinction between federal and unitary states has long remained the primary axis for comparative analyses of subnational state structures.[1] In Germany and France, though less in the United States, infrastructures for urban government and politics now fundamentally alter the consequences of this distinction. Among the eleven urban regions, infrastructures devoted specifically to urban governance account for more of the variation in supralocal initiatives than such organizational features of states at higher levels.

To analyze the logics that drive this localization and the significance of its variants, this chapter considers the effects of policy initiatives from above on the outcomes discussed in the last chapter. I first set forth hypotheses about the general processes and the variations to expect. To compare supralocal policy initiatives in pursuit of local economic development, environmental protection and place-based equity, I then map these measures forward to the local level.

The Logics of Decentralization

Localization marks a sea change in prevailing ideas about how policy making should be done. Where turn-of-the-century analysts of economic and state organization like Taylor and Weber once stressed the virtues of formality and hierarchies, contemporary organization theorists look to decentralized arrangements and informal networks for improvements in efficiency, effectiveness and responsiveness.[2] Decentralized policy grows not only out of this recognition but also out of institutional processes that have always been intrinsic to policy, and out of the political interests that give shape to policy and implementation. The substantive domains of supralocal policies, the organization of states at the top, and other existing infrastructures of local government often alter these influences on initiatives from above. Yet even these nation-centered influences often

---

[1] Paul Peterson, *The Price of Federalism* (Washington: The Brookings Institution, 1995).

[2] See, e.g., George Frederickson, "The Repositioning of American Public Administration," *PS: Political Science and Politics* 23(4) (1999): 701–711; Joel Handler, *Down from Bureaucracy* (Princeton: Princeton University Press, 1996); Oliver Williamson, *The Economic Institutions of Capitalism* (New York: Free Press, 1985).

reinforce the dependence of policy making on local arrangements and choices.

General Logics. Even as the localization of policy challenges received notions of governmental institutions, the "new institutionalism" in political science and other fields has furnished several ways of understanding this process. Partly intrinsic to the institutions of policy making, localization stems from efforts to improve policy performance as well as from the politics of economic and other interests. Much of the literature on each of those influences retains the simplifying assumption that elites at the heights of states dictate policies, objectives and even state structures. To account fully for localization requires an analysis that incorporates attention to local aims and choices.

Intrinsic institutional attributes of the modern state make localized discretion of some sort virtually impossible to root out from policy. Research on the implementation of policies from welfare programs to criminal codes shows that "street-level bureaucrats" engage in substantial policy making of their own.[3] Legislators themselves typically prefer elements of this sort in policy. The need for flexible adjustments among objectives, the likelihood of unforeseen difficulties, and the shifting contexts of policy over time make it reasonable for legislative elites to entrust powers to alter specific aspects of policy to those who carry it out. The territorial dimension of policy provides one of the most pervasive imperatives for localized decision making.

Any local setting presents a unique geographic political, economic and social context that policy makers from above can seldom expect generic statutory categories fully to address.[4] Without localized elements, policies handed down from above could hardly adapt to the distinctive environmental conditions, local markets, private firms and social structures of a specific urban political economy and to the links that connect markets and social life there to other places. For instance, consider the sheer volume of information to be processed, and the number of conflicts to be resolved, were the legislature of a sizeable advanced industrial country to take onto itself current local responsibilities to legislate comprehensive, detailed maps of land uses for all metropolitan regions. This daunting prospect

---

[3] Michael Lipsky, *Street-Level Bureaucracy* (New York: Russell Sage, 1980).
[4] For one of the most sweeping arguments to this effect, see James Scott, *Seeing Like a State* (New Haven: Yale University Press, 1998).

highlights why, in Europe as well as in the United States, control over urban land uses remains "the greatest arena for the exercise of local [governmental] autonomy."[5]

At the same time, localized decision making has grown out of what Frederickson calls "administrative conjunction" among policies and official bodies. Someone has to decide how highways and transit lines can accommodate users of new public university facilities, how redevelopment in a downtown shopping district should respect or adapt to mandates for historical preservation, how the activities of supralocal bodies charged with economic development and environmental protection can be reconciled. The more that policies in related fields proliferate, and the stronger the conjunction among domains, the more this density of policies generates new imperatives for local resolution. When local and supralocal officials both participate in determinations like the precise location of a new highway or transit line, this conjunction links different levels of government in ways that often qualify formal administrative hierarchies. Within an urban region that faces common problems, the multiple local jurisdictions that typically divide up the urban space often must coordinate with one another or come together in collective action. Throughout the advanced industrial world urban and regional planning has emerged as one of the most important local means to this end.

The path dependency inherent in policy and politics has reinforced each of these decentralizing logics. Just as historical processes ensure that the choices of one period shape the opportunities of the next, similar dynamics reinforce the positions of specific places in patterns of policy choices. Groups within cities, like the coalition that imposed growth restrictions in San Francisco in the 1970s, may benefit from favorable environmental and market conditions beyond the immediate control of anyone.[6] But this "place luck," like Machiavelli's *fortunà*, rarely amounts to luck alone. Prior decision makers found a city to take advantage of natural conditions, build infrastructure to secure the city a place in translocal markets, and may preserve or enhance local environmental conditions. Even when initial choices of this sort have come about arbitrarily, "increasing returns" from them affect the rationality of subsequent decisions.[7] Enhancements to a

---

[5] Paul E. Peterson, *City Limits* (Chicago: University of Chicago Press, 1981), p. 25.

[6] Richard DeLeon, *Left Coast City* (Lawrence: University of Kansas Press, 1992).

[7] W. Brian Arthur, *Increasing Returns and Path Dependence in the Economy* (Ann Arbor: University of Michigan Press, 1994); Paul Pierson, "Increasing Returns, Path Dependence and the Study of Politics," *American Political Science Review 94*(2) (2000): 251–268.

city in the present can convince subsequent decision makers that it is cost effective to invest in the city in the future. Through such enhancements, current local officials can secure additional leverage over later decisions at all levels. Thus sophisticated infrastructure and ample environmental amenities may do more than lobbying to attract a national research institute to a city.

Within the scope of these broad processes, distinct strands of institutionalist thought supply different accounts of why elites at heights of states have chosen to pass growing amounts of policy-making authority to lower levels. For functional analysts like Williamson and principal-agent theorists,[8] decentralization often represents the best way to effectuate elite ends. Similar to such arrangements as contracting out and franchising, localized policy enables those at the top to save themselves the cost of carrying out the policy. They need only monitor the local actors to ensure that the policy is carried out. For analysts of public choice, rational calculations of self-interest among actors at the heights of states drive decentralization. Elite legislators maintain control over decisions for which they want to claim credit but pass unpopular decisions along to lower levels. In the "decentralization of penury," for instance, national governments facing fiscal constraints can pass decisions about government spending downward to spare legislators from having to disappoint competing constituencies.[9] Similarly, the constraints of a supranational government like the European Union can furnish national legislators incentives to pass decisions to subnational governments.[10]

Although decisions about localization are no doubt a matter of values as well as of intentions, the combination of functional and political theories furnishes a rich set of propositions about how decentralization might vary.[11] A full account, however, must supplement the "top-down" per-

---

[8] See Oliver Williamson, *Markets and Hierarchies: Analysis and Antitrust Implications* (New York: Free Press, 1975); Armen Alchian and H. Demsetz, "Production, Information Costs, and Economic Organization," *American Economic Review 62* (1972): 777–795; Michael Jensen and William Meckling, "Theory of the Firm: Managerial Behavior, Agency Costs, and Capital Structure," *Journal of Financial Economics 3* (1976): 305–360.

[9] Jeffrey Anderson, "Business Associations and the Decentralization of Penury," *Governance 4* (January 1991): 67–93.

[10] Gary Marks, Lisbet Hooghe and Kermit Blank, "European Integration and the State," paper presented at a conference on the politics and political economy of contemporary capitalism, Humboldt University, Berlin, 1995.

[11] Cf. Peterson, *Price of Federalism*.

spective typical of both theories with the "bottom-up" view that is also indispensable to understanding the sources and consequences of decentralization. With increasing regularity, local initiatives have turned supralocal programs into instruments of local strategies.[12] When entrepreneurs like Mayor Lee have drawn on these programs, the ends pursued in the community may have little to do with the politics or even the aims of the original legislation. One local coalition may carry out public housing to provide cheap, quality shelter for its lower- and middle-income residents. Another may employ the same policy to warehouse poor people displaced through gentrification. Entrepreneurship in supralocal arenas may even enable local actors to shape policy at higher levels to suit local ends. All told, the combined effects of local and supralocal entrepreneurship from below may shape the substance of policy as decisively as the decisions of national legislators. The more that decentralization vests responsibility for policy with local decision makers, the more inadequate it is to relegate the local role to implementation of decisions reached at higher levels or even to agency on behalf of a supralocal principal. A decentered state requires decentered analysis.

Variations According to Types of Policy.   These influences differ with the type of policy domain.[13] The importance of *place* to the content of policy fosters both functional and interest-driven logics on behalf of localization. So may demands for responsiveness to local markets or political forces. These sources of localization differ among developmental, environmental and distributive domains of policy.

Increasingly, policies aimed at aggregate economic growth have been understood in terms of local as well as supralocal components. Despite disagreement over the level of government where decisions about devel-

---

[12] This interdependence with supralocal infrastructures of policy and government sets limits on "local autonomy" (Mike Goldsmith, "Autonomy and City Limits," in *Theories of Urban Politics*, David Judge, Gerry Stoker and Harold Wolman, eds. [Thousand Oaks: Sage Publications, 1995], pp. 228–252) as an indication of local capacities for governance.

[13] Although Peterson in particular has summarized ways that these conditions differ within the United States, his analysis has important shortcomings. Because he confines his attention to one country, his account lacks adequate attention to how much difference even those institutions that are specific to the United States may make. And because he presumes that policy can be "made" only at one level or another, rather than jointly, his view of the potential for localization remains incomplete.

opmental policy should take place,[14] analyses usually converge around both the need for supralocal participation and the disadvantages of too extensive a supralocal role. Political logics rooted in local interests reinforce the likelihood of both local and supralocal influences on these decisions.

In an economy that relies on the decisions of firms and markets, as the literature on "fiscal federalism" has emphasized, localized elements can bring basic advantages for developmental policies.[15] The advantages stem largely from the way localization enhances the power of private markets in relation to policy makers. The more that public decision making about development is local, the more that multilocational or mobile firms and others can take advantage of opportunities or threats to exit from one setting to another to gain leverage over policy. Greater information about local circumstances often places policy makers within a city in a better position than higher-level decision makers to accurately judge competing concerns, local markets and local preferences. Local decision makers also face incentives to be responsive not only to interlocal markets but also to local business-government relations, to local civil society and to local democratic processes. When developmental policies require wholesale restructuring of local land use, property ownership and civil society, as urban regeneration often necessitates,[16] then localized decision makers may also be essential to mobilize other local actors outside the government around developmental aims.

At the same time, other components of developmental policies require binding systems of interlocal cooperation, if not measures from above.

---

[14] From a variety of perspectives, American scholars have argued that the localized policy making that increasingly typifies U.S. practices helps promote local economic development (Peterson, *Price of Federalism*; Barry Weingast, "The Economic Role of Political Institutions," *Journal of Law, Economics and Organization 11* (1995): 1–311; Ann Bowman and Michael Pagano, *Cityscapes and Capital* [Baltimore: Johns Hopkins University Press, 1995]). Other U.S. and international analyses emphasize the need for national policy initiatives or structures (e.g., John Donahue, *Disunited States* [New York: Basic Books, 1996]; and Daniel Treisman, "Political Decentralization and Economic Reform: A Game-Theoretic Analysis," *American Journal of Political Science 43*[2] [1999], 488–517).

[15] E.g., Wallace Oates, *Fiscal Federalism* (New York: Harcourt Brace Jovanovich, 1972); Charles Tiebout, "A Pure Theory of Local Expenditure," *Journal of Political Economy 44*(5) (1956): 416–424; Peterson, *Price of Federalism*.

[16] Alan Harding, John Dawson, Richard Evans and Michael Parkinson (eds.), *European Cities Towards 2000* (Manchester: Manchester University Press, 1994); Dennis Judd and Michael Parkinson (eds.), *Leadership and Urban Regeneration* (Newbury Park, CA: Sage Publications, 1990); H. V. Savitch, *Post-Industrial Cities* (Princeton: Princeton University Press, 1988); Jerry Webman, *Reviving the Industrial City: The Politics of Urban Renewal in Downtown Lyon and Birmingham* (New Brunswick, NJ: Rutgers University Press, 1982).

Physical infrastructure such as roads, airports and power lines often necessitates policies conceived at scales wider than urban regions.[17] Accounts of the "endogenous" sources of economic growth also demonstrate the benefits from collective investments to promote technological innovation and its application.[18] In this way, supralocal support for universities, research, development, training and education can contribute to economic expansion. For places that face clear disadvantages in translocal markets for development, such as sites of declining industries, governmental action can redirect societal resources to aid in local economic restructuring or to limit its consequences.

In this mix, logics of political interest and influence are also at work. The local politicians and local businesses that pursue developmental policies, as well as social movements and others opposed to those policies, may do so at the heights of the state as well as within city regions. Not only grants to localities for economic development but also national programs for education and infrastructure can take their shape as much from these local initiatives as from elite objectives. Parallel mobilization around similar concerns, or logrolling around diverse local issues, furnishes local representatives and groups with a common basis for this wider collective action.

In distinct ways from developmental policies, policies toward the environment and natural resources have required localized elements. The role of decentralization here goes beyond the accommodation of preferences. In the zoning of land, the creation of a park, the preservation of woods or the protections of a historic district, places and their physical attributes help define the substance of policy itself. Throughout local settings, the concerns relevant to land use relate to each other in myriad ways. Sometimes a tract of open space may require strict protection. Other times a similar tract may supply the best available site for needed new housing, and the need for open space may be filled by other means. Local proceedings thus accommodate not only markets and preferences but also the diversity of local circumstances to which general policy must be applied. Participation at the local level helps to resolve these substantive issues. Even the computerized systems of geographic information that now

---

[17] Peterson, *Price of Federalism*, p. 27.
[18] E.g., Robert Barro and Xavier Sala-i-Martin, *Economic Growth* (New York: McGraw-Hill, 1995); Gene M. Grossman and Elhanan Helpman, *Innovation and Growth in the Global Economy* (Cambridge, MA: MIT Press, 1991).

assemble comprehensive, minute data bases about land use cannot eliminate the difficulty of making these choices without localized elements. No
computer program can accommodate the vast array of local demands and
the extended processes of local deliberation that would be necessary to
make these choices at a national level.

At the same time, environmental policies often address regional,
national and ultimately global problems. In policies to control pollution
or to protect open space across and among urban regions, consistency
across the territory often depends on regulatory initiatives at wider scales.
Protective measures at these levels of government can overcome the jurisdictional and other constraints on what individual communities can do to
combat partly external environmental harms. Uniform supralocal actions
prevent localities from shirking the costs of protecting metropolitan land,
controlling automobile usage or keeping a river clean.

Distinctive logics of political interest and influence also shape environmental policy. As environmentalist groups have emerged with a prominent
place in policies at higher levels,[19] grassroots groups have mobilized
around defense of property rights among home owners, around other local
issues and around more general environmental initiatives.[20] At both levels,
businesses and other economic interests have often, but not always,
opposed environmental measures.[21] Multilevel coalitions around environmental policies such as efforts to curb sprawl often embrace both business
groups in pursuit of profits and farmers interested in incentives for land
preservation.[22]

Finally, distributive elements, which often go far beyond merely "redistributive" elements, address equity as an overall dimension of markets and
policy. Equity between people living in different places is intrinsic to these
policies. A long-standing critique of U.S. federalism stresses far-reaching
functional reasons to lodge distributive aims and programs at the national

---

[19] Russell Dalton, *The Green Rainbow* (New Haven: Yale University Press, 1994).

[20] Elliot J. Feldman and Jerome Milch, *Technocracy versus Democracy: The Comparative Politics of International Airports* (Boston: Auburn House Publishing Co., 1982); Barry Rabe, *Beyond NIMBY* (Washington: Brookings Institution, 1994).

[21] Cf. Sidney Plotkin, *Keep Out: The Struggle for Land Use Control* (Berkeley: University of California Press, 1987).

[22] On the example of the Portland region, see Christopher Leo, "Regional Growth Management Regime: The Case of Portland, Oregon," *Journal of Urban Affairs* 20(4) (1998): 363–394; Paul Lewis, *Shaping Suburbia* (Pittsburgh: University of Pittsburgh Press, 1996).

level.[23] To address inequities that cross jurisdictional lines like the division between cities and suburbs or the wider regional disparities of the United States necessitates authoritative norms or funding schemes that span unequal jurisdictions. Otherwise, mobile firms and privileged labor can flee jurisdictions that limit inequities for those that do not. Disadvantaged groups, through migration to jurisdictions that pay more attention to equity, can impose additional regulatory or fiscal burdens on those places.

It would be a mistake to assume, as arguments about the need for supralocal distributive policies sometimes have, that higher-level decisions would suffice to guarantee equity among people or places.[24] The placement of services *within* an urban region often matters as well. Concentrated cheap housing, inadequate neighborhood schools and minimal cultural and social initiatives within neighborhoods can turn the disadvantages of individual families and persons into social, cultural and economic exclusion for whole neighborhoods. The better schools, environmental conditions and shopping opportunities in neighborhoods of privileged citizens can reinforce the advantages of these groups. Markets for development and processes of political influence not only reflect but also often compound these influences from policy. In a society already pervaded by unequal chances, local choices in these processes play as essential a role for equity between neighborhoods as supralocal choices do for equity between cities. However much local efforts to foster this equity raise living costs and lower potential earnings for the poor, as U.S. analysts have sometimes contended,[25] equity across a metropolitan area would be difficult to imagine without some such efforts.

Conflicting logics of political interest have shaped distributive policy. Across Europe as well as the United States, business interests as well as political elites concerned to "decentralize penury" have repeatedly assaulted the social welfare and other policies that have promoted territorial and other forms of equity. The growing influence of arguments and interests in favor of economic internationalization appears to have

---

[23] E.g., Grant McConnell, *Private Power and American Democracy* (New York: Knopf, 1966); Alice M. Rivlin, *Reviving the American Dream: The Economy, the States, and the Federal Government* (Washington: Brookings Institution, 1961); Peterson, *Price of Federalism*.

[24] Peterson in particular treats local and supralocal policies toward distributive concerns as mutually exclusive rather than as potentially complementary.

[25] E.g., Peterson, *City Limits*; Pietro S. Nivola, *Laws of the Landscape* (Washington: Brookings Institution, 1999).

accelerated this trend.[26] At the same time, governing parties on the left in Germany and France, as elsewhere in Europe, have retained important distributive elements in national policy making.[27] Despite the limits that U.S. students of urban politics have often stressed on the capacities of local political configurations to pursue equity,[28] both European local governments and occasional coalitions in U.S. urban centers have stressed this objective.[29]

Table 3.1 summarizes the most general inferences that can be drawn from this summary discussion. In all three domains, localized elements play essential functional roles in policy and its realization. At the same time, other functional considerations require various kinds of supralocal elements in each domain. At both local and supralocal levels, political logics often reinforce these functional rationales.

National Variations. Although national institutional patterns might be expected to make a difference in supralocal policies, comparative analysis of these patterns must look beyond institutional features like federalism and executive-legislative relations at the heights of states. National infrastructures for local government and politics can have different implications for local outcomes than these traditional institutional characteristics. In comparing France and Germany in particular, these two sets of implications are precisely opposed to each other.

As influences on local policy, the territorial structures of states need to be considered along with such aspects of vertical organizational integration as separation of powers and bureaucratic centralization. A long-standing line of organizational analysis stresses how greater vertical integration fosters coordination among elites and suppression of

[26] See Wolfgang Streeck, "Neo-voluntarism: A New European Social Policy Regime?" in Gary Marks, Fritz W. Scharpf, Phillipe C. Schmitter and Wolfgang Streeck *Governance in the European Union* (London: Sage, 1996), pp. 64–94; Bill Jordan, *The New Politics of Welfare* (London: Sage, 1998).

[27] See, e.g., Carles Boix, *Political Parties, Growth and Equality* (Cambridge: Cambridge University Press, 1998); Geoffrey Garrett, *Partisan Politics and the Global Economy* (New York: Cambridge University Press, 1998).

[28] Clarence N. Stone, "Urban Regimes and the Capacity to Govern," *Journal of Urban Affairs* 15(1) (1993): 1–28; Peterson, *City Limits.*

[29] On European examples see, e.g., George Steinmetz, *Regulating the Social* (Princeton: Princeton University Press, 1993). On U.S. examples, see, e.g., Phillip Nyden and Wim Wievel, *Challenging Uneven Development* (New Brunswick, NJ: Rutgers University Press, 1991); Pierre Clavel, *The Progressive City* (New Brunswick, NJ: Rutgers University Press, 1986).

Table 3.1 *Functional and Political Sources of Local and Supralocal Roles, by Dimensions of Policy*

	Supralocal	Local
Promotion of service-based growth (without industrial legacies)	Depends; essential to aspects of physical infrastructure, to redirect resources to build human capital, often to respond to wider mobilization	Depends; often essential to adapt to markets; important to accommodate and mobilize local interests
(regeneration in settings with industrial legacies)	Essential to redirection of wider societal resources, sometimes to respond to wider mobilization	Essential to adapt to markets, accommodate and mobilize local interests
Policies to provide environmental goods	Depends; essential for territorial consistency, important to aggregate environmental goods, often essential to respond to wider mobilization	Essential to adapt environmental ends to local conditions, to accommodate and mobilize local interests
Limits on local spatial advantage, disadvantage	Essential to equitable territorial distribution of unequal resources among localities, sometimes to respond to wider mobilization	Essential to equitable territorial distribution within locality, often to accommodate and mobilize local interests

conflict.[30] For these reasons, the high vertical integration of the French state should enable the strongest, most consistent intervention through policy making from above. The continued centralization of the national government, the limits to separation of executive and legislative powers and the persistent hierarchies of national administration should help foster the most effective initiatives in all three domains (Table 3.2(a)).

Federal territorial arrangements in the United States and Germany give intermediate-level governments a stronger role in policies.[31] In both

---

[30] Paul Pierson, *Dismantling the Welfare State?* (New York: Cambridge University Press, 1994), pp. 32–39; Frintz Sharpf, "The Joint Decision Trap: Lessons from German Federalism and European Integration," *Public Administration* 66 (1988): 239–278.

[31] Since the new regional governments in France lack authority or resources outside of limited domains like education, their addition has not fundamentally altered this contrast. See *infra*.

Table 3.2 *Expected Variations in Supralocal Intervention as a Consequence of Supralocal State Structures and Infrastructures of Local Government and Politics, by Types of Policies*

(a) National and Intermediate Levels

	Germany (Moderate Vertical Integration with Equalization)	France (High Vertical Integration)	United States (Low Vertical Integration)
Promotion of development	Somewhat weaker (unless economic decline of *Land*)	Stronger (consistent)	Somewhat stronger (contingent by state)
Environmental policies	Somewhat stronger (contingent by *Land*)	Stronger (consistent)	Weaker (contingent by state)
Distributive policies	Somewhat stronger (contingent by *Land*)	Stronger (consistent)	Weaker (contingent by state)

(b) Infrastructures of Local Government and Politics

	Germany (Centralized Policy, Decentralized Administration, Limited Intergovernmental Entrepreneurship)	France (Centralized Policy and Administration, Local Intergovernmental Entrepreneurship)	United States (Decentralized Policy and Administration, Local Intergovernmental Entrepreneurship)
Promotion of development (generally)	Somewhat weaker (consistent)	Stronger (contingent)	Somewhat stronger (contingent)
(postindustrial regeneration)	Stronger (consistent)	Stronger (contingent)	Weaker (consistent)
Environmental policies	Stronger (consistent)	Stronger (contingent)	Weaker (consistent)
Distributive policies	Stronger (consistent)	Stronger (contingent)	Weaker (consistent)

Note: Consistency and contingency refer to amount of domestic variation among places.

countries, the resulting difficulties of coordination and competition should weaken capacities for supralocal policy. In Germany the parliamentary system, the role of *Land* governments in the Bundesrat and the constitutional system of financial equalization partly compensate for the limited vertical integration. In realms of policy like environmental and distributive measures, these features should enhance capacities for consistent, somewhat strong supralocal intervention. In developmental policies, equalization among German *Länder* also imposes constraints on policy that U.S. state governments do not face. Although these practices redirect fiscal resources to those *Länder* in relative economic decline, other *Länder* face limits on financial and other resources.

In the United States, vertical integration remains the lowest. Constitutional equalization among the federal states plays no formal part in state structures. Separation of powers and fragmented national and state administrations further limit organizational capacities for coordinated policy from above. In the absence of territorial equalization, U.S. state governments that are engaged in developmental efforts also confront fewer constraints from national institutions than do their German counterparts. As a result, those states not faced with decline may be able to muster more resources around developmental policies.

National infrastructures of local government and politics complicate and even contradict these expectations about institutional capacities to make policy from above. Beside centralization in both policy making and administration, these infrastructures encompass opportunities for local intergovernmental entrepreneurship. In Germany, this infrastructure should help overcome the limits of federalism. In France, it should introduce elements of localized contingency not apparent from arrangements at higher levels. (Table 3.2(b)).

Consider the implications from the German infrastructure. Despite federal, decentralized administration, centralized parties and organized interests formulate comparatively centralized policies. The national system of local bureaucratic administration helps frame and carry out those policies. Local intergovernmental entrepreneurs face relatively few discretionary opportunities to influence these policies from below. In environmental and distributive matters these conditions favor supralocal intervention similar to that in France. At the same time, because these policies impose more standardization on localities, supralocal developmental initiatives confront stronger constraints. Only in efforts to address postindustrial decline might the highly organized translocal interests of the German institutional infrastructure foster comparatively strong capacities to mobilize policies effectively around aims in any single place.

In a contrasting way, the French infrastructure of local government and politics qualifies the effects of vertical integration at the commanding heights of the state. The centralized governmental structures of the French state have played more varied roles in the pursuit of policy within urban regions. With organized political and societal interests like those of the German system less prominent in French national policy, local governments and political entrepreneurs have shaped more idiosyncratic local policies and outputs. Although authorizing legislation itself likely reflects these local influences, local intergovernmental entrepreneurship and local discretion furnish the primary avenues of influence. Despite the persistent pervasiveness of supralocal intervention even after the reforms of the 1980s in France, these opportunities enable the choices within localities to depart from one another or even to undermine national policies.

Analysts of the U.S. infrastructure for local government and politics, by contrast, have rarely stressed institutional patterns different from those at higher levels.[32] In the comparative absence of highly organized parties and economic interests, elaborate centralized policy making, or centralized administration, supralocal governments have sought less to control land use, carry out postindustrial regeneration or address social equity in local policy. At the same time, the supralocal programs that exist often operate in ways that depend on the initiatives of local intergovernmental entrepreneurs like Mayor Lee. In the developmental arena, the opportunities that such programs present can enable multiple supralocal policies to be mobilized systematically around local objectives.

Except in the United States, these infrastructures of local government and politics imply different patterns of local outcomes from those that follow as a result of institutions at higher levels of the state (Table 3.2). Both the strength of supralocal initiatives and the variations in those initiatives between localities within each country should differ in ways that reflect these sets of influences. Comparison of the policies actually carried out should establish which set of influences has the most important consequences for these initiatives.

Subsequent sections of this chapter assess these hypotheses for all three policy domains. In each domain, I ask how much the elaboration of parallel policies brings about similar variations regardless of national institutions. Where nation-specific practices made a difference in outputs or policies, I inquire whether patterns of vertical integration or infrastructures of local government and politics affected this difference. Finally,

---

[32] See, e.g., Peterson, *Price of Federalism*; Steven L. Elkin, *City and Regime in the American Republic* (Chicago: University of Chicago Press, 1987).

I assess how essential were the choices of local actors themselves to all of these supralocal policies and their consequences.

The Expanding Supply of Legal Authority: An Overview

The development of policy in all three domains shares a similar core. Since the Second World War, in all three countries, a proliferation of legislation has contributed to the logics I have traced. It would be difficult to separate out how much this growing "legal supply" has followed specific functional or political dynamics.[33] Yet, overall, this legislation manifests not just an elaboration of supralocal mandates and controls, but an expansion of the opportunities for localized governance.

Elements of land use regulation are in some respects as old as cities. Prescriptions of this sort can be found in early Roman law.[34] German principalities of the eighteenth and nineteenth centuries developed the first rudiments of what would evolve into a complex, nationally legislated system of localized regulation (Table 3.3). Local authorities often supervised the local use of space through the broad legal capacities of *Polizeirecht*. With the dramatic urbanization that accompanied the industrial revolution in Germany, principalities increasingly formalized authority for local officials to regulate setbacks from streets and other aspects of local development. Under the Weimar Republic, bolstered by new constitutional authorizations to regulate property and expropriate land, the national government passed the first legislation at that level to regulate the growing efforts of local officials to supervise local development. The Nazi government issued both the first German natural protection legislation and initial decrees to regulate urban design at the national level. After the war, individual *Land* governments undertook to regulate the rebuilding and with it the design of German cities. The new federal constitution incorporated much of the Weimar language.

In contrast with Germany, such public efforts as the reconstruction of Paris under Baron von Haussman in the 1860s remained an aberration in nineteenth-century French cities. Even in the early twentieth century,

---

[33] Nancy Burns, *The Formation of American Local Governments* (New York: Oxford University Press, 1994), p. 95.

[34] Jean-Bernard Auby and Hugues Périnet-Marquet, *Droit de l'urbanisme et de la construction*, 4th ed. (Paris: Montcrestien, 1995), p. 10.

Table 3.3 *Initial German Planning and Regulatory Authorizations*

Development of police powers (*Polizeirecht*) (principalities)	18th, 19th centuries
Setback Laws (*Fluchtliniengestze*), other specific laws (principalities)	1868-early 1900s
Weimar Constitution (1919) (authorized expropriation [Art. 155], imposed social duty on property [Art. 153])	1919
National Settlement Law (*Reichssiedlungsgesetz*)	1919
National Housing Law (*Reichsheimstättengesetz*)	1920
Laws or decrees for construction, forms of construction, historic protection, natural protection, regional planning, highways	(Nazi legislation)
Rubble removal, reconstruction Law at *Land* level	1948–1949
Basic Law, followed by advisory opinion of Constitutional Court	1948, 1952
Highway, Street Laws	1953 (BW 1964) (N 1962) (NRW 1961)
Construction Law (*Bundesbaugesetz*) (followed by laws at *Land* level)	1960 (BW 1972) (N 1974) (NRW 1984)
Construction and Land Use Law (*Baunutzungsverorndnung*) (followed by laws at *Land* level)	1962 (BW 1965) (N 1974) (NRW 1970)
Regional Planning Law (*Raumordnungsgesetz*) (followed, and in North Rhine-Westphalia preceded, by Planning Laws at Land level)	1965 (BW 1971, first plan 1983) (N 1966, first plan 1973) (NRW 1950, first plan 1970)
Amendment to Construction and Land Use Law limiting large stores outside urbanized areas	1968
Urban Renewal Law (*Städtebauförderungsgesetz*)	1971
Waste Treatment Law (*Abfallbeseitigungsgesetz, Abfallgesetze*)	1972, 1986 (NRW 1973, BW 1975, N 1986)
Landscape Protection Laws (*Landschaftschutzgesetze*)	BW 1972, NRW 1975
Forest Law	1975 (BW 1985) (N 1978) (NRW 1980)
Natural Protection Law (*Naturschutzgesetz*)	1976 (BW 1975) (N 1981) (NRW 1951)
Historic Protection Laws (*Denkmalschutzgesetz*)	1980 (BW 1971, N 1978, NRW 1980)

BW: Baden-Württemberg; N: Lower Saxony; NRW: North Rhine-Westphalia.

when the national government established local authorities to plan and authorize subdivisions (Table 3.4), local regulatory efforts besides historical protections continued to have little effect on urban development in most places. Only after World War II, when the expansion of *les trentes*

Table 3.4 *Initial French Planning and Regulatory Authorizations*

Protection of historic monuments	1913
Authorization of mandatory city planning	1919
Subdivisions authorized	1924
Law on the conservation of sites and monuments	1930
Establishment of construction permits and regulatory authority	1943
Authorization of communal expropriation for private use	1953
Authorization of comprehensive urban plans	1955
Creation of first planning districts (ZUP)	1958
National urban planning code	1961
Authorization of historic districts (Malraux Law), preemptive purchase in designated urban zones	1962
Establishment of *schéma directeurs, plans d'occupation des sols, zones d'amenagement concertés*	1967
National construction code	1969
Supermarket regulation (Law Royer)	1970
Fee for exceeding local height restrictions	1975
Nature protection law	1976
Decentralization of construction, planning authorities	1982–1983
Modifications to decentralized authorities	1985–1986
Coastal protection and development law	1986
Law of orientation for the city (addressing disadvantaged neighborhoods)	1991
Landscape protection law	1993
Framework law on regional planning	1995

glorieuses brought economic modernization for the first time to much of the provinces, did local and national officials begin to elaborate frameworks to steer local development in many cities. Although national state representatives in territorial offices retained the leading formal role under these early legal frameworks, the procedures increasingly incorporated and regulated relations among other local actors as well.

Historical comparison of this evolution with Germany's casts new light on one of the most important features of the French decentralization in the 1980s. From a top-down perspective, these reforms might easily be portrayed as an effort simply to relieve the national state of responsibilities. But key elements among them, especially the passage of authority for construction and planning to municipal officials, served more to expand a domain of policy that up to that point had remained limited in scope. Especially in the context of the increasingly elaborate codes for construction, urban planning and environmental regulation, this measure amounts to one element in a longer-term legal transformation toward localized systems of multilevel policy making. The new authorities meant a shift toward the more decentralized practices of the German federal state.

The multiple levels of policy making that French officials had elaborated largely from above emerged in the German case more from below. Beginning only slightly earlier, new legislation in Germany had introduced a growing array of centralized elements. Since the 1950s, the federal and *Land* governments had enacted several new systems of rules and authorizations that both extended local opportunities to make policy and imposed new local obligations. Under discussion among experts since the 1930s, the federal construction law of 1960 first instituted a national legal basis for local planning and permit authorities. Broader programs of regional spatial planning, new procedures for urban renewal, initial frameworks for construction of physical infrastructure and the natural protection laws of the 1970s built on this foundation. In most of these areas, under terms specified in the Basic Law, the federal government passed the national legislative frameworks, but the *Länder* assumed the authority to elaborate rules under these frameworks.

Since the 1950s, successive enactments at the European level added to these nation-specific legal structures in Germany and France. The most directly relevant of these measures to the policy domains at issue here either built on preexisting national policies or made piecemeal additions.[35] In the environmental domain, where the European Union increasingly developed an island of quasi-federal authority, these measures supplemented national measures the most. In addition to the requirement of environmental impact assessments for a wide array of manufacturing and development projects and other mandates to undertake research and provide information,[36] council directives set standards for water pollution, air pollution, waste management, toxic chemicals, noise pollution and species protection.[37] In developmental and social domains, the market-

---

[35] In other, southern European countries, where environmental and other policies were less developed, European policy had a more extensive effect (Antonio La Spina and Giuseppe Sciortino, "Common Agenda, Southern Rules: European Integration and Environmental Change in the Mediterranean States," in J. Duncan Liefferink, Phillip Lowe and Arthur P. J. Mol [eds.], *European Integration and Environmental Policy* [London: Belhaven Press, 1993], pp. 217–236).

[36] Council Directive OJ No. L 175 of 5/7/85.

[37] Stanley P. Johnson and Guy Corcelle, *The Environmental Policy of the European Communities*, 2nd ed. (London: Kluwer Law International, 1995).

making prescriptions of European institutions influenced not only national and intermediate governments but also the opportunities that local governments faced. More directly relevant programs, such as the structural funds, the regional development funds, the ERASMUS Program and European transportation planning, supplemented national programs of supralocal intervention.

At the level of individual U.S. states, only occasionally supplemented by federal authorities, similar local authorizations have accumulated over the same period (Table 3.5). In Connecticut, North Carolina and Wisconsin this process proceeded in largely parallel ways. In each state the first authorizations for zoning, planning and construction regulation emerged by the 1920s. As occurred in Europe, however, only after the 1950s did local regulation under these authorizations proliferate. Further legislation not only elaborated these authorities but added legal frameworks to govern subdivisions, water, sewers, redevelopment and regional planning at the local or metropolitan level. In the 1970s and 1980s additional provisions authorized institutional mechanisms to govern historic districts, farmland preservation and other specialized matters.

Under a variety of Left and Right coalitions, even under both dictatorial and democratic governments, parallel frameworks of policies, procedures, expertise and organizations have emerged. The overarching trends still highlight the more general institutional dynamics that have brought similar arrangements in different national contexts. The rise of environmental policy has consistently played a role in these trends. Formal lists of legislative initiatives provide only the sketchiest information about how these supralocal initiatives varied with the different policy domains or infrastructures of local government. To confirm the more general tendencies and illuminate these variations will require a closer examination of supralocal initiatives and what these efforts accomplished.

Supralocal Policy in the Growth of Service Centers

An entire range of initiatives at national, intermediate and European levels furnished much of the substance of developmental policy for the eleven service centers. Both state structures at higher levels and national infrastructures of local government and politics influenced the effective shape of these policies. Even as these initiatives and structures imposed from above altered the possibilities for local action, the entrepreneurial activity

Table 3.5 *Initial U.S. Planning and Regulatory Authorizations*

Building regulation, inspection	Connecticut 1902 (Fire Code), 1945 (Building Code), North Carolina 1905, Wisconsin 1913
City or town planning	Wisconsin 1909, Connecticut 1917, North Carolina 1919
Zoning	Wisconsin 1917, North Carolina 1923, Connecticut 1924
Water supply regulation	Connecticut 1915, Wisconsin 1919, North Carolina 1955
Housing code	Connecticut 1905, Wisconsin 1929, North Carolina 1939
Housing authorities	Wisconsin 1935, Connecticut 1936, North Carolina circa 1945
Sewer regulation	Connecticut 1935, North Carolina 1955, Wisconsin circa 1950
Subdivision regulations	Connecticut 1947, North Carolina 1955, Wisconsin 1955
Urban redevelopment	Wisconsin 1943, Connecticut 1949, North Carolina 1951
Regional planning commissions	Wisconsin 1939, Connecticut 1947, North Carolina 1961
Solid waste management	(Federal 1965) Connecticut 1958, North Carolina 1973, Wisconsin 1967
Farmland preservation	Wisconsin 1977, Connecticut 1978, North Carolina 1985
Historic districts	Wisconsin 1977, Connecticut 1978, North Carolina 1989
Hazardous waste management	(Federal 1976) Connecticut 1980, North Carolina 1989, Wisconsin 1991
Groundwater regulation	Wisconsin 1983, Connecticut 1989, North Carolina (watersheds only) 1989

that gave local reality to supralocal policy often sprang from the urban regions themselves.

Supralocal Policies and the Effects from National Infrastructures.
Increasingly, developmental policies that strive for growth through technological innovation and advanced services typify advanced industrial societies. Especially in urban service centers, developmental efforts reflect supralocal initiatives to boost such activities as education, research, health,

administration, tourism and sales. The variations in these initiatives among the cities of Germany, France, and the United States offer a basis to compare the influence from national state structures with that from infrastructures of local government.

Any consideration of these policies must take into account several ways that economic analysis has established that policy could contribute to service-led growth in a metropolitan area. First, location theory has long stressed that decisions about physical infrastructure that are subject to public control, such as the siting of airports, highways and rail stations, allocate market opportunities among places.[38] For firms and for well-to-do workers in fields like management, research and sales, cities that are well positioned in transportation networks offer the lower costs of cheaper mobility.

Second, as innovation has played a greater role in growth, "human capital" has become increasingly important to advanced industrial society.[39] Institutions of education, research and applied research have emerged as potential sources of both national and urban growth. Supralocal governments usually either retain formal administrative control over many universities and hospitals or exercise indirect control over their institutions through funding for crucial activities. Either way, these institutions attract private support as well as resources from the rest of society to a city. Local institutions that diffuse innovations from national or international networks – such as a typical teaching hospital – hold much of the same promise for local economic benefits as institutions that generate entirely new innovations. Both the educated workforce and the chance for ties to institutional centers of innovation attract new businesses.

Third, by assuring services for existing residents, bringing in prosperous workers and rendering a city more attractive to visitors, supralocal policies can help turn cities into centers of consumption.[40] A downtown that draws shoppers from a wide region or tourists from abroad brings new business for local merchants in the short term and can attract new residents in the long term. Much of the growth linked to universities often

[38] Alfred Weber, *Theory of the Location of Industries*, trans. C. J. Friedrich. (Chicago: University of Chicago Press, 1929).

[39] Grossman and Helpman, *Innovation and Growth*; Robert E. Lucas, Jr., "On the Mechanics of Economic Development," *Journal of Monetary Economics* 22 (1988): 3–42.

[40] Susan Fainstein and Todd Swanstrom, *The Tourist City* (New Haven: Yale University Press, 1998); John Urry, *Consuming Places* (London: Routledge, 1995); and the essays in vol. 35, nos. 5–6, of *Urban Studies* (1998).

stems from the opportunities that educational centers offer potential residents to participate in the arts, intellectual activity, sports and other cultural opportunities.

Finally, initiatives on behalf of urban redevelopment and housing at supralocal levels can contribute directly to growth. Development and redevelopment create new urban spaces, and public or publicly sponsored housing expands the housing market. The tax and other incentives that U.S. advocates of urban development like Porter have recommended for businesses that locate in depressed downtowns furnish more indirect means to similar ends.[41]

The operative policies of this sort for a given setting grew out of the combination of local decisions with initiatives from above. Supralocal policies can thus be compared for the strength or extent of the initiatives themselves and for their part in this wider array of policies. In either comparison, the analysis requires forward maps of policy from the elite level to complete the backward map from the results. Opposing hypotheses about supralocal policy toward these cities follow from the vertical integration of the state and from the infrastructures of local government and politics. The greater vertical integration of the French state at higher levels of government might seem to favor the most consistent, most effective supralocal intervention on behalf of development. But the German infrastructure of local government and politics fostered stronger initiatives to aid declining urban regions and more consistency in developmental policies toward service centers. The German service centers in fact enjoyed more gradual, more uniform patterns of growth and conformed more to regional tendencies than did either their French or U.S. counterparts.

My analysis of these efforts begins with the initiatives at supralocal levels that comprised part of French, German and accompanying EU policies. I then turn to parallel American influences. Finally, my analysis considers what role local political entrepreneurship played.

a. French and German Developmental Policies. Table 3.6 compares the direct manifestations from French and German policies since the 1960s toward physical and administrative infrastructure, toward the expansion and application of human capital (in universities, research institutes and hospitals), toward downtown commercial renewal and toward new housing developments. The outputs verify the importance of supralocal policies to

[41] Michael E. Porter, "The Competitive Advantage of the Inner City," *Harvard Business Review* (May—June 1995): 55–71.

Table 3.6 *Local Consequences of Supralocal Initiatives and Programs*

	France				Germany			
	Clermont-Ferrand	Montpellier	Nancy	Rennes	Bielefeld	Freiburg	Göttingen	Münster
Physical infrastructure	Airport, highways, regional rail	Airport, highways, TGV	Airport, highways, normal rail	Airport, highways, TGV	Highways, rail lines, subway system	Highways, rail lines	Highways, rail lines	Highways, rail lines, airport
Government	Regional capital	Regional capital	Departmental capital	Regional capital	City government only	Subregional administrative center	Administrative center for county	Subregional administrative center
Higher education	Universities (+16,106), 2 *grandes écoles*, south campus	Universities (+33,250), 5 *grandes écoles*, north campus	Universities (+13,686), 6 *grandes écoles*, Vandoeuvre campus	Universites (+26,853), 2 *grandes écoles*, Beaulieu campus	New university (+14,812), east campus; *Fachhochschule*, 2 others	University (+13,163), downtown; 4 others	University (+30,133), next to downtown; 1 other; (also 5 Max-Planck-Institut)	University (+32,645), downtown; *Fachhochschule*, 4 others
Health services	Regional hospital center	Regional hospital center, medical institutes	Regional hospital center	Regional hospital center	Total city beds: 2,922	Total city beds: 2,648	Total city beds: 2,703	Total city beds: 3,705
Downtown renewal	Centre Jaude (1970s)	Polygone (1960s–1970s), Antigone (1970s–1990s)	Joffre-Sebastien (1960s–1970s)	Columbia (1960s–1970s)	Northern downtown (1969–early 1980s)	Projects throughout downtown (1970s–1980s)	Eastern ring (late 1960s), inner city (1970–mid1980s)	Downtown renovation (1978–mid1908s)
Major housing projects	Numerous scattered projects	La Paillade (1960s–1970s), Antigone (1970s), others; coastal new towns (1960s–1970s)	Hauts-du-Lièvre (1950s–1970)	Villejean ZUP, South ZUP, others (1950s–1970s)	Sennestadt, Baumheide, Schildesche, Brackwede, others (1950s–1970s)	Weingarten, Landwasser, others (1950s–1970s)	Leineberg, Holtenser Berg, Grone (1960–1970s)	Aaseestadt, Coerde (1960s)

Sources: For university figures, see Jefferey M. Sellers, "Place, Postindustrial Change and the New Left," *European Journal of Political Research* 33 (1998): 187–217; German hospital beds from Deutscher Städtetag, *Statistisches Jahrbuch Deutscher Gemeinden 1992.*

local growth. At the same time, the established infrastructures of local government have different implications for these policies from patterns of vertical integration at the heights of the state. Federalism and related arrangements in Germany imply less consistent, less extensive supralocal interventions than in France. Infrastructures of local government and politics should make for more consistent but also for less extensive ones.

The territorial planning that had evolved in France from the 1960s onward clearly mobilized supralocal governments more around development in the French cities. Regional service centers stood at the center of the national economic policies crystallized most clearly in the planning documents of the Gaullist period. Elites at the national level fashioned administrative, economic, infrastructural, educational and technological policies with consistent territorial ends in mind. To counter the overwhelming political, social and economic predominance of Paris, and to bring economic expansion and its fruits to the most backward regions of the provincial "desert," planners coordinated these policies around construction of regional centers for postindustrial services. The centralized, unitary French state, the active role of the state in many economic sectors and the dominance of state-created elites in key political, administrative and economic positions helped make these efforts possible.[42] Without these supports, a coherent reallocation of national resources would have been far more difficult to realize. Even after the decentralization of the 1980s, planning beyond the metropolitan level remained the prerogative of the national government. Neither departmental governments nor the new regional governments received authority to carry out such efforts. Increasingly, the territorial planning schemes that the state established to structure its own efforts evolved into documents to ratify regular intergovernmental negotiations.[43]

In contrast with these arrangements, but consistent with the German infrastructure of local government, the territorial planning that emerged over the same period throughout western Germany elaborated a more standardized set of prescriptions. For the market position of these cities

[42] Peter Hall, *Governing the Economy* (New York: Oxford University Press, 1986); Andrew Schonfield *Modern Capitalism* (New York: Oxford University Press, 1965); Ezra Suleiman, *Politics, Power and Bureaucracy in France* (Princeton: Princeton University Press, 1974).

[43] Hall, *Governing the Economy*; Jean-Pierre Gaudin, *Gouverner par contrat* (Paris: Presses de Science Po, 1999).

in relation to the many others in their respective states, this institutionalized standardization within the *Länder* would prove decisive. Building on a broad authorization in the Basic Law (Art. 72) to "equalize living conditions," federal planning legislation held out the general goal of "balanced economic, social, cultural and ecological conditions" for these regional efforts (ROG Art. 2 [1]2). Regional planning in pursuit of this end mostly built on and reinforced existing hierarchies of cities. To allocate functions among localities prescriptively, the system relied on classifications from descriptive geographic theories of central places, growth poles and spatial proximity.[44] Planners designated the four service centers *Oberzentren* (highers level centers) for a surrounding planning region that included the metropolitan area. As this system reaffirmed the equivalent importance of all *Oberzentren*, including those in neighboring regions, it denied any *Oberzentrum* a wider monopoly on transportation nodes, educational services or other spurs to local growth.

Several additional features of policy making reinforced these constraints. In Germany, in contrast with France, the regional policies that *Land* and federal governments overlaid on this scheme generally provided business subsidies for settlement either on the periphery of these metropolitan areas or in other cities like those of the Ruhr.[45] The German subsidies to towns or cities within these metropolitan areas not only worked at cross-purposes with the main thrust of regional planning but also remained somewhat more modest than French counterparts.[46]

---

[44] See Gérard Marcou, Hans Kistenmacher and Hans-Günther Clev, *L'Aménagement du Territoire en France et en Allemagne* (Paris: La Documentation Francaise, 1994), p. 83.

[45] Overviews of policies addressed to the Ruhr include Jeffrey Anderson, *The Territorial Imperative* (Cambridge: Cambridge University Press, 1992); Rolf G. Heinze, Helmut Voelzkow and Josef Hilbert, *Strukturwandel und Strukturpolitik in Nordrhein-Westfalen* (Opladen: Leske + Budrich, 1992); Paul Ktemmer and Klaus Schubert, *Politische Maßnahmen zur Verbesserung von Standortqualitaten* (Berlin: Duncker and Humblot, 1992); Organisation for Economic Cooperation and Development (OECD), *Regional Policies in Germany* (Paris: OECD, 1989).

[46] In Montpellier, a local business guide (Annie Dalbin, *Montpellier Affaires* [Montpellier: Éditions M, 1991], pp. 60–70) listed several different types of subsidies available: a *Fonds Régionalisé d'Aide aux Initiatives Locales pour l'Emploi* (in the state-region contract for 1989–1993), an *Aide pour le Renforcement des Équipes Dirigeantes* (financed under the same auspices), a *Fonds Régional d'Aide au Conseil* (also part of the state-region contract), a *Fond Régional d'Études de Faisabilité* (by the region), an *Aide Régionale à la Création d'Entreprise* (a loan from the region for up to 5 years), an *Aide aux Demandeurs d'Emplois Créateurs ou Repreneurs d'Entreprises* (a state grant), a *Fonds Départmental d'Initiative des Jeunes et des Femmes* (another state grant), and several types of grants from the Agence Nationale pour la Valorisation de la Recherche, including a 50 percent subsidy up to 400,000 francs to

Other policies with clear territorial implications, such as decision making about where to expand educational facilities, also pursued a hodge-podge of goals.[47] With less of research in the hands of governmental agencies and institutes,[48] and often with less governmental participation in leading sectors of technological innovation than in France,[49] German officials also possessed fewer capacities to induce relocations of these activities.

The contrast between the vertically integrated state at higher levels in France and the federal organization of the German state only partly accounts for these differences in policy. French elites seeking to redirect resources at the national level lacked the difficulties of coordination among the *Länder*, as well as the constraints of constitutionally mandated fiscal equalization among these bodies. But the large individual German *Länder* like North Rhine-Westphalia had imposed planning frameworks within their territories that could have redirected large amounts of resources. Subnational schemes of this sort probably bore more of the responsibility for any constraints on supralocal interventions to spur growth.

The federalism of Germany also left more ample room for intermediate governments to pursue inconsistent strategies than was possible in France. The German constitutional order assigned individual Länder responsibility for making the critical decisions in matters of education, technology, construction and spatial planning.[50] These intermediate bodies also looked to divergent political logics and different problems. North Rhine-Westphalia, the biggest site of declining manufacturing and mining and a bastion of Social Democratic hegemony since the mid-1960s, had mobilized technological and spatial policies more aggressively; Baden-

search for foreign partners. The German supralocal subsidies to outlying communes in the Münster and Bielefeld metropolitan areas as well as close to the east German border in the *Kreis* surrounding Göttingen never paid more than 15 percent of costs. These French subsidies often offered half or more support for specific tasks like feasibility studies and up to 35 percent support for creation of new firms in depressed outlying areas.

[47] See L. Cerych and Paul Sabatier, *Great Expectations and Mixed Performance: The Implementation of Higher Education Reforms in Europe* (Trentham, Stoke-on-Trent: Trentham Books, 1986).

[48] In 1988, only 34 percent of the total German budget for research and development ($25 billion) was in public hands, compared with 50 percent of the French ($18 billion) and 49 percent of the United States ($138 billion) (Eugene B. Skolnikoff, *The Elusive Transformation* [Princeton: Princeton University Press, 1993], p. 23).

[49] For a fuller comparison of national practices, see Nicholas Ziegler, *Governing Ideas* (Ithaca: Cornell University Press, 1998).

[50] See Basic Law §§ 83, 91a.

Württemberg and Lower Saxony had done so less.[51] In North Rhine-Westphalia the location of new educational facilities had followed a logic of compensation for local manufacturing decline; in the other states the expansion of universities and other schools reinforced the status of established educational centers.[52] Any consistency in the local results of the disparate German service centers would have to have transcended the consequences from these divergences in policy at intermediate levels.

Different national patterns of urban settlement had in part resulted from these influences and in part qualified them. Parisian dominance in French social, economic and cultural life had no equivalent in Germany, and the backwardness of regions like Languedoc-Roussillon and Brittany in the early 1960s far exceeded that of the regions around Göttingen or Freiburg. The less dense urban structure of France had also favored concentration of postindustrial services in midsize places like these. In western Germany, with 14 cities over 500,000 in population, and more than 150 over 50,000, there was no need to concentrate physical infrastructure, human capital and other spurs to development in there midsize cities. In France, with less than half the number of cities in either category, midsize cities like Rennes and Montpellier remained the largest urban centers for many regions. Preexisting cultural and social heritages associated with earlier provincial capitals added to the "place luck" of these settings.

As a result of these multiple influences, many of the supralocal programs remained less ambitious in the German settings (Table 3.6). Less extensive intervention of this sort from above clearly helps to account for the lower levels of growth. All the French cities except Nancy received new functional responsibilities in the postwar period as seats of regional governments. The German cities retained their previous, more limited status as, at most, the regional administrative centers for *Regierungsbezirke* (subregions) beneath the *Land* level, and in Bielefeld and Göttingen local or metropolitan governments only. As central nodes of transit, the French cities had received major regional airports and even the new high-speed train (*train à grande vitesse*, or TGV). Even their location on main transportation corridors failed to bring similar priority for the German cities. The French cities also benefitted from decentralization of the national specialized schools (*grandes écoles*) and research institutes that located in them.

---

[51] Ulrich Jürgens and Wolfgang Krumbein (eds.), *Industriepolitische Strategien: Bundesländer in Vergleich* (Berlin: Edition Sigma, 1991).

[52] See Cerych and Sabatier, *Great Expectations*, Ch. 3.

No such elite institutions, except for the five branches of the Max-Planck-Institut in Göttingen, accompanied the expansion of higher education in the German cities. The national French initiatives manifest in local policies also generally extended the developed space of cities more than in their German counterparts. In Montpellier, Nancy and Rennes, the university had expanded largely on new campuses established at a distance from the city center. Among the German universities only the entirely new school established in Bielefeld had followed this pattern. In Montpellier and Rennes, downtown projects had extended the local commercial center beyond the Old Town. In the German cities, renewal mostly reconstructed or rehabilitated the Old Town. Although high-rise peripheral housing estates marked the public housing programs of both countries into the 1970s, the massive projects of La Paillade in Montpellier, Haut du Lièvre in Nancy and the southern addition to Rennes demonstrated how the French *Zones d'Urbanisation Prioritaires* (ZUP) of the 1950s and 1960s created more extensive developments of this sort. During the first decades after the war, these more extensive initiatives also contributed to an industrial deconcentration in France that hardly took place at all in Germany.[53]

The contrast in the average extent of supralocal intervention followed from national influences at both higher and lower levels. The greater inconsistency of the French outputs underscored the limited significance of German federalism. Concentrated outputs from state initiatives in Montpellier and Rennes helped bring about more dramatic growth than in the other French cities as well as in the German ones. With regional capitals, early TGV stations, massive university expansion and immense

---

[53] The arrival of Citröen at Rennes in 1953 set off a sharp rise in local jobs there, and over the next two decades other firms, such as ITT (telephones), SGS ATES (semiconductors), and SPLI (textiles), installed new facilities in the agglomeration (Patrick Le Galès, *Politique Urbaine et Développement Local* [Paris: L'Harmattan, 1993], pp. 150–151). In Montpellier, IBM first set up a plant in 1963, then subsequently expanded its local facilities to become one of the largest local employers. Although Michelin had remained headquartered in Clermont-Ferrand since the beginnings of the firm early in the century, the postwar expansion of the firm into the leading international tire producer drove a parallel expansion in that city into the 1970s. Even though local firms, like Dr. Oetker in Bielefeld, had also often expanded over this period, no major firms moved to establish similarly large new plants in the German cities. Parisian technocrats undoubtedly helped to encourage the deconcentration in France through assurances of support, if not through direct advocacy. The expansionist supralocal initiatives addressed to the local level confirmed these assurances with concrete incentives to relocate.

new housing and commercial projects in the downtowns, both cities received more of the benefits from supralocal efforts than did either Clermont-Ferrand or Nancy. The preexisting urban structure scarcely made this result inevitable from the outset. Gaullist officials could have chosen Nancy rather than Metz as the regional capital and could have constructed more university buildings in both Clermont-Ferrand and Nancy. The officials could also have diverted more national resources from, say, Lyon or Grenoble. The choices they made instead contributed directly to the sharp disparities in growth among the French cities. In discrete domains, such as the expansion of universities, supralocal policies in Germany brought about different consequences in different cities. But in none of these instances did the German elites coordinate multiple new expansionary policies as much around any place.

Only in efforts to counter postindustrial decline had German supralocal intervention clearly exceeded that in parallel French settings. In Bielefeld, supralocal territorial initiatives at the *Land* level had done more than either the French or the U.S. government at higher levels to forestall urban decline as major portions of local manufacturing jobs departed. These efforts had helped the city to maintain steady levels of population and income like those of the other German cities.

Beginning in the 1960s, supralocal assistance and local initiatives to mobilize it had redirected resources to new projects in Bielefeld. At that time several of the local industries, including machine tool manufacturers, a large textile works and a bicycle maker, had either already moved out or were preparing to do so. To counter these losses the Social-Liberal government employed a scaled-down version of strategies applied in larger Ruhr cities like Essen and Dortmund. The *Land* established a new university on a campus to the west of the city, and a *Fachhochschule* devoted to training and retraining of workers in one of the former manufacturing zones to the east. Territorial reorganization brought both the university campus and several towns in the immediate area within the city limits and nearly doubled the overall population. Local officials also sought and secured large subsidies of *Land* moneys for several major projects. By the late 1980s, the city had acquired a pedestrian mall lined with big department stores, a subway and an immense new civic center. Further supralocal money flowed into local museums and the conversion of crumbling former factories into parks. At first outside the center, then on smaller tracts throughout the city, local planners and nonprofit housing companies constructed massive quantities of publicly financed housing. Conflicts forestalled even more ambitious initial plans for an airport and new highway arteries. Even in the mid-1990s, after funds for urban renewal had been cut out in the other German cities, the *Land* continued to provide support for rebuilding downtown Bielefeld.

These efforts stood in sharp contrast to the more limited supralocal initiatives for both of the French cities that underwent postindustrial decline. The new regional governments had also taken on a stronger role than had the departments and municipalities in the provision of subsidies for new or arriving businesses.[54] Yet in Nancy and Clermont-Ferrand, supralocal initiatives into the 1990s had so far failed to compensate for the local losses that had followed the flight of manufacturing and related industries. Since the problems the central state had addressed in the area around Nancy lay chiefly in mining areas beyond the metropolitan area, the initiatives there had centered outside the central city. In Clermont-Ferrand deindustrialization and urban decline had clearly reinforced each other. The central city population had begun to fall in the late 1970s, as the extensive Michelin facilities there continued to prosper. In 1983, however, the company introduced the first in a series of worldwide cutbacks. Over the next ten years the local workforce for the company fell from over 30,000 workers to around 15,000 – a reduction of all manufacturing jobs in the city by a fourth even without the corresponding losses among local suppliers.

Despite the losses, initiatives of the sort that had effectively replaced departing industry with new activities in Bielefeld had failed by the mid-1990s to materialize in Clermont-Ferrand. New "poles" of development had yet to be drawn from outside the region, and extensive incentives had only produced two or three new local firms with around a hundred new jobs. Younger residents continued to depart.[55] Spatial initiatives like the efforts that had sustained Bielefeld had remained weak.[56] The new univer-

---

[54] Pierre Kukawka, "Le rôle des régions dans le développement économique," in Serge Wachter (ed.), *Politiques Publiques et Territoires* (Paris: L'Harmattan, 1989), pp. 113–130.

[55] Christophe Beslay, Philippe Bernard and Évelyne Cavet, "Clermont-Ferrand – La difficile transition d'une régulation privée à une régulation institutionelle" (Université de Toulouse le Mirail, 1994), pp. 58, 84.

[56] Part of the problem lay in the failure of the main institutional actors to coordinate. A nationally publicized rivalry between Roger Quilliot, the Socialist mayor, and Valéry Giscard d'Estaing, the regional president after 1986, was only one of the several conflicts within and between parties that had hindered cooperation.

sity and research facilities had expanded only modestly since the early 1980s; the national University 2000 program, begun in 1990, brought Clermont-Ferrand a new engineering school and other facilities.[57] But other cities, like Montpellier and Nancy, had acquired larger new facilities and new European-oriented institutes that Clermont-Ferrand still lacked. National officials twice postponed the possibility of connecting the city to the TGV. In the mid-1990s fewer supralocal subsidies went into the city's local museums and cultural activities than had gone into the other French cities. These shortcomings perpetuated those of earlier national programs for urban reconstruction (Table 3.6). Less redevelopment had taken place downtown. The Centre Jaude, a downtown mall, opened three years after its counterparts in the other cities. The outlying university campus of les Cézeaux remained small and relatively isolated.[58] Only the extensive public housing the Socialist administration of Clermont-Ferrand had undertaken surpassed efforts in the other French cities.

The limits of these efforts lessened the significance of the measures undertaken by supralocal officials. Although the central state intervened to manage the effects of restructuring on workers, this intervention aggravated rather than alleviated the decline of the city. In the formal agreements between the Michelin Company, worker representatives and the officials who sanctioned the layoffs, the Fonds Nationale de l'Emploi (FNE) committed itself to help finance the relocation of foreign workers, early retirement of other workers and reclassification of still others. In some years these services for former Michelin employees took up more than half of the total expenses by the FNE.[59] At the same time that these measures limited the rise in local unemployment, they precipitated the decline in population. By the mid-1990s, as the extent of the cuts became clear, other supralocal actors and funds mobilized to address the decline of the local economy. As part of one of the agreements with central officials in 1991, Michelin itself agreed to create a separate corporation with an initial investment of 90 million francs in support of local development. Territorial field offices of the national state, regional and

---

[57] Syndicat Intercommunal d'Étude et de Programmation de l'Agglomération Clermontoise (SIEPAC), *Schéma Directeur de l'Agglomération Clermontoise: Diagnostic, Parti d'Aménagement* (Clermont-Ferrand, 1994), p. 39.

[58] In recognition of this fact, the regional plan for 1994 announced a project to connect the new campus more closely to the city (SIEPAC, *Schéma*, p. 39).

[59] Beslay, Bernand and Cavet, "La difficile transition," pp. 64–65.

departmental governments, and regional government-business partnerships, also assembled funds and organized initiatives to bring new activities.[60] A detailed assessment by local scholars found few tangible consequences from these efforts.[61]

In Bielefeld, German planning manifested the potential of the infrastructures of local government to compensate for postindustrial decline. The comparatively strong organization of labor and parties in North Rhine-Westphalia undoubtedly contributed to this result. In the more devastated cities of the Ruhr, similar policies had succeeded less convincingly.[62] But even in Bielefeld the *Land* government had accomplished no more than to compensate for losses. The consistent effect of equalization posed a stark contrast to the French outputs. Although interventions of central state actors and regions in France had sometimes succeeded more than in Clermont-Ferrand or Nancy,[63] inconsistency clearly plagued French efforts at postindustrial regeneration.

No account of how the supralocal policies toward urban development in France and Germany have evolved since the 1970s would be complete without attention to the expanding role of the European Union. Viewing policies at that supranational level from the standpoint of urban outcomes in these cities opens up an altered perspective on the EU from that of analyses centered on national states.[64] The most pervasive influence European policy had at this metropolitan level was probably indirect. As European institutions laid the foundations of transnational markets, the

---

[60] In the largest fund, the national field offices brought together 11 million francs from the European Union and other money from national sources for a total of 32 million francs. Clermont Auvergne Développement, for instance, combined representatives from Michelin, Electricité de France and other major regional enterprises with the Chamber of Commerce and Industry and municipal officials. The president, Pierre Maillet, was director of the Var-Développement organization that had created Sophia-Antipolis, the premier technological park in France; the chief executive was an ENA (École Nationale d'Administration) graduate. The organization drew on national networks these officials had developed in efforts to find investors (Beslay, Bernard and Cavet, "La difficile transition," p. 77).

[61] Besley, Bernard and Cavet, "La difficile transition," p. 77.

[62] Jeffrey Andersen, *The Territorial Imperative* (Cambridge: Cambridge University Press, 1992).

[63] Wachter, *Politiques Publiques et Territoires.*

[64] For various examples of top-down perspectives, see, e.g., Andrew Moravcik (ed.), *Centralization or Fragmentation?* (New York: Council on Foreign Relations, 1998); Marks et al., *Governance in the European Union.*

resulting expansion in trade and commerce confronted local governments and businesses with new opportunities to pursue development and with new competition to attract mobile firms and residents.[65]

Although European funds and related measures also played a direct role in local policy, up to the mid-1990s this element remained a modest influence at best. Typical of European policy toward cities, effective supranational contributions of this sort to local policy depended at least as much on initiatives within and among localities as on measures taken from above.

European Union policies on behalf of economic and social cohesion and transportation networks played the most important direct roles in urban development.[66] For the French cities in particular, the Structural Funds and other sources furnished financial aid to the surrounding region that could be mobilized on behalf of urban development. Beginning in 1994, the European Regional Development Fund and Cohesion Fund singled out Clermont-Ferrand as a target for Aid to Declining Industrial Areas (Objective 2) in Auvergne. Longwy next to Nancy and Sète next to Montpellier won approval as targets for similar regional aid. Parallel funds went to sites outside the urban region itself, but within the wider region around Rennes, Münster and Göttingen. Areas on the fringes of the urban regions around Freiburg and Montpellier, as well as within the wider regions surrounding Nancy and Rennes, received funds designated to foster development and adjustment of rural areas in decline. In both France and Germany smaller sums from designated structural and cohesion funds also went to specific objectives such as small and medium enterprise support, technical assistance and combating drought. Especially after 1996, in every region except the one around Göttingen, other funds aimed at wider, cross-border regions supplemented these. By the late 1990s, Nancy and Montpellier had also gained new developmental advantages as nodes along high-speed train routes that the EU had designated as funding priorities. Support from the EU also fostered a growing array of formalized educational, scientific and cultural

---

[65] It remains difficult to separate out European policy as an influence on these markets. The opening of Eastern Europe, the development of new technologies that facilitated mobility, the spread of just-in-time production, the growth of transnational business organization and widespread shifts in local orientations also furnished new impetuses to developmental initiatives.

[66] See European Commission, *Towards an Urban Agenda in the European Union* (Brussels, 1997), Report COM(97) 197, p. 8.

exchanges.[67] The urban regions that could draw on such funds clearly gained advantages in developmental policy. Montpellier, for instance, had secured funds from the Integrated Mediterranean Programs and others to expand the local airport, to help build a massive conference center and to support a network of metropolitan technology parks.[68] Largely through the efforts of regional governments, Clermont-Ferrand, Nancy and Rennes had also secured substantial funds.

But consistent with the multilevel character of EU policy making, the actual role of supranational funding remained both limited and contingent. In the early 1990s, EU subsidies comprised so small a portion of municipal budgets as to play an essentially symbolic role.[69] Even within the regional programs of the Structural Funds, EU financing generally remained a fraction of the total amounts. Before 1997, in all of the French cities and two of the German ones, national and other governments financed over 95 percent of even the EU programs under the Structural Funds.[70]

In the substance of the programs supported, even more than in the total sums involved, decisions reached below proved decisive. In all of these cities, EU programs generally went to developmental measures that other national, regional or local actors had devised and already supported. At national, intermediate and local levels, institutions and planning priorities were usually already in place. These policies, and ultimately the national systems of local government that influenced them, remained the ultimate determinants of what the EU funds could accomplish.

---

[67] Exchanges with numerous partner cities had grown into regular, if largely symbolic, events in all the European settings. Especially in the domain of research and education, European Union programs of exchange like ERASMUS, EUREKA and equivalents in specialized professional formation had spread to most of these cities.

[68] André Donzel, "Montpellier," in Harding et al., *European Cities Towards 2000*, pp. 144–160.

[69] The only direct EU subsidies to local governments in the 1990s that my study of budgets in these cities revealed had occurred in Nancy. There the EU had paid 130,855 francs to support installation of traffic signals. Total expenses in this category for the fiscal year had amounted to 6.7 million francs. Montpellier had also secured funds from Brussels in the form of a grant to the region Languedoc-Roussillon for expansion of the airport outside the city – according to several local respondents through the connections of Mayor Frêche to Jacques Delors through the Socialist party.

[70] See www.inforegio.org (October 10, 2000). In the regions around Bielefeld and Münster the percentage was higher or impossible to calculate, but the programs applied to areas beyond the urban region itself. Even in 1997–1999, as the EU contributions rose, the contributions from other sources persisted at no less than 54 percent of the total.

124

In France, the limits to EU policy enabled other priorities than those in the main Structural and Cohesion Funds to dominate territorial policy. Largely through efforts at the regional level, Auvergne had by 1997 garnered the highest per capita contribution from EU Structural and Cohesion Funds for Clermont-Ferrand and other industrial areas.[71] Funding for Lorraine also increased. But somewhat higher levels of grants from the EU could scarcely overcome the decisive opportunities that French national programs gave to the regions like those around both Montpellier and Rennes. An official assessment of the Structural Funds for 1989–1993 also pointed to greater difficulty in administering these Funds in Auvergne and Lorraine. Both ranked among the lowest performing in Europe in terms of EU expenditures per new job.[72] Within the regions, the study found deficits in management and appraisal and, to a lesser degree, in community partnership and in programmatic coherence. Both of the more successful regions had mobilized the EU grants more effectively. Montpellier and its surrounding region had won EU support to build on a central position in international transportation networks and employed Structural Funds more efficiently to create jobs. Brittany received as high a rating in the Commission's official assessment for the use of Structural Funds as any French region.

Among the German cities, the standardized system of regional planning and the infrastructure of local government imposed limits to EU subsidies beyond the criteria for the Funds themselves. At the same time that German *Länder* administered these funds more consistently than French regions, EU assessments observed that the *Länder* had "transferred" pre-existing regional policies into this process.[73] In larger *Länder* like North Rhine-Westphalia, new strategies to spur regional innovation preserved the same priorities that limited growth in places like Münster and Bielefeld. The Plan North Rhine-Westphalia passed in 1995 continued to stress development in the Ruhr (now designated as part of the German "European metropole"). As a result, even planners in the Münster region, despite

---

[71] Including Section 2 and Section 5b subsidies, Auvergne received 647 ECU per person, compared with 144 in Lorraine, 114 in Languedoc-Roussillon and 27 in Brittany.

[72] Ernst & Young, *Ex-Post Evaluation of the 1989–1993 Objective 2 Programmes: Synthesis Report* (Brussels: 1994), pp. 84–87.

[73] European Inforegio, *Evaluation of Research, Technological Development and Innovation-Related Actions under Structure Funds* (Brussels, 1999), p. xiv, see also Ernst & Young, *Ex-Post Evaluation*.

their forecast of continued local growth, anticipated that the city would lose service activities to the larger nearby cities.[74]

Even in cities where European funds made more of a difference in local policies and outcomes than in these service centers,[75] choices at lower levels have decided the character and the ultimate fate of supranational developmental policies. As a result, European supralocal initiatives have either mirrored the distinctive patterns of domestic developmental efforts or succumbed to the influence of those efforts. In France during the 1980s and 1990s, a growing commitment of Structural and Cohesion Funds to Clermont-Ferrand and its region could not overcome the national and subnational developmental priorities in favor of Montpellier and Rennes or the entrepreneurship of local and intermediate governments on behalf of those cities. In supranational as well as domestic initiatives addressed to urban economic development in Germany, planning priorities and political entrepreneurship continued to reinforce hierarchies formalized as long as thirty years before.

b. U.S. Developmental Policies. Analysis of the U.S. developmental policies at supralocal levels presents fewer complexities. No transnational governments have been even indirectly involved, and infrastructures of local and supralocal governance share similar features. Supralocal governments not only have intervened less, but they have not formally coordinated territorial policies as the European states did. For this last reason, the parallel infrastructural, educational and administrative concentrations that brought growth in and around both Madison and Durham (Table 3.7) may seem to present a puzzle.

The expansion of services and physical infrastructure in these settings parallel those of the rapidly expanding French service centers. Massive amounts of societal resources came from elsewhere to build these cities. Since the emergence of extensive policy making at the state level in the Progressive era and the New Deal, expanding governments had brought a largely continuous boom to the Wisconsin state capital of Madison and to the metropolitan regions surrounding the capital of North Carolina in Raleigh. The state universities in Madison and in Chapel Hill next to

---

[74] Ministerium für Umwelt, Raumordnung und Landwirtschaft des Landes Nordrhein-Westfalen, *Landesentwicklungsplan Nordrhein-Westphalen: Entwurf* (Düsseldorf, 1994), p. 14; Regierungspräsident Münster, *Gebietsentwicklungsplan Regierungsbezirk Münster – Teilabschnitt Münsterland* (Münster, 1994), p. 17.

[75] See, for instance, the examples in Harding et al., *European Cities Towards 2000.*

Table 3.7. *Local Consequences from Supralocal Programs and Initiatives, U.S. Settings*

	Durham	Madison	New Haven
Physical infrastructure	Highways, major airport (Raleigh-Durham)	Highways, regional airport	Highways, minor regional airport
Government	[State Capitol in neighboring county]	State Capitol	City government, judicial seat
Higher education (private nonprofit) [increase of college students in central city, 1960–1990]	University of North Carolina, North Carolina Central University (Duke University, Durham Tech) [+11,952]	University of Wisconsin [+29,801]	(Yale University, 4 others) [−68]
Federal research and development obligations, 1991 (millions)	$128.1 (Duke), $111.5 (UNC-Chapel Hill)	$179.1 (UW-Madison)	$152.5 (Yale)
Health services (private nonprofit)	UNC Hospital (Duke Hospital)	UW Hospital	(Yale-New Haven Hospital, 1 other)
Downtown renewal	Extensive clearance (1950s–1970s)	Limited clearance, but new office construction, pedestrian mall (1960s–1970s)	Clearance, projects throughout downtown (1950s–1970s)
Housing (major projects into 1970s)	Small and midsized complexes around downtown (1950s–1970s)	Small and midsized redevelopment projects (1960s–1970s)	Fair Haven, other small and midsized complexes in downtown (1940s–1970s)
Federal funding, 1996 (per person)			
Housing and Community Development	$98	$255	$264
Individual housing assistance	$10	$8	$45

Sources: Higher education figures from U.S. Census Bureau, *SMSA Reports, 1960, 1990*; research and development data from U.S. Census Bureau, *Statistical Abstract of the United States 1994*, p. 611; housing funding from Gaquin and Littman, *1998 County and City Extra*, pp. 866, 954, 998.

Durham engaged in massive expansions of educational, research and health facilities. Especially in Madison, the numbers of students exploded. Even Duke University, in North Carolina, though a private institution, benefitted from one of the largest injections of federal research and development funding to any university as well as from its nonprofit, nontaxable status under federal laws. Although the technical colleges in Madison and their equivalents in New Haven had existed since earlier in the century, Durham also acquired an equivalent institution. Interstate highways and regional or "hub" airports established corridors for spatial development as well as critical infrastructural connections to other cities. In Durham especially, urban clearance made way for new complexes of offices and businesses. Even as urban renewal devastated much of existing neighborhoods in downtown Durham, and generated smaller amounts of downtown housing than were destroyed, new development as a result of this process contributed to growth.[76]

State and federal governments in Durham went beyond even these efforts. Along with other examples throughout the advanced industrial world,[77] the Research Triangle Park in southern Durham County emerged by the 1980s as a successful center of research and administrative activities on national and global scales. Established by North Carolina in 1958 after the example of Silicon Valley, the park had brought offices or laboratories for the federal Environmental Protection Agency and the National Institute for the Humanities to Durham alongside IBM and other private and nonprofit enterprises. By 1990 local experts estimated that the park had generated some 52,000 jobs in the area, or a fourth of the total increase over the past thirty years.[78] As Castells and Hall have argued in the case of Silicon Valley and similar centers, governmental activities had, by providing such assets as the universities, the local physical infrastructure and a nearby administrative center, made the success of the park possible. Even

---

[76] Other supralocal policies addressed more to consumers and businesses rather than to local policy makers contributed to these local outcomes. Massive federal subsidies through tax deductions and loans for mortgages dwarfed the subsidies the French and German governments established to promote construction of individual homes (Arnold Heidenheimer, Hugh Heclo and Carolyn Teich Adams, *Comparative Public Policy*, 3rd ed. [New York: St. Martin's Press, 1990], Ch. 4).

[77] Manuel Castells and Peter Hall, *Technopoles of the World* (London: Routledge, 1994).

[78] Harvey A. Goldstein and Michael I. Luger, "Technologieparks und die Umstrukturierung der städtischen Raumökonomie," in Hans G. Helms (ed.), *Die Stadt als Gabentisch* (Leipzig: Reklam, 1992), pp. 134–152, see p. 140.

in the absence of an institution like the Research Triangle Park, the resulting conditions could have drawn national and international organizations to the area.

Like Clermont-Ferrand and Bielefeld, both the central city and the surrounding metropolitan area of New Haven had lost much of the manufacturing at the core of its earlier economy. Again like the French city, New Haven had failed to replace its formerly thriving industry with new service-based prosperity. Unlike in Clermont-Ferrand, however, supralocal policy makers mobilized around the transformation of local land use. The unusually large scholarly literature on Mayor Lee and subsequent urban redevelopment in New Haven documents these efforts thoroughly.[79] From the 1950s through the 1970s, the city stood at the center of perhaps the most ambitious urban renewal program in the United States for a place its size, as well as amid regional construction of the interstate highway system. The privileged place of the city in the policies of higher levels of government continued through such efforts as the Model Cities program and even beyond the decline of federal involvement after 1970. As late as the mid-1990s, federal funding for housing and community development as well as for individual housing assistance in New Haven exceeded levels in Durham and Madison. Meanwhile, tax incentives and other benefits in federal Empowerment Zones and brownfields programs directed resources at distressed inner-city areas. As fiscal intervention from the federal government receded, the state government stepped in to provide more external support than in the other cities. In 1992, the city reported 53 percent of its revenues as coming from intergovernmental sources, compared to 37 percent in Madison and 28 percent in Durham. The state government supplied 86 percent of this money in New Haven, compared with 83 percent in Madison and 43 percent in Durham. State tax breaks for businesses in the downtown added to the federal incentives for investment.

---

[79] Robert A. Dahl, *Who Governs?* In: *Power and Democracy in an American City* (New Haven: Yale University Press, 1961); Raymond E. Wolfinger, *The Politics of Progress* (Englewood Cliffs, NJ: Prentice-Hall, 1974); G. William Domhoff, *Who Really Rules? New Haven and Community Power Reexamined* (New Brunswick, NJ: Transaction Books, 1978); Norman I. Fainstein and Susan S. Fainstein, "New Haven: The Limits of the Local State," in Susan S. Fainstein, Norman I. Fainstein, Richard C. Hill, Dennis Judd and Michael P. Smith (eds.), *Restructuring the City*, 2nd ed. (New York: Longman, 1986), pp. 27–79; Clarence N. Stone and Heywood Sanders, "Re-examining a Classic Case of Development Politics: New Haven, Connecticut," in Clarence N. Stone and Heywood Sanders (eds.), *The Politics of Urban Development* (Lawrence: University of Kansas Press, 1987), pp. 159–181.

Only during the 1980s had efforts of this sort finally helped to stem the tide of investment and residents out of the central city. Even this modest success remained precarious. Comparison with both the more successful U.S. service centers and the postindustrial reconstruction of Bielefeld demonstrate why these efforts failed. The extensive transformation in the fabric of the city had hardly changed the situation of New Haven within wider systems of physical infrastructure and governmental provision. The airport remained a minor regional facility. The elimination of all but judicial functions in New Haven County had effectively demoted the city as an administrative center. Bielefeld had also acquired a new university and technical college, and the universities in most of the other settings had expanded by ten thousands or more students. Although Yale University expanded its facilities and research activities too, and emerged as the city's predominant economic institution, its growth remained far more limited. The number of college students in New Haven actually dropped slightly between 1960 and 1990, and the university drew fewer federal research dollars to the city than did either the University of Wisconsin-Madison or the two major schools in metropolitan Durham. Although the extent of urban clearance dwarfed that in the European cities, public supralocal resources devoted to housing, though high for the United States, remained low by European standards (see *infra*). Subsequent chapters will show how the local strategies to implement these supralocal measures further undermined aspirations to bring growth.

The direct initiatives in Table 3.7 represent only the most concrete manifestations from a broader range of supralocal policies. All three U.S. state governments added packages of tax breaks and other incentives to attract and retain businesses.[80] Although considerable research has shown the growth that such policies fostered to be at best limited and contingent,[81] North Carolina and other Sun Belt states supplemented these incentives with right-to-work laws that weakened unions. The end to legal segregation in Durham, as throughout the South, also helped enhance the

---

[80] Cf. Peter K. Eisinger, *The Rise of the Entrpreneurial State* (Madison: University of Wisconsin Press, 1988). Articles 92–94 of the European Union Treaty prohibited a wide range of parallel efforts as "state aids" presumed to distort markets (Commission of the European Communities, *Third Survey of State Aids in the European Community* [Luxembourg: European Community, 1992]). Although decisions over the 1990s under these provisions increasingly challenged various public subsidies to local industries, they had little immediate impact on decisions in these settings.

[81] For a nuanced assessment, see Donahue, *Disunited States*, Appendix A.

attractiveness of the universities and employment markets there to mobile professionals from other regions.

In the United States as in Europe, developmental policies at national and intermediate levels played unmistakable roles in patterns of prosperity and decline. Despite the more limited scope of public institutions and policies at these levels in domains like governmental administration, higher education, health care and housing, informal coordination brought greater concentrations of new services to Madison and Durham than to their German counterparts as well as to New Haven. Even as supralocal interventions in aspects of the urban political economy in the postindustrial U.S. city surpassed equivalents in most American cities of similar size, those measures fell short of the ones that had forestalled decline in Bielefeld.

c. Local Political Opportunities to Influence Supralocal Policies. Thus far, the discussion has analyzed these supralocal initiatives as interventions from the top down. Important differences in these policies can also be understood partly as the result of simultaneous influences from the bottom up. National infrastructures of local governance, in offering different opportunities for this influence, have enabled local actors to shape supralocal policy in divergent ways. The characteristic tendencies of policy already tested reflect national contrasts in collective representation of local interests through parties, interest groups and other means. But opportunities for intergovernmental entrepreneurship on the part of individual governments and other actors also account for patterns of supralocal intervention. Differences in these opportunities help to explain how supralocal initiatives came to be coordinated around growth centers in the United States; how French supralocal priorities persisted even as authorities decentralized; and how German supralocal policy limited both favors and disadvantages for these cities.

In the U.S. settings, precisely this local initiative helps explain how a fragmented, decentralized state with little supralocal planning could produce postindustrial concentrations. The universities, governed either privately or by state boards, generally made decisions to expand unilaterally. But most other policies, including the location of new state government offices in Madison, depended in part on local initiatives. The origins of the most ambitious instance of public-private collaboration in the three settings, the Research Triangle Park, exemplifies how local elites mobilized supralocal policies and resources for their own purposes. In the early 1950s two local actors, University of North Carolina professor Howard

Odum and Greensboro developer Howard Guest, had pushed similar ideas for a research park on a site equidistant from Raleigh, Chapel Hill and Durham.[82] Citing the example of Route 122 in Cambridge, Guest campaigned for the idea among local corporations and school officials. When a group presented the idea to Democratic governor Luther Hodges after his election in 1954, Hodges established two committees to look into the matter. Despite initial reluctance among local businesses, the three main universities in the area cooperated with Guest after 1958 through a nonprofit foundation. Using the services of a forest official from Duke and a separate private company, Guest and another private developer bought up the land.[83] After Governor Dan Moore (another Democrat) gave the federal government 500 acres of land in the park during the 1960s, the arrival of federal agencies helped to draw IBM and other prominent corporations. According to one account, Governor Terry Sanford capitalized on campaign debts from the 1960 presidential race to win a commitment to move federal offices to the park. Into the 1980s, officials at the local universities continued to lead efforts to attract new research facilities.

As juridical creations of the state governments, localities in the U.S. settings often depended on supralocal measures to pursue urban objectives. But state and federal programs to build public housing, carry out urban renewal and shape translocal transportation networks frequently relied on local participation in decisions. In the 1940s and 1950s, local business and civic leaders had created redevelopment commissions and housing authorities to take advantage of new housing and redevelopment programs at the federal level. As these activities continued into the 1960s, New Haven obtained support for social services through the Model Cities Program. Beginning in the 1970s, as the flow of federal funds slowed dramatically, all three cities maintained active programs under federal Community Development Block grants, Urban Development Action Grant (UDAG) measures and Section 8 housing subsidies.[84] In most of these programs, in

---

[82] This account draws on Jean Bradley Anderson, *Durham County* (Durham: Duke University Press, 1990), pp. 412–415.

[83] The purpose of the purchase was kept secret to avoid having to pay inflated prices.

[84] Including education, which was only on budget in New Haven, the combination of state programs and grants for the city for 1995–1996 came to just over 50 percent of the combined general and special funds budget for the city. Federal grants paid only 3.6 percent of local revenues budgeted. In Durham, overall intergovernmental revenues for that year amounted to only 13 percent of general funds appropriations and less of others. In Madison (in 1992), these revenues supplied 27 percent of general expenditures.

addition to formal applications on the basis of specific projects, lobbying at supralocal levels aided in this success. As federal funds declined, state government programs increasingly replaced them.

New Haven regularly acquired larger shares of funds from both federal and state programs than did Madison or Durham. Like other states in the region, Connecticut had generally undertaken to do more on behalf of its cities than had state governments outside the Northeast. Since the days of Mayor Lee, moreover, New Haven had also acquired consummate skills in the game of federal grantsmanship. Traditions of machine politics in a long-time Democratic state probably helped secure support from above. Under President Reagan in the 1980s, scandals at the federal Department of Housing and Urban Development (HUD) revealed connections to the Democratic Congress and the bureaucracy that had helped influence grant decisions in favor of New Haven.[85] Networks in national business and foundation communities, often enhanced through Yale ties, reinforced these means of influence in the private sector.[86] In redevelopment alone, Fainstein and Fainstein estimate the federal expenditures from the 1950s into the 1970s at $160 million.[87] Even in the 1990s the city continued to receive more than twice as many funds from the federal Community Development Block Grant program, or more than $5 million in 1995–1996, than did either of the other two cities.[88] Parallel efforts at the state level that year had brought New Haven $4 million in grants for various capital improvements in roads and pavement, compared to just over $300,000 in Durham and only $50,000 in Madison.[89] These funds more than surpassed the somewhat higher contributions of federal sources to local transportation networks in the other two cities.[90]

Even in the 1960s, the clientelistic opportunities in French central-local relations contrasted less with the U.S. pattern than the formal legal powers of the French state suggested. Within cities, state actors would seldom

---

[85] Jefferey M. Sellers, "Grounds of Democracy: Public Authority and the Politics of Metropolitan Land in Three Societies" (Ph.D. diss., Yale University, 1994), Ch. 3.

[86] Fainstein and Fainstein, "New Haven," pp. 27, 38–39.

[87] Ibid., p. 49.

[88] See below for more details on this and other grants with distributive consequences.

[89] This last figure is for 1992.

[90] Durham had received the most in federal transportation grants, predominantly $1.4 million to study new transit systems, and even Madison had received a total of $960,000 in federal transportation grants. But New Haven, despite the absence of federal funds for other transportation, had devoted its $720,000 in federal grants for transportation capital improvements to a new runway at the local airport.

exercise the exclusive control they did over construction of the vacation villages along the coast. From the late 1950s, local elites in Rennes and to a lesser degree in Nancy formulated and began to carry out strategies of local development in advance of much of Gaullist planning. Modernizing mayors like Freville in Rennes and counterparts in Grenoble had employed the technical and planning services of the field offices of the central state to organize and carry out local strategies.[91] Even in Montpellier, where state officials had originated the large downtown project called the Polygone, the municipality had assumed responsibility for much of the implementation. In Clermont, by contrast, the lateness of urban renewal and the limits on *grands ensembles* like those in the other French cities demonstrated how cities could also forego the path of aggressive modernization.

In the wake of decentralization, relations among the numerous institutionalized actors with new or stronger roles (regions, departments, organized groups of communes) took the form of contractual funding agreements among different levels. At the same time as this process reconfirmed a strong supralocal role, it institutionalized and extended political opportunities for local officials. Formerly issued from elite circles of bureaucrats, planning now took place through joint arrangements to sponsor physical infrastructure or other measures. The list of roadway projects in the Regional Contract for 1994–1998 in Lorraine, for instance, featured some forty specific forms of new construction on area roads. For most of these the state paid a third to half the cost. The region would add a third, and the relevant department from another fifth to a fourth.[92] Although governments of all political hues participated in these relations, ample room existed for political logics to enter the process. In Clermont-Ferrand, Montpellier and Rennes, for instance, partisan tensions often marked relations between departmental or regional governments of the Right and central city governments of the Left. In Montpellier, the regional government elected in 1986 had cut funding for a huge new opera and convention center in the city, forcing the municipality to obtain money

---

[91] Especially when structures in a region did not favor a single solution, such as in the choice between Metz and Nancy as the site of important official functions, political logics could enter into the strategies of Parisian planners. Local elites in Nancy blamed the choice of Metz for the main east-west autoroute A4 on a mayor of Metz who was serving as a minister at the time.

[92] André Lefebvre, *Nancy et son Agglomération: Contribution a une Reflexion d'Ordre Stratégique* (Nancy, 1995), Annexe 8.

for the operation from the central state. Further contractual ties linked municipalities to the large public banks like the national Caisse des Dépôts et Consignations (CDC). These institutions both financed local projects of semipublic development companies and provided general loans to cities. At the same time that the CDC and other banks attained means for control over local initiatives through these arrangements, the localities themselves acquired financial resources and a vested supralocal interest in development.[93] Pursuit of program benefits from the bottom up also pervaded administration of European programs. Even as programs like the Structural and Cohesion Funds imposed criteria for funds from the top down, cities like Montpellier could still secure funds and other privileges from European policy through the entrepreneurship of local and intermediate governments. Regional leaders like Jacques Blanc of Languedoc-Roussillon and later Valéry Giscard d'Estaing of Auvergne helped assure benefits for their own constituencies through prominent roles on the European Council of Regions.

In Germany, constraints on the opportunities for this sort of intergovernmental entrepreneurship limited the chances for cities to override the dictates of frameworks for planning. Unlike its U.S. counterpart, the German federal government rarely participated in developmental policies except through the establishment of broad policies and frameworks for the *Länder*. Specific decisions typically resided with the *Land* governments or their representatives at regional levels beyond metropolitan areas. Whatever competition for supralocal resources did take place generally occurred at those levels. Although opportunities existed there to obtain funding and infrastructure, the system of spatial planning increasingly constrained these chances for influence in rigid frameworks. Designated *Oberzentren* like each of these cities received equal priority in the allocation of facilities and funds. At the same time, the systematic revenue sharing that dominated local finance remained impervious to local entrepreneurship. Beneath the constitutionalized system of fiscal equalization among the *Länder*, additional formulas for revenue sharing equalized finances available to communes within each *Land*.[94] Although these cities received

[93] These financial authorities do not, however, appear to have been used to exert microlevel control over the projects undertaken.
[94] For an overview of this system, see Gérard Marcou, Hans Kistenmacher and Hans-Günther Clev, *L'Aménagement du Territoire en France et en Allemagne* (Paris: La Documentation Francaise, 1994), Ch. 6.

between 32 and 47 percent of the revenues for their operating budgets from the *Land* or federal government, the bulk of that sum in each case came from the system of equalization for tax revenues.[95]

Within the restricted bounds of this system, individual *Länder* still varied in the degree that developmental programs remained susceptible to initiatives from below. In North Rhine-Westphalia, the site of the Ruhr crisis as well as an SPD bastion, policy making at this intermediate level constrained local initiatives more. As Table 3.3 suggests, *Land* officials there had acted earlier and more systematically to structure local use of those resources through planning. Even the biggest single public initiative in Bielefeld, the new university, came about more through the initiative of an expert commission (led by Helmut Schelsky) at the *Land* level that sought to address a regional shortage of educational facilities than as a result of local lobbying.[96] Here as in the other two *Länder*, support for specific projects like new infrastructural measures depended on the same sorts of categorical grants and particularized decision making as in the United States and France. But planning at the *Land* level typically imposed integrated priorities in ways that constrained how much any community could gain from these measures. Both Lower Saxony and Baden-Württemberg had engaged in less directive planning, introduced comprehensive planning later and built fewer restrictive specifications about growth for particular communities into supralocal plans. Local entrepreneurial initiative in these settings could sometimes qualify the consequences of *Land* policies. Although North Rhine-Westphalia supported such programs as public housing more aggressively than did the CDU-governed Baden-Württemberg,[97] Freiburg had engaged in extension urban reconstruction and sponsored large new housing projects over much of the postwar period.

In the 1990s, as the need to fund east German reconstruction weighed increasingly on the system of intergovernmental finance, all three *Länder*

---

[95] Thus in the early to mid-1990s these cities (Bielefeld, Freiburg, Göttingen and Münster) received 32, 44, 37 and 47 percent of their tax and related income from the Land or the federal government. But 11, 22, 9 and 13 percent of these sums came from the equalizing *Schlüsselzuweisungen*, and 16, 13, 13 and 26 percent from apportioned shares of the income tax.

[96] Peter Lundgreen, *Reformuniversität Bielefeld, 1969–1994* (Bielefeld: Verlag für Regionalgeschichte, 1994), pp. 23–30.

[97] Wolfgang Jaedicke and Helmut Wollmann, "Wohnungsbauförderung im Bundesländervergleich: Macht Landespolitik einen Unterschied?" *Stadtbauwelt* (1983): 437–443.

converged toward fewer discretionary grants. This trend followed the dominant tendency in the supralocal policy of both France and the United States toward lower levels of developmental spending. Even Socialist decentralization in France went along with a sharply reduced supralocal role in renewal and housing policy. The growth of European funding for developmental policies only partly qualified these trends. Granted through a process of applications from national and subnational actors, European support depended on lobbying at least as much as did national policies. Successful grantsmanship in French cities and regions depended partly on location in poor regions, but partly also on political capacities to obtain and carry out grants.[98] In Germany, the same planning frameworks that limited this entrepreneurship within domestic policy making hampered enlistment of surrounding regions and *Länder* in campaigns for European resources.

These persistent limits on intergovernmental entrepreneurship in Germany help to account for the constraints on growth in the cities there. In both the fragmented supralocal authorities of the United States and the vertically integrated state of France, greater entrepreneurial opportunities enabled cities like Rennes, Montpellier, Madison and Durham to secure developmental advantages from below.

In all three countries, policy makers at supralocal levels had parallel means available to bring growth to service centers like these. Variations in the use of those means made much of the difference in local patterns of growth. Not only state organization at national and intermediate levels but also the divergent infrastructures of local government and politics shaped the employment of those means. More in Germany than in the other countries, local policies in these disparate cities followed similar patterns. There uniform constraints and tendencies toward equalization offset the territorial variations that federalism might otherwise have fostered. Under both the centralized, unitary state structures of France as well as the decentralized federal structures of the United States, supralocal policies addressed to development in urban regions varied more. In both countries these variations helped produce the greater divergences in service-led growth. Local discretion to instigate and implement higher-level initiatives informed most developmental policies. Limits to this discretion reinforced the comparative uniformity of the German initiatives and of the outputs that

---

[98] Cf. Marc Smyrl, "European Policies, Regional Programs, Local Politics: Implementing European Community Regional Policy" (Ph.D. diss., Harvard University, 1997).

137

ensued. Greater opportunities in the United States for local entrepreneurship and growing ones in France gave rise to a wider variety in supralocal efforts to bring local growth. In both countries the success of those efforts was a riskier proposition.

Environmental Policies at Supralocal Levels

Environmental objectives have furnished much of the impetus toward localization of policy. Both functional and political logics make local components crucial to these policies. At the same time, for policies of this sort to be consistent or address translocal issues, supralocal components are often indispensable. In bringing about the most consistent local environmental protection of the three countries, the German infrastructure of local government overshadowed German federalism even more in this policy domain than in developmental matters. U.S. and French policies, though dependent to different degrees on supralocal components, left local policies similarly contingent on local initiatives.

Despite the growth of European norms in numerous environmental domains,[99] policies at national and intermediate levels still dominate translocal influences on efforts to achieve urban sustainability. Those international elements that have emerged as potential influences on urban environmental policy in Europe and beyond have done so mostly after these national and subnational policies were in place. Beginning with a Green Paper on the urban environment in 1990 and the start of the Sustainable Cities Project in 1993, the European Union introduced a series of encouragements to cities to engage in sound environmental practices across a wide range of policy domains.[100] Even more than for developmental policy, European measures in support of urban environmental aims relied directly on decisions within and among cities. Usually bypassing national and even intermediate governments, measures from the early 1990s onward established means that would allow individual city governments and international networks of cities to cooperate and compete in pursuit of sustainable development. From 1991 the Directorate General for the Environment, aided by an Expert Group on the urban environ-

---

[99] For an overview of European intervention as of the mid-1990s, see Philip C. Schmitter, "Imagining the Future of the Euro-Polity with the Help of New Concepts," in Marks et al., *Governance in the European Union*, pp. 121–150.

[100] See European Commission, *Progress Report of the European Commission's Expert Group on the Urban Environment, 1993–1996* (Brussels, 1997).

ment composed of officials from community environmental ministries, sought to accumulate and disseminate knowledge about local environmental policy and contributed to networks of conferences, support and communication with the European Sustainable Cities and Towns Campaign. In these actions, the EU helped bolster wider international urban environmental initiatives like the promotion of Local Agenda 21 from the 1992 Rio Conference and the International Council for Local Environmental Initiatives (ICLEI). Advocated by the Expert Group, a "greening" of the Structural Funds made parts of this support available for more direct financing of local environmental initiatives.

Without stronger components in actual national or subnational policy, these accumulating initiatives could not themselves alter patterns of land use policy that had already been established. Even into the 1990s, EU environmental mandates related to urban policy remained confined to discrete domains like waste management and biodiversity or to procedural requirements like environmental impact statements.[101] EU Structural Funds directed at these settings have continued to allocate only small proportions of overall totals to environmental measures.[102] Although cities like Freiburg and Madison participated actively in international conferences, exchanges and networks, the consequences of these activities for local policy choices depended even more than did international funds on how local officials chose to draw on examples and support from other cities.

My analysis of top-down initiatives will focus on one subset of the *protective* policies that represent the most characteristic form of environmental measures related to land use. By means of either positive initiatives like creation of parks or negative constraints like regulation, such measures protect the natural resources of a metropolitan area, and related cultural resources, from environmental harms due to development. Protections on forests, on open space, on exurban sprawl, on historical structures and on parklands comprise the clearest instances of such policies.[103] A full account

---

[101] Johnson and Corcelle, *European Environmental Law.*

[102] Up to 1997, in none of these urban areas did Structural Funds go to budgeted environmental expenditures. In North Rhine-Westphalia, however, just under a third of a smaller 7.9 ECU program for small and medium enterprises went to environmental measures. A fourth of the Structural Funds that went to the Ruhr Valley were also budgeted for environmental improvements in industrial areas.

[103] Protection for pedestrians and bicycle users and even mass transit also prevent environmental damage from automobiles. But only pedestrian zones clearly impose a direct constraint on other forms of possible development. A similar logic of protection applies to policies toward preservation of clean air and water.

of the supralocal influences on these policies must encompass more than the measures that higher levels of government imposed directly. Direct impositions of this sort, such as regulatory rules addressed to new construction, restrict or condition the *supply* of land available in development markets. Through other measures that influence the *demand side* of those same markets, supralocal policy makers can exert similar or complementary effects that are often just as crucial. New roads and mass transit can render centralized urban settlement either more or less costly for individual consumers. Restrictions on the placement of amenities like shopping can make development in outlying areas less of an environmental threat. Reconstructed downtowns that attract residents to the urban center can diminish market pressures for outlying new development.

The following analysis of the role these supralocal policies played revolves around the same questions as those posed for developmental policies. First, I inquire what actions supralocal governments undertook to influence environmental outputs like those found in Chapter 2. Second, I consider how far local actions shaped or even decided the ultimate consequences of any supralocal measures. Finally, I assess whether the patterns of supralocal measures within each country reflect influences from infrastructures of local governance or the effects from different degrees of vertical integration at higher levels of the state.

Germany. German protective policies toward land use exemplified how the infrastructure of local governance could overshadow structures at intermediate levels of the state as an influence on policy. Legal prescriptions at the national level had imposed a growing array of policies that local actors in all three *Länder* applied. Although manifestly dependent on local practices of interpretation and application, the resulting policies proved more consistent, and more consistently effective, than those in either France or the United States.

Although German principalities had initiated earlier protections on such sensitive environmental domains as the Black Forest, land use policies at the national level had accumulated only over the postwar period. Since the interwar period, professional planners in the local governments of cities and in technical university faculties across the country had worked to develop these rules. Already in 1960, the first national construction code prescribed limits to construction in the so-called outer areas beyond urbanized parts of the metropolitan area (BBauG § 35). Spurred by such nationwide environmentalist organizations as BUND, as well as by a pro-liferation of local movements, the national Social-Liberal coalition of the 1970s extended environmental policies into numerous areas. These efforts culminated in the mandate of the Natural Protection Law of 1976 that losses of natural areas to development be compensated through creation of new protected natural areas (NaturG § 8).

An array of policies in other domains reinforced these constraints on new development in urban peripheries and ecologically sensitive lands. In the domain of transportation, a gas tax six times as high as that in the United States has supplemented a variety of measures that limit and control automobile use or promote public transit.[104] Prohibitions on con-struction of larger supermarkets outside urbanized areas limited shopping opportunities that might invite more dispersed housing. Even in 1995, one report found only 22 percent of retail sales space in western Germany outside urbanized areas.[105] Subsidies for farmers discouraged conversion of agricultural land.[106] Finally, systems of urban and regional planning that developed at local and *Land* levels over the 1950s and 1960s received national sanction under a national law of 1965. Additional laws under the Social-Liberal coalition prescribed legal frameworks for urban renewal itself. Such measures systematically encouraged city governments to relieve pressures for exurban expansion through new development in already urbanized areas.

From the perspective of many local actors, this national regulatory framework had by the 1990s overshadowed both local markets and much of local decision making. Significantly more than their counterparts in either Montpellier or New Haven, elites and activists in and around Freiburg identified the legal rules there as more important than market forces as influences on patterns of land use.[107] In my interviews in

---

[104] John Pucher and Christian Lefèvre, *The Urban Transport Crisis in Europe and North America* (Houndmills, Basingstoke: MacMillan Press, 1996), Ch. 3.
[105] Helmut Bunge and Rolf Spannagel, "Standorte im Wettbewerb – Revitalisierung oder Auszehrung der Innenstädte," in Joseph Lachner, Thomas Nassua and Rolf Spannagel (eds.), *Entwicklung des Handels in den neuen Bundesländern* (Berlin: Forschungsstelle für den Handel, 1995), pp. 35–74, see p. 41.
[106] Nivola, *Laws of the Landscape*, pp. 29–30.
[107] In response to a standardized question, 42 percent found the rules ("*Bau- und Pla-nungsrecht*") to be more important than "market forces." Only 26 percent in Montpellier and 34 percent in New Haven chose a similar assessment (Sellers, "Grounds of Democ-racy," p. 504).

the German city most agreed with the observation of a mayor from an outlying town that "market forces mustn't go beyond what the rules allow." Rather than determine the content of the rules, observed a local legal expert, "Market forces generally follow the legal rules." An architect on the City Council made clear where the importance of the rules lay. "Market forces," he explained, "follow the availability of places to build." The rules controlled markets by restricting where – and whether – new construction could be built. "When there's no available land, prices go higher."

Such statements reflected prevailing attitudes in Freiburg toward national prescriptions as well as those prescriptions themselves. Variations occurred more at the local than at the *Land* level. Federal commissions that studied application of land use planning rules in both the 1980s and the 1990s found wide differences in the strictness of enforcement, but less among *Land* governments than among *Regierungsbezirke*, or regional administrative offices for oversight.[108] Local and metropolitan officials in the four services centers echoed these observations. Even in greater Freiburg, some respondents observed more lenient enforcement in outlying towns of the metropolitan area than in the central city.

A look at how development evolved in the German metropolitan areas from the 1960s into the 1980s affirms the importance of local decisions in these policies and ultimately in the comparative success of German protections on land. Not only did local actors diverge in the strictness with which they applied the rules, but they often had already reoriented land use markets around protective goals by the time the legislation of the 1970s was introduced.

An index that measures shifts in development over time throughout each metropolitan area offers a more precise means to analyze these effects than the overall indicators of outcomes in Chapter 2. The index of new housing that I created for this purpose compared the patterns of housing construction for successive nine- or ten-year periods with the pattern of existing housing at the beginning of each period. For each metropolitan town, the index divided the proportion of all metropolitan housing units constructed over the relevant period by the proportion of preexisting met-

---

[108] Bundesministerium für Raumordnung, Bauwesen und Städtebau, *Kostensenkung und Verringerung von Vorschriften im Wohnungsbau* (Bonn, 1995), p. 77; Hellmut Wollmann (ed.), *Rechtstatsachenuntersuchung zur Baugenehmigungspraxis*, Heft Nr. 03.110 (Bonn: Bundesministerium für Raumordnung, Bauwesen und Städtebau, 1985).

ropolitan housing stock in the town.[109] If the index stood at 1, the town had received precisely the same amount of metropolitan construction in that period as it had already received. A reading above 1 signified that development had shifted toward the town; below 1, that development had moved away.[110]

This index enabled a straightforward comparison of how metropolitan development responded to attempts to protect environmentally sensitive areas. If the index for a town rose with the distance of that town from the urban center, generating a positive correlation with the index, new development had dispersed. A negative correlation with the index would indicate that new housing had shifted back toward the central city. Similarly, negative correlations with proportions of open space or forest land, and with agricultural land, would demonstrate that new development had

---

[109] Mathematically, the index for each town in a metropolitan area corresponds to:

$$\frac{(c_i/C_i)}{(t_{i-1}/T_{i-1})},$$

where c_i = the housing units constructed in that town over period i, C_i = overall construction of housing units in the metropolitan area over that period, t_{i-1} = the total housing units in the town at the beginning of period i, and T_{i-1} = the total housing units in the metropolitan area at the beginning of period i.

To calculate the index for the French metropolitan areas, I used the total housing units in the five censuses from 1962 through 1990. Since these figures from each census specified the values of t_{i-1} and T_{i-1}, I calculated $c_i = t_i - t_{i-1}$ and $C_i = T_i - T_{i-1}$. For the German and U.S. settings, changing municipal boundaries and less frequent censuses over the same period necessitated an alternative approach. In these two countries, responses to a recent census (1990 in the U.S., 1987 in Germany) provided data on the age of housing units that could be taken as an archaeology of how development had evolved over the preceding three decades. Totals of housing constructed in successive periods could be assigned values of c_i and C_i. The total housing units in the latest census, or t_f, provided the information to estimate

$$t_{i-1} = t_f - \left(\sum_{i=1}^{n}(c_i)\right),$$

where n = the number of periods $(i, j, k, \ldots)$ between t_{i-1} and t_f. A parallel calculation for aggregate metropolitan figures produced an estimate for T_{i-1}.

[110] Differences in census categories and municipal boundaries necessitated adaptations in each country. For instance, subtraction of the total housing in a previous census from the total in the latest census leaves out housing constructed through replacement of existing stock. A total based on the estimated date of construction fails to take into account housing that has been replaced. These anomalies cannot account for variations between settings with similar practices. I also verified the results in France and New Haven with parallel calculations based on alternative formulas.

shifted away from these other objects of land use protections. An average of all three correlations furnishes a general indicator of land use protections. Since markets as well as policies have influenced development, analysis of this data must take account of changes in demand alongside the restrictions that policies might place on supply. Where available, evidence of market constraints should supplement other indications of control through policy. Without rising prices for exurban land or a heavy volume of overall construction, a shift in development toward the center could have grown out of subsiding market demand.

This analysis demonstrates a correspondence between control of sprawl in the German urban regions and policy interventions since the 1960s. Especially in North Rhine-Westphalia, metropolitan and regional planning under auspices of the *Land* government had begun to shift patterns of development well before the legislation of the 1970s. Particularly in relation to indicators for peripheral and forested land, housing in and around Münster and Bielefeld manifested the results (Figure 3.1). Centralized settlement in these metropolitan areas was by no means foreordained. During the 1960s in Münster, a positive correlation between the housing index and the environmental indicators demonstrates that development was shifting out into the urban periphery and into forested areas. But over the next decade, the *Land* government introduced both regional plans for urban areas and a new law for the protection of landscapes. The federal government passed Forest and Natural Protection Laws and imposed increasingly strict limits on placement of new shopping facilities outside urbanized areas. At the same time, urban renewal in the city centers and expansion of municipal boundaries into the periphery gave central-city officials new powers over exurban development markets. As a result, despite persistent or rising rates of construction, average correlations with the environmental indicators fell. Around Münster, development shifted back to a slightly negative average relation with these figures. Although none of the protections applied explicitly to agricultural land, the shift away from the urban periphery and from forested communes was all the more dramatic. Around Bielefeld, the average correlations of development with the indicators besides farmland included also moved significantly lower. After 1978, with the natural protection legislation fully in place and a revised forest law at the *Land* level, protections on non-agricultural land continued to tighten. Although in both urban regions new development took place increasingly through conversion of farmland, the newly developed housing continued to concentrate closer to the urban

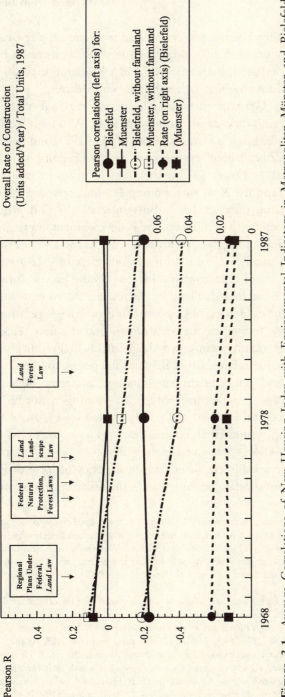

Figure 3.1 Average Correlations of New Housing Index with Environmental Indicators in Metropolitan Münster and Bielefeld, 1958–1987

Note: Pearson correlations measure average relation of New Housing Index by commune with distance from city center, with proportion of cadastral land in forest for 1979; and with proportion of cadastral land in agriculture for 1979. Housing figures calculated from age of housing units given in responses to 1987 Census. Correlations employ statistics by town for the city and surrounding *Landkreise* (counties) (*n* = 39, Bielefeld; *n* = 49, Münster). For more detailed data analysis see Jefferey M. Sellers, *Federalism and Metropolitan Governance: The Case of Urban Sprawl, the Environment and Planning* (forthcoming).
Sources: Statistical Office for North Rhine-Westphalia.

center than it had under historic patterns. Despite slightly lower overall rates of construction during this period, the demand for housing in both exurban peripheries persisted. Between 1980 and 1990, land prices in the surrounding jurisdictions rose faster than in the central cities.[111]

In the other two German metropolitan areas, regional planning under the federal framework came somewhat later. Although Baden-Württemberg initiated its first plan at the *Land* level in 1971, and another in 1983, the "South Upper Rhine" region surrounding Freiburg issued its first plan only in 1980. In Lower Saxony the *Land* government legislated its first plan in 1982, and the *Kreis* surrounding Göttingen issued its own plan under this scheme only in 1987. But especially in and around Freiburg, local protections had directed new development away from forests, agricultural land and peripheral areas as early as the 1960s (Figure 3.2). Into the 1970s, steady or even rising overall rates of construction accompanied largely consistent control. In the 1980s, except for the increased conversion of agricultural land in Göttingen, the average correlations point to a slight tightening of this control. Protective legislation at the national level, new forest laws in both *Länder* and the new regional plan for Freiburg and vicinity reinforced this control. In Freiburg as in North Rhine-Westphalia, accumulating demand for peripheral land over this period pushed land prices in the surrounding *Landkreise* higher in comparison with those of the central city.[112] In Göttingen during the 1980s, however, the central city had made only limited land available for development within its municipal boundaries.[113] There prices in the central city rose in relation to the surrounding area.

By the 1980s a remarkably consistent national policy of local protections had brought about similar consequences in the urban regions of three

[111] In Münster the ratio of construction-ready land prices in the central city to prices in the rest of the metropolitan area fell from 4.48 to 4.03 over this period; in Bielefeld the same ratio dropped from 1.95 to 1.41 (data from North Rhine-Westphalia Statistical Office).

[112] Here the ratio of prices for construction-ready land in the central city to prices in the surrounding *Landkreis* fell from 1.96 in 1975 to 1.42 in 1990 (Sellers, "Grounds of Democracy," p. 645).

[113] Since *Land* statistics on Göttingen do not separate out the figures for the central city from those for the rest of the *Landkreis*, these figures are not precisely comparable to those elsewhere. In 1970, the ratio of city prices for construction-ready land to prices for the entire *Landkreis* stood at 1.27. Over 1986–1990, this ratio averaged 2.15. At the same time, the amount of construction-ready land that changed hands in the city fell from over 300 to under 100 square meters per year (Niedersächsisches Landesamt für Statistik, *Baulandverkäufe und Baulandpreise in Niedersachsen 1970* [Hannover, 1971]; Niedersächsisches Landesamt für Statistik, *Kaufwerte für Bauland 1990* [Hannover, 1991]).

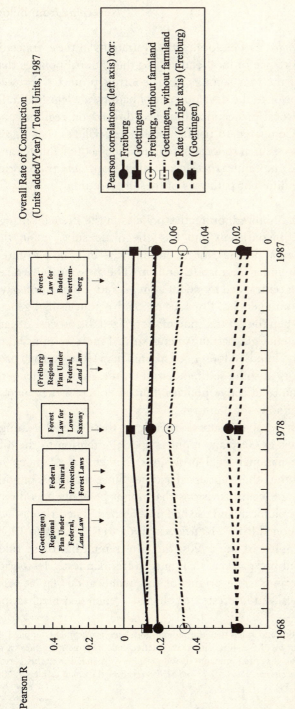

Figure 3.2 Average Correlations of New Housing Index with Environmental Indicators in Metropolitan Freiburg and Göttingen, 1958–1987

Note: Pearson correlations measure average relation of New Housing Index by commune with distance from city center; with proportion of cadastral land in forest for 1979; and with proportion of cadastral land in agriculture for 1979. Housing figures calculated from age of housing units given in responses to 1987 Census. Correlations employ statistics by town for the city and surrounding *Landkreise* (counties) (*n* = 75, Freiburg; *n* = 29, Göttingen). See Sellers, "Federalism and Metropolitan Governance."
Sources: Statistical Offices for Lower Saxony (Göttingen), Baden-Württemberg.

different German *Länder*.[114] The local action variations in these trajectories suggest the importance of local choices for the national policies that emerged. In three of the four settings, local controls protected forested and peripheral land prior to the development of nationwide legislation. In Münster, systematic local protections followed directly on regional and national initiatives. Compared to national and local policies, *Land* governments proved less essential to local outcomes. Since both Münster and Bielefeld belonged to the same *Land*, local rather than *Land* trajectories must account for the different pathways of these two settings.

France. As Chapter 2 showed, protective policies in the French settings had generated more inconsistent and less effective results. As in the domain of developmental policies, local contingencies in France fostered greater variation than under German federalism. The growing departures of the 1980s from the centralized model of administrative regulation gave new shape to these contingencies. Previous protective policies had generally succeeded only when the central state monopolized the process of carrying them out. The emerging arrangements turned more responsibility over to local actors and imposed looser constraints than German legal prescriptions. Local actors in some settings seized on these arrangements to carry out modestly more effective policies, but by doing so they aggravated the disparities among local efforts.

To analyze how the evolving supralocal role in these French settings diverged from parallels in Germany requires special attention to the difference between the national legal provisions that embodied much of supralocal policy and the other supralocal actions. Since the 1950s in both countries, the supply of legal provisions that might be applied as direct protective constraints on local land use had proliferated. The French *Code d'Urbanisme* had ballooned from 216 pages in 1964 to 919 pages in 1988. Yet even at the beginning of the 1990s, the constraints that these rules imposed on local land use markets in France were manifestly less strict than Germany constraints. The origins of the qualifications lay at least partly in the same localized interests that shaped French decentralization

---

[114] Changes in the subsidies and rules that the federal and *Land* governments applied to housing cannot account for these shifts either. Legislative encouragement to the sort of owner-occupied housing that predominated in the periphery expanded over this period (Hans-Artur Hassis, *Bodenpreise, Bodenmarkt und Stadtentwicklung* [Munich: Minerva Publikation, 1987], pp. 70–71).

in general.[115] The result would help perpetuate both the administrative regulation and the entrepreneurial opportunities of the infrastructure for local government.

Local elites and activists in greater Montpellier offered a view of national legislation that at least partly typified other French settings. Where the Germans had emphasized the constraints the rule imposed, the French emphasized how the rules "adapted to markets," how it was "necessary to satisfy the market" or to "listen to the market." Even those who asserted that the central city had controlled market forces also noted that "the small communes in particular lack the means to counterbalance the market." The regulatory texts themselves helped promote this flexibility. Beyond the wide array of "dérogations" (departures) that national legislation authorized,[116] the rules contained fewer unqualified statements of protective purposes like those in the German Construction Law. The ambiguities of a prolix, dense thicket of legal prescriptions also detracted from efforts to pursue consistent policies. Sixty percent of the elites and activists in and around Montpellier, compared with 44 percent in greater Freiburg and 30 percent in greater New Haven, agreed with the statement that the substantive rules were "too complicated to apply effectively."[117] At the same time, respondents expressed comparative ambivalence toward the formal texts themselves as a source of authority.[118]

Under the centralized infrastructure of local governance that prevailed in France into the 1970s, national officials and their territorial representatives generally played a more decisive role than did legislated rules in the pursuit of policies at the local level. Even after the reforms of the 1980s, national actors continued to dominate specific components of protective policy more than even the *Land* officials did in Germany. National ownership had spared the volcanic hills in the Puy-de-Dome park to the west of Clermont-Ferrand and the domainal forests outside Nancy and

---

[115] Catherine Grémion, "Décentralisation An X," *French Politics and Society 9* (3–4) (Summer/Fall 1991): 32–42.

[116] For instance, L. 123–1, R. 111–20, R. 421–15 *Code de l'Urbanisme* (1988). See Auby and Périnet-Marquet, *Droit de l'urbanisme*, pp. 288–291.

[117] Sellers, "Grounds of Democracy," p. 521.

[118] Fifty-four percent, compared with 39 percent in greater Freiburg and 33 percent in greater New Haven, agreed with the assertion that it was "more important for a judge to attain justice than to conform to the written law" (Sellers, "Grounds of Democracy," pp. 519–520).

Rennes from pressures for development.[119] Even after decentralization, laws to protect major historical and natural sites and to enforce related restrictions on land use remained under the administration of national officials.[120] The National Architects of France had established, and continued to administer, historic districts under the Malraux Laws that submitted much of the Old Towns in Montpellier, Nancy and Rennes to an especially strict regime of regulation and rehabilitation.[121]

The influence of central officials extended well beyond any such discrete areas. The powers to approve local decisions and to resolve disputes that were accorded the prefect and other national officials retained a role in contested decisions in and around Montpellier that went well beyond the role of even the *Land* government and its territorial representatives in the Regierungspräsidium of Freiburg. In the set of thirty-five land use controversies that the elites and activists of Montpellier volunteered from the 1980s, national actors of some sort had been involved in 86 percent. In a total of 66 percent, respondents ascribed those actors either "decisive" or "considerable" influence on the result. In a parallel set of thirty-four controversies, the *Land* government and its representatives in greater Freiburg had gotten involved in 59 percent, but they had exercised similar degrees of influence in only 29 percent. As might be expected, the German federal government remained predominantly uninvolved, with a direct role in only 12 percent of the controversies and limited influence in only half of those. But even the departmental government for the subregion surrounding Montpellier, a body with much less authority than national officials, had begun to approach the *Land* government of Freiburg in importance.[122] In the more routine, less contested matters that comprised the bulk of intergovernmental activity, the national French actors maintained a similarly distinctive role. Not only in the smallest controversies but also in everyday networks of consultation and contacts, these officials retained a promi-

---

[119] Since its creation in 1975, the National Land Conservancy had also secured protection through ownership of some 400,000 hectares of shorefront property in 300 sites (Claude Dubillot, "M. Barnier veut protéger 30% du littoral français," *Le Monde* [February 18, 1995]: 10).

[120] Auby and Marquet, *Droit de l'urbanisme*, pp. 231–232, 249–250.

[121] The German procedures for historical protection (*Denkmalschutz*) administered at the local level had probably restricted inner-city development less.

[122] Sellers, "Grounds of Democracy," p. 158. Respondents found that the new regional government that decentralization had created for Languedoc-Roussillon had no more than "limited" influence in any controversy. They deemed the department "considerable" or better in influence on 17 percent of all controversies.

150

nent position. In the central city as well as in the smaller peripheral towns, local officials looked to supralocal actors more frequently than had their counterparts in Freiburg.[123]

At the national and intermediate levels of the French state, unitary, centralized authorities might appear to possess the means to bring about more effective environmental policy making than in Germany. This conclusion would fail to take account of the systematic influence from infrastructures for local implementation on the application, and ultimately on the explicit aims, of national rules. Attitudes in and around Montpellier toward the rules reflected practices that often enabled local actors to put national policies to use for their own purposes. Some employed these opportunities to carry out protections, but others worked to subvert or limit national policies.

The other policies that shaped the demand side of land use markets in France also provided less reinforcement to land use control than in Germany. In contrast to most northern European countries, postwar France concentrated its transportation policies on "a vast programme of investment in roads and the automobile" that remained uncoordinated with land use policies.[124] Programs to provide financial incentives for property ownership added to incentives for city dwellers to move to the urban periphery. Until the 1990s, efforts to control the spread of shopping centers into the periphery remained as limited and contingent as direct protections on land. The Royer Law, passed in 1973 at the urging of threatened artisans and retailers in the downtowns, had instituted a system to regulate supermarkets by means of commissions at the departmental level. Composed of representatives from organizations of consumers and shopkeepers as well as local officials, these commissions received authority to disapprove supermarkets beyond a moderately large size.[125] Yet around Clermont-Ferrand, Montpellier and Nancy, as throughout France, these arrangements had not halted the spread of large stores and discount outlets into the urban periphery throughout the 1980s. Political favors, even rumored bribes to local officials on the commissions, helped to undermine the process.[126] In the 1990s the national government

---

[123] Sellers, "Grounds of Democracy," p. 167.

[124] Pucher, Lefèvre and Lefèvre, *Urban Transport Crisis*, p. 65.

[125] Auby and Périnet-Marquet, *Droit de l'urbanisme*, p. 131.

[126] John T. S. Keeler, "Corporatist Decentralization and Commercial Modernization in France: The Royer Law's Impact on Shopkeepers, Supermarkets and the State," in Philip G. Cerny and Martin Schain (eds.), *Socialism, the State and Public Policy in France* (New York: Methuen, 1985), pp. 265–291.

intervened repeatedly to tighten this law.[127] Moreover, some of the most generous farm subsidies in the EU discouraged agricultural conversion but had not prevented the extensive sale of farms around cities like Clermont-Ferrand and Montpellier.[128]

The first efforts of national officials to apply protective policies to metropolitan development in these settings demonstrated the difficulties that local arrangements posed. In the late 1960s and early 1970s, at about the same time that Germany had instituted a system of regional planning, French territorial officials in each of these metropolitan areas pursued similar efforts. In 1972 for Rennes, in 1973 for Nancy, and in 1977 for Clermont-Ferrand, the prefect and local field offices had issued regional plans (*schémas directeurs*). These documents set out future uses of space for the city and the communes surrounding it. Maps designated areas of forest and farmland to be protected as well as new land to be developed. A parallel measure in Montpellier never gained approval. Although local officials at that time possessed little formal authority over issuance of the regional plan, squabbles between communes had been enough to undermine an officially prepared plan.

Even where these plans had passed, however, the documents had little apparent effect on protected areas. North of Clermont-Ferrand, a new housing project named "Les Mauvaises" (the naughty ones) exemplified how clientelistic ties and limited capabilities for enforcement undermined the prescriptions of the plans. The project took its name at least partly from its location in an area the regional plan had designated as protected forest.

Parallel statistics to those in the German metropolitan areas demonstrate this failure. Consider the patterns of development since the 1960s in Montpellier alongside those in Rennes, the other French metropolitan area where pressures for growth had persisted into the 1980s (Figure 3.3). Throughout the 1960s in both metropolitan areas, the traditional centralized pattern of settlement remained the decisive influence on patterns of new housing. The intensive construction associated with the buildup of regional capitals and educational services concentrated in the urban centers. At the same time, inadequate infrastructure in the urban

---

[127] In 1993, Prime Minister Balldur imposed a moratorium on new supermarkets. Even before then, regulation appears to have somewhat braked commercial expansion in the urban periphery (Bernard Dezert, Alain Metton and Jean Steinberg, *La Périurbanisation en France* [Paris: SEDES, 1991], Ch. 8).

[128] Nivola, *Laws of the Landscape*, pp. 29–30.

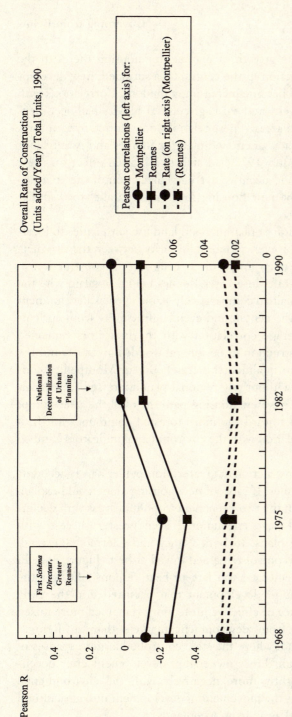

Figure 3.3 Average Correlations of New Housing Index with Environmental Indicators in the Most Rapidly Growing French Metropolitan Areas, 1962–1990

Note: Pearson correlations measure average relation of New Housing Index for housing added per year during each period by commune with distance from city center; with proportion of cadastral land in forest for 1970 (periods 1962–1968 and 1968–1975) and for 1988 (periods 1975–1982 and 1982–1990); and with proportion in agriculture of the population residing in ordinary households in 1962 (periods 1962–1968 and 1968–1975) and proportion in agriculture of active employed cantonal population in 1982 (1975–1982 and 1982–1990). Change in housing for each period represents total at beginning of period minus total at end of period. See Sellers, "Federalism and Metropolitan Governance."

Sources: INSEE, *Recensement Général de la Population de 1962;* id., *Recensement Général de la Population de 1982: Évolutions démographiques;* id., *Recensement Général de la Population de 1990: Évolutions démographiques;* id., *Communoscope* (1988): Ministry of Agriculture, *Census de l'Agriculture 1970.*

periphery helped limit the growth of markets for housing there. In the 1970s, as rates of construction in the central area subsided, new development moved outward and became increasingly random. Correlations with distance from the central city and with agricultural activity had been negative in both metropolitan areas. These relations now shifted toward zero. The protections of the state-sanctioned plan for Rennes and twenty-four surrounding communes after 1972 had at best a limited effect on these overall patterns. The strong negative average correlation of the environmental indicators with the new housing index rose parallel to a similar movement in Montpellier.

After the decentralization of planning and land use authorities to localities in the early 1980s, however, a modest disparity between the two metropolitan areas began to open up. With a rising rate of construction in both urban regions, the shifts in greater Rennes help to explain why the density gradient there remained comparatively stable. As new development moved back, away from the center, and even slightly away from agricultural communes, the average correlation with the indicators remained negative. Intensified construction in peripheral wooded areas beyond the reach of the regional plan qualified this trend. But in Montpellier construction rates had risen without any regional plan addressed to patterns of metropolitan land use. As new housing patterns over the 1980s crept increasingly outward and toward the more forested communes north of the city, the average correlation with the environmental indicators climbed above zero.

The more intensive construction in greater Montpellier hardly accounts for this contrast with Rennes. If rates of new housing alone could explain the degree of control, then the two French metropolitan areas with declining growth rates should have encountered even greater success with state-sanctioned regional plans. In both Nancy and Clermont-Ferrand, however, the evidence of control remained mixed at best (Figure 3.4). In both settings, the plans emerged too late to bear responsibility for the more centralized patterns of development that persisted into the early 1970s. Thereafter, evidence of effective protections remained more mixed despite fewer pressures from development markets than in Rennes. Around Clermont-Ferrand, where the state controlled larger expanses of metropolitan land through direct ownership, development after decentralization correlated slightly more negatively with the environmental indicators. Around Nancy, the movement of development into agricultural areas canceled out a trend away from woodlands.

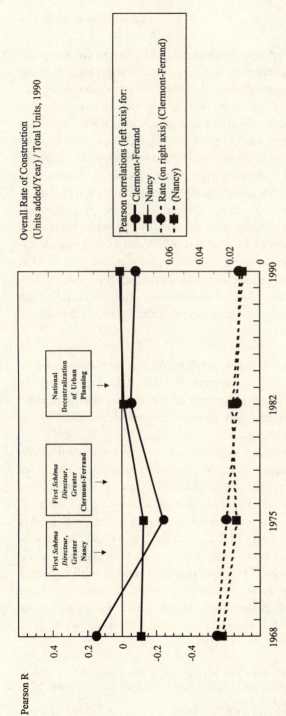

Figure 3.4 Average Correlations of New Housing Index with Environmental Indicators in French Metropolitan Areas with Declining Growth Rates, 1962–1990

Note: Pearson correlations measure average relation of New Housing Index for housing added per year during each period by commune with distance from city center; with proportion of cadastral land in forest for 1970 (periods 1975–1982 and 1982–1990) and for 1988 (periods 1975–1982 and 1982–1990); and with proportion in agriculture of the population residing in ordinary households in 1962 (periods 1962–1968 and 1968–1975) and proportion in agriculture of active employed cantonal population in 1982 (1975–1982 and 1982–1990). Change in housing for each period represents total at beginning of period minus total at end of period. See Sellers, "Federalism and Metropolitan Governance."

Sources: INSEE, *Recensement Général de la Population de 1962;* id., *Recensement Général de la Population de 1982: Évolutions démographiques;* id., *Recensement Général de la Population de 1990: Évolutions démographiques;* id., *Communoscope* (1988): Ministry of Agriculture, *Census de l'Agriculture 1970.*

The protective policies of the regional plans had succeeded modestly at best. Only after the infrastructure of local governance decentralized did slight effects on actual patterns of urban development in urban regions like Rennes emerge. Once metropolitan markets for development appeared in the 1970s, regulation based on the plans proved too difficult to impose at all in greater Montpellier and was generally ineffectual elsewhere. Only in the schema for the communes immediately surrounding Rennes, as the next chapter will show, did these earlier arrangements assert clearly effective controls. During the 1980s and early 1990s decentralization and other measures only partly resolved these difficulties. New arrangements enabled local initiatives in settings like Rennes and perhaps Clermont-Ferrand to attain a modicum of success. Around Montpellier, new development undermined the hope for preservation even more than before. Within the narrower central jurisdictions of Montpellier and Rennes, local elites had also seized increasingly on opportunities after decentralization to pursue pedestrian zones, farmland preservation and parks. Elites in the other cities had done so less.

The United States. In the American settings, protective measures relied even more on local choices. Successful protection still depended frequently on initiatives from above. With incentives and resources that promoted local efforts, state governments grafted more central elements onto the infrastructure of local governance.

Although national policies and institutions have pervasively influenced land use in the United States, efforts to control metropolitan land have emerged almost entirely at state and local levels. National constitutional property rights, going beyond similar provisions in France and Germany, imposed constraints on policy and reinforced the place of local market actors.[129] From the earliest years of U.S. zoning law around the turn of the century, state and local innovators attentive to constitutional challenges had modified the original German planning models with variances and other qualifications to local regulatory powers. As local initiatives in this domain proliferated in the 1980s, the Supreme Court tightened constitutional scrutiny.[130] At the same time, unlike in countries such as

---

[129] Judith Garber and David Imbroscio, "The 'Myth of the North American City' Reconsidered: Local Constitutional Regimes in Canada and the United States," *Urban Affairs Review 31*(5) (1996): 595–624.

[130] See, e.g., *Dolan v. City of Tigard*, 114 S.Ct. 2309 (1994).

Germany, in the United States control over land use rarely emerged as an object of direct federal legislation. As late as the 1970s, efforts to legislate additional federal policies on metropolitan land use fell victim to the power of prodevelopment lobbies and to the absence of organized business constituencies with interests rooted in the downtowns.[131] By the 1990s, the Republican Congress was considering new reinforcements to property rights.

Although the national government undertook policies in other environmental domains, state governments enacted the supralocal policies addressed to protection of land. In the absence of broad constitutional authorization for local government, like the one in Germany, state legislation in all three states established legal authorizations as well as other tools for new domains of local policy. In all three U.S. settings, however, local actors still usually determined whether open space was protected, whether urban sprawl was slowed or even how much of wetlands received protection. A similar localization pervaded protective policies even in states that mandated more extensive planning or substantive results, like Oregon or Florida.[132] Unlike in the German or the French settings, the local elites of the U.S. settings could readily identify which towns within the metropolitan area controlled land use more strictly, and which did not. In greater New Haven, respondents in the more exclusive suburbs consistently rated the rules as more important than market forces, even as those in the central city espoused the opposite view.[133] Respondents in and around Durham pointed to Chapel Hill as stricter; those in Madison, to the central city itself. Although state or federal bodies sometimes reviewed local decisions in such discrete areas as housing, wetlands protection and water pollution,[134] direct interventions of this sort played a more limited role in the United States than in Germany and France. In two-thirds of the disputes that elites and activists mentioned in and around New Haven, these respondents attributed to state or federal officials limited or no influence on the outcome.

Other supralocal policies, in fueling demand for exurban growth, added market pressures for further development to the other difficulties of environmental protection. Combined with an array of loan supports, the

---

[131] Sidney Plotkin, *Keep Out* (Berkeley: University of California Press, 1987).

[132] Raymond Burby and Henry May, *Making Governments Plan* (Baltimore: Johns Hopkins University Press, 1997).

[133] Sellers, "Grounds of Democracy," pp. 528–530.

[134] Ibid., p. 167.

federal income tax deduction for mortgage interest offered U.S. consumers the strongest array of incentives for home ownership among the three countries.[135] Since the 1950s, with the support of growing suburban congressional constituencies, the federal Interstate Highway Program and other national policies furnished physical infrastructure and subsidies for the process of suburbanization.[136] Usually with the cooperation of local officials, state transportation departments in all three U.S. settings had laid out new roads that created further opportunities for developers to carry out this process. An array of other transportation policies in the United States, from low gasoline taxes to lesser support for public transit, fostered greater support for forms of settlement based on high auto usage.[137] Retail regulation of the sort that urban shopkeepers had helped bring about in Germany and France posed no obstacle in the United States to the growing departure of retail from the downtowns for suburban malls. In addition, lower agricultural subsidies than in Europe furnished farmers with fewer disincentives to convert farmland.[138]

These national tendencies leave the comparative control over exurban development as well as other environmental measures in Madison in need of explanation. If this city had spent less on parks and had protected its forestland and farmland less than most of the German cities had done, it still did so more than most other places. Also, local officials had stemmed the loss of open space beyond Madison's municipal boundaries with comparative effectiveness, confining the dispersal of settlement to nearly as slow a rate as in the German cities. State enactments as well as local initiatives played vital roles in these successes.

As the evolution of development throughout the metropolitan area demonstrates (Figure 3.5), these protections emerged over an extended period following the introduction of countywide planning in the early 1970s. Only after Wisconsin enacted additional planning powers and offered incentives in support of local planning did development register increasing signs of control. In the first decade of the Dane County Planning Commission, planning may even have helped spur the spread of

[135] Cf. Peter Marcuse, "Determinants of State Housing Policies: West Germany and the United States," in Norman I. Fainstein and Susan S. Fainstein (eds.), *Urban Policy Under Capitalism* (Beverly Hills, CA: Sage Publications, 1982), pp. 83–115.

[136] Kenneth Jackson, *Crabgrass Frontier* (New York: Oxford University Press, 1985); John H. Mollenkopf, *The Contested City* (Princeton: Princeton University Press, 1983).

[137] Pucher and Lefèvre, *Urban Transport Crisis*, Ch. 10.

[138] Nivola, *Laws of the Landscape*, ibid.

peripheral development. Over this period, the average correlation of new housing with environmental indicators rose from negative toward zero. Although new housing shifted slightly away from farmland, it also began to depart from the previous centralized pattern, and it moved sharply into agricultural lands. Beginning in the late 1970s, however, new tools enabled planners to assert increasing control over development within as well as outside the central city. City officials received extrajurisdictional authority to zone as well as powers to annex.[139] In addition, the state granted new tax breaks to farmers who agreed to preserve agricultural land.[140] However little effect Chapter 2 showed these measures to have had on losses of agricultural land across the state, local actors in and around Madison drew on the new resources to assert increasingly effective control over metropolitan development. Within the expanding city limits, development had dispersed to a degree well beyond that of similar-sized German cities. But outside, the average correlations of new housing with the environmental indicators now shifted slightly downward and away from zero. In the late 1980s this trend accelerated even as the overall rate of development intensified. Supralocal measures played a significant if by no means the only role in this comparative control over sprawl.

In greater Durham and greater New Haven somewhat sketchier metropolitan statistics indicated generally less successful control (Figure 3.5).[141] Only in and around Durham did the central city take advantage of annexation powers and extraterritorial jurisdiction similar to those in Wisconsin.[142] Long only sparsely populated, the outskirts of the metropolitan area surrounding Durham began to exhibit serious symptoms of sprawl in the late 1970s. Growing proportions of new construction were concentrated in outlying areas toward Chapel Hill, the Research Triangle Park and the northern part of Durham County. Over the next decade, the introduction of planning and zoning over the entirety of both counties culminated in the establishment of a rural buffer in one and a growth boundary in the other. Backed in part by state authority for extraterritorial zoning, these new local initiatives help to account for the falling average

---

[139] 93-94 Wis. Stats. 62.23 (7a); 66.021.

[140] 93-94 Wis. Stats. 62.075.

[141] For periods before 1990, published census reports did not break down statistics for unincorporated areas in North Carolina. Before 1980, figures for all Connecticut towns were also unavailable. The absence of statistics dating to 1970 in each case, as well as the comparative lack of material on actual land use, limits what can be concluded from this data.

[142] 1987 N.C. Stats. 160A-46; 160A-360.

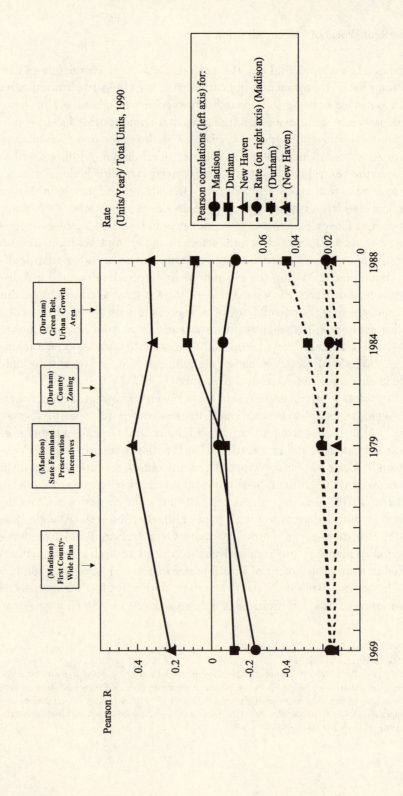

Rate
(Units/Year)/ Total Units, 1990

Pearson correlations (left axis) for:

Madison ●
Durham ■
New Haven ▲
Rate (on right axis) (Madison) ●----
(Durham) ■----
(New Haven) ▲----

(Madison)
First County-
Wide Plan

(Madison)
State Farmland
Preservation
Incentives

(Durham)
County
Zoning

(Durham)
Green Belt,
Urban Growth
Area

Pearson R

1969   1979   1984   1988

0.4

0.2

0

-0.2

-0.4

0.06

0.04

0.02

0

correlation of the late 1980s even as the overall rate of new construction accelerated.

In greater New Haven the shift of development toward the periphery and toward environmentally sensitive areas persisted. In the absence of supralocal policies, localities had also exercised less effective control over metropolitan markets. New development continued to correlate at $r = .42$ with the distance from the urban center. Towns with more open space and more agricultural activity received growing concentrations of new development. The smaller, more exclusive suburbs like Madison and Woodbridge scaled back or kept steady their own rates of new construction. Surging construction shifted to the less wealthy towns with more agricultural land, like North Branford and Bethany, and to working-class suburbs like East Haven. Rising relative prices confirmed the market pressures in these new centers of real estate development.[143] The central city itself continued to attract only small amounts of new housing.

Other contrasts beyond supralocal policies undoubtedly contributed to these divergences.[144] But more uniformly effective protection of land in the U.S. settings would most likely have required more supralocal

[143] Sellers, "Grounds of Democracy," p. 677.
[144] Denser settlement in greater New Haven, and polycentric metropolitan patterns around both that city and Durham, made a shift of new housing back toward the center more difficult to bring about than in greater Madison. But note that similar preexisting patterns in Bielefeld had not brought about this comparative result.

Figure 3.5 Average Correlations of New Housing Index with Environmental Indicators in Metropolitan Madison, Durham and New Haven, 1960–1988
Note: Pearson correlations employ New Housing Index for housing added per year by town ($n = 59$, Madison; $n = 13$, Durham; $n = 15$, New Haven). In all three settings this index relies on ages of housing given in answers to 1990 census questionnaire. For Madison, the environmental indicators derive from Planning Commission figures for proportion of town in crops or pastures for 1980 (1960–1969 and 1970–1979) and 1990 (1980–1984 and 1985–1988); and for proportion of town in forest for 1980 (1960–1969 and 1970–1979) and 1990 (1980–1984 and 1985–1988). For Durham and New Haven, the indicator of farmland uses the proportion of resident workers in agriculture in the census of 1980. For New Haven, the indicator for forest relies on the estimated proportion of land in open space in 1984; no estimate of forest or open space by town for metropolitan Durham was available. See Sellers, "Federalism and Metropolitan Governance."
Sources: U.S. Census Bureau, *1990 Census of Population and Housing: Social and Economic Characteristics*, State Reports; Dane County Planning Commission; South Central Regional Council of Governments, *Growth and Change: Issues for the 90's* (North Haven, CT, 1988), p. 26.

intervention of at least the type present in Wisconsin.[145] Not only fragmentation but also legal provisions at federal and state levels fostered the constraints on supralocal intervention characteristic of U.S. local governance. At the wider metropolitan level as well as within the central cities, lapses and inconsistencies were a predictable outcome.

Other local environmental policies beyond control of land use, like the provision of bicycle paths and public transit or the promotion of recycling, depended in more straightforward ways on local efforts. Yet even the national system of metropolitan land use regulation in Germany emerged from divergences among urban regions. Consistent with implications from the infrastructure of local government and politics there, increasingly standardized policies at the national level brought more and more uniform local results even among different federal *Länder*. Application of those rules by the disparate local governments appears to have been indispensable to this consistency. In both centralized, unitary France and the federal, decentralized United States, control over the various dimensions of sprawl came about only through a combination of initiatives from below with instruments from above. Localized elements present more in some French urban regions than in others altered the policies handed down from above. The resulting protective policies varied more than parallel German efforts according to local contingencies. In the United States, the effective local policies depended the most on local choices, and the least on either supralocal governments or standardized rules. But new supralocal components helped enable a surprising degree of control in and around Madison and the beginnings of effective local regulation in and around Durham.

Supralocal Policy and Place-based Disadvantage

Place-based concentrations of advantages and disadvantages within urban regions depend on a wide range of policies. Decisions within cities play a critical role in assuring that these policies secure equity among places. Since the 1970s, local components in these policies have often grown more as a result of reduction than as a consequence of expansion in initiatives from above. Of the two dimensions of territorial equity, the disadvantages faced by underprivileged and segregated groups have

---

[145] Cf. Burby and May, *Making Governments Plan*; Leo, "Regional Growth Management Regime"; Myron Orfield, *Metropolitics* (Washington: Brookings Institution, 1996).

162

historically given rise to the most active national and intermediate-level governmental efforts.[146] As Chapter 2 showed, both American cities and French counterparts like Montpellier and Nancy manifest neighborhoods of aggravated, segregated disadvantage. The German cities and French counterparts like Rennes and Clermont-Ferrand have managed to avoid this fate. Not just differences in supralocal policies, but local decisions about how to carry out and supplement those policies produced these local outcomes.

Contemporary patterns of racial and socioeconomic segregation build on long-standing legacies. In addition to the evolving social and spatial structures that the next chapter will examine within these urban regions, supralocal policy has directly and indirectly shaped these patterns. Beyond the welfare, employment and incomes policies that help to define the disadvantages that underprivileged groups share in relation to others, an array of policies also pertain directly to the places in which these groups and others live.[147] First, planning and land use policies sometimes deal directly with the residential integration or segregation of these groups. In addition, public policies to provide affordable housing provide a specific source of potential benefits but also of potential segregation from the remainder of society. As a result, determinations as to whether this housing would be confined to separate neighborhoods or spread around the city maintained at least as powerful an influence over segregation as decisions as to the amount of housing. Finally, other policies that encouraged or discouraged privileged groups to separate themselves from the disadvantaged could also contribute to or alleviate ghettos of the disadvantaged. Policies from the top down have often done more to help others avoid disadvantaged groups than to help those groups integrate into society.

As in the case of urban environmental policy, emerging policy making structures above the level of nation-states played little direct role. From the late 1980s onward in particular, budgetary pressures linked to the construction of a common market and currency in Europe help to account for reductions in national expenditures on housing and other social policies. But as a result of wider economic and political trends that themselves drove market making in Europe, these reductions were already well under way.

---

[146] The closest any supralocal government came to forbidding segregated elite settlement was the German prescription of territorial equalization discussed *infra*, p. 115.

[147] See Douglas S. Massey and Nancy A. Denton, *American Apartheid* (Cambridge, MA: Harvard University Press, 1993), pp. 42–57; Jackson, *Crabgrass Frontier*, pp. 190–230.

Although the EU began by the mid-1990s to direct studies, pilot programs and initiatives under the Structural Funds to problems of social exclusion and segregation in European cities, these programs had no immediate effects on the cities in this study.[148]

Germany.   Across the German cities, the integration of neighborhoods was clear and comparatively uniform. Even larger, more diverse German cities like Hamburg remained relatively integrated in comparison with U.S. metropolitan areas. Although unemployment was on the rise throughout Germany in the early 1990s, the combination of more egalitarian wage policies and more expansive social benefits secured the largest share of the income distribution of all the three countries for the most disadvantaged German groups.[149] At the same time, governments in all four cities undertook local policies to prevent or minimize pockets of disadvantage. Rooted only partly in supralocal mandates, these efforts again reaffirmed the predictions from the infrastructure of local government over expectations as a result of the federal state structure at the top.

In all four German settings, planners and others portrayed the mixture of housing as one of the goals of local policy. In my standardized survey of elites and activists in Freiburg, the respondents placed stronger, more consistent stress on the need to provide housing for both foreigners and poor people than did either their French or their American counterparts.[150] Although prescriptions from above figured in these local preferences, the legal supply of authority could only partly explain the local norms. At most, the postwar German constitution had explicitly authorized legislation to "unify living conditions over the territory of a *Land*"; regional planning laws prescribed measures to secure "balanced economic, social, cultural and ecological relations" in places where these were not present; and the code that regulated construction and planning spoke broadly of "socially just land use."[151] None of these nor other rules mandated integration of housing explicitly; nor did they explicitly assign rights to the large, growing number of foreign residents who faced major impediments to

---

[148] European Commission, *Towards an Urban Agenda*, pp. 10–11.

[149] In 1989, the Gini index for Germany stood at 28.1. The lowest 20 percent of earners earned 9 percent of the total or 1.8 percent more than their French counterparts (World Bank, *World Development Report 1999/2000*, pp. 238–239).

[150] Jefferey M. Sellers, "Norms in the Politics of Housing for Minorities," *Ethnic and Racial Studies 19* (3): 585–608.

[151] Basic Law Art. 72 (2) 2; ROG Art. 2 (1) 2; BbauGB Art. 1 (5).

political citizenship and social assimilation. Each provision could easily be read to prescribe measures short of requiring socially and ethnically integrated neighborhoods. Although local planners sometimes cited these prescriptions as the reason for their initiatives, the rules depended on local interpretations for this effect. As the next chapter will show, other national policies like administration of public schools supplemented direct regulation of land use with largely uniform systems of services.

Through the provision of public housing that could be put to use for the purpose of integrated settlement, national and intermediate-level governments exerted a more concrete effect on local policies. In this domain, federalism and the divergences in party control that it permitted had produced significant differences among local outcomes. Although subject to federal laws, and supported throughout the German *Länder*, public housing in Germany had received more support under *Land* governments of the Left. The longtime SPD-led government in North Rhine-Westphalia had provided more extensive subsidies for this housing than longtime CDU-led counterparts in Baden-Württemberg or Lower Saxony.[152] Although conservative Münster had sought and received less housing as a result of these subsidies than social-democratic Bielefeld, both had received more than either of the other German cities. In 1987 social housing comprised 22 percent of all housing units in Münster and 28 percent in Bielefeld. Although Freiburg had pursued social housing actively as well, the total remained at 19 percent there, while Göttingen had attained 16 percent. With substantial proportions of housing in this category in all four cities, the location of these units could still have fostered either integration or segregation. It was in these decisions about location that parallel policies achieved the most similar results.

During the late 1980s and early 1990s in all four settings, local decisions increasingly came to determine even the amount of new social housing. As subsidies at other levels generally shrank,[153] a legislated forty-year limit on the amount of time housing could remain subject to social restrictions quietly ran out for many units built shortly after World War II. Between 1987 and 1996, the proportion of housing in this category in

---

[152] Jaedicke and Wollmann, "Wohnungsbauförderung im Bundesländervergleich." Needs linked to greater urbanization in North Rhine-Westphalia fostered support even independently of party influence.

[153] Michael Harloe, *The People's Home? Social Rented Housing in Europe and America* (Oxford: Blackwell, 1995), p. 471.

these cities dropped by as much as 8 percent.[154] Although all the city governments undertook efforts to compensate, the Red-Green government in Freiburg did the most. Even as the city carried out a large, off-budget housing development on its former sewerage farm, its on-budget expenditures on housing persisted at 12 million DM/year. This total local investment far exceeded not only the 1 million DM in Göttingen, but the 4 million DM in the larger cities of Münster and Bielefeld. Nowhere, however, did these local efforts come close to compensating for the losses.

Although the variation in social housing reflected differences between the *Länder* as well as between the cities, local governments here pursued territorial equality consistently. National policies limited segregation, but local policy makers furnished much of the substance of those policies. Increasingly, these local actors had assumed responsibility not only for the avoidance of concentrated disadvantage but also for the overall level of local social provision.

France. In France, wages and social policies contributed to levels of income inequality somewhat higher than those in Germany but still much lower than those in the United States.[155] Despite this intermediary position, the French cities differed most in the degree that neighborhoods of concentrated disadvantage had emerged. The most centralized, unitary state of the three might have been expected to carry out the most consistent policies. The infrastructure for local government and politics had ultimately made more of a difference for initiatives from above in this domain than had the vertical integration of the state at higher levels. This infrastructure enabled local officials to exercise more autonomy within national programs and to act more as intergovernmental entrepreneurs in quest of supralocal support for local aims.

As in other areas, the legal supply of authority for planning and land use in France prescribed no clear policy toward disadvantaged areas. If the German legal provisions were at best ambiguous, similar provisions in France did not exist. Although the opening paragraph of the *Code de l'Urbanisme* proclaims "promotion of equilibrium among populations" as a goal

---

[154] In all these cities, the level of social housing declined drastically in the 1980s. By 1996 the level had reached 11 percent in Freiburg and only 9 percent in Göttingen. Officials in Münster asserted that 6,000 social housing units a year were being privatized.

[155] Here the Gini index of 32.7 stood 4.6 points higher than in Germany, and the lowest 20 percent of earners took in 1.8 percent less of the total income. World Bank, *World Development Report.*

(Art. L-110), none of the French officials cited legal norms to justify policies toward local concentrations of poverty, unemployment and ethnic difference. Even those elites and activists who explicitly endorsed housing for socioeconomically disadvantaged and immigrant groups did not refer to national rules. Although across these urban regions the national educational system had established from above such formally uniform services as schools, this had not prevented the emergence of disparities between school populations similar to those of urban neighborhoods.[156]

The considerable variations in the amount, the character and the placement of public housing contributed as much as any other influence to the different degrees of isolation that disadvantaged residents of these cities faced. Centralized, unitary state structures at the top limited the extent to which different intermediate governments could affect local levels of public housing. But local intergovernmental entrepreneurship and more effective application of resources from above made much of the difference between urban regions that federalism did not. In Rennes, where the city government had engaged in some of the most extensive solicitation of supralocal resources and the most aggressive local planning, fully 22 percent of housing units in 1990 were publicly subsidized. In Clermont-Ferrand, where a Socialist local majority had rule for several decades, the proportion stood at 17 percent. But in Nancy, where a government of the Right had dominated, only 14 percent of housing belonged in this category. In Montpellier, where a rightist administration gave way to a Socialist one at the same time as in Rennes, only 12 percent of housing fell into this category. Public housing in such Rennes developments as the South ZUP or planning district also provided more spacious quarters, more green space and amenities and more convenient services than the same facilities in a development like La Paillade in Montpellier.

Just as local decisions about where to place publicly subsidized housing made the biggest difference for the consistent integration of the German cities, choices of location proved decisive for the emergence of different degrees of segregation in France. Decisions reached by the early 1970s established foundations for the segregation of 1990. In Rennes and Clermont-Ferrand, local administrations working in cooperation with national administrators had seen to it that the massive infusions of subsidies to be devoted to new housing in all the French cities would be applied to developments dispersed around the city in convenient locations. In

---

[156] See Chapter 4.

Montpellier and Nancy, the new housing took the form of massive, out-lying housing estates like those on the outskirts of such cities as Paris and Lyons. La Paillade on the edge of Montpellier and Hauts-du-Lièvre near the city limits of Nancy each absorbed most of the local publicly subsidized housing. As the gentrification that both local governments also helped sponsor raised housing prices throughout much of both cities, minorities and the unemployed found themselves forced by housing prices if not by evictions into these new neighborhoods.

Over the 1980s and early 1990s the Socialist government introduced programs to remedy disadvantages in places like La Paillade and Haut du Lièvre. A national minimum income payment (or *revenu minimum d'insertion*) stabilized the decline in the buying power of the poor residents.[157] The Besson Law of 1990 required departments to establish programs to house low-income families. A 1991 law (*Loi d'Orientation pour la Ville*) formalized arrangements for planned housing in a program of contracts between local and central governments. Along with efforts to rehabilitate existing housing, the state undertook to provide more services and improve schools in disadvantaged neighborhoods.[158] These efforts did little to rearrange the neighborhoods themselves. At the same time, the national code continued to promote gentrification of the Old Towns.[159] Subsidies for housing declined and were shifted to encouragement of property ownership rather than of rental housing.

As in Germany, the reduction in national resources for new housing also reinforced the relative importance of local efforts to better the situation of the worst-off neighborhoods. These efforts generally combined the local resources available to upgrade housing and neighborhood conditions with discretionary resources from national programs to improve education, to subsidize public transportation or to support housing rehabilitation and construction.[160] Faced with cutbacks to supralocal funding for

[157] Michel Piotrkowski, "Le Haut-du-Lièvre: Un quartier à repenser," in Gérald Cahen and René Louis (eds.), *Nancy* (Paris: Autrement, 1990), pp. 110–111.
[158] Begun as early as 1977, these efforts were consolidated in the 1990s as "City Policy." These efforts had only limited effects. See Jean-Claude Boyer, *Les banlieues en France* (Paris: Armand Colin, 2000), p. 150; A. Anderson, *Politiques de la ville, de la zone au territoire* (Paris: Syros, 1998).
[159] L. 313-4 *et seq.* R-313-4 *et seq.*
[160] On-budget expenditures into the 1990s, for instance, reflected the ongoing efforts of the new Socialist-led coalition in Montpellier after 1977 to compensate for previous legacies. To improve conditions in the housing estates, the local government invested in social centers (*Maisons pour tous*) located in those neighborhoods. Nancy and Rennes had

housing, local governments looked to modest rehabilitation rather than public construction, introduced larger proportions of private housing into developments with publicly subsidized units and sought to reintegrate poor neighborhoods through such means as transportation and commercial projects.[161] As the segregation of 1990 indicates, these efforts did not reverse the disparities in local outcomes between segregated cities like Montpellier and Nancy and more integrated ones like Clermont-Ferrand and Rennes.

Even under the more centralized state of Gaullist France, local influences set policies administered from the top down along divergent trajectories. The more decentralized practices of the 1980s and 1990s placed greater emphasis on the local governments to make decisions. As a result, the infrastructure of local governance enabled contrasts in policy among the French cities to make a larger difference in policies toward territorial equity.

The United States. Within U.S. urban regions, the most uniform and strongest levels of ethnoracial and socioeconomic segregation prevailed. Policies of national and state governments helped bring about this outcome. An array of economic and social policies contributed to the greatest income disparity among the residents of any advanced industrial country.[162] In the midst of a complex, contradictory welter of national and intermediate measures, higher-level governments had undertaken limited efforts to improve the situation of the most disadvantaged urban neighborhoods. Local choices had always given shape to these efforts, and increasingly took over the definition of policy.

In the absence of higher-level policies in favor of territorial equity, some of the most influential supralocal policies in the United States had in fact helped bring about and entrench segregated concentrations of the disadvantaged. For most of the twentieth century in the United States, policies

---

invested a third or less of this sum in similar centers, and Clermont far less. Budgets showed a total of 33.3 million francs in the *Maisons pour tous* in Montpellier, compared with 11.2 million francs in social centers in Rennes, 9.6 million francs in both categories in Nancy, and only 1.9 million francs in *Maisons de quartier* in Clermont-Ferrand.

[161] Rennes established a light-rail system to strengthen links among neighborhoods; Montpellier constructed a new stadium to bring more visitors to La Paillade.

[162] The Gini index in 1994 stood at 40.1. The lowest 20 percent of earners received only 4.8 percent of total income, only slightly more than half that of the same group in Germany. World Bank, *World Development Report*. On U.S. inequality, see Claude S. Fischer et al., *Inequality by Design* (Princeton: Princeton University Press, 1996), pp. 129–170.

embedded partly at state and federal levels furthered the residential isolation of African Americans. Backed by national constitutional rulings, the notorious Jim Crow laws and segregated school systems of the South established the racial demarcations that ran through metropolitan Durham. Local policies and private strategies, such as the enforcement of restrictive covenants for home owners and the discriminatory practices of the Federal Home Owner's Loan Corporation, the Federal Housing Corporation and the Veterans' Administration, applied directly to private decisions about land use.[163]

The civil rights movement had ended legally sanctioned discrimination of this sort across the United States, but without ending residential segregation. Starting in the 1950s, Supreme Court decisions, congressional civil rights legislation, state court decisions and state legislation established the basis for far-reaching challenges to racial discrimination. Especially in matters of public education, litigation in federal courts presented one of the most powerful means of influence for the local civil rights movement in Durham.[164] Lawsuits also aided subsequent local efforts to reduce segregated patterns in the two northern school systems. In the 1980s, a warning from the Office of Civil Rights in the Reagan Justice Department provoked Madison officials to move toward achieving more integrated schools. In Connecticut, too, a court decided in 1977 that unequal school funding violated state constitutional rights. In turn, a 1992 lawsuit effectively challenged the reformed system. As a result, the Connecticut General Assembly established voluntary arrangements for metropolitan cooperation among school systems in greater New Haven and across the state.[165] In comparison with the German policies toward land use, however, the basic limitations of U.S. federal and state civil rights laws remained apparent. Attentive to discrimination among people rather than to conditions of places, the courts and legislatures stopped short of prescribing racially or socioeconomically integrated neighborhoods.

Other national and state policies reinforced the disadvantages of poor and minority neighborhoods. Encouragements to suburbanization implicitly promoted desertion of the inner-city neighborhoods, where the con-

---

[163] Massey and Denton, *American Apartheid*; Jackson, *Crabgrass Frontier*.

[164] Anderson, *Durham County*, Ch. 19; William Keech, *The Impact of Negro Voting*, 2nd ed. (Westport, CT: Greenwood, 1981) (copyright 1968), p. 66.

[165] Kathryn McDermott, "Regionalism Forestalled: Metropolitan Fragmentation and Desegregation Planning in Greater New Haven, Connecticut," in Clarence Stone (ed.), *Reforming Urban Education* (Lawrence: University of Kansas Press, 1998), pp. 46–48.

centrations of the disadvantaged grew. Federal urban renewal programs of the 1960s and 1970s often harmed the interests of inner-city residents and deepened the isolation of these areas. Consistent with the opportunities for local intergovernmental entrepreneurship in U.S. policy making, local actors determined much of the substance of these programs. This local participation frequently contributed to urban agendas in ways that further burdened the poorest neighborhoods. Under loose federal critieria and coordinated state and local policies, urban renewal and highway construction devastated such working-class and minority neighborhoods as Wooster Square in New Haven and Hayti in south Durham.[166] In New Haven, local initiatives under the federal Model Cities program took rare steps toward advancing the interests of inner-city residents.[167] But these initiatives had ended abruptly in the 1970s there, and they bypassed Durham and Madison altogether. Although the state government of Connecticut also channeled large sums to schools in downtown New Haven, the local character of U.S. public education precluded the more systematic standardization and redistribution of the European school systems.

In comparison with both other countries, the amount of publicly owned or financed housing in the American urban regions remained small. Federal housing programs had never supplied nearly the proportion of new housing as was built in Europe and had barely avoided elimination under the budget axes of both the Reagan and Clinton administrations.[168] Although public housing stock in 1990 manifested considerable local differences in the pursuit of supralocal housing funds, the smaller U.S. amounts enabled far less control over housing markets than in Europe. In New Haven, the longtime federal participation of local officials had raised the total amount of housing under the auspices of the City Housing Authority to 5.5 percent of all housing units. In Durham and Madison, city housing authorities controlled only 2.8 percent and 1.1 percent of all units. In all three cities up to the 1970s, however, public housing had concentrated in poor and minority neighborhoods and generally had reinforced segregation. Even in Madison, a public housing project in Bram's Addition stood at the core of the poorest neighborhood.

---

[166] Fainstein and Fainstein, "New Haven"; Anderson, *Durham County*, p. 409.
[167] Fainstein and Fainstein, "New Haven," p. 54.
[168] Paul Pierson, *Dismantling the Welfare State?* (New York: Cambridge University Press, 1994), pp. 87–95.

By the early 1990s, reforms at the federal level cut back housing and welfare assistance to disadvantaged groups; in Wisconsin, the pioneering Wisconsin Works program of 1992 anticipated the end to a federal welfare entitlement. State and federal initiatives aimed at alleviating segregation and its effects remained small and incremental. In continued local programs under Community Development Block Grant and Housing and Urban Development Section 8 programs, housing rehabilitation and renovation acquired new importance. In these and other programs, New Haven continued to reap the benefits of effective grantsmanship. The city maintained four times the level of federal assistance for private housing as in the other U.S. cities (cf. Table 3.7), won more extensive federal grants under the Community Development Block Grant program (CDBG), participated in other programs administered by the Department of Housing and Urban Development, gained tax breaks for development in federally designated Enterprise Zones and secured regulatory relief as well as subsidies for conversion of brownfields for development. The Connecticut state government also helped insure completion of affordable housing projects like the Ninth Square project downtown during the 1990s and initiated a judicially administered program to mandate more affordable housing in the suburbs. Federal programs administered in New Haven and Madison now aimed explicitly to scatter public housing into white working-class neighborhoods. In New Haven as elsewhere, however, these programs drew fewer direct expenditures from federal and often state budgets than had earlier initiatives. In neither Madison nor New Haven, for instance, did scattered-site housing programs acquire more than two dozen new units a year.

In seeking new resources for low-cost housing in the face of dwindling support from either higher level, New Haven and Durham had increasingly begun to look elsewhere. In the Ninth Square project, intended to bring a new mixture of publicly supported and private housing to downtown New Haven, Yale University had assumed a leading role. Beginning in the mid-1980s, in a move increasingly common among U.S. cities,[169] the Durham city government raised additional off-budget support for housing and neighborhood development in bond markets. Up to 1996, general obligation bonds worth a total of $2.7 million per year now surpassed either supralocal assistance or on-budget expenditures as a source

---

[169] Alberta Sbragia, *Debt Wish: Entrepreneurial Cities, U.S. Federalism, and Economic Development* (Pittsburgh: University of Pittsburgh Press, 1996).

of support for affordable housing, rehabilitation and neighborhood development.

Even alongside such efforts, the array of supralocal programs in all three cities still had no more than incremental effects on the consistent patterns of spatial socioeconomic and ethnic segregation. Even the greater initiative that New Haven had shown in its quest for supralocal policies to remedy the problems of its depressed areas could not overcome the other policies and other forces that entrenched these metropolitan patterns.

Despite the obvious importance of supralocal components to effective distributive policies, local elements remain critical in this domain. In all three countries, local participation has grown in importance relative to that of governance at higher levels of the state. Alongside expansion in certain types of local capacities, retrenchment or disengagement at higher levels has foisted more responsibility on local authorities. Differences among federal units contributed to variations in these policies among the German and American cities, but effective policies toward territorial equity diverged even more among the French cities. As in the other domains, local contexts and the infrastructures of local government and politics account most convincingly for these patterns.

From Supralocal Policies to Urban Governance

Supralocal policies clearly shape outcomes in urban regions, but local choices often decide how this influence occurs. Institutional dynamics associated with the elaboration of policy making at higher levels of government have placed growing emphasis on this local decision making. In environmental and developmental domains, local agents have often shouldered the burden of realizing policies set out at higher levels. In domains of social policies like housing, actions from below have often followed retrenchment from above. The growth of localized elements in all three domains has made infrastructures of local government and politics increasingly critical to understanding local variations in the operative substance of measures at higher levels. These institutional infrastructures have often accounted better for domestic divergences in effective policies than the organizational forms of states at higher levels.

Infrastructures of local government and politics undoubtedly reflect such national policy choices as the strong social and environmental emphases in Germany and the predominance of economic growth over social equity in the United States. But these institutional infrastructures

Table 3.8. *Comparative Extent and Consistency of Supralocal Initiatives, by Types of Policies*

	Germany	France	United States
Promotion of development where limited industrial legacies	Weak	Strong	Moderate
	(consistent)[a]	(contingent)[a]	(contingent)
Influences on domestic variations	*Supralocal, local*	*Local*	*Supralocal, local*
Postindustrial regeneration	Strong[a]	Weak[a,b]	Moderate[a,b]
Influences on domestic variations	*Supralocal, local*	*Local*	*Supralocal, local*
Environmental policies	Strong[a]	Moderate[a,b]	Moderate to weak[a,b]
	(consistent)[a]	(contingent)[a]	(contingent)
Influences on domestic variations	*Local*	*Local*	*Supralocal, local*
Distributive policies	Strong[a]	Moderate[a,b]	Weak
	(consistent)[a]	(contingent)[a]	(consistent)[a]
Influences on domestic variations	*Supralocal, local*	*Local*	*Supralocal, local*

[a] Different from predictions on the basis of national and intermediate state structures.
[b] Different from predictions on the basis of infrastructures for local government.

ultimately add up to much more than the sum of policies from above. In each domain, these patterns have influenced local variations in supralocal measures as much as or more than the differences in the vertical integration of the state at higher levels (Table 3.8). An analysis that looked only to the character of the state at higher levels would have missed the remarkable consistency of developmental, environmental and distributive policies among the German cities, and the equally remarkable contingency of all three types of policies in the French cities. Such an account would have also failed to predict the stronger German supralocal measures in pursuit of postindustrial regeneration, environmental policy and equity among places. Despite several anomalies, an analysis that looks to infrastructures of local government and politics accounts far better for the patterns in supralocal measures. Where it does not, as in the supralocal environmental measures in the United States and the unexpectedly weak environmental and distributive measures in France, departures from traditional propensities of local government and policy account for most of the unexplained variation. The particular circumstances of cities like New Haven and Clermont-Ferrand, or isolated national departures from more general propensities, explain a smaller portion.

In Germany, the infrastructure of local government and politics made at least as much of the difference for policies toward these cities as federalism, and sometimes more. In discrete areas of developmental and housing policies, efforts did vary among the *Länder*. But the national legal supply, the interlocal fiscal equalization and the comparative constraints on local political entrepreneurship imposed consistent outputs in all three domains. In protective environmental measures and efforts to alleviate spatial disadvantage, supralocal elements played a comparatively strong role even as local policy makers made many of the decisions. In developmental policies, except in the postindustrial regeneration of Bielefeld, supralocal constraints limited the extent of supralocal intervention.

In France, the decentralization of the 1980s had altered the effects of both infrastructures of local governance and higher-level institutions on supralocal policies. In environmental and distributive measures as well as efforts at postindustrial regeneration, the central government had stepped back at least partly from its traditional dominant role. Only occasionally, as in and around Rennes, had local actors compensated fully for this withdrawal. But even before decentralization, local political entrepreneurship and divergences in the local application of policies toward development and public housing had left the substance of higher-level policy dependent on local contingencies. Comparison with the more uniform results in Germany highlights the striking variations that resulted. In every domain except development, French officials had undertaken not only less uniform, but generally less extensive supralocal policy.

Among the U.S. cities, supralocal interventions continued to conform for the most part to a more uniformly decentralized infrastructure. Predictably aggressive developmental strategies for Durham and Madison combined political entrepreneurship from below and informal coordination from above. The resulting urban concentrations of physical infrastructure and services did more to foster growth than in the German cities. In the rather exceptional efforts at regeneration in New Haven, but also

Table 3.9. *Importance of Supralocal and Local Elements in Effectiveness of Supralocal Policies*

	Germany	France	United States
Developmental policies in settings without industrial legacies	[*Limited effectiveness*] S: extensive regional and *Land* planning L: important	[*Effective*] S: extensive nationally led mobilization L: (increasingly) important	[*Effective*] S: extensive, discrete state and federal policies L: essential
Postindustrial regeneration	[*Mostly effective*] (Bielefeld) S: extensive *Land*-level policies of conversion L: essential	[*Ineffective*] (Clermont-Ferrand) S: contradictory national policies L: (increasingly) important	[*Mostly ineffective*] (New Haven) S: national, state policies in several areas L: essential
Environmental policies	[*Mostly effective*] S: (increasingly) extensive national policies L: essential	[*Contingent effectiveness*] S: national policies in discrete areas L: essential to most effective policies	[*Contingent effectiveness*] S: few national, some state policies L: essential to any effective policies
Distributive policies	[*Mostly effective*] S: directly and indirectly related national and *Land* policies L: essential	[*Contingent effectiveness*] S: indirectly related national policies L: essential to effective policies	[*Ineffective*] S: highly limited, contradictory national and state policies L: essential to most effective policies

Note: Overall outcomes from policies and markets in brackets. S = Supralocal policy making and governmental initiatives; L = Local or metropolitan activities.

in the protective policies that had expanded in Madison and later in Durham, supralocal measures diverged from the more systemic patterns. But the limited initiatives of higher-level governments to redress the conditions of the most disadvantaged neighborhoods conformed to the lower expectations for this infrastructure.

The more difficult questions concern how far the supralocal measures addressed to these settings succeeded, and how important local elements of any sort were to success or failure. For an initial answer to these questions, it is now possible to compare the outcomes of Chapter 2 with a map of supralocal policies forward to the local level (Table 3.9). Successful outcomes suggest, though they cannot fully verify, that the supralocal efforts were effective. Even where the supralocal policies were generally ineffective, like the efforts to foster territorial equity in and around New Haven, specific measures that were still furnish a basis to assess the role of different levels of government.

This analysis leaves little doubt about the need for local elements. However important the supralocal measures themselves were to achieving the outcomes that policy makers at higher levels sought, local components were usually crucial to successful supralocal initiatives. In protective policies toward land and efforts to alleviate neighborhood disadvantage, local actors generally played a role whenever policies appear to have been effective. Even postindustrial regeneration in Bielefeld, like its less successful counterpart in New Haven, depended on the ceaseless efforts of local officials to win supralocal benefits and reshape markets. Only in the urban developmental policies of Gaullist France did local decisions appear less essential, but even in that domain local actors had assumed increasingly pivotal roles. In three distinct types of advanced industrial states, parallel functional, political and institutional logics of decentralization had brought about largely similar, even convergent tendencies toward multilevel policy. Even where supralocal policies had increasingly dictated local ones, as in German controls on urban sprawl, local elements remained essential to the realization of supralocal measures.

A full analysis of the policies and their effectiveness will require greater scrutiny of the metropolitan settings that were the targets of supralocal measures. Increasingly, local efforts to bring about development, environmental quality or territorial equity go beyond the initiatives at the higher levels of governments. The ways that these efforts synthesize disparate supralocal elements often make sense only from below.

4

<hr>

Governing within Urban Regions

In the multilevel governance of contemporary urban regions, the urban contexts themselves amount to much more than ground zero. Even the intendants of Louis XIV, the prefects of Napoleon or the Gauleiter of Nazi Germany, when they sought to address the conditions of specific cities, often found themselves at the mercy of local politics, markets and social conditions. In the advanced industrial countries of today, efforts within urban regions to mobilize and manage these conditions have acquired new status and importance. Beyond legal mandates, monetary incentives, institutional supports and formal devolution from above, accumulating initiatives from below compel this urban governance. In Europe and North America, it transcends differences between national states and economies. For every dynamic American mayor like Richard Lee in New Haven, counterparts like Edmond Hervé in Rennes or Rolf Böhme in Freiburg have asserted parallel prerogatives. Within the service centers of advanced industrial societies, parallel political formations have emerged to contest this governance, and sometimes to cooperate. On one side stand coalitions of liberal groups and minorities in the United States, Social Democrats and Greens in Germany and Socialists and other Left parties in France. On the other belong conservative and centrist political groups often linked to business interests. Increasingly, local entrepreneurs have built regimes of governance outward from central cities into urban regions.

Not only local and supralocal initiatives but also an increasingly international diffusion of ideas among localities has fostered this proliferation of local policy. The protagonists of urban governance within urban regions, however, face not only the diverse supralocal policies outlined in the preceding chapter but an array of other conditions. To govern effectively from below, local actors rely on political coalitions in the electoral process, on governing coalitions among other elites or social movements and on interlocal dynamics of cooperation or competition with surrounding towns. Local agency plays a critical role in each of these aspects of urban governance. At the same time, local participants in governance must work within infrastructures of local government and politics anchored at higher levels of states and must take account of the social and spatial arrangements distinctive of each urban region.

This chapter charts the evolving strategies of governance among policy makers within the eleven cities and analyzes how several of these conditions beyond supralocal policy and local-state relations have altered these strategies. After an outline of how infrastructures and contextual influences can be expected to operate, I survey and analyze the local choices in each central city. I conclude with consideration of how interlocal policies and markets within these urban regions contributed to urban governance.

Toward an Analysis of Local Choice

Whether it is the power of business, the need for prosperity or the dictates of the nation-state, hierarchical approaches to urban political economy stress imperatives linked to translocal forces. To presume these imperatives, however, would preclude a full analysis. Local choices might after all make a difference in local outcomes. Within urban regions, these choices could combine the broad objectives of growth, environmental quality and distributive equity in any of several ways. The priorities of the leading political and governmental officials within the central cities play critical roles in these choices. Political and governmental institutions within the urban political economy, but anchored in infrastructures at higher levels of the state, help define the identities, interests and rules of the game for these officials. Resources and constraints inherent in the social and spatial structures of urban regions also impose internal conditions on local choices. Beyond the central city, interlocal governance as well as interlocal markets usually add a metropolitan dimension to the work of urban coalitions. My preliminary analysis of local choices and these influences on them will consider each of these elements in turn.

For purposes of this analysis, the objectives that local officials and others have pursued must be considered separately from analysis of the coalitions that sought those ends. Just as similar coalitions facing divergent circumstances might organize around different ends, different coalitions might also seek similar objectives. Local efforts to address the three broad objec-

Table 4.1. *Types of Urban Policy Syntheses*

	Growth	Distributive Equity	Environmental Goods
Growth	X		
Social service delivery		X	
Ecological			X
Upscale	X		X
Local Fordist	X	X	
Social-Ecological		X	X
Comprehensive	X	X	X

tives of development, environmental quality and social equity might conceivably seek any of seven permutations (Table 4.1). Strategies of localized governance that emphasize only one of the three aims date largely from the years before the proliferation of policy from above and the accompanying changes within urban regions. Consistent with the contentions of global city and public choice theorists, American analysts frequently identified local *Growth* as the main objective of coalitions or "machines" devoted principally to expanding development.[1] In Europe, urban governments devoted to *Social Service Delivery* for middle- and working-class residents built localized governance around a competing distributive aim.[2] An alternative model for the recent era of greater environmental awareness might be expected to oppose an *Ecological* agenda to either of these others. In fact, as the overview of outcomes has already suggested, local policy makers attentive to environmental objectives have usually integrated these ends with one or both of the others. Changes in supralocal policies, along with other shifts within and among urban political economies, have contributed to this shift. As a result, urban coalitions have increasingly sought *policy syntheses* rather than single objectives.

[1] John Logan and Harvey Molotch, *Urban Fortunes: The Political Economy of Place* (Berkeley: University of California Press, 1987); John Logan, Rachel Bridges Whaley and Kyle Crowder, "The Character and Consequences of Growth Regimes," *Urban Affairs Review* 32(5) (1997): 603–630.

[2] Keith Dowding, Patrick Dunleavy, Desmond King, Helen Margetts and Yuonne Rydin, et al., "Regime Politics in London Local Government," *Urban Affairs Review* 34 (4) (1999): 525–528; Jon Pierre, "Models of Urban Governance," *Urban Affairs Review* 34 (2) (1999): 372–397.

Among the possible permutations, an *Upscale synthesis* most clearly fits the logic of a hierarchical, global economy. Not only might elements of environmental sustainability go along with new development, but so long as environmental policies permitted some growth, the two aims might even reinforce each other. In an Upscale synthesis, however, the combination would work against distributive equity. Both developmental and environmental policies would predominantly serve the interests of privileged residents and firms. Developmental policies would attract professionals and executives from elsewhere. Environmental goods would enhance this attraction and maintain the political and market loyalty of consumers and voters. This combination of amenities and development, calibrated to draw and maintain the privileged, would preclude distributive concerns.

In opposition to this synthesis, policy makers have available three ways to combine distributive equity with other objectives. The logic of the global economy might seem to make all three difficult, if not impossible. The oldest alternative, most familiar from the postwar era of growth in Europe, would combine developmental initiatives with efforts to distribute the benefits from development to disadvantaged groups.[3] In harnessing local distributive policy to the local benefits from growth, this *Local Fordist synthesis* displays the characteristic logic of the era when rising wages from mass production helped finance expanding welfare states and growing consumer demand.[4] Though regarded with skepticism among urban analysts in the United States, this synthesis closely approximates the sustained strategies of certain Social Democratic governments at the local level under northern European welfare states.[5] As mandates from above have combined with other influences to bring a growing environmentalist element to urban political economies, other combinations of aims have replaced the Local Fordist synthesis.

A local government that could withstand economic pressures in favor of developmental policies might realize the *Social-Ecological synthesis* that

---

[3] See, e.g., the account of Stockholm in Peter Hall, *Cities in Civilization* (New York: Pantheon, 1998), or the earlier efforts in German cities (George Steinmetz, *Regulating the Social* [Princeton: Princeton University Press, 1993]).

[4] This characterization has become associated with Theories of Regulation. See Robert Boyer (ed.), *The Regulation School: A Critical Introduction*, trans. Craig Charney (New York: Columbia University Press, 1990); Mickey Lauria (ed.), *Reconstructing Urban Regime Theory* (London: Sage, 1997).

[5] See Pierre, "Models of Urban Governance."

Green theorists have often favored.[6] This combination would integrate the efforts of green movements to secure environmental quality with the preoccupation of social-democratic politics for social equity. Alongside social and other policies addressed generally to the interests of ethnically and economically disadvantaged groups, this synthesis would aim to alleviate place-related disadvantages. Both environmental goods and equitably distributed benefits from those goods would go along with social aims. Often proposed as a "post-Fordist" alternative to the traditional emphasis of the Left, such a synthesis would directly challenge any pressures from the global economy for development and urban growth. For those who paint global capitalism as an ineluctable hierarchical influence, a sustained, successful challenge of this sort is hard to imagine.

Analogous difficulties would confront a *Comprehensive synthesis*, or one that emphasized the pursuit of all three aims at once. Given the potential benefits from successful policy in all three areas, it would hardly be surprising if growing numbers of local politicians throughout the advanced industrial world laid claim to such a synthesis. Along with new development to expand the urban economy, they could assure that the benefits of growth went to the disadvantaged as well as the privileged and make high levels of environmental amenities widely accessible. But the global economy and associated pressures might take the most immediate toll on precisely this strategy. The need to attract more mobile, more privileged firms and residents through development would pull in the direction of Upscale strategies. A governing coalition that resisted that pull might have to give up on realistic hopes for continued growth.

The localized choices in these syntheses usually accumulate over time within a metropolitan setting, and they depend to varying degrees on policies handed down from above. Although comparative urban analysts may dispute whether or when the making of these choices takes place by means of urban regimes, growing local participation in policies and markets clearly elevates local governmental officials to crucial actors in these choices. The leaders of electoral coalitions that have amassed political power in the central city typically play critical, though not always decisive, roles in these choices. But as Mollenkopf has elaborated, urban governance requires more than simply election to the most important political offices

---

[6] Alain Liepitz, *Green Hopes*, trans. Malcolm Slater (Cambridge: Polity Press, 1998); Margit Mayer and John Ely (eds.), *The German Greens* (Philadelphia: Temple University Press, 1998).

of the city. Even a coalition that attains electoral dominance must also "build working relationships with major centers of public and private power whose cooperation is necessary for carrying out policy."[7] At the least, this second task entails the construction and maintenance of a governing coalition around the objectives of coalition leaders. Increasingly, as subsequent sections will make clear, governing coalitions depend on regimes of interlocal relations business-government relations and movement incorporation.

To one degree or another, urban policy syntheses and the local coalitions that pursue them depend on local choices. Even when local political leaders themselves do not dictate these choices, locally embedded constituencies, clienteles, traditions and institutions often do. Many such local institutions, as parts of wider systems, incorporate translocal influences into local decision making. Systems of parties and political ideologies comprise one of the most recognized such influences. Studies of "Progressive" or Left coalitions in Europe as well as in the United States exemplify the possibilities of localized political choices.[8] American studies of these formations highlight both "red" components that follow the traditional emphasis of European Social Democratic parties on distributive equity in housing and services, and "green" elements of Green parties that work for local ecological policies and against development.[9] Analysts of both European and U.S. urban politics have often identified dominance by the Right with pro-growth or business interests opposed to social and environmental policies.[10] As the discussion of alternative policy syntheses suggests, these generalizations capture only the broadest tendencies in the influence of parties. On the Left, closer analysis will show local parties to have both supported and opposed growth and even to have sometimes

---

[7] John H. Mollenkopf, *A Phoenix in the Ashes* (Princeton: Princeton University Press, 1992), p. 5.

[8] John Walton, "Theoretical Methods in Comparative Urban Politics," in John Logan and Todd Swanstrom, (eds.), *Beyond the City Limits* (Philadelphia: Temple University Press, 1990), pp. 243–257.

[9] E.g., Richard DeLeon, *Left Coast City* (Lawrence: University of Kansas Press, 1992); Peter Hall, *Cities in Civilization* (New York: Pantheon, 1997); Steinmetz, *Regulating the Social*.

[10] Stephen Elkin, *City and Regime in the American Republic* (Chicago: University of Chicago Press, 1986); Clarence N. Stone, *Regime Politics* (Lawrence: University of Kansas Press, 1989); Susan S. Fainstein, *The City Builders* (Oxford: Blackwell, 1993); Monique Pinçon-Charlot, Edmond Preteceille and Paul Rendu, *Ségrégation urbaine* (Paris: Éditions Anthropos, 1986); Patrick Le Galès, *Politique Urbaine et Développement Local* (Paris: L'Harmattan, 1993).

neglected social equity. On the Right, Christian Democratic and other parties have sometimes opposed growth, and sometimes supported both environmental quality and social equity.[11]

Much of the reason for these variations traces to nation-specific influences that go beyond the supralocal policies and central-local relations analyzed in the last chapter. Translocal organizational forms, often anchored in legislation from above, also shape the ends, resources and constraints of local government and politics within a city. In the arena of local electoral competition, national parties that organize extensively within a city weld the elements of a coalition together. Less frequent elections and fewer elected positions exacerbate the obstacles to dominance but assure a dominant coalition greater capacity to surmount challenges. Within the local government, just as at the national level, greater vertical integration enables a dominant electoral coalition to assert unified control over the public bodies of the local state. Institutional fragmentation leaves elected officials with less capacity to do so. Finally, the Tiebout model of inter-local competition has highlighted the importance of the fiscal base for local government finance as an influence on local choices.[12] Local governments that rely on raising taxes depend not only on the support of local constituencies that could revolt against taxation or leave but also on competition with other localities in interlocal markets for businesses and residents. To accomplish any objectives at all under this system, urban coalitions may have to pursue growth. Local governments that can count on revenues independent of locally imposed taxation face only the constraints that supralocal systems of public finance impose on local choice. Under this type of infrastructure, leading local coalitions can more easily put revenues to use for ends unrelated to growth.

---

[11] For similarly qualified findings see, e.g., George Boyne, *Constraints, Choices and Public Policies* (Westport, CT: JAI Press, 1996); Dowding et al., "Regime Politics in London"; Margit Mayer, "Restructuring and Popular Opposition in West German Cities," in Michael P. Smith and Joe R. Feagin (eds.), *The Capitalist City* (Oxford: Basil Blackwell, 1987), pp. 343–363.

[12] Charles M. Tiebout, "A Pure Theory of Local Expenditures," *Journal of Political Economy* 64 (1956): 416–424; Paul E. Peterson, *City Limits* (Chicago: University of Chicago Press, 1981); Keith Dowding, Peter John and Stephen Biggs, "Tiebout: A Survey of the Empirical Literature," *Urban Studies 31* (4–5) (1994): 767–797. A closely related literature integrates the Tiebout analysis into studies of "fiscal federalism." David E. Wildasin (ed.), *Fiscal Aspects of Evolving Federations* (Cambridge: Cambridge University Press, 1997); Teresa Ter-Minassian (ed.), *Fiscal Federalism in Theory and Practice* (Washington: International Monetary Fund, 1997).

Table 4.2. *Supralocal Infrastructures for Local Government and Politics, with Implications for Capacities of Dominant Coalition*

	Germany (Administrative Localism, Political Centralism)	France (Administrative Centralism, Political Localism)	United States (Administrative Localism, Political Localism)
Features of infrastructure			
Conditions related to sustained local electoral dominance by Left parties (party and electoral systems)	Strong party organizations, infrequent elections	Strong majoritarian coalitions, infrequent elections	Weak or nonexistent party organizations, frequent elections
Vertical integration of local government	Varied but generally high	High	Varied but generally low
Independent fiscal resources of local governments	Least dependent on local tax decisions, national system of equalization	Less dependent on local tax decisions, moderate equalization	Varied but generally dependent on local tax decisions, little equalization
Consequences for comparative capacities			
Maintenance of winning electoral coalition	Generally stronger	Stronger	Generally weaker
Control over administrative tasks	Generally stronger	Stronger	Generally weaker
Insulation from external local challenges	More	More	Less

Each of these elements within urban governance has its own logic. Together, they complement the wider institutional patterns already evident from central-local relations (Table 4.2). In Germany, despite variations among the *Länder* in local government forms, each element reinforced capacities to organize and mobilize the local government around equity and environmental policy.[13] Almost by definition, a strong party system depended on high levels of party organization within cities. In contrast with a majoritarian electoral system, proportional representation in

[13] For a clear introduction in English to the intricacies of German local government, see Arthur Gunlicks, *Local Government, in the Federal Republic of Germany* (Durham: Duke University Press, 1986).

local councils as well as at other levels of the state assured multiple parties some voice within local institutions. Electoral periods of from four to seven years, and limited numbers of elective offices, furnished ample opportunities for an elected majority to elaborate governing strategies. By the 1980s strong Green parties had joined the highly organized traditional Social Democrats on the Left in the party systems of German cities. Local administrative hierarchies also unified local governmental functions in all areas under the council, department heads and local chief executive. Although governmental forms varied by *Länder*, a national civil service and similar administrative templates for local officials helped reinforce parallel practices of vertical integration across the country. Finally, as Figure 4.1 indicates, the system of local finance made German city governments less dependent on locally raised taxes than either their U.S. or French counterparts.[14] The four central cities drew an average of 35 percent of their operating receipts from locally raised taxes, but those taxes that the municipality could adjust accounted for only 21 percent. Fiscal equalization of the business tax reduced the difference that even these local adjustments could make.

In France, the national infrastructure of local government imposed an administrative centralism analogous to that of the national state. National governmental forms and party systems offered opportunities to dominate that paralleled and in some respects exceeded those in Germany. At the local level, where only local council members were elected, the electoral system fostered stable council majorities behind the mayoral candidate whose party list won that election. Even after the winner-take-all rules of the Gaullist period were eliminated, a two-round majoritarian system limited proportional representation and encouraged parties to combine forces.[15] Although party organization at the local level remained less extensive,[16] the Communist and Social Democratic Left had long occupied a prominent position in the party system. Rather than a strict separation of

---

[14] See Paul Spahn and Wofgang Föttinger, "Germany," in Ter-Minassian, *Fiscal Federalism*, pp. 226–248. For an international overview of local government finance, see John Norregaard, "Tax Assignment," in Ter-Minassian, *Fiscal Federalism*, pp. 49–72.

[15] Kenneth Benoit and Kenneth Shepsle, "Electoral Systems and Minority Representation," in Paul Peterson (ed.), *Classifying by Race* (Princeton: Princeton University Press, 1995), pp. 50–84.

[16] Stephane Dion, *La politisation des mairies* (Paris: Economica, 1986); Jefferey Sellers, "Grounds of Democracy: Public Authority and the Politics of Metropolitan Land in Three Societies," Ph.D. diss., Yale University, 1994.

authorities, prescribed forms for administration through mayoral *adjoints* from the council and administrators perpetuated unified control under the mayor and the dominant coalition. A national civil service for local government reinforced these administrative capacities, though less systematically than in Germany.[17] Since the decentralization of the 1980s, French local governments depended somewhat more than their German counterparts on locally raised revenues (Figure 4.1).[18] Except in Montpellier, where the local government had transferred to the capital budget funds that the other cities maintained as operating expenses, taxes with rates subject to local determinations contributed 30 or 31 percent of the operational budgets.

Despite the greater variety of local governmental forms that the states authorized, U.S. administrative and political organization shared common traits. The frequency of the biennial local elections and the much larger number of officials that voters selected separately required any coalition to prove itself constantly in the electoral arena. The majoritarian cast of most such elections helped discourage stable electoral formations. In Wisconsin and North Carolina, as in most U.S. states, nonpartisan rules banned formal participation by parties in local politics. Even in Connecticut, where the electoral rules allowed parties, political "machines" like the one in New Haven lacked the central organizing role of German parties in local party competition.[19] As a result, not only traditional Left parties like those of western Europe but political parties in general remained weak, if not absent. In each central city, decentralized, fragmented patterns of political and governmental organization compounded the difficulties of maintaining coalitions. A welter of commissions and boards exercised authority in functionally specific areas like education, often on the basis of separate elections. Whatever the governmental form, councils generally shared formal decision-making power with the local executive. The civil service comprised at most a weak, locally determined element of local administration, and was not present at all in Durham. Finally, more than in either other country, local fiscal capacities in the United States depended on local political support and local tax receipts

---

[17] Michael Keating, *Comparative Urban Politics* (Aldershot: Edward Elgar, 1991), p. 55.

[18] M. Keating and A. Midwinter, "The Politics of Central-Local Grants in Britain and France," *Environment and Planning C: Government and Policy 12* (1994): 177–194.

[19] For an instructive exception to this rule in Ann Arbor, see Samuel Eldersveld, *Party Conflict and Community Development* (Ann Arbor: University of Michigan Press, 1995).

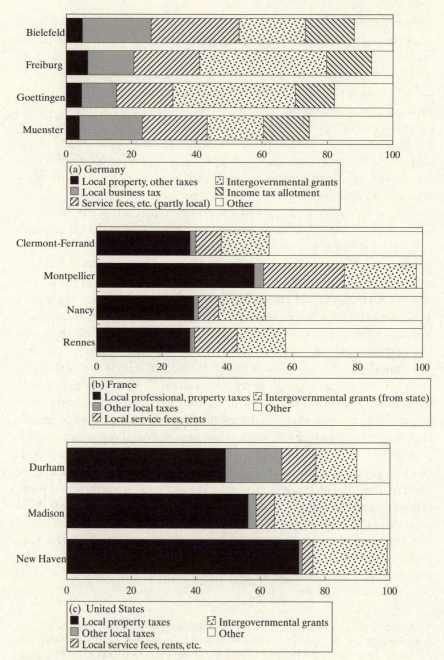

Figure 4.1 Locally Raised Taxes and Other Sources of Operating Revenues, 1990s (Calculated from Municipal Budgets)

(Figure 4.1). With the category of educational expenditures excluded, the three U.S. central cities looked to locally raised taxes for between 58 and 73 percent of their operating expenses. Even their capital budgets, though financed mostly through borrowing as in all three countries, relied on bonds that lacked the backing their European counterparts received from governmental guarantees.

In each country, the local elites and activists engaged in building dominant coalitions faced distinct sets of opportunities, cognitive and normative orientations, and identities. In both German and French local government, stronger party systems, facilitative electoral rules and infrequent electoral tests enhanced the chances of consolidating and maintaining a winning electoral coalition over time. Vertically integrated local government, long electoral periods, party coalitions and more secure fiscal resources improved the chances for an elected coalition to muster an effective governing coalition. Many of these elements operated partly by minimizing opportunities for opponents to veto policies or to organize alternative coalitions. In the United States, weaker or nonexistent local parties, multiple offices and frequent elections made it more difficult to build victorious, lasting coalitions and offered opponents more chances to mount challenges. Even electoral coalitions that overcame these obstacles confronted the low vertical integration of the government, the constant threats to local fiscal resources and the numerous veto points. These elements of the institutional infrastructure compounded the difficulty of maintaining an effective governing coalition within the government.

Increasingly, as the urbanized areas expanded, governance within the central city became inextricable from relations with other metropolitan towns. Considered only as a set of local intergovernmental relations, these horizontal ties require a full account of urban governance to encompass elements beyond government and politics in the central city. As the Tiebout model also makes clear, this dimension must ultimately encompass the metropolitan markets as well as the governmental arrangements that are crucial to the substance of governance. Only with this dimension taken into account can the effects of allocating such goods as schools, shopping and environmental quality, and ultimately the reasons for allocations of those goods, be understood.

Urban governance has also shaped the social and spatial structures that figure prominently as influences on urban politics. Over time, even as pervasive ethnoracial and class divisions and dispersed, segregated settlement have fostered interests in Upscale syntheses, local or localized decisions have contributed to these influences. The next three sections of this chapter chart postwar urban governance up to the mid-1990s in each of the eleven cities. My accounts draw on interviews with local actors; on local budget, administrative and electoral statistics; on the extensive documentary and journalistic records of local policy; and in most instances on accumulated secondary research. The analysis of these trajectories will demonstrate the relevance of institutional infrastructures for local government and interlocal governance and verify the importance of local social and spatial structures. Close attention to these other influences will help to define the limits as well as the significance of local choice.

The German Central Cities: Ecology, Equity and the Limits to Growth Politics

By the environmental as well as the social yardsticks of Chapter 2, the German central cities had attained the most consistent results. In job and income growth, the German outcomes had neither matched the rates of most French and U.S. settings nor stood out as much from surrounding regions. Bielefeld had avoided the decline typical of postindustrial settings, but only Freiburg had grown consistently in the central city and the surrounding region. To a greater degree than in the other two countries, supralocal policies in Germany help to account for these results. Higher levels of government offered strong incentives for local actors to undertake environmental measures, provided much of the means to pursue social equity and furnished less concentrated supports to new growth through physical infrastructure and related measures. Yet political coalitions within the German central cities also influenced outputs and outcomes. Parallel results came about partly through parallel trajectories of local policy making and politics. Similar infrastructures of local government and politics reinforced these trajectories.

Despite major differences in the dominant coalitions, party politics in the four German cities had evolved over the four decades since 1956 along broadly similar lines. The parallels reflected the growth of national parties to the main role in defining the composition of local councils (Figure 4.2). By the 1960s, reinforced through proportional representation in each setting, the SPD and the CDU had emerged on the Left and the Right to dominate the party system. The FDP and various local groups had declined but remained an often pivotal influence between the largest blocs. Beginning in the 1970s, as the composition of the local economy and the

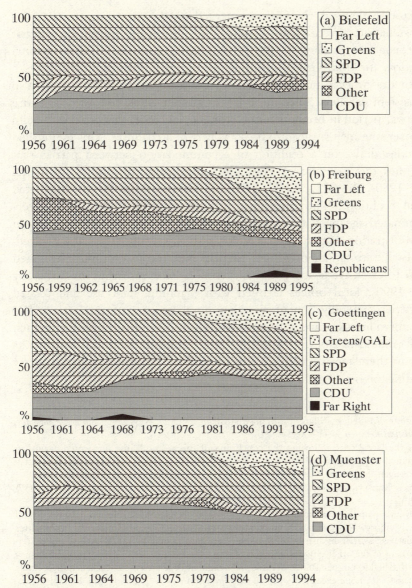

Figure 4.2 Composition of Local Council in German Central Cities, 1950s–1990s (Evolution in Cumulative Percent of Seats)

electorate changed, the Greens emerged in all four settings to alter this constellation. In a trend common to university towns throughout Germany,[20] expanding Green parties brought about a narrow council majority for "Red-Green" coalitions by the mid-1990s in all four cities.[21]

In the process and institutions of government itself there were also consistent parallels. Since the 1980s in all four cities, and over the entire postwar period in Freiburg and Göttingen, any party that aspired to build a governing majority had to do so as part of a coalition. This established practice draws on a tradition of accommodation between parties that "defines the structure of West Germany's party system."[22] Up to the late 1980s, the SPD, CDU, FDP and smaller voter groups dominated local coalitions. The emergence of Left majorities altered but rarely eliminated the need for constant compromises between the parties. In administration, largely similar bureaucratic apparatuses had also evolved. In each setting, major efforts to plan and reconstruct the city dated back to extensive postwar reconstruction or to even earlier initiatives. By the 1990s, local offices charged with planning, land use and related activities generally contained larger numbers of staff and usually had greater administrative expenses than their counterparts in the French and American cities.[23] Especially large numbers of local bureaucrats saw to the extensive local systems of land use information and property administration.[24]

---

[20] Jefferey M. Sellers, "Place, Postindustrial Change and the New Left," *European Journal of Political Research 33* (1998): 187–217.

[21] In the late 1990s, following the conclusion of this research, the left would again lose council majorities and/or control of the mayor's office in all four cities. In these cities, however, the margin of defeat for the Red-Green coalition remained narrow.

[22] Peter Katzenstein, *The Semi-Sovereign State* (Philadelphia: Temple University Press, 1986), p. 40.

[23] Overall, planning staff numbered 10.2 per 10,000 residents in Bielefeld, 10.6 per 10,000 in Freiburg, 11.9 per 10,000 in Münster and 6 per 10,000 in Göttingen. In the latter, however, a separate district office of the *Land* government exercised supervisory powers present in the other city governments. Among the French cities only Rennes and Nancy, with 8 and 9 staff per 10,000 in these and a number of related areas, exceeded these levels. In the U.S. none exceeded 5 per 10,000. Expenditures on planning and its implementation ranged from $43 per resident to $91 per resident in the German cities. Among the French cities only Rennes, with $44 per resident, exceeded a level of $16 per resident. U.S. cities did not budget parallel expenses in this area.

[24] Offices in this area counted between 4.2 and 6.4 staff members per 10,000 residents. Among the other cities with separate staff figures in the area only Rennes with 5.8 per 10,000 and Nancy with 4.0 per 10,000 so much as approached this level. (Clermont and Montpellier appear to have counted these offices along with others.)

Closer examination of what these local actors did leaves little doubt about their importance to the comparatively favorable environmental and social outcomes of the German central cities. Wherever local results diverged, as in the stronger growth that came to Freiburg, the causes could usually be traced to local initiatives.

Freiburg. The central city of Freiburg had emerged with the most impressive combined outcome among those studied. Alongside the most extensive environmental amenities and comparatively small concentrations of advantage and disadvantage, Freiburg had also grown to a degree uncommon among larger German cities. Although the local governmental infrastructure and policies of Baden-Württemberg contributed to these results, policies and other choices within the central city clearly made much of the difference.

In the principality of Baden, as elsewhere in Germany, the local origins of systematic city planning traced well back into the nineteenth century.[25] Initial planning efforts were made by officials in Freiburg under the Weimar Republic and Nazi regime, but reconstruction following the destruction of two-thirds of the Old Town in World War II gave the main impetus to the development of comprehensive planning. Even in the 1990s, a visitor to the newly constructed local planning office still passed through halls lined with photographs of the wartime devastation and the subsequent restoration. Because the South German form of local government gave strong executive authority to a nonpartisan mayor elected every eight years alongside the local council elected every five years, this separately elected figure exercised a continuous influence over both coalition building and the broad directions of local choices. With Eugene Keidel from 1962, and with former State Secretary Rolf Böhme after 1982, a

---

[25] On the early history of Freiburg, see Heinz Kneile, *Stadterweiterungen und Stadtplanung im 19. Jahrhundert* (Freiburg Universitätsbuchhandlung, 1978). On postwar politics and policies and policy, see Dieter Apel and Tim Pharoach, *Transport Concepts in European Cities* (Aldershot, England: Avebury Ashgate, 1995); Benno Heinrichsmeier, "Sozialräumliche Differenzierung in Freiburg im Breisgau" (Ph.D. diss., Albert-Ludwigs-Universität zu Freiburg i. Br., 1982); Rolf Böhme, *Je mehr wir haben, desto mehr wir wollen* (Bonn: Verlag J. H. Dietz Nachfolger, 1994); Freiburg im Breisgau, *Freiburg – Westentwicklung 1987* (Freiburg im Breisgau: H. Rebholz, 1988); Hans-Arthur Hassis, *Bodenpreise, Bodenmarkt und Stadtentwicklung. Beiträge zur Kommunalwissenschaft 23* (Munich: Minerva Publikation, 1987); Netzwerk Dreyeckland E.V., Politische Buchhandlung Jos Fritz, and Stadtzeitung für Freiburg, *Stattbuch Freiburg Dreyeckland* (Freiburg: Walter Marx, 1985); and publications of the Freiburg Amt für Statistik und Einwohnerwesen.

Social Democratic mayor developed local agendas in cooperation with majorities in the local council. Into the 1980s, and in particular for passage of the comprehensive plan made official in 1980, the mayor, local planners and the SPD relied on alliances with the CDU. Beginning at the end of the 1970s, however, the Greens capitalized on ecological and social challenges to developmental policies to build a growing following among younger, more educated voters. By 1989 parties of the Left had attained a slight majority on the Freiburg council, and the Greens had acquired one of their largest local followings in Germany. In 1994, the Greens surpassed the SPD to become the largest local party of the Left.

Each of the shifting political coalitions contributed to persistent patterns in local policies and markets. Even by the late 1980s, local environmental initiatives had garnered Freiburg a regular designation in the media as the "'ecological capital' of the Republic."[26] Any city as old as Freiburg that had retained as much of the Black Forest within its city limits might be expected to have done so through a tradition of preservation (see Figure 4.3). Prior to the national legislation of 1960, the first comprehensive plan of the city in 1954 reiterated a commitment to maintenance of both agricultural land and forestland. From the 1970s through the early 1990s, local officials elaborated a wide array of ecological policies that went well beyond preservation. Pedestrian zones, inaugurated in 1969, grew to cover the entire Old Town. Bicycle paths more than doubled in length. Extensions of bus and trolley service maintained an unusually strong role for public transit. Discouragement of commercial development beyond the urban center and of housing outside major urban nodes helped retain settlement patterns more conducive to these alternatives to the automobile. Other local measures introduced extensive noise protection measures, and 30-kilometer speed limits on nearly all secondary roads. These policies earned Freiburg recognition in the UN Habitat Report of 1995 and elsewhere as a model of sustainable urban development.[27] At the same time, the city proceeded to build new park facilities like the massive Seepark in the high-rise residential neighborhoods of Betzenhausen and Landwasser. Newly planted or preserved forests more than made up for losses in land to development. Preservationist practices grew over the 1970s and 1980s

---

[26] Rolf Obertreis, "Ökotopia im Schwarzwald," *Baden-Württemberg*, Sonderheft 1 (1988): 64.

[27] United Nations Conference on Human Settlement, *Report of the United Nations Conference on Human Settlement* (New York: Oxford University Press, 1995), pp. 318–319; Apel and Pharoach, *Transport Concepts in European Cities*.

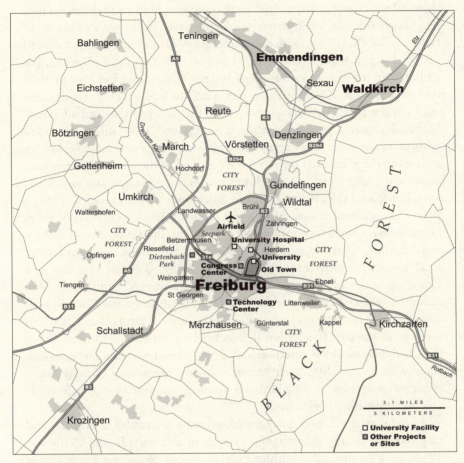

Figure 4.3   Freiburg

into a regular feature of planning for new development in and around the center. Although the Greens and local movements had helped provoke many of these policies (see Chapter 6), the policies themselves had usually begun long before the Red-Green majority emerged.

The success of Freiburg in attracting new residents and carrying out new development made the city stand out even more from the other German cities. If the livability that the environmental measures helped create contributed to this result, local officials since the election of Keidel in 1962 had also endeavored repeatedly to bring in new businesses and residents. In the 1960s, along with university expansion in the downtown,

195

these efforts centered around the construction of high-rise housing in new neighborhoods like Weingarten and Landwasser to the west of the main rail line. By the 1970s, with the elaboration of national authorities and financial supports for urban renewal as well as for regional planning, the emphasis in the initiatives that produced the Comprehensive Plan of 1979 turned to ways to reinforce the urban center as a regional center of commerce and services, or *Oberzentrum*. Both the plan and the array of neighborhood renewal projects within it envisioned new, often gentrified housing in the older inner areas and a range of peripheral neighborhoods, including newly annexed towns on the outskirts of the city. Urban renewal, additional commercial zoning, downtown parking garages and new highways reinforced the attraction of the downtown for businesses and shoppers. Even as local contestation often modified implementation of these plans, similar objectives continued to prevail into the 1990s. Mayor Böhme and his allies, often over intense opposition from the Greens and other local groups, pushed through such long-discussed projects as the new Congress and Convention Center in the downtown, close to the rail station; a widened version of the B31 highway through the Black Forest; and a massive housing project on the former sewage farm ("Rieselfeld") to the west of the city. In addition to a technology center and other facilities that had helped draw international firms like the computer company Iomega to a small high-tech sector, publicity promoting the city could point to an average of 10 additional hectares per year being made available for expanding businesses.[28]

As the data in Chapter 2 suggested, growing inequality in earnings and employment usually accompanies growth of this sort. In the 1970s and 1980s, as a number of wealthier neighborhoods along the Black Forest became more exclusive, the gentrification of older living quarters in the Old Town and surrounding neighborhoods had helped spark protest movements and given rise to the Greens. But although land prices persisted at levels close to those of much larger German cities, local officials had also persistently sought to equilibrate social inequalities among neighborhoods. Ever since Freiburg had first elected an SPD mayor, its local officials had been acquiring an unusually large proportion, for a city in Baden-Württemberg, of publicly supported or social housing, and increasingly had spread the municipally owned units around the city. In the Rieselfeld project of the 1990s, planners continued to insist on a mix of

---

[28] Freiburg im Breisgau, *Addressbuch Freiburg 1996* (Freiburg im Breisgau, 1996), p. 29.

housing types that included a large proportion of publicly subsidized units. The coordinated strategies of transit, land use and commercial development that had encouraged denser settlement also served a social purpose. In an award-winning presentation to a national competition of its overall strategies of development during the 1970s and 1980s, Freiburg's City Planning Office identified as its main strategic purpose to rectify the disadvantage of the traditional working-class neighborhoods built since the late nineteenth century in the areas to the west of the main rail line.[29] Trolley lines, new parks and shopping opportunities in these areas, as well as in the more distant and newer developments like Landwasser, not only served the interests of the areas' lower-income residents directly. The improvements also attracted new residents and, up to 1980 at least, brought about a steady amelioration in the social status of such neighborhoods as Landwasser and Betzenhausen.[30] To a lesser degree, these advantages also benefitted the declining neighborhoods near the center where the comparatively small local population of disadvantaged minorities concentrated. The city had also undertaken such specific initiatives for its minorities as a housing project for the native gypsy population and a representative council for the growing noncitizen residents of Turkish, Yugoslav and Italian background.[31]

By the early 1990s, then, Mayor Böhme and the new Red-Green majority in the Freiburg council presided over well-established, consistently implemented local measures in all three domains. As a result of the attraction of the Black Forest and a growing region, local restrictions on markets probably posed less of a threat to expansion than in most German cities. The strong position of the mayor in the South German form of local government also helped Mayor Böhme and his predecessor to overcome the divisions between parties that might otherwise have hampered collective action. Local efforts proved essential to realize these advantages.

Münster. If the growth in Münster had remained somewhat below the rate in Freiburg, Chapter 2 found similar environmental and even social results. Strikingly, the Right controlled the local government here even

---

[29] Freiburg im Breisgau, *Freiburg – Westentwicklung 1987.*

[30] Heinrichsmeier, "Sozialräumliche Differenzierung in Freiburg im Breisgau," p. 122.

[31] Jefferey M. Sellers, "Norms in the Politics of Housing for Minorities: Evidence from a French, a German and a U.S. Metropolitan Area," *Ethnic and Racial Studies 19*(3) (1996): 599.

more firmly than the Left dominated the local government in Freiburg. This business-oriented, conservative coalition thus carried out a synthesis that much of the literature on urban governance has associated with Progressive coalitions. Although partly the consequence of supralocal policies, this strategy also had local roots.

For Münster too, the activities of the local government long preceded the emergence of federal frameworks for localized policy. Municipal preservationist restrictions on development dated back to the turn of the century, and city planning to 1920.[32] As a longtime seat of bishops and the regional center for the Catholic Church, however, Münster had also long provided local majorities for the CDU and earlier religious parties. In the absence of a separately elected mayor under the local government form in place in North Rhine-Westphalia up to 1999, council majorities alone determined control of the executive in Münster. Throughout the postwar era up to 1984, despite sweeping changes under way in the local political economy, the CDU held an absolute majority. Even after the number of voters supporting the party slipped beneath 50 percent that year, the CDU managed to retain power for another ten years through a coalition with the FDP. Only in 1994, when the FDP fell below the 5 percent threshold to enter the council, did the growing support for the Greens among university students and other younger voters produce a majority for the local Left. Up to this point, the local government had amassed a well-established set of strategic choices in all three domains.

Even as the Greens had hammered persistently at the road-building propensities of the departing majority, CDU officials could legitimately boast about environmental initiatives that went far beyond any mandates from above. Protection for green zones could be traced back to a city plan of 1920, and formal preservationist restrictions on development to 1904.[33] In 1966 the city instituted, and in 1979 it expanded, a "Green Plan" to integrate local environmental measures. The preservationist components

---

[32] Münster, *Münster Stadterneuerung* (Münster, 1991), p. 16; Heinz Heineberg and Alois Mayr, "Räumlich-strukturelle Entwicklung Münsters und Probleme der Stadtplanung seit 1945," in Franz-Josef Jakobi, (ed.), *Geschichte der Stadt Münster*, vol. 2, (Münster: Aschendorff, 1993), p. 296. On the history of planning and politics in Münster, see also Münster, *Grünordnung Münster* (Münster, 1980); Münster, *Flächennutzungsplan: Kurzfassung des Erläuterungsberichtes* (Münster, 1983); Münster, *Verkehrsbericht Münster* (Münster, 1993); Münster, *ökologisch Leben und Wohnen in Münster* (Münster, 1995); and the extensive essays in Jakobi (ed.), *Geschichte der Stadt Münster*, 3 vols. (Münster: Aschendorff, 1993).
[33] Heineberg and Mayr, "Räumlich-strukturelle Entwicklung"; Münster, *Münster Stadterneuerung*, p. 16.

of this plan centered around a system of seven broad "Greenways" (*Grünzüge*) of protected open space that radiated out from the Old Town like the spokes of a wheel (Figure 4.4). A proliferating system of parks, private gardens and landscape restrictions anchored and helped reinforce this plan. Often drawing on subsidies that the *Land* government in North Rhine-Westphalia offered for development, city officials sponsored local parks, such as a massive recreational area around the Aasee south of the university, and offered public funds in support of private green spaces. The plan also guided an extensive program that employed new paths, bicycle racks and other encouragements to generate one of the highest rates of bicycle ridership in the country. Environmentalist and preservationist policies toward the Old Town played an integral role in these initiatives. If the Red-Green coalition would introduce the formal goal of an auto-free downtown, the previous local government had already carried out most of the necessary measures to implement it. In Münster, in contrast to the more aggressive initial postwar reconstruction in Freiburg and most other German cities, a local ordinance from 1950 required strict adherence to the original architectural and urban structures. Efforts to renew the downtown in the 1970s and early 1980s took the form of subsidies for private, preservationist gentrification rather than the stronger public intervention attempted in Freiburg. From a modest beginning in 1969, pedestrian zones had spread throughout the city by the early 1980s. Although the city had given up its trolley in the postwar period, it continued to support a frequent bus service. By the early 1990s, 30-kilometer speed limits applied throughout much of Münster's residential areas.

Especially up to 1994, developmental policies enshrined in a Comprehensive Plan elaborated over 1975–1981 consistently fostered the growth of Münster as a regional service center (*Oberzentrum*).[34] If these measures had generated less growth than they had in Freiburg, local protagonists of these policies in Münster also had to overcome the disadvantages of a surrounding *Land* in postindustrial decline. Especially from the 1950s through the 1970s, local actors drew on the comparatively interventionist *Land* policies of North Rhine-Westphalia. Stronger housing supports from this level than in Freiburg helped enable such new high-rise neighborhoods as Aaseestadt and Coerde, then Berg Fidel and Kinderhaus. Especially in the 1970s, the *Land* had also helped bring new firms and institutions to the city. Investment credits helped attract international

---

[34] Münster, *Flächennutzungsplan*.

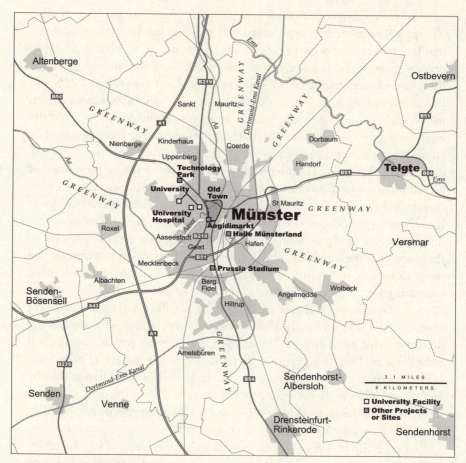

Figure 4.4 Münster

businesses like Armstrong Cork and Wyeth Pharmaceuticals from the United States. The university and its hospital undertook massive construction, including a new medical center. The city itself carried out parts of these projects, administered the downtown renovation and built such new service complexes in the downtown as a combination of parking, shops, offices, restaurants and housing in the Aegidimarkt. Under joint CDU and FDP control in the late 1980s and 1990s, the local government undertook an increasingly diverse array of developmental measures on its own. It extended commercial and industrial zones; redesigned zones for such entertainment facilities as the Stadthalle and the Prussia Stadium;

expanded peripheral shopping centers in such areas as Coerde and Aaseestadt; initiated a technology center, then the Technology Park; developed housing in peripheral neighborhoods like Gievenbeck; and sought to strengthen the urban center with more highways in the periphery and more parking in the downtown. Alongside such initiatives, one of the lowest business tax rates among German cities helped win Münster occasional recognition in national business periodicals as one of the country's most "business-friendly" cities.[35] At the same time, local constraints that had restricted development over the postwar era persisted. Even under the CDU and FDP, local business observers continued to complain about inadequate amounts of commercially zoned land and burdensome local regulatory restrictions, and the local Left lamented the paucity of funds for new housing.

Whatever the shortcomings of local distributive measures in comparison with the demands of the Left or the accomplishments of the Freiburg coalition, low levels of segregation and high levels of social housing persisted. Even as the postwar CDU government in Münster took less advantage of public subsidies for housing than the nearby municipality of Bielefeld, the Social Democratic government of North-Rhine Westphalia continued to make more generous subsidies available than the *Land* government in Freiburg. At the same time, from the initial postwar high-rises to the planned district of Gievenbeck in the 1990s, the planners under the CDU-led government also sought a mix of social housing with other, private forms of ownership. This position on segregation in Münster belonged to a more general social thrust in local policy. Local budgets continued to supplement such components of the German welfare state as support for working parents, children and the aged.[36] Although the SPD and the Greens pointed out deficiencies in local policy toward housing privatization and toward foreigners, these qualifications only partly altered the overall thrust of a strong local social policy.[37]

[35] This and the following sentences are taken from Marion Kamphuls, "Standorte im Vergleich: Beschränkt aussagefähig," *Wirstschaftsreport Münster 1988/1989* (Münster, 1989), pp. 57, 58.
[36] A model program of subsidies for self-help groups in diverse social spheres had earned the city the accolade of CDU Labor Minister Blüm as the "self-help-friendliest city in the Republic" (Münster, *Wirtschaftsreport Münster 1988/1989*, p. 8).
[37] The housing policies of the Right during the 1990s emphasized privately owned dwellings more and social or rental housing less than would the Red-Green coalition. At the same time, the CDU and FDP came under fire for refusing to commit more resources to

With extensive environmental and even social measures already in place beside the developmental ones, the Red-Green coalition of 1994 ushered in surprisingly limited alterations in the overall local policy synthesis. If the more active intervention of a *Land* under Social Democratic control contributed to the similarity of results in Münster with those in Freiburg, local actors consistently played the decisive role in local outcomes. Only in certain social policy domains did the efforts of the 1980s and early 1990s fall well short of parallel efforts in Freiburg. Difficulties in the wider regional economy, however, left local developmental efforts in Münster somewhat less successful.

Bielefeld. In Bielefeld, close by Münster, where manufacturing had once dominated and still persisted as an influence, local actors confronted economic and political conditions less evident in the other German central cities. Still, both the environmental and the social results there compared favorably with French and American counterparts. Throughout most of the postwar era, the local SPD had dominated the local coalitions that shaped these results in Bielefeld much as the CDU had in nearby Münster. Especially since the end of the 1970s, contestation from the Greens on the Left, from local citizen movements and from the CDU and its allies on the Right had helped forestall the development of more comprehensive local strategies.

In Bielefeld too, localized policies had emerged well before the elaboration of federal planning and land use rules. In the absence of planning before World War II, haphazard patterns of exurban development predominated.[38] But the destruction of 45 percent of all the housing stock and most of the Old Town precipitated new efforts to organize and control

housing and otherwise assisting the growing but comparatively small numbers of local asylum seekers and other immigrants in the city. Debates over local budget priorities in the years leading up to the 1994 election exemplify these critiques. See Münster, *Zum Haushalts dan 1991, 1992, 1993, Stellungnahme–der Ratsfraktionen* (Münster: Press- und Informationsamt der stadt Münster, 1990, 1991, 1992).

[38] Diethelm Düsterloh, "Oberzentrum Bielefeld," in Alois Mayr and Klaus Temlitz (eds.), *Bielefeld und Nordost-Westfalen* (Münster: Geographischen Kommission für Westfalen, 1995), p. 168. For additional sources on Bielefeld, see George Wagner, *Wohnraum für Alle: Der Soziale Wohnungsvau in Bielefeld, 1950–1990* (Bielefeld: Verlag für Regionalgeschichte, 1991); Bielefeld, *Erläuterungsbericht zum Flächennützungsplan* (1978); Bielefeld, *Räumliches Stadtentwicklungskonzept: Entwurf* (Bielefeld, 1992); Hartmut Hein (ed.), *Ausgerechnet Bielefeld* (Münster: Westfälisches Dampfboot, 1991); Ulrich Mai, "Bodenpreise, Stadtflucht und Stadtpolitik," in Mayr and Temlitz, *Bielefeld und Nordost-Westfalen*, pp. 181–193.

development. Over the course of these efforts, except for the interlude of an "antimarxist" majority made up of CDU, FDP and several small parties from 1952–1956, the SPD dominated the local government. Beginning in the 1970s, when the party lost its absolute majority, cooperation with the CDU or the FDP became necessary in order for the SPD to assemble council majorities. At the same time, local neighborhood movements and, from 1979, one of the first powerful Green or "alternative" Left parties in Germany emerged to challenge existing local policies in development, the environment and other domains. At first in occasional votes, and eventually through open cooperation, the Greens and the SPD began to work together. In 1989, a new voter group on the Right called the "Citizen Union for Bielefeld" (Bürgergemeinschaft für Bielefeld; BfB) emerged to garner nearly 10 percent of the vote. Although composed of conservative businesspeople, a splinter of the CDU and localistic traditionalists, the BfB also appealed to other alienated voters: "In Bielefeld we don't need the Republicans," the chairman proclaimed, in a reference to the small German right-wing party with Nazi associations; "We have the Citizen's Union."[39] In coalition with the CDU, the new formation wrested control of the local council from the Left. Following intense contestation over this coalition's plans for development and other areas, the Red-Green coalition between SPD and the Greens returned to power in 1994. New electoral coalitions had thus shaped local policy making repeatedly since at least the beginning of the 1970s.

The most consistent local policies molded by these influences lay in the social dimension. Except for the reconstruction of the downtown, the pre-eminence of large new social housing developments in the strategies of the postwar local governments had brought about what amounted to a service delivery strategy over most of the 1950s and 1960s. Even in the 1990s, a local exhibit sponsored by city planners portrayed the provision of social and other forms of housing as the central element in the history of Bielefeld's land use policy.[40] If Münster had taken only limited advantage of the comparatively generous housing subsidies in North Rhine-Westphalia, Bielefeld and other Social Democratic cities capitalized on these resources and on closer ties to the governing SPD to build up more extensive stocks of publicly subsidized housing.[41] From the 1950s to the end of the 1960s,

[39] Christian Presch (1991). "'... Denn sie wissen nicht was sie tun': Stadtplanung à la Bielefeld," in Hein, *Ausgerechnet Bielefeld*, p. 171.
[40] Wagner, *Wohnraum für alle*.   [41] Ibid., p. 154.

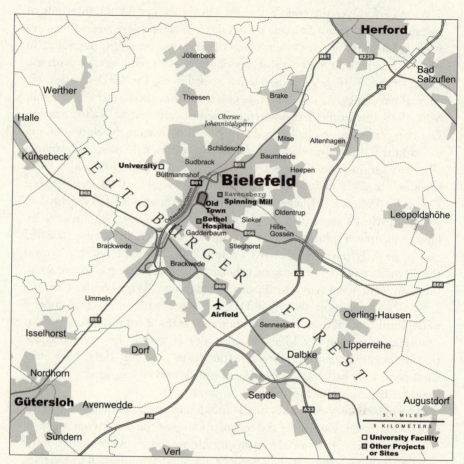

Figure 4.5   Bielefeld

the new satellite city of Sennestadt, with 6,000 rental and owner-occupied units, set the pattern for housing developments in Brackwede, Stieghorst, Baumheide, Schildesche and Bültmannshof. Even in the 1980s and 1990s, as the subsidies for social housing fell and the forty-year-long social protections on postwar housing expired, the city continued to integrate social units with the growing proportions of owner-occupied ones.[42] Along with this mix, improvements to neighborhoods, speed limits in residential neighborhoods, the resettlement of industry in the periphery and supra-

[42] Ibid., pp. 110–117.

local subsidies for housing modernization helped ease segregation in the downtown.[43] Ultimately the attempts to address social disparities also extended to the growing numbers of foreigners in the city. Industries concentrated in Bielefeld had originally brought in large numbers of foreign workers, but the efforts of the city to aid refugees and other immigrants also helped make it a haven for these groups. An unusually broad array of services guaranteed living space for quotas of foreigners, provided special assistance to foreign renters, mediated conflicts with native Germans and furnished additional medical, educational and other social aid.[44] The Right majority of 1989–1994 cut back local subsidies for disadvantaged groups in mass transit and retraining,[45] but even in 1993, at the end of this period, overall expenditures for such services as schools, social security, health and recreation took up from two to eight percent more of the operating budget in Bielefeld than they did in the other German cities, for a total of 44 percent.

Over the same period, many of the other developmental initiatives that had promoted prosperity in Freiburg and to some extent in Münster encountered more contestation, greater institutional and economic obstacles and, ultimately, less success. Although often under discussion in local circles as early as the immediate postwar period, these efforts first began to come to fruition with initiatives at the *Land* level in the 1960s.[46] Over this time, local planners pushed not only the new university that the *Land* decided to build in 1965 but also such projects as an autobahn through the city, a major regional airport and a new subway. From 1968 to 1985, department head Jügen Hotzan integrated these initiatives with ambitious plans for reconstruction in the downtown as well as for extensive new housing construction. Anchored in the comprehensive plan that Bielefeld developed from 1973 and finally passed in 1978, the largest single urban renewal project in the Federal Republic extended some 150 hectares from the train station to the northern part of the small Old Town. Alongside the new residential areas in the periphery, new commercial and industrial zones in neighborhoods like Oldentrup helped draw the factories of firms like Kochs-Adler and Ostermann from the downtown. More than in

[43] Düsterloh, "Oberzentrum Bielefeld," pp. 186–187.
[44] Bielefeld, *Situation der Bielefelderinnen und Bielefelder auslänischer Herkunft* (1994).
[45] Presch, "'. . . Denn sie wissen nicht,'" p. 173.
[46] Uwe Lahl, "Der Interruptus Coccus Bielefeldis," in Hein, *Ausgerechnet Bielefeld*, pp. 153–156. Presch ("'. . . Denn sie wissen nicht'") also summarizes the history of large projects in Bielefeld.

Münster, local fiscal limitations forced city officials to rely constantly on grants and subsidies from above. Even in the 1980s, as concern about local economic decline persisted, efforts to promote local business persisted.[47] As the city encountered difficulties attracting development to replenish its coffers, and incurred debt obligations in efforts to borrow for developmental initiatives, fiscal constraints compounded political ones.

Under the coalition of the Right that entered office in 1989, a new set of ambitious plans for the proclaimed "Economic Metropole" built on the aims of the comprehensive plan. Under their "Spatial Urban Development Conception," local planners proposed additional expansion of both commercial and residential zones, the new Stadthalle in the downtown, extensions to the city subway, a new development corridor along a widened B66 to the west, new local facilities for the Bundespost and Deutsches Telekom and other projects.[48] To promote economic development more generally, the government established the private Economic Development Corporation, a technology and innovation center and a center to advise local firms on opportunities in European programs.[49]

If its initiatives for local development helped ward off the losses in jobs that beset the French and American postindustrial settings, Bielefeld's successes rarely approached those of Freiburg or Münster. The commercial and shopping zone that emerged from the 1970s in the downtown renewal district generated modest revenues by comparison with these other cities, and industry continued into the 1990s to depart. Comparative business surveys traced the causes to "[a lack of] sufficient commercial and industrial surfaces. . . . high tax rates, bad traffic connections, regulatory uncertainties, and up to 1990 an unfavorable 'climate' between Council and Administration on the one hand and business on the other."[50] Especially in larger projects, what one local commentator termed "Interruptus Coccus Bielefeldis" (Latin for "Bielefeld delay bug," but also a play on the term for aborted sexual intercourse) plagued local development.[51] The

---

[47] Amt für Beschäftigungs- und Wirtschaftsförderung Bielefeld, *Wirtschaftsförderungsbericht 1987* (Bielefeld: Amt für Beschäftigungs- und Wirtschaftsförderung Bielefeld, 1987).

[48] Presch, "'. . . Denn sie wissen nicht'"; Florian Mausbach, "Bielefeld muss sich konzentrieren." In Mayr and Temlitz, *Bielefeld und Nordost-Westfalen*, pp. 443–447.

[49] Amt für Beschäftigungs- und Wirtschaftsförderung Bielefeld, *Wirtschaftsförderungsberichte 1990, 1991* (Bielefeld: Amt für Beschäftigungs- und Wirtschaftsförderung Bielefeld, 1990, 1991).

[50] Düsterloh, "Oberzentrum Bielefeld," p. 178.

[51] See Lahl, "Der Interruptus Coccus Bielefeldis"

often irregular flow of supralocal subsidies, the indebtedness of a city government locked into overly ambitious financial commitments and the limited tax base all imposed constraints on projects.[52] But recurrent opposition within the community and the city government often proved decisive. In the 1970s and 1980s, local forces from neighborhood associations to the Greens to the CDU had altered the plans that Hötzan advocated almost beyond recognition. Their opposition had contributed to defeat of the regional airport, stopped the construction of an autobahn interchange on the downtown site of the original Ravensberg cloth factory, helped to delay construction of the local subway for seven years and exposed scandals surrounding the purchase of land and buildings for renewal. In the 1990s, local planning restrictions or delays had contributed to the loss of the planned postal distribution center, a rail freight center, a mail-order center and an IKEA market as well as of numerous new roadways.[53]

Yet local opponents to development had only partly translated such successes into positive local environmental measures. Even the ambitious scheme for development in the Comprehensive Plan of 1978 had retained protective restrictions on such green areas as the Teutobürger Forest, discouraged the dispersal of settlement across the landscape and protected open space.[54] At the same time, planners under the Right coalition of 1992 noted the continued failure to realize a greenbelt around the city in more than parts.[55] Into the 1990s, as preservation and natural protection moved to the center of local planning, both the Left and the Right coalitions supported efforts to build or extend parks like the Johannisbachtalsperre and to convert the former Ravensberg spinning mill into a park and museum. Partly to secure supralocal resources for its efforts at revitalization, the city government had often committed itself to grandiose developmental goals that crowded out more environmentalist aims. A small but expensive subway had substituted a short underground tunnel for more extensive trolley and bus service; resources for four-lane highways supplanted extensions to the network of bicycle paths; intensive reconstruction in renewal areas replaced the more preservationist measures carried out in Münster. Because the more extensive plans that opponents to development had fought incorporated local public transit, downtown pedestrian zones and

---

[52] See generally Presch, "'Denn sie wissen nicht.'"
[53] Düsterloh, "Oberzentrum Bielefeld," pp. 178–179.
[54] Bielefeld, *Erläuterungsbericht zum Flächennutzungsplan*, pp. 60–61, 75–76.
[55] Bielefeld, *Räumliches Entwicklungskonzept*.

even elements of historical preservation, the setbacks to local developmental policies also hindered extension of environmental amenities.

Not only *Land* initiatives but also Bielefeld's coalitions contributed to the extensive measures to secure social equity and the significant environmental initiatives. The Right coalition of 1989–1994 proved unable to alter these established local priorities. But since the 1970s political contestation had undermined developmental strategies and limited even the effective extent of environmental measures. In Bielefeld, political shifts similar to those in the other German cities contributed to the emergence of a Red-Green coalition but had not enabled the Left to remain dominant. If the resulting policies still went beyond those of other postindustrial settings, either more secure majorities as in Münster or a mayor-led coalition as in Freiburg might have enabled more extensive policies.

Göttingen. In Göttingen too, growth up to 1989 remained limited despite effective policy in the other domains. Again, local efforts accounted for much of the local results. As in Bielefeld, shifting party coalitions and conflict within the government had hampered local policy making.

Prior to the federal schemes, local efforts to plan, promote and regulate urban growth here had proceeded even further than in the other German cities.[56] As early as 1899 the city had passed an initial zoning scheme. In 1929 the local government had started to craft a local development plan, and under the Nazis had passed both a general city plan and a development scheme for the Old Town. Göttingen also escaped the destruction that World War II brought to other German cities. Over the decades after the war, however, local governmental structures in lower Saxony complicated efforts to form coalitions to carry out the earlier plans. Along with the mayor and deputy mayors appointed following council elections, the parties in the council selected an *Oberstadtdirektor* – essentially a city manager – every twelve years to head city administration. Up to 1991, shifting party alliances and recurrent squabbles among these

---

[56] Hans-Dieter Von Frieling, "Der Bau des Gehäuses," in Kornelia Duwe, Carola Gottschalk and Marianne Koerner (eds.), *Göttingen ohne Gänseliesesl*, 2nd ed. (Gudensberg-Gleichen: Wartberg Verlag, 1989), pp. 18–31, see pp. 22–27. On the history of planning and politics in Göttingen, see the other essays in Kornelia Duwe, Carola Gottschalk and Marianne Koerner (eds.), *Göttingen ohne Gänseliesel*, 2nd ed. (Gudensberg-Gleichen: Wartberg Verlag, 1989); Göttingen City Planning Administration, *Altstadtsanierung, 1969–1979* (Göttingen, 1980); Göttingen City Planning Administration, *Grün in Göttingen* (Göttingen, 1981); Göttingen City Planning Administration, *Göttingen 2000* (Göttingen, 1991).

Figure 4.6 Göttingen

officeholders had often prevented consistent lines of policy. Despite a steadily declining share of local vote totals, the FDP played a pivotal role in these developments. From 1948 into the late 1960s, the council had chosen FDP mayors alongside a nonpartisan *Stadtdirektor*. Following election of an SPD mayor and *Oberstadtdirektor* in 1968 as well as the national Social-Liberal coalition, the SPD and FDP in 1970 entered into a coalition that lasted until 1979. In that year, FDP member Rolf Vieten, a deputy administrator under this arrangement, assured himself election as the next *Oberstadtdirektor* by leading a realignment of his party with the CDU. The resulting coalition maintained a governing majority up to 1986, when, with the growth of the Greens, the Left secured its first council majority. Over the next year and a half, Vieten aggravated relations with council members across the political spectrum with behavior so erratic and imperious that the deputy mayors accused him of being "neither personally nor professionally suited to the office."[57] In 1987 the requisite three-fourths majority of the council voted to oust him, and in 1988 the SPD, CDU and FDP, but not the Greens, voted to name Hermann Schierwater of the SPD as *Oberstadtdirektor*. Schierwater worked with various coalitions up to 1991. After the victory of the the the Red-Green coalition in 1991, he worked with a Left majority.

Under these shifting coalitions, a commitment to environmental amenities emerged as the most notable constant of local Göttingen strategies. As early as 1953, local officials had worked together with surrounding communities to develop the first metropolitan or municipal plan in Germany for protection of green areas, plant species and watershed supply.[58] Following extensive reforestation in the 1950s, a "Green Plan" established in conjunction with the Comprehensive Plan of 1965, and extended in 1975, consolidated a citywide system of land use protections. Over the next twenty years governing coalitions added continually to these measures; by 1992 the Red-Green coalition had extended natural or landscape protections to 62 percent of the municipal territory.[59] Efforts to create new parks and recreational areas had already stretched back to late in the previous century. By 1959, the city laid out a system of narrow, radial "green axes" along the Leine River from north to south, through Oststadt and Geismar to the east and through Grone to the west. Over the next decades extensive new sports and garden facilities in places like the Kiessee shores preserved and expanded these axes. Göttingen budgets in the 1990s showed even bigger expenditures per capita on parks than were made in either Freiburg or Münster. The Old Town, having already escaped destruction from Allied bombing, also obtained more protection through historic preservation than did the downtowns of most other German cities. As early as 1968, a local ordinance established restrictions of this sort for an array of buildings. Over the 1970s, local antidevelopment movements won further limitations on the expansion of commercial services in the downtown, on the construction of access roads and parking garages there

[57] *Göttinger Tageblatt*, October 17–18, 1987, p. 1.
[58] Göttingen City Planning Administration, *Grün in Göttingen*, p. 5.
[59] Göttingen City Planning Administration, *Göttingen 2000*, p. 32.

and on alterations to historic buildings. By the time of the final renewal project, begun in 1978, gentrification had assumed the restorative, privately sponsored form that predominated in Münster. Although Göttingen's bicycle paths, pedestrian zones, public transit and 30-kilometer speed limits remained somewhat less extensive than their counterparts in cities like Freiburg and Münster, the Red-Green coalition and its predecessors had also worked to expand local policies in these areas.[60]

More than in Freiburg or Münster, however, local contestation and protective measures imposed growing constraints on developmental policies in Göttingen. In the early 1960s, as new University and University Hospital facilities and a new Max-Planck Institute for Biochemistry extended the urbanized area of the city to the north, local officials mobilized around plans to build the city into an *Oberzentrum* for the surrounding region. Alongside new neighborhoods at Holtenser Berg and Grone, the city surrounded the new research and educational facilities with additional housing, with a shopping center in Weende and with a four-lane connector (A 388) to the A 7 autobahn. The 1965 Comprehensive Plan and a 1970 Plan for the Old Town also set out programs of construction that included a ring road around the inner area, new parking facilities for the downtown, new department stores and gentrification of housing as well as pedestrian zones and historical protections in the Old Town.[61]

Over the next decade, neighborhood opposition, local antidevelopment movements, squatting by students and ultimately skepticism in the local council itself brought growing modifications to these plans. In 1974 a revised inner-city plan drastically scaled back the parking garages and commercial space for the Old Town; as actually implemented, this plan would make even more modest changes.[62] After 1978, initiatives by the FDP and CDU under Vieten had failed to alter a general trend toward restricted conversion of land either for new commercial and shopping opportunities or for new housing. The market that developed for inner-city commerce proved too small to support major department stores like Hertie and contributed to a comparatively low tax base among cities in Lower Saxony;

[60] W. Theine, R. Losert, H. Mazur and R. M. Miller, *Verkehrliches Leitbild Göttingen: Bestand, Bewertung, Massnahmenvorschläge* (Hannover: Planungsgemeinschaft Dr. Ing. Walter Theine, 1994).

[61] Von Frieling, "Der Bau des Gehäuses," pp. 28–31.

[62] Hans-Dieter von Frieling, "Erneuerung oder 'Kahlschlagsanierung'? Der Umbau der Göttinger Innenstadt seit 1960," in Duwe, Gottschalk and Koerner, *Göttingen ohne Gänseliesesl*, pp. 132, 136.

demand for new housing drove local prices as high as in any similar sized city in the *Land*. Under the Red-Green coalition after 1991, new residents and service clienteles from the former East Germany added a further 100,000 new consumers to potential regional markets and aggravated demand for new housing.[63] Repeated studies that local planners commissioned up to the mid-1990s stressed how limited local developmental responses to this demand had so far been.[64]

Concerns about social and spatial equity surfaced repeatedly in local policy making, but often with ambiguous consequences. Lower Saxony, like Baden-Württemberg, provided less supralocal support for social housing than did North Rhine-Westphalia. Göttingen had employed those resources regularly in new housing developments built around the city but had not compensated as much as Freiburg had for the limits to supralocal resources. The new peripheral neighborhoods of the 1960s had included important components of social housing. Local opposition to urban renewal had precipitated increased proportions of social and other affordable housing to accommodate the students, foreigners and others who already lived in the Old Town.[65] But the overall proportion of social units stood at only 14 percent in 1987, and even the Red-Green coalition had failed to prevent this type of housing from falling to 8 percent of the total by 1996. Partly as a consequence, planning in Göttingen had gone somewhat less far toward alleviating disparities among neighborhoods than in the other German cities. Segregation persisted at levels that approached those of the more equilibrated French cities. The well-to-do neighborhoods of the Oststadt in the shadow of the Göttingen Forest retained their more exclusive social composition and even garnered more than an equal share of environmental amenities and protection from development. Local policies on behalf of the growing number of foreigners remained limited as well. A separate, elected council to represent these residents had existed since the 1970s but had secured little special attention from the majority for the needs of this group. Local planners under the Red-Green coalition

---

[63] Dr. Lademann and Partner, *Zentrale Standorte für den Einzelhandel* (Hamburg: GWH Dr. Lademann and Partner, 1994), p. 93.

[64] In addition to the *Göttingen 2000* report and those by Lademann and Partner and W. Theine (*supra*), see Institut für Entwicklungsplanung und Strukturforschung, *Wohnungsversorgung und Wohnungsbaubedarf in der Stadt Göttingen* (Hannover, 1994).

[65] Similar to Münster, Göttingen also appears to have undertaken few of the special initiatives for local immigrant minorities in areas like housing evident in Freiburg and Bielefeld.

212

pointed to foreigners as around half of the apartment seekers for whom the coalition sought to provide new housing.[66] The local administration continued to make several dozen apartments available annually for this and other disadvantaged groups. At the same time, officials acknowledged that they had found it "as good as no longer possible to take care of" the needs for affordable housing.

In Göttingen the pursuit of all three ends confronted not only limits to local finances but the constraint of scarce, expensive land. The *Land* government had influenced these efforts with resources and commands from above, but to a somewhat lesser extent than in North Rhine-Westphalia. In the absence of a stable majority coalition among the national parties or a sufficiently powerful mayor, local political conflicts and the absence of cooperation had often hampered local policy in all three areas. These conflicts had imposed especially strong constraints on local developmental measures. Despite these constraints of the late 1980s and early 1990s, the local government had continued to carry out policies analogous to those of the other German cities toward both environmental ends and social equity.

Among the German cities, similar local choices as well as supralocal constraints helped bring about the similarities in local outcomes. Even in developmental matters, where the local policy syntheses diverged the most, local policies in Freiburg remained limited in ways comparable to those in Bielefeld and Göttingen. Supralocal policies toward domains like housing and environmental protection imposed more uniform mandates. Supralocal regulation of developmental planning constrained local economic initiatives more. The system of local public finance assured more funding for equity and environmental protection and generated less of a fiscal imperative to pursue development. Even under these distinctive external conditions, the similarities grew partly from parallel local influences. The strong national civil service within local government, the common centralization of municipal administration under the local council and executive, the similarities in local party systems and the comparative infrequency of municipal elections maintained parallel conditions for local policy making in all four German settings. In each place, local antidevelopment movements in the 1970s and Red-Green council majorities by the 1980s or 1990s precipitated the buildup of measures to enhance environmental outcomes and address social equity.

[66] Göttingen, *Sozialwohnungsbericht* (Göttingen, 1996), pp. 1, 4.

Even in Münster, where the CDU and FDP had maintained a majority in the council until 1994, local policies had mostly followed a similar trajectory.

These broad similarities should not obscure the significant divergences among local syntheses, and different local choices contributed to these. By the late 1980s and early 1990s the combined local strategies in Freiburg and Münster encompassed significant elements in all three domains. In Bielefeld and Göttingen, where efforts to promote new development lagged, the local synthesis came closer to the Social-Ecological type. Partly because of financial constraints, local social and environmental measures there fell somewhat short of those in the two settings with the most growth. Especially for Freiburg, the benefits of location had helped to make the difference in local policy. But other advantages that both Freiburg and Münster had enjoyed also played significant roles in their comparative success. A sustained majoritarian coalition in Münster and a powerful mayor-led coalition in Freiburg had enabled more consistent pursuit of local syntheses despite local opposition. In both settings, despite the comparative equalization of German municipal finances, local prosperity had assured the government additional financial resources for policies and implementation in all three areas. Ideological contrasts between the stronger Left in Freiburg and the stronger Right in Münster made surprisingly little difference for the objectives or the success of these local efforts.

The French Central Cities: Divergent Syntheses, Different Results

None of the French central cities had maintained the range of environmental goods in most of the German cities, and fewer had addressed place-based disadvantages effectively. But outcomes among the French settings generally diverged more than among the German ones. Rennes had combined steady growth and comparative equity with considerable environmental amenities. Montpellier had retained less spatial equity but enjoyed more rapid growth. Nancy and Clermont-Ferrand had each fared less well in two of the three categories. Policies at supralocal levels played a diminishing role in these trajectories. Especially with the decentralization of the 1980s, local choices and dominant municipal coalitions proved decisive for many of the results. Despite the uniform French legal infrastructure for local government, local governing coalitions embedded their different strategies for pursuit of the three ends in divergent constellations of institutions.

For local leaders intent on building and maintaining dominant coalitions, such as Georges Frêche in Montpellier or Edmond Hervé in Rennes, the institutional infrastructure that had developed since the last years of the Fourth Republic in France offered major advantages. Beyond the opportunities for central-local intergovernmental entrepreneurship seen in the last chapter, the organization of politics and government at the local level itself favored those elites who could obtain political power. Electoral coalitions coalesced around a single list usually composed of candidates from more than one party (Table 4.3). The mayoral candidate headed this list, and if his or her slate won, would be elected by the council. To attain a majority of seats, a coalition needed only to obtain the highest vote total of any slate in a second electoral round. Once elected it could count not only on five years of secure tenure following each election but on a local government more unified than those in Germany under the local councils, a less established national civil service within the local bureaucracy and electoral mechanisms that made it easier to maintain a winning margin. Against the background of relatively similar political economies, these conditions alone enabled the leaders of a winning coalition considerable leverage over local policies. The fiscal reforms that accompanied decentralization, by making more of local revenues than in Germany dependent on locally determined taxes, offered stronger potential incentives to pursue growth. At the same time, discretionary grants from above and a modest program of financial equalization furnished additional resources for local governments to pursue various ends.

Rennes. Among the cities outside Germany, Rennes had by the early 1990s most clearly combined comparative territorial equity and environmental quality with steady growth. Policies of the Left coalition in power after 1977 decisively influenced these outcomes. But local choices under the Center-Right coalition of the first postwar decades laid much of the foundation.

The local institutions that evolved to carry out local strategies long predated the decentralization of the 1980s. World War II helped precipitate this early mobilization. With 58 percent of Rennes destroyed, local officials faced a need for reconstruction similar to that in most German

Table 4.3. *Composition of Local Councils in Central City, 1953–1996 (Mayors in Capital Letters; Periods of Left Control Shaded)*

Local Elections	Clermont-Ferrand	Montpellier	Nancy	Rennes
1953	MONTPIED (SFIO, rad. soc.) (16); PC (8); RPF (3); RGR (2); indep., MRP (8)	ZACARELLI (PC) (9); SFIO (4); indep. left (6); rad. soc. (7); MRP (3); indep. (8)	PINCHARD (PC) (6); SFIO (4); RFR-UDSR (3); mod., indep. (11); RPF (11); Apol. (4)	FRÉVILLE (PC) (8); SFIO (6); MRP (10); indep., UNR (13)
1959	MONTPIED (SFIO, rad. soc.) (36)	DELBEZ (indep., Rad., UNR, MRP (36); PC (1))	WEBER (PC) (6); SFIO (3); MRP (2); Rad. (2); indep. (14); UNR (8); no label (2)	FRÉVILLE (MRP, others) (37)
1965	MONTPIED (SFIO, cent. l., no label) (37)	F. DELMAS (indep., MRP, UNR, Rep.) (37)	WEBER (indep. rep., UNR, div. l., MRP) (37)	FRÉVILLE (MRP, others) (37)
1971	MONTPIED (PS, div. l., rad.) (37)	F. DELMAS (CDP, UDR, Dem. Center, rad. indep., div. l.) (37)	M. MARTIN (mod., div. l., PS, cent. opp., rad.) (37)	FRÉVILLE (Dem. Center, UDR, indep. soc., Rad., indep. rep.) (37)
1977	R. QUILLIOT (PS, PC, MRG, div. l.) (43)	G. FRÊCHE (22 PS, 13 PC, 5 rad. l., 2 PSU, 1 gaull. l.)	COULAIS (mod., UDF, UDF-CDS, RPR, UDF-PR) (41)	E. HERVÉ (24 PS, 12 PC, 4 rad. l, 2 UDB, 1 UJP (?))
1983	R. QUILLIOT (PS, PC, div. l., MRG, Ecols) (44)	G. FRÊCHE (PS, PC, div. l., MRG, PSU) (45); Right (RPR, UDR-PR, CNI, UDF-rad.) (14)	A. ROSSINOT (UDF, div. rt., RPR, CNIP, no label) (45); Left (PS, PC) (7); div. rt. (1)	E. HERVÉ (PS, PC, MRG, PSU, UDB, div. l.) (45); Right (RPR, UDF-CDS, UDF-PR, div. rt., UDF-rad.) (14)
1989	R. QUILLIOT (PS, PC, Maj. p., MRG) (45); Right (UDF, RPR) (8)	G. FRÊCHE (PS, PC, div. l., MRG, PSU, AD) (46); Right (div. rt., UDF, RPR) (8); Nat. Front (3); Greens (2)	A. ROSSINOT (div. rt., RPR, UDF-rad., UDF-PR, UDF-CDS, CNI) (43); PS (5); Greens (3); Nat. Front (2)	E. HERVÉ (PS, PC, div. l., MRG, UDB, other) (46); Right (UDF-CDS, RPR, UDF-PR, div. rt.) (8); Greens (4); Nat. Front (1)
1995	R. QUILLIOT (PS, PC, div. l., Ecols., LCR, extr. l.) (42); Right (div. rt., UDF, RPR) (13)	G. FRÊCHE (PS, PC, div. l., ref. PC, Ecol., MDC) (48); Right (UDF, RPR, div. rt.) (10); Nat. Front (3)	A. ROSSINOT (UDR-rad.) (39); Left (PS, PC) (7); Div. (7)	E. HERVÉ (PS, PC, Ecols, AREV) (47); Right (12)

Apol.: Apolitical; AD: Association of Democrats; AREV: Red-Green Alternative; CDP: Center Democracy and Progress; CDS: Social Democratic Center; Ecols.: Ecologists (besides Greens); CNI(P): National Center of Independants and Peasants; League of Revolutionary Communism; MDC: Movement of Citizens; MRG: Left Radicals; MRP: Popular Radical Movement; PC: Communists; PS: Socialist party; PSU: Unified Socialist party; RGR: *Rassemblement* of the Republican Left; RPF: *Rassemblement* of the French People; RPR: *Rassemblement* for the Republic; SFIO: (Socialists); UCF-PR: Republican party; UDB: Union for Breton Democracy; UDF: Union for French Democracy; UDF-CDS: Center for Social Democracy; UDR: Democratic Union for the Republic; UNR: Union for a New Republic.

Source: *Le Monde* election listings.

cities.[67] In advance of most similar French cities, local officials had created semipublic development companies in the 1950s (see Ch. 5) and a public planning agency for the metropolitan region (AUDIAR) in 1970. From 1953 to 1977, a coalition under Mayor Henri Fréville presided over policies that took on an increasingly Upscale orientation. At first allied with the local Socialists, Fréville shifted increasingly toward the Center and in his last term during the 1970s toward the Right.[68] After 1977, building on the support of growing local constituencies among postindustrial service workers and students, the Left coalition under Edmond Hervé dominated the local government. During these years, the government continued to extend local developmental policies, but it also stressed social equity and, increasingly, the quality of the local environment. In doing so, the Hervé administration built not only on the new politico-administrative environment of decentralization but also on tendencies that had already distinguished the Fréville government from conservative counterparts in other French cities. As Le Galès notes,[69] Hervé and his allies continued to rely on the same social milieus of progressive Catholic networks and civil servants as the dominant coalition of the previous period.

Under Fréville local policies largely maintained the exclusive developmental focus of a growth coalition. Rennes had emerged as a regional capital, had acquired massive additions to its universities and *grandes écoles*, and from the 1950s into the 1960s had attracted Citröen, Kodak, SGS-Fairchild and other major manufacturers. Local officials often played an active role in these efforts, and, at the same time, they assisted the national and parapublic actors in the city in an extensive program of new housing, physical infrastructure and ultimately commercial construction. From 1958, the "Directive Urban Plan" prepared for the local council by the Parisian architect Louis Arretche guided these efforts;[70] the Comprehensive Plan approved in 1975 consolidated them. In the new zones of

---

[67] Alain Bineau, "La maîtrise publique du developement urbain rennais," in Alain Guengant, (ed.), *Les nouveaux coûts d'urbanisation* (Rennes: Agence d'Urbanisme et de Développement Intercommunal de l'Agglomération Rennaise [AUDIAR], 1989), p. 62. For accounts of planning and politics since the postwar period, see also Louise Blin and Jeanne Labbe, *Le District de Rennes: Un territoire des hommes* (Rennes: CRDP de Bretagne, 1993); Le Galès, *Politique Urbaine et Développement Local*; District of Rennes, *Politique foncière du District de Rennes* (Rennes, 1993); District of Rennes, *Schéma Directeur* (Rennes, 1994); Rennes, *Plan d'occupation des sols: Rapport de présentation* (Rennes, 1976, 1989, 1994).

[68] Le Galès, *Politique Urbaine et Développement Local*, p. 160.

[69] Ibid., pp. 193–194.

[70] Bineau, "La maîtrise publique," p. 64.

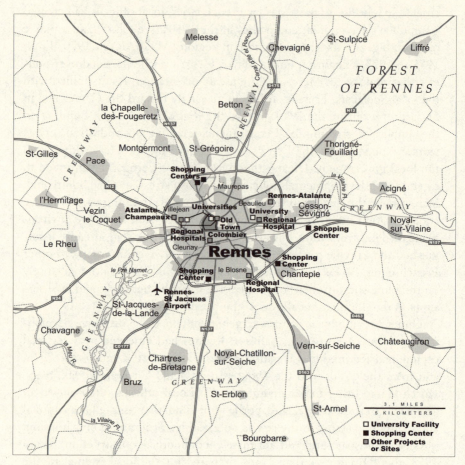

Figure 4.7 Rennes

Beaulieu to the east of the Old Town and Villejean to the west, new campuses housed the extensions to the university and the new state and regional administration. In other new urban neighborhoods, such as Maurepas and Le Blosne, massive planning districts or "priority zones for urbanization" (ZUPs) provided sites for the new housing units that appeared at a rate of around 3,000 a year between 1954 and 1970. A network of concentric ring roads within the central city and the beginnings of a four-lane autoroute around it redirected local traffic. In addition to new shopping centers along this route to the north and the south, and renovations in the Old Town, Arretche planned and the local para-public company began to construct a massive commercial and office center at Colombier on the site of a former army barracks.[71] After 1970, the creation of a metropolitan district of Rennes and AUDIAR expanded these initiatives into a number of surrounding communes.

The Left coalition of Hervé entered office after the most intensive growth had given way to moderate expansion. In the 1980s and 1990s, Hervé and his allies faced declining supralocal revenues but expanding legal tools for development. Drawing on the more circumscribed agenda for future development already in the Comprehensive Plan of 1975, as well as on a campaign based partly on critiques of strategies since the 1960s, the new administration qualified but maintained the previous emphasis on growth. Although AUDIAR and local officials continued to promote construction of new housing and commercial facilities, these efforts shifted increasingly to projects in the surrounding towns of the district of Rennes. A new technology park in Rennes-Atalante drew on proximity to the university in Beaulieu to attract public and private research facilities. This project proved so successful that in the 1990s the city added an extension to the Atalante site on the Villejean campus. By 1995 the four-lane autoroute had been extended around the entire circumference of the city. In the urban center, planners scaled back the Colombier project from three towers to one but carried out plans to establish the mall there as a major new center for shopping and other commercial activities. Throughout the downtown, new housing increasingly filled the gaps left between the planned zones of the 1960s.

The shift from Right to Left in 1977 might have been expected to affect the attention local policy makers paid to social equity even more than to developmental policy. Even up to 1977 Rennes had secured comparatively high levels of publicly subsidized housing among the four French cities. At the same time, local participants in planning at Rennes, including Fréville himself, had already worked against the propensities of national housing officials in the Gaullist era to sponsor smaller, homogenous, collective housing in the city.[72] The earliest postwar public housing projects in Cleunay and Maurepas reflected the high-rise, islolated manner of construction that would typify French housing estates. But by the late 1960s, especially in the massive ZUP at Le Blosne, lower-density settlement, mixtures among different types of public subsidies and higher levels of

[71] Ibid., pp. 67–68.   [72] Ibid., p. 69.

neighborhood amenities predominated. Despite the intensification of commercial construction and gentrification in the downtown, the attractiveness of the housing estates helped forestall growing concentrations of the disadvantaged in the ZUPs.

Under Hervé the city government took advantage of these conditions to elaborate a more extensive social agenda. Intensifying its efforts to capitalize on diminishing subsidies for housing, the coalition mandated that one-third of the new housing in the Colombier would now have to be of this type. In other, smaller construction projects around the city, planners also mixed subsidized housing with other forms. Drawing on national resources, local initiatives renovated neighborhoods like Cleunay and Maurepas and spread amenities like sports and cultural facilities around the city. Other initiatives sought to provide housing for students and seniors. By the mid-1990s, with the support of AUDIAR and the district, local efforts to support housing and other social initiatives took place largely at the metropolitan level. The district had almost matched the overall levels of support that the city itself provided for metropolitan programs to build publicly subsidized housing.[73] Programs funded at this level, often with assistance from the national government, addressed needs of gypsies and other migrants, students, seniors and the most disadvantaged families.[74]

The environmental and preservationist policies of the 1990s had emerged through efforts under both coalitions. If the Fréville administration had stressed development over ecological concerns, it still left legacies that would enable comparatively effective policies under Hervé. The national government had approved protections for a historic district in the Old Town in 1966, and even the 1958 plan had envisioned protection against high-density development in the old center. The more compact development that the plan had prescribed helped limit the loss of open space, and the intercommunal *Schéma Directeur* of 1974 for the district also set out a program of development for the wider metropolitan area that included protection for agricultural land and several green axes. But it was only under Hervé that environmental concerns, as one element in the local "quality of life," emerged as a distinct, important objective in local policy. In the 1990s, more city budget funds went to land use administration and

---

[73] *Programme Local de l'Habitat: Diagnostic* (Rennes: District of Rennes, 1994), p. 36.
[74] District of Rennes, *La Politique Locale de l'Habitat de l'agglomération rennaise* (Rennes, 1995).

enforcement than were expended in any other French city.[75] Although urbanization had grown to eliminate all farmland within the city boundaries by the 1990s, a program of reforestation raised the proportion of wooded land. Parks emerged as a major component of local efforts to enhance the quality of life. By the 1990s expenditures in this area surpassed not only their levels in the other French cities but also in several of the German cities.[76] Downtown, the Rennes government expanded the pedestrian zones of the Old Town. In the early 1990s, alongside an already extensive bus service, local officials also secured national funds for the first new trolley or "VAL" line from the northwest corner of the city through the center to Le Blosne in the south. At the district level, a "Landscape Plan" in 1994 consolidated an extensive and increasingly effective system of land use controls and transportation schemes for much of the wider metropolitan area.[77]

Here, as in the other domains, the coalition under Hervé had altered the emphases of its Center-Right predecessor at the same time as it built on previous efforts. The environmental policies as well as their consequences remained less extensive than in most of the German cities. Still, the combined strategies pursued under Hervé by the early 1990s encompassed significant efforts in all three domains. Like Freiburg and Münster, Rennes benefitted from the expanding region that surrounded it and from the fiscal benefits of comparative local prosperity. But despite the constant presence of the national government in the policy making of Rennes, the central city government had elaborated and carried out distinctive local strategies of its own. Localized initiatives played an increasingly decisive role in the overall outputs of even supralocal policy.

Montpellier. The stronger growth and considerable environmental amenities within Montpellier went along with higher levels of sociospatial exclusion. As in Rennes, the decisions of the dominant local electoral coalitions played an increasing role in these outcomes. A remarkably similar

---

[75] Rennes spent $44 per person on planning and implementation, equivalent to levels in Freiburg and Bielefeld but compared with no more than $16 in the other French cities. Personnel in this area per resident, at 8 per 10,000 people, also exceeded the level in other French and American cities besides Nancy.

[76] Rennes spent $84 per resident in this area, more than double the level in the other French cities and higher that in Bielefeld or Münster.

[77] District of Rennes, *Schéma Directeur.*

progression of coalitions to that in the other French city had in this instance elaborated more consistently Upscale strategies.

Local policy making had emerged later in Montpellier. Proposed city plans in the 1920s and later under the Vichy government had never reached the stage of implementation,[78] and no wartime destruction forced major choices about reconstruction. Only after 1960, when a mass influx to the city of refugees from the former Algerian colony as well as the initiatives of the central state gave rise to rapid growth, did the elements of local planning and related policies clearly emerge. From 1959 to 1977, Mayor François Delmas dominated local politics at the head of a Center-Right coalition. Initially nonpartisan, Delmas eventually sided with the national Gaullist party and served as a minister in the Pompidou government. In 1977, as Edmond Hervé came to power in Rennes, the Socialist Georges Frêche, in an alliance with Communists and Radicals, wrested municipal control from Delmas. Like Hervé, Frêche drew on both discontent among established local elites with the development policies of the previous administration and the support of the expanding postindustrial service workers and students. Over the next twenty years, Frêche and his coalition consolidated a dominant role in an increasingly elaborate system of local policies.

Even more than they did in Rennes, developmental policies stood at the center of this system in Montpellier. The Delmas administration and its predecessors had played a significant role in the measures that brought rapid growth to Montpellier up to the mid-1970s. At the beginning of that decade local officials had proclaimed "the blue ribbon for development" as a municipal slogan and already held out a goal to make the city into a regional metropole analogous to Toulouse or Marseille.[79] Without an overarching scheme like the one in Rennes to guide local choices, however, Montpellier's efforts toward this goal remained mostly piecemeal reactions

[78] Service Regional de l'Inventaire de Languedoc-Roussillon, G. Fabre, ed,. *Montpellier 985/1985: Paysages d'Architectures* (Anduze: AZ Offset, 1985), p. 76. On the history of planning and politics in Montpellier, see also Roger Brunet, Lóic Grasland, J. Pierre Garnier, Robert Ferras and J. Paul Volle (eds.), *Montpellier Europole* (Montpellier: RECLUS, 1988); Gérard Cholvy (ed.), *Histoire de Montpellier* (Toulouse: Éditions Privat, 1989); André Donzel, "Montpellier," in Alan Harding, Jon Dawson, Richard Evans and Michael Parkinson (eds.), *European Cities Towards 2000* (Manchester: Manchester University Press, 1994), pp. 144–160; Georges Frêche, *La France Ligotée* (Paris: Pierre Belfond, 1993); Jerome Milch, "Paris Is Not France" (Ph.D. diss., Massachusetts Institute of Technology, 1973); Montpellier, *Révision du Plan d'Occupation des Sols de Montpellier* (1990).
[79] Milch, "Paris Is Not France," p. 392.

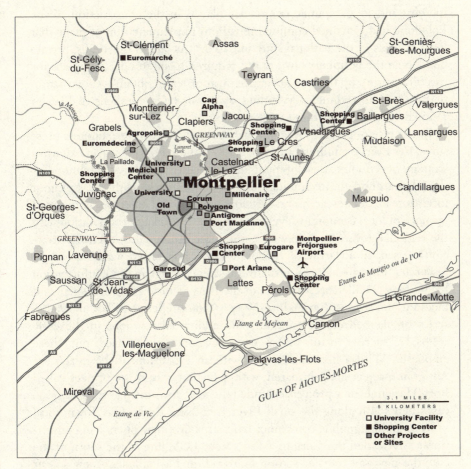

Figure 4.8   Montpellier

to initiatives from outside. The city had helped attract IBM and other firms through preparation of new industrial and commercial zones. It had participated in the choice to locate the new university expansion and the regional medical center on campuses to the north of the center. It had helped bring about the new peripheral housing estate at La Paillade. It had largely carried out the massive downtown commercial and administrative complex of the Polygone on an abandoned military training ground next to the Old Town. An intercommunal association formed in 1965 coordinated economic development in the periphery. But the role of local officials in local projects had remained a largely passive one. Even the part

223

the city and its parapublic companies played in the construction of the Polygone had remained confined mostly to implementation of plans that local officials of the national state initiated.[80] As late as the 1970s, private builders in the periphery "[were] not required to submit detailed plans for careful scrutiny by the city government in order to obtain a construction permit."[81] The rudimentary zoning of the first Comprehensive Plan in 1975 did little to alter these tendencies.

In the face of greater local authority as well as growing economic pressures, the Frêche administration elaborated these efforts into an extensive strategy of economic development and new construction. A "Technopole" centered around the technology and industrial parks with the strongest local domains of research and development activity emerged as the centerpiece of local economic development policy. Through cooperation with the regional government as well as the intercommunal district, the strategy focused on an array of corporate parks concerned with biomedical research ("Euromédicine"), agricultural science ("Agropolis"), information technology ("Millénaire," the site of the IBM facility) and other small and medium enterprises. Ratified in the new Comprehensive Plan of 1984, a series of planned districts (ZACs) and additional revisions in the early 1990s, a succession of major new developments carried out these emphases. With a first phase, then with an expansion of the mixed-use Antigone project and ultimately with a further mixed-use project called Port-Marianne, new projects extended the new downtown at the Polygone east, then south along the small River Lez. Next to the Old Town, local officials and parapublic companies built a massive new opera and convention center called the Corum; along a new TGV line in the south of the city, the new rail transfer station Garosud; in La Paillade, a new soccer stadium. Renovation and rehabilitation spread throughout the city. Local projects attracted prestigious architects like Claude Vasconi, Ricardo Bofill and Richard Meier to the city. Additions to the hospitals, the universities, the *grandes écoles*, the airport and TGV service continued to foster growth in the local economy. Frêche and other local representatives lobbied aggressively and often successfully for regional, national and European support for these initiatives.

---

[80] Françoise Hudon-Moreau, "La Zone d'amenagement concerte du polygone a Montpellier: Conception – programme – realisation" (Ph.D. diss., Université Paul Valery de Montpellier, 1981).

[81] Milch, "Paris Is Not France," p. 398.

Environmental measures increasingly emerged with a place alongside development. In Montpellier, with no regional dimension like the one around Rennes, and lower commitments of resources to parks or land use controls, these policies had remained somewhat less effective. Under Delmas, the government had secured the preservationist architectural protections of the Safeguarded Sector in 1967[82] and had added new parks of some 7 hectares to an inherited network of 121 hectares.[83] Under Frêche, the municipality expanded environmental measures further. Despite considerably lower expenditures than in Rennes or the German cities for parks as well as for regulatory enforcement and land use administration,[84] the new measures brought about significant environmental improvements. Zoning restrictions in the plan of 1984 preserved much of local agricultural land. Although the 1990 revision cut these protections, other new zones, municipal purchases and expansions to the park system enabled the city to retain a small amount of forestland. As the local government created a total of 121 hectares of additional parkland in over fifty sites, the Comprehensive Plan set out "green corridors" along the Lez to the east and the Mosson to the west.[85] In the Old Town, the Frêche administration quadrupled the length of pedestrian zones over the 1980s and early 1990s to a total just short of that in Göttingen. Although efforts to build bicycle paths remained limited, the city cooperated with the bus company under control of the district to extend service and even build special bus lanes in the downtown. With assistance from supralocal sources, a new tramway was built in the late 1990s across the city, providing regular service from La Paillade and the northwest through the central rail station to Millénaire.

The Frêche administration faced steeper odds in its efforts to reverse the comparatively stark social disparities in Montpellier's previous development. Under Delmas and his predecessors, the city had not only built considerably fewer subsidized housing units than under Fréville in Rennes, but it had concentrated the subsidized housing in exclusive areas of the urban periphery to the south and west. The single "new town" on the ZUP of La Paillade, on a former aristocrat's estate totally isolated from the downtown, housed closed to half of all subsidized-housing units built up

---

[82] Cholvy, *Histoire de Montpellier*, p. 390.   [83] Montpellier, *Révision*, p. 48.

[84] In the 1990s the city budget recorded less than $5 per person for planning administration and less than $17 per person for parks and natural protection.

[85] Montpellier, *Révision*, pp. 48–49, 72–78.

to 1978. These patterns of development left a clear divide between the areas of industrial facilities and housing estates to the south and west and the rest of the city to the north and east.[86] With its low priorities for social and cultural funding, the Delmas administration had aggravated the difficulties of living in disadvantaged areas.[87] The Frêche coalition made highly publicized efforts to redress these circumstances. In housing itself, the city added 2,800 subsidized units from 1975 to 1982 for a total of 8,700.[88] Fully 2,400 of the new units were built outside of La Paillade. Antigone stood at the center of these efforts. A counterpoint to the new offices and mall of the Polygone, this new mixed-use development brought 300 subsidized housing units to the heart of the new eastern downtown. In La Paillade, in the southern neighborhoods of subsidized housing and in the remaining working-class areas of the Old Town, local officials drew on national funds to carry out renovations and rehabilitation. Frêche himself touted municipal initiatives to disperse a concentration of foreigners in one of the cités of La Paillade, to house French nationals of Arab heritage and to provide special language and educational services for the minority children of La Paillade under a national program.[89] At the same time, programs like new local cultural centers or "Houses for All" (*Maisons de tous*) scattered funding and facilities for sports and associative activities throughout the city, and improvements in public transit enhanced access to the center.

The difficulties that confronted these efforts stemmed not only from the legacies of the Delmas coalition but also from contradictions in the policy of the new administration. Whatever the initial importance Frêche save redressing social disparities, he ultimately aimed more "to conjugate in the present tense economic success and the quality of life."[90] With the Technopole, the Corum and even Antigone, appeals to high-tech researchers, executives, entrepreneurs and tourists took precedence. Highly publicized but limited gestures had failed to prevent the growing concentrations of foreigners and poor people outside the center. Rents for even the subsidized units the city administered in Antigone remained at significantly higher levels than in La Paillade,[91] and both the second phase

---

[86] Roger Brunet, "Production et environnements d'une europole," in Roger Brunet, et al., *Montpellier Europole*, pp. 30–31.
[87] Milch, "Paris Is Not France," pp. 400–401.
[88] Montpellier, *Révision*, p. 29.   [89] Frêche, *La France Ligotée*, pp. 223, 227.
[90] Ibid., p. 212.
[91] At the end of the 1980s rents of the municipal housing company averaged 9.12 francs per

of that project and the subsequent development at Port-Marianne eliminated the emphasis on social units. Elsewhere in the downtown, as in the neighborhood of Saint Ursule, renovation forced gentrification and the exodus of minorities and the unemployed.[92] Despite the publicity that the city gave its efforts to address the needs of disadvantaged neighborhoods, local officials had declined to apply for supralocal support under the national program instituted in 1990 for this purpose.[93] Into the early 1990s, overall operating expenditures on social programs, education, public health and sports facilities continued to occupy less of the municipal budget than in any other French city and nearly ten percent less than in Rennes.[94] While the other French cities were spending from 15 to 21 percent more on these areas than on economic development, Montpellier was spending only 2 percent more.

The emphasis under Frêche on development and amenities for *cadres* and entrepreneurs largely undermined efforts to alleviate disparities among neighborhoods and even limited the extent of local environmental measures. At least into the early 1990s, the contradiction reinforced more an Upscale synthesis than a fully Comprehensive one. Locational advantages had made successful developmental policies even easier in Montpellier than in Rennes, and growth itself produced resources for new policies that offset the lower average income of the city. Tensions surrounding the larger populations of Muslims and North Africans than in Rennes may have helped foster more Upscale emphases, but choice among local officials proved crucial.

Nancy. In both of the other French central cities, more consistent majorities had dominated the local councils over the forty-five years of the postwar era. Local officials in both Nancy and Clermont-Ferrand wrestled with the declines that beset their cities over much of this period. In Nancy, Center-Right coalitions had at the same time helped produce environmental goods and neighborhood disparities like those of Montpellier.

---

square meter every month in La Paillade, but 11.68 in Antigone and other central units (Laboratoire Logement, *Observatoire de l'Habitat*, Édition 1990 [Nancy: Association Laboratoire Logement, 1990], p. 167).

[92] Gérard Gasselin, "Une opération d'amélioration de l'habitat: Le cas de Montpellier," *Bulletin de la Société Languedocienne de Géographie 14*(4) (1988): 421–453.

[93] *Midi Libre*, December 18, 1990, p. X7a.

[94] This calculation includes municipal expenditures in budget chapters 943 (education), 944 (social and educational works), 95 (social services), and 945 (sports and beaux arts). In

Both World War I and World War II had generally spared Nancy from serious damage. But as in Rennes and the German cities, planning had begun well before the emergence of national frameworks. As early as the German occupation in 1942–1943, local officials had marked out areas of the downtown for renewal and begun to buy up the land.[95] Even prior to receiving legal authority to issue binding Comprehensive Plans, local officials had drawn up a proposal in 1946, which was approved in 1954, designating goals for downtown development. In the 1950s the industrialist and engineer Raymond Pinchard and in the 1960s the *docteur* Pièrre Weber had presided over Center-Right coalitions that laid the foundations of local developmental policy. Pinchard, a technocrat who proclaimed his goal "to construct human happiness" (*construire le bonheur humaine*), took an early lead in the creation of institutions to carry out postwar planning. His efforts led to the first effective plan for the city in 1956, the establishment of an intercommunal district of twelve communes in 1959 and the institution of the parapublic development company SOLOREM (Société lorraine de l'économie mixte d'aménagement urbain) in 1960. The district would help to create a separate agency, the Agence de Développement et d'Urbanisme de l'Agglomération Nancienne (ADUAN), that furnished much of the technical expertise for planning in the city region.

By the time André Rossinot and his coalition took office in 1983, his administration could build on a long-standing tradition of support for the Center-Right among downtown businesspeople, local professionals and even many of the service workers who had switched to the Left in other French university towns. Only the centrist coalition that included several Socialists in 1970 and 1971 had broken the continuous electoral dominance of Center-Right slates.[96] The unusually narrow city limits of Nancy

---

Rennes and Clermont, the local government spent 25 percent in these categories as opposed to 9 percent and 4 percent for economic development (chapter 96). In Montpellier, the city spent 15 percent and 13 percent in the two categories. Even in Nancy, where the city spent 19 percent and 4 percent, respectively, more of local expenditures went into social service delivery. Per capita expenditures reflected similar disparities.

[95] René Taveneaux, *Histoire de Nancy* (Toulouse: Privat, 1990), pp. 467–468, 472. On politics and planning in Nancy, see also Agence de Développement et d'Urbanisme de l'Agglomération Nancienne (ADUAN), *Atlas de l'agglomération nancienne* (Laxou: Éditions de l'est, 1994); Gérald Cahen and René Louis, *Nancy* (Paris: Autrement, 1990); André Lefebvre, *Nancy et son Agglomération* (Nancy: n.p., 1995); Nancy, *Plan d'Occupation des Sols: Rapport de présentation* (Nancy, 1995); Jean Vartier, *Histoire de Nancy* (Paris: Mazarine, 1980).

[96] The centrist slate, taking the name "Nancy Capital," capitalized on disappointment over the complicity of municipal officials in the 1969 decision to make Metz rather than Nancy the site of the new regional capital.

228

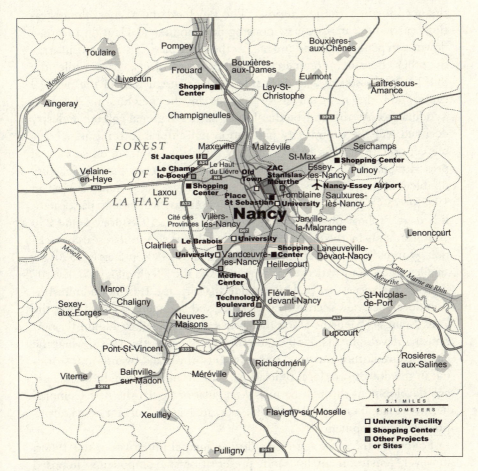

Figure 4.9 Nancy

enhanced this dominance. The downtown elites and businesspeople who had furnished regular neighborhood majorities opposed to the Left in Rennes and Montpellier made up a bigger proportion of the electorate here.

Beginning with Pinchard, successive coalitions took up new development as a constant theme. The first postwar plans had stressed the construction of new housing, the redevelopment of old manufacturing areas along the Meurthe and implantation of administrative offices and the need for new traffic arteries.[97] The Pinchard and Weber administrations carried out massive new housing development at Haut du Lièvre, a downtown pedestrian zone and mall at the Place St. Sebastien, and an array of other housing, commercial and office projects. Meanwhile the SOLOREM assumed a leading role in the construction of the medical center and the new university campus in the neighboring town of Vandoeuvre. At the end of the 1960s, as the regional mining industry declined and the central city population fell, efforts to bring new commerce, offices and research to the city intensified. Seizing on supralocal prescriptions embodied in the 1973 *Schéma Directeur*, the municipality doubled the rate of new office construction to 9,000 units a year in 1968–1975.[98] Outside the city, a "Technopole" or technology park established at Brabois on the Vandoeuvre campus in 1978 drew some 250 establishments by the mid-1990s in such fields as scientific research, technology transfer and other services.[99] In the late 1980s and early 1990s, as smaller technology parks at St. Jacques II and the "Technology Boulevard" built on the success of Brabois outside the city, the Rossinot administration developed new recreational facilities and commercial activities at the ZAC Stanislas-Meurthe along the river and continued to administer new housing developments of 500 and more units. Since the 1970s, when the city approved office and hotel towers twenty-three and twenty-four stories tall in the downtown, local officials had also frequently sought to encourage development through permissive regulation. Even the new Comprehensive Plan, first issued in 1986, operated as a "servant to vigorous property development."[100]

Following the most aggressive developmental initiatives of the 1960s, however, environmentalist and preservationist components imposed growing qualifications on these policies. In a tightly bounded, urbanized jurisdiction, the initial efforts along these lines focused on historic preservation. From the early 1970s several neighborhood associations and even members of the governing electoral coalition had raised protests against plans for urban redevelopment and artery construction in the downtown. Appeals to the minister of culture brought a halt to the tallest of the towers in the downtown and by 1976 had secured among the largest Safeguarded Sectors in France, covering 10 percent of the municipal territory. Although

---

[97] Taveneaux, *Histoire de Nancy*, p. 468.   [98] Ibid., p. 469.
[99] ADUAN, *Atlas*, pp. 60–61.   [100] Nancy, *Plan d'Occupation des Sols*, p. 46.

pedestrian zones in the city remained limited, subsequent planning increasingly incorporated preservationist and ecological concerns of local groups into schemes for development. A process of revisions to the Comprehensive Plan begun in 1989 institutionalized concerns to "safeguard, indeed reinforce the green fabric of the city," and to "better preserve or restore the coherence of the urban image."[101] Nancy had already constructed an assortment of new parks over the late 1970s and 1980s. The new "Green Plan" incorporated in the revision affirmed protections for existing parks and trees and committed the city to creating 40 additional hectares of green space.[102] City officials also looked increasingly to the district for measures to preserve forests, build bicycle paths and extend the bus system.

Even more than the analogous synthesis under the Left in Montpellier, this emerging combination of developmental and environmental policies retained an Upscale cast. Alongside aggressive downtown gentrification, the new housing of Le Haut du Lièvre brought a similar polarization as La Paillade. Claiming "territorial limits of the city" as a justification for the location, the Pinchard administration situated the immense, elongated blocks of 2,800 housing units on an elevated site at the northwest edge of its jurisdiction.[103] Distant and difficult to reach from the downtown, the estates began to harbor an increasingly unstable, disadvantaged population shortly after their completion in 1970. Subsequent construction of subsidized housing in the city had remained confined to small, scattered apartments, leaving many of the surrounding communes with larger shares of subsidized units.[104] At the same time, urban renewal in older downtown neighborhoods drove large numbers of minorities and poor residents to seek housing in Le Haut and other peripheral estates; developers of the Place St. Sebastien had even "expelled" or relocated residents from there to the commune of Jarville.[105] In the early 1980s, as the degradation of neighborhood conditions in Le Haut du Lièvre became unmistakable, the city launched improvements in conjunction with the national Commission Sociale de Développement des Quartiers. In addition to physical renovations, a neighborhood office coordinated the installation of a stronger

---

[101] Ibid., p. 5.   [102] Ibid., pp. 239–248.

[103] Taveneaux, *Histoire de Nancy*, p. 470.

[104] In 1990, for instance, public housing in Tomblaine comprised 26 percent of principal residences, and in Jarville 33 percent, but in Nancy only 17 percent.

[105] Vartier, *Histoire de Nancy*, p. 312.

police presence, the administration of financial aid to local residents, credits for meals, initiatives in local schools and a program of cultural activities.[106] As in Montpellier, the municipal parapublic housing company imposed limits on concentrations of foreigners and opened up housing space for students and others. Even these efforts remained limited in comparison with other cities. Local expenditures on education, sports and public health in the early 1990s remained only 19 percent of operating expenditures, or 6 percent less than in Rennes.

The policies that the Center-Right coalition of Rossinot and his predecessor carried out in Nancy came the closest among all these European cities to the neoliberal program of many American settings. An Upscale agenda explicitly embraced strategies that Frêche and his coalition in Montpellier had made limited, contradictory efforts to reverse. Gentrification had helped Nancy maintained the highest per capita income of the French cities and enabled the city to secure higher levels of environmental amenities than it otherwise would. The declining population and the narrow central city jurisdiction had fostered these strategies but had also placed fiscal and territorial constraints on how far the city could pursue them.

Clermont-Ferrand.　After 1980 the industrial city of Clermont-Ferrand had suffered the biggest losses in population and revenues of any of those studied. Even relative to other cities in the same country, environmental outcomes stood at lower levels than in the German manufacturing center of Bielefeld. Neighborhoods had polarized with postindustrial restructuring here, but up to the early 1990s this result remained more limited than in Montpellier or Nancy. A long-dominant Socialist coalition had contributed to this outcome with the strongest emphasis among the French cities on social equity. At the same time, the coalition had undertaken more limited developmental efforts and minimal environmental initiatives.

Although urban plans for Clermont-Ferrand had been issued both in the Napoleonic era and in 1924, such documents had made little difference for the city's patterns of development up to the 1950s.[107] Not only

---

[106] Michel Piotrkowski, "Le Haut-du-Lièvre: Un quartier à repenser," in Cahen and Louis, *Nancy*, pp. 104–111; Maurice Blanc and Monique Legrand, "La participation des habitants dans la rehabilitation des quartiers d'habitat social," in Dominique Colas (ed.), *L'État de droit* (Paris: Presses universitaires de France), pp. 89–110.

[107] A. G. Manry, *Histoire de Clermont-Ferrand* (Clermont-Ferrand: Mont-Louis, 1975), p. 365. Other sources on the politics and planning in Clermont-Ferrand include Christian

did World War II spare the city from destruction and the consequent need for reconstruction, but from the late nineteenth century through the first half of the twentieth, the heavy, paternalistic hand of Michelin had also dominated and even partly supplanted decision making in the city. For its workers, who furnished the main source of local population growth, the company constructed close to 8,000 new housing units as well as sports facilities, hospitals and schools. Building on properties that eventually grew to half of the municipal territory, the company gradually extended its "factory city" from the north of the Old Town to the old village center of Montferrand and the city limits.[108] Within the city government itself, the Left had dominated politics since the 1920s. Beginning with the installation of Gabriel Montpied as mayor following the Liberation of 1945, the Socialists dominated the Left majority. From 1971 onward, Roger Quilliot, a former mayoral adjoint who had also taught as a Camus scholar at the local university, replaced Montpied at the head of the mayoral coalition. Under Quilliot, a coalition of Socialists, Communists and radicals enjoyed comfortable electoral majorities in local elections up to 1995, when Valéry Giscard d'Estaing, the former president of the Republic, nearly won the second electoral round. Only an electoral alliance with the local Greens, who had won 6 percent of the vote in the initial round, enabled Quilliot to eke out a victory.

Asked about the existence of "municipal socialism," Quilliot frequently replied that he knew of Socialist mayors and nothing more.[109] Yet much like its counterpart in Bielefeld, the Socialist coalition in Clermont-Ferrand had long pursued the classic "municipal socialist" goals of social service delivery. Although the city government had built small amounts of housing as early as the interwar period, it assumed growing responsibilities in this area after the formation of the first local public housing company in 1953. Bolstered through the efforts of Quilliot as a senator and ultimately as the head of the national association of public housing

Lamy and Jean-Pierre Fornaro, *Michelin-ville: Le logement ouvrier de l'entreprise Michelin, 1911–1987* (Nonetter: Éditions Créer, 1990); Christophe Beslay, Philippe Bernard and Évelyne Cavet, "Clermont-Ferrand – La difficile transition d'une régulation privée à une régulation institutionelle" (Université de Toulouse le Mirail, 1994); Clermont-Ferrand, *Clermont-Ferrand en chiffres 1994* (Clermont-Ferrand, 1994); Roger Quilliot, *Misères et grandeur des maires de France* (Paris: Albin Michel, 1997); Syndicat Intercommunal d'Étude et de Programmation de l'Agglomération Clermontoise (SIEPAC), *Schéma Directeur de l'Agglomération Clermontoise* (Clermont-Ferrand, 1994).

[108] Lamy and Fornaro, *Michelin-ville*, pp. 45–52.
[109] Quillliot, *Misères et grandeur*, p. 172.

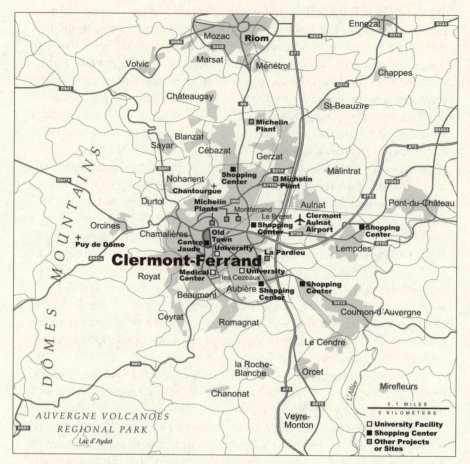

Figure 4.10 Clermont-Ferrand

companies,[110] Clermont-Ferrand had secured the highest proportion of social housing units in any of the French cities. Although high-rise developments in ZUPs like Neyrat, Flamina and La Gauthiè contained up to 15,000 housing units in a single neighborhood, both the city government and Michelin had also scattered developments around the south and center as well as to the north of the city. Local officials not only had lobbied to reduce the size of ZUPs but also had contributed municipal resources to

[110] Ibid., p. 55.

234

provide an array of meeting facilities, cultural centers, sports facilities and shopping opportunities in the new neighborhoods.[111] Into the 1990s, as restructuring precipitated levels of unemployment as high as 24 percent and concentrations of foreigners up to 28 percent in these developments,[112] local officials continued to work to minimize the disadvantages of the worst-off neighborhoods. A panoply of programs assisted residents of the most depressed neighborhoods and helped disadvantaged people in search of housing.[113] The Communal Center for Social Action (CCAS) supplemented the array of state financial aids for the elderly, the poor, and youth with local sociocultural centers, homeless shelters and a larger proportion of municipal expenditures. Under a special contract between local and supralocal governments, the CCAS also addressed the needs of local foreigners for literacy, education, employment and cultural opportunities. Overall, municipal expenditures in an array of categories for education, sports, social services and public health took up 25 percent of operating expenses in the 1990s, virtually the same proportion as in Rennes.

From the 1950s, local developmental policies grew alongside these efforts. Beginning in the 1960s, along with the new housing, the local government established new industrial zones at Brezet near the Michelin factories. In the 1970s it commenced urban renewal and rehabilitation in the old center with the major regional mall of the Centre Jaude. Under the decentralization of the 1980s the government initiated an extension of Brezet and a new technology park at La Pardieu. In the early 1990s, with the collapse of employment as Michelin phased out production in the city, Quilliot had helped secure such additional projects as a number of new research institutes, new university facilities, a new TGV station, an extension of the east-west autoroute through the city and national planning designations that enabled the city to receive EU funds for regional economic reconversion. An intercommunal organization emerged to coordinate joint metropolitan efforts to promote cooperation. Although the comparatively low tax rates in the city might be seen as a further spur to development,[114] local officials continued to voice complaints about developmental opportunities. Quilliot claimed that he had had to offer his resignation to then-Prime

---

[111] Ibid., pp. 110–111.   [112] SIEPAC, *Schéma Directeur*, p. 49.

[113] Clermont-Ferrand, *Clermont-Ferrand*, pp. 118–121.

[114] Statistics compiled by the city showed that its rates for all four of the main local taxes ranked below average in a sample of 23 larger cities that did not share taxes through intercommunal arrangements (ibid., pp. 101–104).

Minister Edith Cresson to win the city more favorable planning designations and a greater part in national programs,[115] and he repeatedly lamented the fiscal constraints and declining national subsidies that his city faced.

Local reluctance to promote development had also done its share to undermine this type of policy. Early in the postwar period, the expansion of Michelin and the university and hospital had helped bring growth to the city without appreciable local efforts. In the regional planning of the 1970s, Quilliot and other local members of the commission of elected officials decried the "forced march of construction" decision of territorial administrators to expand the metropolitan area to a size of 500,000 residents.[116] Also, unlike their colleagues in Rennes and other cities, Clermont-Ferrand's land use administrators had frequently taken a passive stance toward supralocal decisions. Quilliot noted how the local bureaucrats often "hid behind the opinions of the Infrastructure Ministry, or feared the lash of the Ministry's sanctions even when its competencies were not concerned."[117] In the mid-1990s, the total local budget for matters related to planning and local development remained only two-thirds the level in Nancy and a small fraction of the levels in the other cities. In the Old Town, the exception of the Centre Jaude highlighted a general contrast with the more ambitious downtown reconstructions of the other French cities. Local officials chose comparatively modest rehabilitation over either extensive renewal or an expansion of the downtown. Nor did the local government undertake the extensive initiatives under way in cities like Montpellier and Rennes to foster new businesses. Despite a whirl of associational efforts to bring new high-tech jobs, the city had filled its technology park at La Pardieu more with businesses providing traditional services and production than with truly high-tech enterprises.

If the fiscal strains on Clermont-Ferrand detracted from funds to pursue any of the three objectives, environmental policy suffered the most disproportionate effects. In his 1997 memoirs Quilliot placed little emphasis on policy in this area, noting only that his 1995 coalition with the Greens had "integrated the preoccupations of theirs that appeared to us perfectly valid."[118] Up to that time, zoning and other protections had done little to preserve land from development. From 1979 to 1988, agricultural land fell from 48 percent to 15 percent of the land area. Figures from the 1990s

---

[115] Quilliot, *Misères et grandeur*, pp. 206–207.
[116] Ibid., p. 111.   [117] Ibid., p. 91.   [118] Ibid., pp. 133–134.

suggest that the lack of protections stemmed at least partly from lower commitments to staffing offices concerned with planning, regulation and administration of land use. Both overall and in matters of enforcement, fewer local officials worked in these areas in Clermont-Ferrand than in any other French city.[119] Although the portion of land owned by Michelin had dropped from a half to only a fifth, the 8 percent of land in possession of the city itself remained two percent less than in the other French cities. Partly as a result, Clermont-Ferrand had maintained much less extensive parks than the similarly large cities of Montpellier and Rennes.[120] The city had devoted comparatively high per capita expenditures to parks, had expanded pedestrian zones in the Old Town, had supported an active metropolitan bus system and in the late 1990s had briefly obtained funding to build a local tramway similar to the one in Montpellier. But the Greens had emerged in 1995 as part of a challenge to a Left coalition that placed environmental ends after social and often economic ones.

The lack of prosperity limited the extent that the local government under Quilliot could pursue any of the three ends. With initiatives to promote new development that even in the 1990s remained more limited than in the other French cities, the Socialist coalition reaffirmed its preferences for service delivery among the alternatives it faced. Despite the location of the city in the most appealing urban settings in France, environmental objectives also came late and in limited fashion.

In contrast with the relative similarity of the policies that evolved in German central cities, the French infrastructures of local government and politics fostered more divergent local choices. In each city longtime coalitions had held onto power and used their position in local government to carry out more distinctive local syntheses of policy. More than with the bureaucracy of the German cities, in France centralization within the local government under the mayor facilitated this control. Unlike the proportional representation of the German cities, majoritarian electoral rules and a politics of majority electoral coalitions reinforced it. Since the early

---

[119] Clermont-Ferrand had staffed these offices at rates of 2.57 persons per 10,000 residents, compared to 2.65 in Montpellier and over 8 per 10,000 in the other cities; 9.5 per 100,000 residents worked in enforcement, compared with 12.0 in Montpellier and 16.14 in Nancy.

[120] Each resident in Clermont-Ferrand corresponded to .48 square centimeters of parkland, compared to 1.57 in Montpellier and 3.79 in Rennes, but only .18 in the much smaller city of Nancy.

1970s, the coalitions in Rennes drew on these conditions to build the most comprehensive strategies. Under the control of coalitions with opposed party identifications, the local governments of Montpellier and Nancy in the 1980s and early 1990s had pursued Upscale syntheses. The governing coalition of Clermont-Ferrand had long maintained the consistent social emphases of the Service Delivery strategy.

The dominant parties of the central city only partly account for these differences in strategy. In Clermont-Ferrand since 1945 and in Rennes after 1977, Left coalitions had persisted in commitments to social equity despite very different track records in other areas. In Montpellier, a Left coalition similar to that in Rennes had followed policies more analogous to those of the Center-Right coalition that controlled Nancy. Although the legacies of the Center-Right coalition that ruled Montpellier up to 1977 help to account for this divergence, Hervé in Rennes had confronted similar legacies. In neither other domain did the dominant party alone correspond even this consistently with the strategies pursued. But the newer Left coalitions contrasted with both the older Left and the Right coalitions in the extent that local officials had carried out environmental objectives along with developmental ones.

Even more than among the German cities, more prosperous, faster-growing cities like Montpellier and Rennes could draw on stronger tax bases and other local fiscal resources to carry out the social, environmental and developmental policies local coalitions chose. By the same token, the declining industrial city of Clermont-Ferrand stood in a measurably worse position than Bielefeld. In France more than in Germany, divergences in the policies of the national government had contributed to the distinctive local trajectories. Both Montpellier and Rennes, as centers of poorer regions, benefitted from efforts since the 1950s to develop the periphery outside Paris. In the wake of decentralization, however, supralocal officials played a less and less critical role in the accomplishments of local coalitions. Increasingly, in developmental as well as environmental and social domains, local choices and local conditions dictated the course as well as the immediate consequences of policy.

The U.S. Central Cities: Variations on an Upscale Theme

The consistent segregation of the three U.S. cities set them apart from their German and half of their French counterparts. In other respects the outcomes for these U.S. cities varied as much as or more than those among the French cities. Madison had combined solid growth with environmental outcomes closest to those of the European cities; Durham had grown even faster but had secured lower levels of environmental goods; and New Haven could claim neither effective environmental provision nor growth. More often than in France and Germany, the choices of local political actors and the makeup of dominant local electoral coalitions accounted for the differences among these variations in the United States. So, as in the European settings, did the governmental and political infrastructures that shaped how these coalitions formed and competed for local power.

In the three U.S. settings, as in most U.S. cities, these infrastructures imposed significantly different conditions than those in Europe for anyone who sought to control the local government, as, for example, Mayor Lee did in New Haven. In contrast with German or French counterparts, a local leader in these settings faced the prospect of having constantly to reassemble coalitions within the electorate as well as among local governmental institutions. In Madison and Durham a winning coalition faced a renewed electoral hurdle every two years, and strictures on political parties in local elections limited the possibilities to institutionalize electoral organization. In New Haven after the 1950s, Democratic dominance had much of the same effect. With a proliferation of local commissions and boards alongside the city councils, and limited means of hierarchical control within the local governments, even leaders of successful electoral coalitions had to make constant efforts to maintain cooperation among the institutional actors within the cities. As in the separate boards responsible for educational policies in all three settings, electoral processes as well as formal responsibilities often vested these other actors with partial autonomy. Finally, election of at least part of the council by wards rather than at large in all three cities institutionalized a potential for fragmentation by neighborhoods.

At the same time, different structures institutionalized partly at state and regional levels in Madison, and to a lesser degree in Durham, could have enabled local coalitions to accomplish more.[121] For Madison, Progressive reforms since the 1950s provided what one local account termed a " 'strong Mayor Council' plan, with a few more restrictions on the Mayor than usual."[122] The nonpartisan mayor elected alongside the council there

---

[121] On U.S. forms of local government, see John Harrigan, *Politics and Policy in States and Communities*, 6th ed. (New York: Longman, 1998), pp. 159–167.

[122] Robert J. Corcoran, *An Administrative History of the City of Madison, Wisconsin* (Madison: Madison Public Library, 1977, mimeograph), p. 12.

retained exclusive appointment powers and considerable administrative authority over the bulk of the local government. Like many American cities in the South and West, Durham maintained the reform institutions of a council-manager system. In this form, a manager appointed by the council has acted as the executive within the city government, and the mayor has served more as the leader of the council. In New Haven, despite such reform practices as a merit system and direct primaries, northeastern traditions of machine politics continued to hold partial sway. The mayor maintained comparatively weaker authority in relation to the council than did the executives in the other cities. Along with party politics itself, ward-based party machinery persisted throughout the postwar period.

As in the European cities, the policy and politics in each of these cities followed common trajectories. In each instance, broad coalitions had emerged in the 1950s and 1960s largely around an agenda of local growth. In each, this objective had persisted into the 1990s even as new coalitions emerged to qualify it with environmental or distributive concerns. More than in Europe, growing numbers of managers and professionals in outlying neighborhoods increasingly shaped electoral coalitions and local policies. To varying degrees, the institutional infrastructure continued to limit the capacity of any coalition to dominate local choices.

Madison.   In Madison, the dispersal of privileged residents and the institutional infrastructure of local government and politics posed the least problem for a dominant coalition. We have seen how this city came closest among the U.S. settings to providing the urban environmental amenities of the German settings, and still grew moderately. From the 1970s, Madison's electoral coalition, the most stable in any of the three cities, had pursued the most sustained set of policies directed at environmental ends at the same time as it welcomed new development. In part because minorities and the poor made up a comparatively small portion of the city's electorate, distributive ends figured only rarely, and then often in contradictory ways, in local governmental choices.

In 1836, even before the institution of planning in the German cities, the plat of the future Wisconsin capital on the Isthmus established Madison as a planned downtown. Even without the added impetus of wartime destruction, efforts to shape the expanding city had punctuated local politics repeatedly throughout the twentieth century.[123] Following along the lines of the widely publicized "suggestive plan" that John Nolen prepared for the city in 1909, Madison initiated a succession of regulatory frameworks: a building code in 1913, zoning in 1927, parks in 1931, the comprehensive Segoe Plan of 1938. Increasingly, these schemes reflected the central position of Madison in the Progressive movement of the inter-war period. After World War II, the city emerged as a bastion of support for the liberal wing of the state Democratic party. The alternating mayoral coalitions that carried out policies from the 1950s reflected this growing dominance as well as the occasional challenges from forces linked to the Republican party. Although mayoral powers stopped short of control over such entities as the school board, they sometimes enabled mayors to take on stronger roles in coalition building than in the other U.S. cities. Ulti-mately, changing neighborhood and socioeconomic structures furnished the basis for a stable new coalition with support from throughout the city (Table 4.4). Through the 1960s the main fault line of Madison politics had separated the east side and central area from the west side (Figure 4.11).[124] To the east and in the center lived the working-class constituencies employed in the plants of manufacturing enterprises like Oscar-Meyer, the processed food producer. To the west lay the privileged suburbs where local elites had begun to move as early as the 1920s. Under Ivan Nestin-gen in the 1950s and Otto Festge in the 1960s, the dominant coalitions had united labor and central support around policies of planning and aggressive development in the downtown. From 1961 to 1965 a conserv-ative coalition under Henry Reynolds, in a challenge that relied on support from the affluent west side, wrested both the mayorship and half the council seats from the predominantly Democratic majority.[125] In 1969 and 1971 the Republican William Dyke also won the mayoral race, but after

[123] On planning and politics in Madison, see Robert R. Alford and Harry M. Scoble, *Bureau-cracy and Participation: Political Cultures in Four Wisconsin Cities* (Chicago: Rand McNally and Co., 1969); Capital Community Citizens, "More Is Less: The Case Study of a City that May Be Growing Too Big for Its Citizens' Good," report (Madison, 1973); Madison Department of Planning and Development, *Downtown 2000* (Madison, 1989); David V. Mollenhoff, *Madison: A History of the Formative Years* (Dubuque, IA: Kendall/Hunt Pub-lishing Co., 1982); William F. Thompson, *The History of Wisconsin*, vol. 6: *Continuity and Change, 1940–1965* (Madison: State Historical Society of Wisconsin, 1988); Madison, *A Land Use Plan for the City of Madison: Plan Report* (Madison, 1985).

[124] Alford and Scoble, *Bureaucracy and Participation*, p. 178.

[125] Ibid., p. 109.

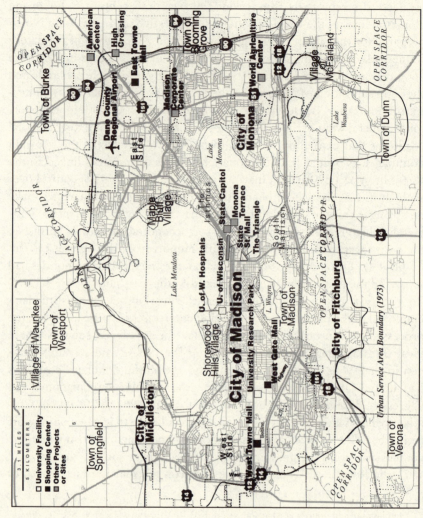

Figure 4.11 Madison

Table 4.4. *Coalitions in Madison City Government, 1950s–1997*

Years	Mayor(s)	Main Elements of Coalition
1956–1961	Ivan Nestingen	Growth coalition with labor, east side, central support
1961–1965	Henry Reynolds	West side, conservative opposition to renewal, development
1965–1969	Otto Festge	Growth coalition with support from labor, central area, east side
1969–1973	William Dyke	Growth coalition with west and east side support
1973–1979	Paul Soglin	Liberal, labor, students and growing suburban support
1979–1989	Joel Skornicka, Joseph Sensenbrenner	Shifting compromises between liberals, business, suburbs and inner neighborhoods
1989–1997	Paul Soglin	Liberals, environmentalists, students, inner neighbor-hoods, suburbs, some business support

both elections he had to work with a divided, predominantly liberal council.

By 1973, a more stable formation had emerged to dominate Madison politics. Paul Soglin, a former radical activist at the University of Wisconsin, fused support from the growing populations on both the east and the west sides with large majorities among the students, poorer residents and urban professionals of the central and southern neighborhoods. In three successive mayoral victories in the 1970s, Soglin capitalized on ties to activists in the university community and to organized labor. Although a pro-development block persisted on the city council, a growing block of votes on the Left furnished Soglin with crucial allies within the city government. In 1979 the former University of Wisconsin chancellor Joel Skornicka, a Democrat, having defeated Soglin aide Jim Rowen in a hard-fought race, initiated a decade of mayoral administrations with explicit pro-development agendas and strong business and suburban support. At the same time, Skornicka and his successor Joseph Sensenbrenner faced divided councils and continued to cultivate ties with labor and many of the downtown civic and activist groups that had supported

Soglin. In 1989, Soglin returned to defeat Sensenbrenner and dominate politics for eight more years. In these later terms Soglin drew extensive support from the suburban neighborhoods as well as the downtown.

Although developmental aims figured more prominently in the policies of the other mayors since 1970, the Soglin administrations had also accommodated and even promoted urban expansion. The city government itself often played a facilitative role, but land use planning brought regular local involvement in projects as well. From the 1940s through the 1960s the University of Wisconsin and the state government accounted for most of the growth in jobs as well as much of the new construction in the downtown.[126] With a few exceptions like the Triangle area, where local officials cleared the principal slum area of the downtown to make way for expansion of the university hospital and other facilities, urban renewal and public housing remained limited. In 1970, under the tenure of the last Republican to serve as mayor, William Dyke, the local government mobilized with downtown businesses against growing threats from peripheral development to issue a plan for development of the city center. A transit mall along State Street from the Capitol to the university, extensive new parking downtown, a new federal courthouse, the civic center complex and numerous large new office complexes in the blocks surrounding the Capitol grew out of these efforts. Following up these efforts under Soglin's first administration, a citywide plan in 1977 laid out a scheme for development in new urban growth centers around malls already built to the east, west and south along the new "Beltline" expressway that circled the outer edges of the city. As the state government moved a major new office building to the western part of the city, the university instituted a major research park, a new medical center and other facilities there.

The later Soglin administration, maintaining the emphasis of Skornicka and Sensenbrenner on new development, continued to orchestrate regular expansion in the office capacity, service installations and physical limits of the city. Skornicka, citing "economic survival" in an era of federal and state budget cuts as the first priority of his administration,[127] had carried out plans for a civic center and introduced tax increment finance (TIF) districts to fund development in the downtown. Sensenbrenner touted his reliance on devices like TIFs to fund new office, retail and housing and pushed successive referenda to bring a new convention center to the

---

[126] Capital Community Citizens, "More Is Less," p. 14.
[127] *Capital Times*, April 8, 1981, p. 39.

city.[128] Soglin rode into office in 1989 on a wave of opposition in a referendum on the long-embattled convention center that Frank Lloyd Wright first proposed to build on Monona Terrace overlooking one of the city's lakes. His administration not only carried out a version of this project but drew on further TIF funding as well as federal CDBG and HOME support for an array of other downtown redevelopment initiatives.[129] At the same time, the city either helped sponsor or guided the construction of such new corporate parks as the American Center, High Crossing, the World Agricultural Center and the Madison Corporate Center on the urban periphery.

As far back as the City Beautiful movement of turn-of-the-century Madison, environmental concerns had supplemented developmental ones. Even during the heyday of growth coalitions in the 1960s, Alford and Scoble noted "a pervasive *moralism* and a concern with *aesthetics* and public amenities."[130] From the start of the twentieth century, the Madison Park and Pleasure Drive Association, and from 1931 the city government itself, had continually added to an unusually extensive municipal system of parks for a U.S. city.[131] Over the 1980s and 1990s local administrations continued to add an array of new parks and nature reserves to this system. Periodically since 1900, but systematically after the institution of countywide planning after 1970, local officials also employed their annexation powers in conjunction with their local planning and zoning authority to assert control of peripheral urban development. After 1971 city officials assumed much of the responsibility to enforce urban growth boundary beyond which Madison refused to provide utility services. By the 1990s, local planners issued detailed area plans that prescribed new development in outlying undeveloped areas. Neighborhood planning of this sort in such areas as High Crossing and the American Center enabled the city to impose impact fees and service obligations on developers and to concentrate new development in specific locations like the intersection of U.S. Highway 151 and Interstates 90 and 94 to the east of the urbanized area. Municipal initiatives toward rehabilitation and redevelopment had helped maintain a stronger nucleus of professional and other residents in the Isthmus

---

[128] *Capital Times*, April 1, 1989, p. 21.
[129] A 1995 summary prepared by local officials listed eight such projects (Wisconsin Community Development Institute, *Community Development Activities in Madison* [Madison, 1995]).
[130] Alford and Scoble, *Bureaucracy and Participation*, p. 113.
[131] Mollenhoff, *Madison*, p. 231.

area than in the other U.S. downtowns. As in many of the European Old Towns, these residents provided clienteles for the State Street mall and mobilized politically in favor of downtown housing, historical preservation, design restrictions and neighborhood amenities.[132] At the same time, in the most extensive efforts among the U.S. cities to foster alternatives to automobile traffic, the local government owned and helped support the Madison Metro bus company and built a growing network of bicycle paths. In the Isthmus and elsewhere in the downtown, the Landmarks Commission and the Design Commission helped secure designation for a growing number of design and historic districts.

Efforts to address distributive equity among neighborhoods, and especially the problems of the poorest residential areas, fared less well. Postwar political agendas in Madison had seldom extended to questions of class.[133] Through such actions as the defeat of a 1950 referendum to build public housing, the white professional constituencies of the city had discouraged the arrival of poor, minority constituencies. When the city secured its first urban renewal funds in the 1950s and early 1960s, it employed them to demolish a neighborhood of blacks and poor Italians in the Triangle area adjacent to the downtown.[134] In the poor, predominantly minority neighborhoods of South Madison, where many of these residents were forced to relocate, more limited redevelopment measures cleared away only part of the housing, constructed replacement low-income housing and added a basic infrastructure of streets, sewers, sidewalks and parks.

But socioeconomic polarization among neighborhoods accelerated dramatically from 1970 to 1990, and the policies of the local government ultimately did little to compensate. In the early 1990s South Madison in particular remained the same pocket of disadvantage as it had thirty years earlier. Following the guidelines of the Land Use Plan of 1977, local officials worked to preserve the mixed racial and social composition in parts of the downtown and to promote the move of commerce, businesses and even state offices to peripheral sites within or near the growth boundary. The combination of controls with encouragements to development helped send land and housing prices higher throughout the city: from 1983 to 1995, the average price of a single-family house climbed 24 percent in real terms. In the well-to-do western neighborhoods prices had risen by two

[132] Madison Department of Planning and Development, *Downtown 2000*, p. 33.
[133] Alford and Scoble, *Bureaucracy and Participation*, p. 105.
[134] Thompson, *History of Wisconsin*, pp. 344–346.

and three times as much. Efforts to preserve the center worsened the disadvantages for poor and lower-income residents. Average valuations in the Isthmus and university areas rose from 87 percent of the city average to one percent below it. Neighborhoods like South Madison, where prices remained as low as before in comparison with the city average (at 65 percent), received more and more of the residents unable to afford housing elsewhere.[135] The limited local scattered site housing supports under the federal section 8 program did little to address these broader trends.

In 1992 the city devoted only 5.8 percent of its operating budget or $35 per resident to social services, and still less to services targeted at the poorest areas. In the capital budget, fully $1.95 million of the $2.28 million designated for housing came from federal and state grants. Even the modest amounts of federal Community Development Block and HOME Program grants that the city applied toward neighborhood housing, business and social services concentrated more in and around the Isthmus than in southern neighborhoods. Despite attempts to integrate the elementary schools of South Madison in the mid-1980s, a majority of children in one school there lived below the poverty level.[136] A succession of commissions and task forces highlighted the continued problems of the area but ventured only minimal remedies.[137] For African Americans, racial discrimination in housing and other markets probably compounded socioeconomic disadvantages. Despite such initiatives as a mild local antidiscrimination ordinance that predated the later national legislation of the 1960s, complaints about discrimination persisted into the 1990s.[138]

All the recent Madison mayors worked consistently with business to carry out developmental policies. Yet even those most in favor of these

---

[135] Data from Madison tax assessments. The 1977 plan had designated South Madison for commercial services to residents of other neighborhoods rather than for residence.

[136] Tom Kaplan, *Madison's Children: Social and Educational Conditions of Children in the Madison Metropolitan School District* (Madison: American Family Insurance, 1993), p. 12.

[137] For instance, several months of discussion in 1990 surrounding a task force that Soglin appointed brought out a litany of complaints about local housing, family support, health services, economic development, inadequate job training and declining commerce (Mayor's South Madison Steering Committee, "Short-range Recommendations for South Madison," report ([Madison, unpublished report, 1990]). The Task Force recommended consolidation of existing neighborhood services, encouragement of home ownership in the area and more study of ways to improve race relations. It also initiated a Little League team (Enis Ragland, "Status of the South Madison Task Force Recommendations," memorandum [Madison, 1997]).

[138] Thompson, *History of Wisconsin*, p. 349; Mayor's South Madison Steering Committee, "Short-range Recommendations," B-10.

policies, such as Skornicka and Sensenbrenner, coordinated their support with a growing array of environmental measures, and the administration of William Dyke at the end of the 1960s had found itself forced to compromise with advocates of these measures on the council. Situated in an appealing site, and favored as the location for the expanding educational and governmental institutions of the state of Wisconsin, Madison had benefitted consistently in both policy domains from the financial resources that local expansion and incoming businesses brought. The somewhat more centralized settlement that local policies had helped foster also reinforced other local efforts to secure better environmental conditions. Smaller numbers of minorities and the poor made the difficulties of these groups easier to address than in many U.S. cities and lessened the chance of racial and class divisions that might have undermined other policies. But with smaller political constituencies in these groups, the dominant coalition addressed their problems with all the more ambivalence.

Durham. In Durham, parallel postindustrial shifts brought more volatile patterns of local politics to the fore. Growth here had accelerated more than in Madison in the 1980s and 1990s, but the environmental outcomes had remained more modest. Into the 1960s, under the legally enforced segregation of the Jim Crow South, the large local African American population had suffered as systematic a disadvantage as any group in the eleven cities. In the decades afterward, both continued racial divisions and the growing suburban interests of this rapidly expanding city would shape shifting electoral coalitions and policies.

As in several of the French cities, formal regulatory institutions in Durham dated from the interwar period. The town had established a planning commission in 1922, zoning and building codes and a recreation commission in 1926 and a series of parks.[139] Beginning with the institution of a city planning department in 1945, Durham built up a sizeable bureaucracy concerned with local land use and development. In the early 1990s, following consolidation of this department with the parallel authorities in Durham County, land use and planning staff per resident exceeded that in

---

[139] Jean Bradley Anderson, *Durham County* (Durham: Duke University Press, 1990), pp. 354, 357–358. Anderson's book offers far and away the most comprehensive account of politics and policy in Durham into the 1980s. Other useful sources include William Keech, *The Impact of Negro Voting* (Westport, CT: Greenwood Publishing, 1968); Durham, *Durham 2005: Comprehensive Plan* (Durham, 1988); Durham City-County Planning Department, *Durham Today* (Durham, 1993).

Madison and exceeded levels in Clermont-Ferrand and Montpellier.[140] The council-manager form of government relied not only on bureaucracies of this sort but on supervision by the appointed city manager.

From the 1960s to the 1990s, elections to the council that appointed this official gave rise to more persistent and serious contestation than in Madison. A coalition composed of predominantly middle-class and leftist elements had usually won local elections. But conservative coalitions linked to the local business community had succeeded in repeated challenges to this formation. With a mayor elected every two years to preside over the council, and council members elected through at-large voting to staggered four-year terms, every new election gave the entire electorate of the city as a body the chance to decide the direction of policy. In matters of local schools, a separately elected board analogous to that in Madison exercised parallel authority that included the setting of school taxes. The dominant local political coalition of the postwar era, a union of white academics and business and labor leaders with the black community, began to break up in the 1950s as the civil rights movement challenged the local racial order.[141] By the 1980s under Charles Markham and Wilbur "Wib" Gulley, a new coalition composed of the liberal Durham Voters Alliance, the Durham Committee on the Affairs of Black People and eventually the environmentalist Sierra Club chapter had emerged to take the place of this alliance. In 1989 this coalition secured election of Chester Jenkins as the city's first African American mayor; in 1993 it swept Sylvia Kerckhoff into office as the first female mayor. At the same time, a coalition with strong ties to the downtown business community had repeatedly challenged this coalition effectively on the strength of the voting in the growing suburban areas within the expanding city limits. In the early 1970s James Hawkins and in 1979 and 1991 Harry Rodenhizer had led these pro-business groups to electoral sweeps that won majorities on the City Council. Rodenhizer, like Hawkins a Republican, also attracted substantial numbers of pro-business and suburban Democrats to slates labelled "Voters for Durham's Future" in 1979 and "Friends of Durham" in 1991. But his coalition repeatedly failed to sustain the electoral support it needed to remain in office more than a term.

---

[140] Overall, staff in this area numbered 5 per 10,000 residents here compared to 4 in Madison, 3 in New Haven and slightly less than 3 in Clermont-Ferrand and Montpellier. Including the somewhat larger county population in the calculation for Durham did not alter this result, but a subsequent downsizing of the department brought the level closer to that of Madison.

[141] Keech, *Impact of Negro Voting*, p. 44.

Table 4.5. *Coalitions in Durham Local Government, 1951–1997*

Years	Mayor(s)	Orientation
1951–1971	E. J. Evans, R. Wense Grabarek	Growth coalition with African American, labor support
1971–1975	James Hawkins	Business-based growth coalition with suburban support
1975–1979	Wade Cavin	African American, liberal, conservative suburban support
1979–1981	Harry Rodenhizer	Business-based growth coalition with suburban support
1981–1985	Charles Markham	Labor, liberal, partial African American, business and suburban support
1985–1991	Wilbur Gulley, Chester Jenkins	Liberal, environmentalist, African American and some suburban support
1991–1993	Harry Rodenhizer	Business-based growth coalition with suburban support
1993–1997	Sylvia Kerckhoff	Liberal, environmentalist, suburban and African American support

If the coalitions of liberal groups had succeeded more often in dominating elections, their policies had rarely checked the long-standing mobilization around new development. The coalition of white and black constituencies from the 1950s had assumed the lead in a more massive urban renewal program than in Madison.[142] Financed to two-thirds through federal funds, but also by local bond issues, a total of seven projects razed the Hayti area and several other longtime black neighborhoods. At the same time, the city opened up land within the urban periphery of the rapidly expanding city to new development. The city annexed the Research Triangle Park, provided the physical infrastructure of roads, water and sewer for it, and raised funds to bring the Durham Technical Institute to the dowtown as a place to train and retrain workers. In addition to support for downtown office construction, local officials sponsored or cooperated with state plans for a traffic loop, extensive downtown

[142] Anderson, *Durham County*, pp. 406–409.

250

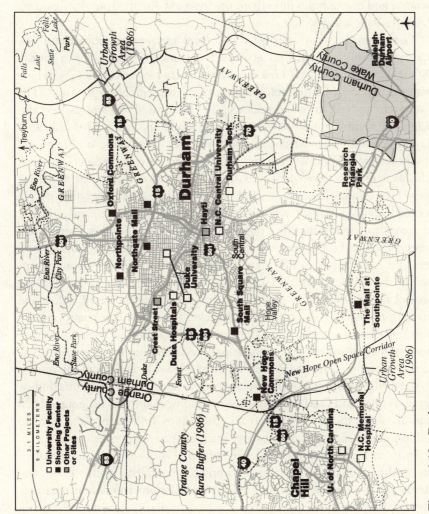

Figure 4.12 Durham

parking and expressways directly to the business district from the Research Triangle Park and Raleigh.

The coalitions that controlled the local government into the 1980s maintained this emphasis on growth. Even under Wib Gulley, a former Public Interest Research Group activist elected over Charles Markham with the support of antidevelopment groups, this emphasis persisted. The Comprehensive Plan issued under Gulley advocated "an aggressive campaign to assemble and/or extend utilities to land appropriate for industrial development," endorsed construction of both "affordable housing" and "high quality 'executive' housing" and gave priority to "projects that will stimulate private development with the greatest employment and long term tax revenue benefits."[143] Public-private initiatives over this period succeeded in building a civic center and hotel, an arts center, and a theater in the central area alongside a number of new office buildings. Outside the center, even as Gulley and others on the council sought to impose new fees and restrictions on new development, city and county planners supported the development of Treyburn, a 5,200-acre industrial and housing project north of the city, as well as a succession of new retail, office and housing projects. Even after Sylvia Kerckhoff led a similar coalition back into power in the mid-1990s, these approvals persisted. Over the objections of local planners, the council approved rezoning for a new 489,000-square-foot plaza around a Wal-Mart at New Hope Commons on the western edge of the city. At least partly due to such decisions, annual industry investments in Durham and the surrounding county had averaged $228 million under these coalitions from 1984 up to 1995, compared to $133 million under the two conservative, business-oriented coalitions.[144]

In its moves to incorporate environmental measures into local policy, the coalition of blacks, liberals and environmentalists in the 1980s and 1990s departed more from its predecessor. The environmental measures of the earlier dominant coalition revolved primarily around creation of parks. In the 1960s, principally as a result of successive local bond issues to raise money for recreation, the city had developed some twenty-four parks.[145] In the 1980s, efforts to add to a system of sixty local parks grew

---

[143] Durham, *Durham 2005*, pp. 27, 35–36.

[144] Annual figures from Greater Durham Chamber of Commerce.

[145] According to Keech (*Impact of Negro Voting*, p. 59), blacks had managed through bond referenda to ensure that these mostly segregated facilities were "more or less" equitably distributed between blacks and whites.

into more comprehensive policies to preserve open space, create green corridors, build bicycle and pedestrian trails and preserve what remained of the original downtown. From 1983 onward, the Urban Trails and Greenways Commission pursued several of these aims alongside county planners. Following the consolidation of city and county planning offices, the Master Plan for Urban Trails and Greenways in 1988 and County Open Space Plan in 1989 established the outlines of local policies. Bonds worth $1.5 million from the county and $3.6 million from the city mainly funded these efforts. At the same time the city introduced impact fees on developers as a source of revenue for parks, open space and physical infrastructure and as an incentive for denser development. In the Comprehensive Plan from 1986, the City Council and its planners had already articulated an overarching policy of growth management that guided these and other efforts. The plan imposed an "Urban Growth Area" boundary beyond which the city agreed not to finance extension of sewer and water service to new development. This Urban Growth Area encompassed a wide swath of undeveloped land "expected to develop an urban character over the next 20 to 30 years."[146] Within the boundary, the city designated areas with sufficient existing city services as "High Priority Growth Areas" and advocated "clustering" of new development in existing "activity centers" like the downtown, the Research Triangle Park, the Duke University area and, in the future, Treyburn.

Distributive policies under the coalition had to contend with the long-standing legacies of Jim Crow. With a few exceptions like parts of the local park system, the racial legal order had subjected the local black population to disadvantages or exclusion in every domain of local social life. From the 1950s successive victories of the civil rights movement secured integration in such domains as housing code enforcement, park access, libraries, cemeteries, schools, hospitals and public appointments. Although protest and litigation rather than elected officials often played the decisive role in these changes, Mayor R. Wense Grabarek took up the demands of local protestors in 1963 with an initiative that desegregated retail establishments and other businesses throughout the city on the basis of voluntary agreements.[147] Gross disparities persisted between white and black neighborhoods in such basic services as water, sewers, sidewalks and schools. The promise of the local urban renewal program to rectify these

---

[146] Durham, *Durham 2005*, p. 38.   [147] Keech, *Impact of Negro Voting*, pp. 85–87.

disparities helped maintain African American support for the dominant electoral coalition, and the black vote proved essential to the passage of bond issues in support of the program. As carried out, however, the program devastated black neighborhoods on a scale well beyond that in Madison. By the end of the program in the 1970s, a total of 4,057 households and 502 businesses, compared to a few hundred households in Madison, had been forced to relocate. The new, often temporary quarters the Housing Authority provided as substitute housing in the southeastern part of the city lay "well away from the prosperous white areas" like Hope Valley to the southwest.[148] Following the demolition, parts of the Hayti neighborhood lay vacant for twenty years. The city had undertaken or encouraged housing only slightly more than Madison. Even in the 1990s, 40 percent of local subsidized housing concentrated in the single neighborhood of South Central Durham.

In the 1980s and 1990s, the local policy synthesis continued to address the needs of the most disadvantaged neighborhoods in ambivalent, contradictory ways. In the wealthy white neighborhoods of northern, western and southwestern Durham, required densities of less than six dwelling units per acre still limited the growth of mixed neighborhoods. As industrial and research firms flocked to outlying sites like the Research Triangle Park and Treyburn, coalition leaders worked to bring new commercial and office facilities to the downtown. These priorities overwhelmed the city programs and the neighborhood-based organizations that addressed the most disadvantaged central neighborhoods. From 1970 to 1990, the metropolitan segregation index for poverty had climbed by 22 points to 45 even as the index for blacks had decreased by 9 points to 57. In the face of dwindling federal HOME and CDBG funds, the coalition won approval of a total of $21 million in neighborhood redevelopment bonds from votes spread over eight years, from 1988 to 1996.[149] But annual capital spending per year on systems of water treatment and transportation persisted at three and four times the level of capital spending on housing and neighborhood revitalization. The public-private initiatives of nonprofit neighborhood companies like the Hayti Development Corporation brought only modest amounts of new commercial and housing development to minority areas like South

[148] Anderson, *Durham County*, pp. 409–410.
[149] Durham City-County Planning Department, *South Central Durham Plan* (Durham, 1995), p. XIV-2.

Central.[150] Consolidation of the county and city schools in the early 1990s helped equilibrate educational finances. A system of neighborhood planning throughout the city enabled planners to solicit, and sometimes to address, the needs of the most disadvantaged areas for amenities and physical infrastructure. But in South Central Durham, the persistent concentrations of subsidized housing maintained the established pattern of disadvantage. Neighborhood planning there brought out complaints about the lack of commercial activity, transit amenities, local employment and ultimately the incompleteness of urban renewal.[151]

Like its counterpart in Madison, the coalition that came closest to dominance in Durham persisted in Upscale measures that overwhelmed its distributive concerns. The suburban, business-oriented coalitions of 1979 and 1991 had also reinforced developmental policies at the expense of other priorities. In both elections pervasive racial divisions reinforced conflicts between downtown neighborhoods and the expanding suburban periphery. In 1979, the conservative coalition swept into office in a campaign that targeted the reluctance of the outgoing council both to approve an east-west expressway through the downtown and to ease building requirements. With compromises that only partly spared minority areas like the Crest Street neighborhood from demolition, the coalition carried out these plans.[152] In 1991, Friends of Durham had capitalized on a scandal surrounding the billing expenses of a former black councilman in the city administration and on opposition to the tax and expenditure policies of the council under Mayor Jenkins to again win heavily in white neighborhoods. This time the coalition issued a downtown revitalization plan that relied heavily on private office and commercial development and delayed the proposals of the Planning Department to introduce new restrictions on peripheral development.

Even when the coalition of liberals, environmentalists and blacks won the election, divisions between suburban whites and the inner-city black community sometimes fractured local policies. African American representatives anxious to expand jobs and distributive programs for their constituencies often found their interests in tension with the desire of suburban environmentalists. In neighborhood planning for South Central

---

[150] In one of the redevelopment areas, HDC built two new shopping centers and 170 housing units.
[151] Durham City-County Planning Department, *South Central Durham Plan*, pp. 69–70.
[152] Anderson, *Durham County*, pp. 449–450.

Durham, local elites and activists expressed more consistent concerns for the jobs and shopping opportunities than for environmental amenities.[153] In the dispute over a building authorization for the Wal-Mart Plaza at Oxford Commons, representatives for the Durham Committee for the Affairs of Black People allied with pro-business conservatives against the rest of the majority coalition and in favor of the project.

As postindustrial transformations turned Durham into a rapidly growing center for research and advanced services, regional as well as local growth helped make ample resources available for the government of Durham to pursue environmental and social aims. Following the advent of legal integration in the 1960s, coalitions of downtown blacks with suburban liberals and eventually environmentalists supplemented developmental policies with a growing array of environmental measures. Not only these new policies but council commitments to distributive equity came repeatedly under challenge. Both Friends of Durham and internal tensions within the more dominant coalition imposed constraints on the pursuit of these goals. In addition to the increasingly dominant interests of suburbanized constituencies within the city, recurrent racial tensions sometimes undermined the progressive coalition and its aims.

New Haven. An industrial city in 1960 like Bielefeld and Clermont-Ferrand, New Haven underwent as precipitous a postindustrial decline as any of the other urban centers. The demographic and economic downtrends, poor environmental conditions and persistent social and racial disparities among neighborhoods typified the larger urban centers of the U.S. Northeast. As in the other industrial settings, the trajectory of local policy in New Haven differed from that in service centers with less extensive legacies from manufacturing. From the 1950s, New Haven attracted national attention from students of urban politics for one of the most aggressive efforts at urban redevelopment in the country.[154] Although the perspective

---

[153] Durham City-County Planning Department, *South Central Durham Plan*.

[154] Dahl, *Who Governs? Democracy and Power in an American City* (New Haven CT: Yale University Press, 1962); Raymond E. Wolfinger, *The Politics of Progress* (Englewood Cliffs, NJ: Prentice-Hall, 1974); William Domhoff, *Who Really Rules? New Haven and Community Power Reexamined* (New Brunswick, NJ: Transaction Books, 1978); Phillip Singerman, "Politics, Bureaucracy and Public Policy: The Case of Urban Renewal in New Haven" (Ph.D. diss., Yale University, 1980); Norman I. Fainstein, and Susan S. Fainstein, "New Haven: The Limits of the Local State," in Susan S. Fainstein, et al. (eds.), *Restructuring the City*, 2nd ed. (New York: Longman, 1980), pp. 27–79; Clarence N. Stone and

of several decades has revealed the limits and shortsightedness of many of these efforts, recurrent developmental initiatives have continued to occupy the center stage of local policy and politics. Larger proportions of minorities and poor people, mostly a consequence of the greater suburbanization outside the city, aggravated the tensions and fiscal pressures linked to postindustrial decline. The typical northeastern inheritances of mayor-council government, machine politics and supralocal urban programs furnished no substitute for the effective local environmental and distributive policies of Bielefeld.

Basic elements of localized policy here were also in place by the 1950s. New Haven had issued its first zoning ordinance in 1926 and its first planning ordinances well before. In 1942 the City Planning Commission approved a plan prepared by Yale professor Maurice Rotival that would guide a comprehensive reconstruction of the urban center. Over the next decade a new redevelopment commission would come into being to carry out these plans. The formal infrastructures for carrying out these policies in New Haven imposed "a fragmented and cumbersome set of government institutions" that corresponded even more than in Madison to a weak-mayor system.[155] In addition to the powers of an array of semiautonomous boards and commissions, a mayor confronted the need to submit appointments and most agency budgets to a council, or Board of Aldermen. Biennial elections by wards tied the alders to specific neighborhoods; local referenda remained far rarer than in the two reformed cities. By the 1950s, however, with the flight of many Republican voters to the outlying towns of the city region, the Democratic party furnished common organizational bases for most of local politics. Democrats maintained solid majorities in mayoral elections from 1953 onward, and Democratic percentages in aldermanic elections ranged regularly between 70 and 95 percent. Single-party dominance left mayors, starting with Richard Lee, with largely similar electoral coalitions (Table 4.6). Electoral allegiances based on "ethnic and neighborhood symbolism combined with the divisible material goods government can dispense" perpetuated the

---

Heywood Sanders, "Re-examining a Classic Case of Development Politics: New Haven, Connecticut," in Clarence N. Stone and Heywood Sanders (eds.), *The Politics of Urban Development* (Lawrence: University of Kansas Press, 1987), pp. 159–181; Mary Summers and Philip Klinkner, "The Election of John Daniels as Mayor of New Haven," *PS: Political Science and Politics* 13(2) (1990): 142–145; Douglas Yates, *The Ungovernable City* (New York: Basic Books, 1977).

[155] Fainstein and Fainstein, "New Haven," p. 36.

Table 4.6. *Mayoral Coalitions in New Haven City Government, 1953–1997*

Years	Mayor(s)	Electoral Coalition
1953–1967	Richard Lee	Democratic growth coalition with white ethnic, professional, minority support
1967–1979	Bart Guida, Frank Logue	Democratic coalition with white ethnic, professional, minority support
1979–1989	Biagio DiLieto	Democratic growth coalition with white ethnic, minority, professional support
1989–1993	John Daniels	Democratic coalition with minority, professional support
1993–1997	John DiStefano	Democratic coalition with white ethnic, professional, minority support

traditional practices if not the organizational forms of U.S. urban political machines.[156] Only the first African American mayor of the city, former State Senator John Daniels, had challenged this system. Backed by a coalition of minority communities and with liberal professional support from the Yale community, Daniels defeated City Development Administrator John DiStefano in the Democratic primary election of 1989 and went on to win two mayoral terms.

The unusual ambition of the Rotival plan, and above all the efforts under Mayor Lee to realize that plan, have brought New Haven developmental policy a central role in debates on the nature of politics in American cities. Fashioning a governing coalition around an accumulation of federal programs and grants, Lee put together perhaps the most extensive effort at urban demolition and reconstruction among American cities of a similar size. The extent of redevelopment projects during this era in New Haven exceeded that of the projects in European industrial cities. Only Allied bombing and the subsequent reconstruction in Europe could compare with the effects on downtown New Haven. The previous mayor had already negotiated with the state to secure the location of the new Interstate 91 to Hartford and to build the Oak Street Connector, an inter-

[156] Ibid.; Wolfinger, *Politics of Progress.*

258

state link to the downtown that would raze the city's worst slum. Under the Lee administration from 1954 to 1968, the city received outside funds that comprised around 30 percent of the aggregate local tax revenues. In 1967 the Redevelopment Administration had grown to about 20 percent of all government employment in the city, with federal funds that totaled nearly half of the city's regular operating budget.[157] In addition to the Oak Street project, renewal projects constructed the Chapel Square Mall along the downtown city green, the Long Wharf district for manufacturing firms and a range of other initiatives around the city. In addition to massive public housing expenditures for the displaced residents, local agencies gained support from the War on Poverty and Model Cities programs. After Lee left office in 1967, the city government and his successors continued to carry out such projects in the face of rapidly declining federal funds and increasingly fragmented local coalitions. Programs like Community Development Block Grants directed what federal resources the city continued to receive into economic development in low- and middle-income neighborhoods.

By the 1980s the deficiencies of aggressive urban redevelopment were already clear.[158] The tax rolls in the renewed areas had increased incrementally at best. Long delays in the projects brought irreplaceable losses. City retail sales had dropped in constant dollars, and new projects like the Chapel Square Mall and the Coliseum had deteriorated and lost money. Property taxes had to be raised regularly to cover payments on a massive debt burden. In the face of these conditions, the city government in the 1980s under Mayor DiLieto commenced a new set of downtown development initiatives based partly on tax abatements for developers as well as on state and federal funds. In addition to a refurbishment of the Chapel Square Mall by the Rouse Company, a federal office building and a reconstructed City Hall, two new office towers went up in the business district. On the limits of the depressed Hill neighborhood to the south of Yale-New Haven hospital, city officials negotiated a new housing, commercial and office development. At Science Park, on the abandoned Winchester rifle factory property, the city worked with Yale University and the state to establish a site for new technology firms near the Yale science campus. The Daniels coalition had won office partly on the basis of challenges to

---

[157] Fainstein and Fainstein, "New Haven," pp. 37–38.
[158] Clarence N. Stone and Heywood Sanders, "Re-examining a Classic Case of Development Politics."

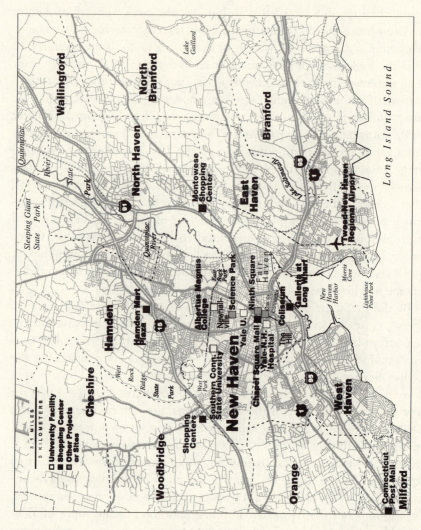

Figure 4.13   New Haven

these developmental initiatives.[159] But the Daniels administration pursued a new air rights mall above the Oak Street Connector, a new tennis stadium on the Yale campus and the Ninth Square complex of housing and commercial and retail development adjacent to the Chapel Square Mall in the downtown. Under John DiStefano, developmental policy took center stage again. In addition to receiving state approval for the largest mall in the region at Long Wharf, local officials developed a hotel, gentrified downtown apartments, renovated the Coliseum, brought improvements to the entertainment district and brought a state FBI headquarters to the city. Per capita city expenditures on planning and development in the mid-1990s stood at nearly double the level in either Madison or Durham.[160] At the same time the city continued to secure federal benefits from Empowerment Zones that provided tax incentives for construction and from brownfield programs that made money available to support environmental cleanups in old industrial sites.

Whatever the shortcomings of developmental policies in New Haven, they clearly set the synthesis here apart from the earlier service delivery strategies of the European industrial cities. As in the other U.S. cities, developmental objectives often overwhelmed attention to social equity. Early redevelopment often devastated poor and minority neighborhoods that helped contribute to the dominant electoral coalition for Lee and his successors.[161] Redevelopment ultimately eliminated some 7,850 housing units over the sixteen years up to 1972 and forced 2,216 businesses to relocate. Fainstein and Fainstein estimate that around a fifth of the city population was uprooted and that new housing "fell more than a thousand units short of demolition."[162] Much like those in Durham and in Madison, the new housing projects in New Haven were located in sites that reinforced established, segregated boundaries. Attempts to introduce scattered-site housing in the 1970s foundered on opposition to integration in white neighborhoods.[163] Other efforts to treat the needs of poor

[159] Summers and Klinkner, "John Daniels."

[160] New Haven spent $146 per resident in this area, compared to $84 in Madison and $70 in Durham.

[161] Fainstein and Fainstein ("New Haven," pp. 45, 49) also note that "blacks were politically inactive in the city," and follow Singerman's suggestion that aldermen had ignored lower income and minority residents in "'receiver' neighborhoods."

[162] Fainstein and Fainstein, "New Haven," pp. 41–42, 47–49.

[163] Ibid., p. 52.

neighborhoods faltered with the death of corresponding federal programs. In the 1960s an independent local agency named Community Progress, Incorporated (CPI), administered the job training and public school services of the War on Poverty on an average annual budget of $4 million. After 1968 the new City Demonstration Agency enlisted bureaucracies in downtown Italian and minority neighborhoods into the Model Cities program. But by the early 1970s CPI had broken up into eight locally administered neighborhood corporations, and by 1974 the Model Cities program was also terminated.

As federal programs in these areas declined from the 1970s to the 1990s, the state supplied part of the difference. The largest such sum, amounting to a third of the regular budget for the city in 1995–1996, came in the form of grants for city education services; an array of smaller grants amounting to just under 10 percent more redistributed other state revenues.[164] Overall expenditures on health, social services and housing here, at $243 per person, came closer than in Madison or Durham to the levels in the European industrial centers with social service delivery strategies.[165] As in other northeastern cities, legacies of machine politics and the local consequences of federal programs enhanced the resemblance.[166] But the total remained well below the $275 per person in roughly the same areas for Clermont-Ferrand, the poorest of the French cities; in relation to the metropolitan area population rather than the central city population alone, this figure would have fallen short by far more. Other French cities and their German counterparts expended $409 or more per person. Budget constraints limited social service expenditures beyond the application of outside funds from the state or federal government. Besides education expenditures, allocations from outside totaled some $7 million more than the total local expenditures for social services of $31 million. This flow of money from outside helped sustain a network of neighborhood development corporations that had survived the cutbacks in federal programs, as well as a larger circle of nonprofits concerned with business, housing and other services.

Partly as a result of the priority assigned developmental efforts, even local policies with strong distributive components did little to address the

---

[164] Figures take from 1995–1996 city budget. Totals do not include payments in lieu of taxes for local nonprofits and state government facilities.

[165] In Madison $70 per person and in Durham $140 per person went to equivalent social expenditures or investments.

[166] Steven Erie, *Rainbow's End* (Berkeley: University of California Press, 1988); David Mayhew, *Placing Parties in American Politics* (New Haven: Yale University Press, 1986).

racial and socioeconomic disparities among neighborhoods. Efforts to carry out the scattered-site "Infill" housing program had provoked a secession movement in the white working-class neighborhood of Morris Cove, and at least one instance of firebombing. By 1995–1996, after cutbacks under DiStefano, the city was budgeting only $242,000 of the social services funds for this program. "Linkage" policies that required developers to provide housing, jobs and recreational or social services as a condition of approvals for large commercial projects and gentrified housing reflected a similar ambivalence. Initiatives of this sort had become a regular practice in cities like Boston.[167] The DiLieto administration promised that 20 percent of the housing in a $300 million "mixed-use" development on the edge of the Hill neighborhood would "be affordable to low and moderate income families."[168] Yet that project centered mostly around an office and conference center and garage next to the Yale-New Haven Hospital. The Daniels administration, elected with the support of a coalition based more heavily in the poor and minority neighborhoods, pursued more redistributive mixes. Under Daniels the city secured federal, state and private funding for the Ninth Square project, a residential development that provided both subsidized and upscale housing adjacent to the Chapel Square Mall. Yet ultimately Daniels too, faced with fiscal and political constraints, looked for solutions in such projects as a downtown mall at the Oak Street Connector and rehabilitation on the fringes of the Yale campus.[169] Under DiStefano local policy shifted away from the downtown and the most depressed areas with such new proposals as a regional mall at Long Wharf along Long Island Sound.

If local policies addressed distributive equity in obviously contradictory ways, environmental measures often failed to find their way onto local agendas. Dedications of land around the turn of the last century had left the city with an armature of large, attractive parks like those at East Rock, West Rock and Lighthouse Point. In the neighborhoods around these parks as well as others north of the Yale campus and toward the town line with Woodbridge, residential zoning of less than six housing units an acre had helped to preserve ample open space and forests in private hands. But

[167] Norman Krumholz and Pievre Clavel, *Reinventing Cities: Equity Planners Tell Their Stories* (Philadelphia: Temple University Press, 1994).

[168] New Haven, *Annual Report 1988* (New Haven: Office of Development Administration, 1988).

[169] Summers and Klinkner, "The Daniels Election in New Haven and the Failure of the Deracialization Hypothesis," *Urban Affairs Quarterly* 27(2) (1991): 202–216.

the strained finances of the city and the desperation of local officials for new revenues had left environmental measures largely unfunded. In the 1990s, New Haven's budgets both for park operating expenses and for enforcement of land use and building code rules remained lower per capita than in either Durham or Madison.[170] Although urbanized areas covered more of its territory than those of the two expanding U.S. cities, new developments on New Haven's available land encountered even fewer objections. Up to the rejection of the Pond Lilly development on the western fringes of the city in 1990, the city's Planning and Zoning Commission had only rarely turned back a project. In the wake of the postwar reconstruction of the city around the interstate highways, policies in support of pedestrians and bicycles as alternatives to the automobile had gone little further than the advisory recommendations of regional planners. With the notable exception of the gentrified Wooster Square neighborhood east of the local rail station in the 1960s, redevelopment had also entailed little attention to historical preservation. By the 1980s, however, an active preservationist group had secured landmark designations for numerous structures, and most renewal projects used or restored existing buildings.

The economic decline of downtown New Haven continued into the late 1990s. Chapel Square Mall lost the last of its anchor stores, and major proportions of the retail and commercial space in the Ninth Square project remained vacant for years. If the city had generally halted its freefall of demographic and market losses, and crime had begun to decrease, fiscal constraints had proven at least as restrictive for policy as in Clermont-Ferrand. In New Haven, far more than they did in Madison and Durham, the surrounding towns of the city region continued to claim the bulk of privileged residents and tax revenues. Divisions between whites and the poor and minority residents of the city imposed constraints beyond those of the European cities. Local infrastructures of government and politics provided few institutional means for bridging those divisions. Only occasionally after Richard Lee left office did the electoral alliances of successive New Haven mayors give rise to coalitions that could dominate the local government. As funds from outside continued to decline, mayors like

---

[170] Expenditures on parks and related matters came to $37 a resident in 1995–1996, compared to $68 a resident in Madison and $43 in Durham. Staff in matters related to planning and land use numbered fewer than any other city except Montpellier, at 3 per 10,000 residents compared to 4 in Madison and 5 in Durham.

Governing within Urban Regions

Biagio DiLieto and John Daniels looked to developmental initiatives to sustain policies toward social equity. The resulting synthesis was contradictory at best.

The local syntheses of the central cities in the United States differed more than those in Germany, but less than those in France. Although local movements and policies devoted to environmental ends had gained increasing prominence in all three U.S. cities, the policies of the central city coalitions in this area diverged the most. Developmental initiatives also varied considerably, but local governing coalitions had sometimes mobilized more intensively around unsuccessful efforts of this sort than where growth in fact occurred. A variety of local efforts, carried out in diverse circumstances, had in each case ultimately reinforced the polarization of neighborhoods. Although the racial compositions and settlement patterns of the U.S. urban regions help to account for these trajectories, infrastructures of local government and politics have contributed to both the similarities and the contrasts.

Clearly, fiscal constraints made more of a difference for U.S. cities than in the more equalized German system of local finance, or even in the French. Although Madison and, by the 1980s, Durham had access to ample resources from local property taxes, New Haven still looked to outside for financial support for most policy initiatives despite a comparatively high tax rate. But over time, as well as between cities, the local governing coalitions also reflected the social composition of the local population more consistently than did their French and German counterparts. To a degree in all three cities, but especially under the two reformed governments, the institutions for assembling electoral coalitions proved indispensable to this result. Instead of parties linked to national organizational networks and locked into longer-term council strongholds, local political formations organized along the lines of pressing policy issues, local social cleavages and segregated neighborhood interests. In the one-party city of New Haven, with the partial exception of the Daniels coalition, the building of governing alliances among splintered neighborhood-based interests entailed a somewhat parallel process. In all three cities, however, greater institutional fragmentation than in Europe left broad initiatives to change policy contingent on coalition building among local officials and governments. Richard Lee and Paul Soglin had succeeded in building stable mayoral coalitions, but neither Harry Rodenhizer, Chester Jenkins nor John Daniels had fully done so. In Durham and New Haven, this failure had repeatedly impeded governance.

Despite the contrasts in these institutional infrastructures, local policy syntheses also shared more similarities than the outcomes of policy might lead one to expect. Developmental policies comprised one of the most significant elements of these syntheses. Even electoral alliances sustained partly on the basis of mobilization against development, such as those under Paul Soglin in Madison, Wib Gulley in Durham and John Daniels in New Haven, governed through coalitions that ultimately supported significant developmental measures. In New Haven, limited local revenues restricted how much the city could pursue these measures. But city officials frequently demonstrated all the more willingness to employ supralocal funding in the 1960s and local tax abatements in the 1980s to generate the necessary revenues. Madison since the 1950s and Durham in the 1990s had little trouble attracting new firms. Yet even in these settings, local officials sought to encourage firms to settle in the city.

The limited distributive policies of all three cities remained partly subordinate to these developmental efforts. In the absence of federal or state participation, the same limits on fiscal resources restricted policy in this area. Local coalition politics also gave rise to different types of limits. In Madison, where white managers and professionals dominated, minorities and poor people proved too small and insignificant a group to wield much clout in the dominant electoral coalition. In Durham, where annexation brought significant numbers of white suburbanites within the city limits as well as inner-city minorities and the poor, periodic, racially tinged protests among suburban whites repeatedly undermined coalitions that drew support from minorities and the poor. In New Haven, where whites had fled in massive numbers to the suburbs, similar pressures were brought to bear on policy making, although more through an exodus of local businesses and residents and external fiscal stress on the city.

As an American city where the social and spatial conditions bore the most resemblance to those of Germany, Madison demonstrates in particular how much difference these conditions both did and did not make. Not only the smaller numbers of poor minorities but more centralized settlement had helped maintain greater numbers of managers and professionals within or with access to the downtown. A comparatively strong mayor and a sizeable local planning bureaucracy carried out a synthesis that helped produce in Madison the most extensive environmental goods among the U.S. settings alongside its considerable developmental policies. Yet even here, the interests of the growing suburban white population within the city imposed greater constraints on local policy than in the

European settings. James Rowen, Paul Soglin's designated successor as mayor, had lost the 1979 mayoral race in a campaign that emphasized the interests of downtown residents and lower-income people in opposition to suburban ones. Unambiguously distributive proposals like new taxes and local rent controls, and opposition to the Beltline highway around the western neighborhoods of the city, cost Rowen votes in the West Side neighborhoods that Soglin had carried. In the 1980s and 1990s, Soglin himself shed the vestiges of his earlier radicalism in favor of fiscal conservatism.

Governance beyond the Central City

As the discussion of Nancy, Rennes and Madison makes clear, policy making on environmental and other matters has often transcended central-city boundaries. In building horizontal relations with other local governments within the metropolitan areas to formulate and carry out policy, local coalitions have increasingly constructed governance arrangements outward from the central city. These arrangements within metropolitan areas amount to interlocal policy regimes. They can be critical to the success of policies and furnish crucial objects for politics. How these regimes work, and often the forces that bring them into existence, depend on the economic and social dynamics that also bind metropolitan regions together and with other places. For this reason, no analysis of governance beyond the central cities can afford to ignore the interlocal dynamics the Tiebout model highlights. On the one hand, I will examine more closely the general consequences of supralocal infrastructures for local government and politics for these processes. On the other, I will consider how interlocal governance within urban regions contributed to urban policy syntheses. In turn, supralocal authorizations, mandates and other provisions for this governance play an important role.

Interlocal Competition and National Infrastructures. The Tiebout model presupposes several processes among localities both within and among metropolitan areas. The account of policy in cities like New Haven, Clermont-Ferrand, Bielefeld and Göttingen has already suggested the fiscal pressures that the model attributes to limited local tax revenues. Peterson argues that the model implies that developmental policies will (and should) be favored in order to attract new residents and new tax revenues to a central city. Environmental and social policies that detract from revenues will be discouraged. The model presumes both that resident tax-payers will move to local jurisdictions with preferred packages of services and taxes and that local officials can and will provide the mix of services and taxes that those taxpayers want.

Both of these aspects of the model depend on infrastructures of markets and policy making that differ between and sometimes within these three countries. Local officials whose revenues do not depend on either the local tax base or political support for local tax imposition should feel few of those constraints that the Tiebout model posits on local services. As Figure 4.1 demonstrates, the national infrastructures make local taxes contingent to very different degrees on conditions that local policy makers can alter. In the country of origin for the Tiebout model – the United States – cities depend on locally raised property taxes for the overwhelming bulk of their operating expenses. In Germany and to a lesser extent in France, frame-works for fiscal equalization or subsidies left much less of local operating revenues dependent on local tax revenues. Taxes that the German city gov-ernments could adjust accounted for only 21 percent of local revenues; and fiscal equalization reduced local leeway to determine even these taxes. Except for one of the French cities, taxes with rates subject to local deter-minations contributed 30 or 31 percent of their operating budgets. In both European countries, moreover, the principal locally determined taxes applied to businesses alone rather than to property in general,[171] and the comparative lack of local discretion over residential property taxes elimi-nated a further cornerstone of the Tiebout model. Finally, especially in Germany, the supralocal policies examined in Chapter 3 imposed obliga-tions and other conditions that indirectly limited the relevance of local fiscal resources for local choices.

Precisely the interlocal competition for businesses and residents that the Tiebout model posits has emerged as a central feature of the postwar era in the U.S. central cities and much of their surrounding regions. Although competition with other metropolitan areas and even national regions played a role in this dynamic, the clearest, most influential com-petition came from the urban regions surrounding central cities. From the aggressive urban renewal of the Lee administration to the efforts of local elites during the Daniels and DeStefano administrations to forestall the

---

[171] In Germany the *Gewerbesteuer*, or business activity tax, and in France the equivalent *taxe professionelle*, garnered well over half of the local finances from taxes set at the municipal level.

death of the Chapel Square Mall, the exodus of businesses and the most prosperous residents to suburban towns loomed constantly over central-city coalitions in New Haven. Market pressures reinforced the limits on amenities and social equity and the repeated mobilizations around growth. Especially before the 1980s, the coalitions in Durham had mobilized around new development partly in competition with faster-growing nearby cities like Raleigh and Chapel Hill. There and in Madison, not only the central city but a number of smaller, less wealthy towns, like Middleton on the west side of Madison and Carrboro in Orange County, had actively sought new development through the 1990s.

Because the local property tax applied to both residences and businesses, however, the U.S. fiscal infrastructure also had different implications for local incentives than did the European business taxes.[172] U.S. local officials faced a need to attract not only businesses that increased the tax base but also residential property owners and their political support. Perhaps even more important, residential property owners had reason to oppose expansion that might place added demands on local infrastructure and even to segregate themselves in jurisdictions of others with similar preferences. In towns where these property owners dominated, such as Woodbridge and Orange around New Haven, local policies constrained new development but maintained high levels of environmental amenities. In towns with a mixture of residential and business taxpayers, like Guilford in the mid-1970s, in Branford in the early 1980s and in Hamden in the late 1980s, local movements based in residential neighborhoods struggled with local officials over development. Poorer towns sought businesses that would provide jobs and services for the residents of the towns that had clamped down on new development. In greater Durham too, the residential areas of Chapel Hill and Orange County retained restrictions on new business development even as Durham continued to pursue major new mall and office complexes.

As the lower levels of exurban segregation in Europe suggest, both social sorting and home owner movements of this sort played more limited roles in the peripheral communes of such cities as Montpellier and Freiburg. But since the decentralization of the 1980s, both French central cities and the communes of their urban peripheries had also engaged increasingly in interlocal competition.[173] In greater Montpellier, the place with the most

---

[172] Peterson, *City Limits*.
[173] For an analysis of this competition see Jonah Levy, *Tocqueville's Revenge* (Cambridge, MA: Harvard University Press, 1998), pp. 140–152.

growth and the least successful interlocal cooperation around planning, this competition pervaded much of the metropolitan area. With such projects as Port Marianne, the central city under Frêche sought to extend the urban area south toward the autoroute along the River Lez. Beyond the city limits along the same river, Michel Vaillat, the rightist mayor of Lattes, initiated a housing and commercial development called "Port Ariane." To the southeast, alongside the expansion of the regional airport at Pérols, the Chamber of Commerce sponsored "Eurogare," a new, multimodal platform for transfer between rail, road, and air transportation. Within the district especially, networks of local elites linked to Frêche and the Left mobilized the organizational resources of the central city around new development. On the Right, Vaillat and his networks linked to the regional government and the Chamber of Commerce and Industry mobilized around competing plans. Outside Clermont-Ferrand in particular, but also outside Nancy, communes had engaged in more haphazard competition. Half-filled office parks had become a familiar feature of the periurban landscape. Around Rennes, however, regional planning since the 1970s had limited this competition more. By the 1990s intercommunal associations of both Rennes and Nancy had quelled interlocal competition with a pooled revenue base from the local business tax.

Within the German metropolitan areas, as the Tiebout model would predict under German conditions, interlocal competition remained the least evident. Beside offering fewer fiscal incentives, supralocal mandates and other policies limited local opportunities to compete. In contrast with both France and the United States, a German ministerial report of the early 1990s emphasized the reluctance of both central cities and exurban communes to authorize new land for any kind of new construction.[174] In the central cities of Bielefeld and Münster, the conservative coalitions of the 1990s pursued developmental policies to forestall losses of jobs to suburban towns. But even regional planners had accommodated the calls of Red-Green coalitions to limit development in the central cities. Outside Freiburg, in one of the fastest growing regions of the Federal Republic, peripheral communes with an interest in either new businesses or wealthy residents sometimes jockeyed to be designated in the regional plan for new housing or infrastructure.[175] But even there, tightening

---

[174] Bundesministerium für Raumordnung, Bauwesen und Städtebau, *Kostensenkung und Verringerung von Vorschriften im Wohnungsbau* (Bonn, 1995), vol. 2, pp. 5–6.

[175] Wulf Tessin, *Stadtwachstum und Stadt-Umland Politik* (Munich: Minerva Publikation, 1986).

regulatory strictures in the 1970s and 1980s imposed limits on such tendencies.

Regional Governance. Against the background of the wide differences in the way supralocal infrastructures shaped interlocal competition, elites and activists in the central cities had frequently built governing coalitions beyond central-city boundaries. As Elinor Ostrom and her colleagues have argued for police services in particular, the "polycentric" urban economy of the Tiebout model can encourage effective governance by means of more localized choices and greater interlocal competition.[176] Other studies of growth management, developmental policies and social equity point to the benefits from arrangements that enable officials to transcend narrow, opposed interests of a particular locality in the pursuit of goods for the entire region.[177] Within the metropolitan area, cooperation or metropolitan policy can address problems that overlap individual town boundaries and that overcome negative externalities from localism and interlocal competition. In the competition with other urban regions for new development, metropolitan regional governance can enable localities to strengthen their position.

The more important this interlocal element is to local policy syntheses, the greater the need to expand analyses of local government and politics into accounts of urban governance. Along with formal metropolitan governance and informal cooperative relations among localities, such an analysis must also take account of how these arrangements shaped markets for residence and development.

a. Interlocal Organization. To make and carry out policies across a city region, supralocal officials might make available and localities could employ any of several formal institutional alternatives. The governments of the municipalities could enter into a formal cooperative arrangement that pooled authorities. A hierarchical government within the

---

[176] Elinor Ostrom, "The Danger of Self-Evident Truths," *PS: Political Science and Politics* 23(1) (2000): 33–44; Robert L. Bish and Vincent Ostrom, *Understanding Urban Government: Metropolitan Reform Reconsidered* (Washington: American Enterprise Institute, 1973).

[177] Paul Lewis, *Shaping Suburbia* (Pittsburgh: University of Pittsburgh Press, 1996); Myron Orfield, *Metropolitics* (Washington: Brookings Institution, 1996); L. van den Berg, E. Braun and J. van der Meer, "The Organising Capacity of Metropolitan Regions," *Environment and Planning C: Government and Policy*, vol. 15, pp. 253–272; C. Lefèvre, "Metropolitan Government and Governance in Western Countries: A Critical Review," *International Journal of Urban and Regional Research* (1998): 9–25.

metropolitan area could assume authority over localities. Or an individual municipality like the central-city government could internalize the problem through annexation beyond its boundaries or through extraterritorial jurisdiction.[178] Though not conceived as part of local government systems, evolving legal and public finance authorities at higher national and regional levels shaped the opportunities for these arrangements. For all of these alternatives, including central-city annexation, proponents in the central city usually had to reach out to other local governments to construct governing coalitions.[179] The usefulness of effective arrangements of this sort is especially clear for policies like environmental management or distributive equity. In these instances, governmental integration enables local officials to overcome local efforts to avoid responsibility for collective problems of the urban region. Coordination among metropolitan towns can even mobilize regional efforts more effectively around developmental efforts.

In the urban regions of western Germany all three means of interlocal governance had been part of regional governance since the 1960s (Table 4.7). Fiscal equalization, supralocal policies and planning mandates from above facilitated these arrangements but rarely dictated them. *Landkreise* or county governments separate from the central city oversaw matters of administration, including construction permits, in the outlying exurban communes. In Göttingen, the *Landkreis* also exercised supervisory jurisdiction over the central city. In each instance, interlocal cooperation and planning predated the institution of a federal framework for regional planning in the 1960s. In each, the plans under this system set out priorities for economic development alongside physical infrastructure and environmental aims. By the late 1980s schemes of this sort around Bielefeld, Münster and Göttingen went so far as to set negotiated targets of new housing for each metropolitan commune. *Landkreis* governments or the regional bureaucratic offices of the *Land* governments themselves (the *Regierungspräsidien*) generally enforced the decisions of these associations. As Chapter 3 demonstrated, these arrangements had a particularly important effect on the management of new development outside the central

---

[178] David Rusk, *Cities Without Suburbs* (Washington: Woodrow Wilson Center Press, 1993).

[179] Vincent Hoffmann-Martinot, "La relance du gouvernement métropolitaine en Europe: Le prototype de Stuttgart," *Revue française d'administration publique* 70 (1994): 499–514; Le Galès, *Politique Urbaine et Développement Local*; Christopher Leo, "Regional Growth Management Regime: The Case of Portland, Oregon," *Journal of Urban Affairs* 20(4) (1998): 363–394; Orfield, *Metropolitics*.

Table 4.7. *Main Institutional Means, Policy Domains and Outcomes of Metropolitan Cooperation, 1970s to Mid-1990s*

	Metropolitan Supralocal Governments	Domains of Cooperation among Main Interlocal Body	Annexation by Central City	Domains of Successful Outcomes
Germany				
Bielefeld	Yes (*Landkreis*)	Growth management (control, growth)	Yes–very extensive	Control
Freiburg	Yes (*Landkreis*)	Growth management (control, growth)	Yes–extensive	Control, growth
Göttingen	Yes (*Landkreis*)	Growth management (control, growth)	Yes–extensive	Control
Münster	Yes (*Landkreis*)	Growth management (control, growth)	Yes–extensive	Control, growth
France				
Clermont-Ferrand	No	Control (minimal)	No	Control (limited)
Montpellier	No	Growth only	No	Growth
Nancy	No	Growth, social equity	No	Growth (limited)
Rennes	No	Growth, control, social equity	No	Growth, control, social equity
United States:				
Durham	Yes (County)	Advisory	Yes–very extensive	Control (limited, belated)
Madison	Yes (County)	Weak	Yes–extensive	Control
New Haven	No	Advisory	No	None

city. In Münster and to a lesser degree in Freiburg, central-city governments had also used the regional planning process to designate peripheral centers of development to alleviate pressures on central cities to expand.

In efforts to manage peripheral development, the territorial reorganization of German local governments in the 1960s and 1970s also proved crucial. Bielefeld and Münster, required by the *Land* government to undertake extensive recombinations of local jurisdictions, grew by 449 percent and 309 percent. Göttingen and Freiburg negotiated increases of 344 and 91 percent with surrounding villages. In each city the newly annexed territories encompassed large expanses of undeveloped peripheral land (Figures 4.3–4.6). To contain sprawl before it started, the local government proceeded to institute protections on those areas. Münster extended its system of green corridors, Freiburg its city forests; all four governments placed local regulatory protections on farmland and natural areas.

In the French settings, municipal jurisdictional boundaries remained overwhelmingly those in place since the Revolution. Since the urban regions usually extended well beyond those boundaries, and both the formal regional and the departmental boundaries were overinclusive, central-city administrations turned increasingly to intercommunal governments to realize agendas. Although the shift to more locally based municipal finance in the 1980s had contributed to greater competition among localities than in Germany, Left governments at the national level in the early and late 1990s elaborated new incentives and formulas for these cooperative arrangements.[180] In Montpellier, Nancy and Rennes, districts composed of the central city and a dozen or more surrounding communes served since 1970 or before to coordinate installation of such new facilities as the university campuses and technology and industrial parks in the urban periphery and of basic physical infrastructure and services. In Montpellier, for instance, surrounding communes had contributed to basic infrastructural services like the airport at Pérols, the metropolitan bus service, the waste disposal system and the system of technology parks. Clermont-Ferrand maintained a looser, more limited intercommunal syndicate for a range of similar purposes, and a myriad of smaller cooperative arrangements saw to specific functions in all four city regions. In the 1990s, acting through local initiatives or under national authorizing legislation, the intercommunal associations of Clermont-Ferrand, Rennes and Nancy stepped up these arrangements. In 1993, the district of Rennes took over from the municipalities the power to raise revenues from the *taxe professionelle*, the most important independent source of local revenues in France. In 1995 communes in the district of Nancy established an "Urban Community" with similar collective tax powers. Around the same time, the syndicate of Clermont-Ferrand became a "community of communes" with power to collect increments to municipal taxes.

---

[180] The Law of Orientation Number 95–125 of February 6, 1992, Relating to Territorial Administration instituted new categories of interlocal organization that included variants with shared tax bases. The Law Number 99–586 of July 12, 1999, instituted additional new incentives.

In Rennes intercommunal cooperation had proceeded the earliest beyond efforts to promote growth and provide basic infrastructure. From its founding with twenty-seven communes in 1970, the district had exercised powers of land use planning in connection with AUDIAR and had regularly accumulated new authorities and communes. By the issuance of a third *Schéma Directeur* in the mid-1990s, the district also extended to thirty-three communes. The course of new development within the district demonstrates how effectively this arrangement assured collective management of growth. Even before the introduction of formal local planning and permitting authorities in the national legislation of the 1980s, cooperation had helped shift development away from protected areas (Figure 4.14). Already in 1968–1975, a period that includes the *Schéma Directeur* of 1973, development in the central city and inner communes corresponded negatively with distance from the center, land in forest and proportions of farm workers. Up to 1982 these correlations persisted as the intensity of development rose, and correlations with distance and agriculture for the metropolitan area converged toward zero (Figure 3.4). In the decade after the district acquired formal land use authority, all three indicators point to greater control than before and more within the district boundaries than anywhere else outside of Germany. At the same time, the district had carried out such cornerstones of local developmental policy as the technology parks at Rennes-Atalante and Atalante-Champeaux as well as local policies toward transportation and physical infrastructure. In an agreement signed in 1982 to aid access to housing for disadvantaged residents, and a further housing convention between the city, parapublic officials and central officials in 1992, the district secured significant local responsibility to furnish subsidized housing, operate facilities for transients and fight the emergence of poor enclaves.

In Clermont-Ferrand, Montpellier and Nancy, the main intercommunal organizations extended across smaller portions of the metropolitan area. Prior to the institution of the Urban Community at Nancy in 1995, these organizations had undertaken more limited activities than were tried in and around Rennes. In the city region of Nancy, where the central city jurisdiction spanned only 15 square kilometers, local officials insisted especially strongly on the need for interlocal coordination.[181] The limited territorial scope of intercommunal arrangements in all three city regions foreclosed systematic efforts to control development outside of a narrow,

---

[181] Lefebvre, *Nancy et son Agglomération*.

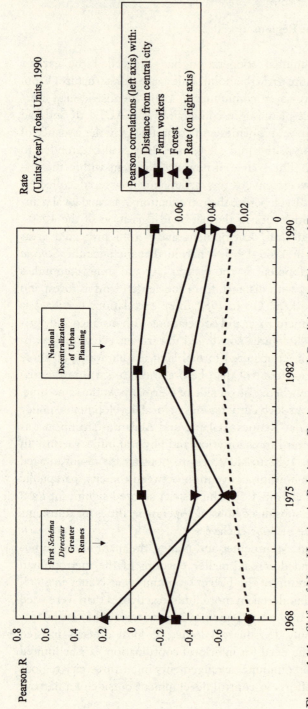

Figure 4.14 Shifts of New Housing in Relation to Environmental Conditions in District of Rennes, 1962–1990

Note: Pearson correlations measure relation of New Housing Index for housing added per year during each period by commune (*n* = 24) with distance from city center; with proportion of cadastral land in forest for 1970 (periods 1962–1968 and 1968–1975) and for 1988 (periods 1975–1982 and 1982–1990); and with proportion in agriculture of the population residing in ordinary households in 1962 (periods 1962–1968 and 1968–1975) and proportion in agriculture of active employed cantonal population in 1982 (1975–1982 and 1982–1990). Change in housing for each period represents total at beginning of period minus total at end of period. For further analysis see Jefferey M. Sellers, "Federalism and Metropolitan Governance: The Case of Urban Sprawl," *Environment and Planning C* (forthcoming).

Sources: INSEE, *Recensement Général de la Population de 1962*; id., *Recensement Général de la Population de 1982*: *Évolutions démographiques*; id., *Recensement Général de la Population de 1990*: *Évolutions démographiques*; id., *Communoscope* (1988): *Ministry of Agriculture, Census de l'Agriculture 1970.*

mostly urbanized circle of communes, and in none of these places did the interlocal organization proclaim explicit policies of this sort. More in Nancy and Montpellier than in Clermont-Ferrand, the metropolitan association continued to mobilize around the developmental policies that gave rise to it. In Nancy the parapublic regional development agency ADUAN, as well as the district, worked to expand the local facilities for research and technology transfer, to promote new enterprises and to encourage higher education and other forms of training.[182] In the 1990s the district had participated in the creation of a "school for biotechnology," a regional management center, a new technology transfer center at Brabois, a program of subsidies for spin-offs by local students and a total of seven corporate parks, as well as regional infrastructure and the revitalization along the Moselle. In Montpellier, where other regional associations, to be examined in the next chapter, undertook more of developmental policy, the district still created industrial and corporate parks, carried out large amenities like the Corum, supported such cultural and sports activities as the symphony orchestra, the music conservatory and the soccer and basketball teams and expanded local bus service. In Clermont-Ferrand, where a proliferation of other organizations had emerged to promote development, the counterpart to these organizations remained more confined to provision of physical infrastructure. Starting in 1994, with studies commissioned under the auspices of nationally authorized Local Housing and Residential programs, the intercommunal organizations in both Clermont-Ferrand and Nancy had begun to address the problems of the most disadvantaged neighborhoods throughout the urbanized areas. But up to 1995 neither program had proceeded to the stage of implementation.

In the U.S. urban regions, localized municipal finance, fragmented local authorities and limited policy mandates fostered interlocal relations that were still more competitive. As metropolitan segregation reinforced the divergences among local interests, cooperative arrangements among localities remained less ambitious and more haphazard. Even in this national context, the comparative success of interlocal governance around Madison and increasingly around Durham indicated that such arrangements could be effective. Both cities took advantage of state authorizations to annex large amounts of unincorporated land in the surrounding counties. By the late 1980s both cities employed refusals to grant utility services to compel developers on the periphery to go along with this policy. Both actively

---

[182] ADUAN, *Atlas*, p. 56.

employed the jurisdiction their state governments had granted to enforce boundaries on exurban growth beyond the city limits. At the same time, both the Dane County Planning Commission and its counterpart in Durham County assumed powers to administer planning directly for parts of the metropolitan area that had not incorporated. After 1988 in Durham County, a combined city-county planning department integrated this peripheral administration with central-city planning; planners in Madison usually cooperated closely with Dane County. Since the metropolitan area surrounding Durham extended into neighboring Orange County and beyond, its governance also required either parallel or coordinated efforts with officials there. Although metropolitan agencies like the Triangle Council of Governments remained advisory, the county and city governments of Durham joined with Orange County, Chapel Hill and other bodies to establish a Triangle Transit Authority in 1989 and a cooperative agreement on an open-space corridor in the New Hope Valley in 1991.

These arrangements had the most direct consequences for the management of growth. In Dane County, the efforts of the city and county governments together help to account for the comparative success of efforts to stem sprawl outside the central city by the 1980s. Although the county authorities also controlled the Madison airport and issued transportation plans, these limited county authorities permitted less of a concerted developmental effort. Outside the Durham city limits, the growth boundary established in the late 1980s probably laid a groundwork for somewhat more effective growth management than the modest result that Figure 3.5 suggests. Another reason for increasingly effective restrictions on sprawl stemmed from regulation in Orange County. There Chapel Hill residents not only had maintained a stricter regime of restrictions on new development within their own city but also had dominated the county zoning board sufficiently to secure a green belt of designated low-density development around the city in 1992. County governments surrounding both neighboring cities had also played little direct role in the measures that brought growth; since Durham County had integrated city and county planning, any such role remained difficult to separate out. In either metropolitan area, only the consolidation of county and city schools in Durham in 1992 addressed the disparities among neighborhoods. Restrictions on development in areas like the Chapel Hill green belt had the coincidental effect of reinforcing prerogatives of wealthy white residents.

In greater New Haven, the regional Council of Governments exercised only advisory authority over metropolitan towns. In the absence of unincorporated land and in the face of opposition among surrounding towns to any manner of central-city annexation, not even county regulatory authorities existed. Municipal zoning with exclusionary consequences had supplied the main tool for control of development. Even in the face of state mandates to rectify the racial and socioeconomic disparities between schools in New Haven and in suburban school districts efforts at interlocal cooperation in that domain had failed.[183] Despite this absence of formal or informal cooperation, municipal authorities in such towns as Woodbridge, Orange and Guilford had effectively preserved low-density settlement. As subsequent analysis will make clear, local movements for growth management in numerous towns reinforced these policies. Successful, systematic efforts of this sort remained confined to the wealthiest towns.

The fragmented regional governance of New Haven typified American urban regions more than did the collective efforts around Durham or Madison. Yet the growth of metropolitan governance in those other U.S. settings followed the international trend evident in France and Germany. The comparative successes of such cities demonstrates the limits of arguments from the Tiebout model in favor of decentralized, fragmented policy making. Especially in the management of new development, metropolitan governance has often overcome the barriers that interlocal competition as well as interlocal coordination pose to the solution of metropolitan problems. Central cities with more successful governance in their surrounding regions have ultimately succeeded better in internal policy.

b. Metropolitan Markets and Exurban Jurisdictions.   Within the general tendencies that Tiebout identified, spatial patterns in the provision of specific urban services or amenities can also influence outcomes through effects on markets.[184] Some such patterns in goods and services like those in public education, take the form of variations among policies and jurisdictions across a city region. Others, like environmental quality and

---

[183] Kathryn McDermott, "Regionalism Forestalled: Metropolitan Fragmentation and Desegregation Planning in Greater New Haven, Connecticut," in Clarence Stone (ed.), *Reforming Urban Education* (Lawrence: University of Kansas Press, 1998), pp. 45–65.

[184] Mark Schneider, Paul Teske and Michael Mintrom, *Public Entrepreneurs: Agents for Change in American Government* (Princeton: Princeton University Press, 1995); Robert Stein, "Devolution and Challenge for State and Local Government," in Ronald Weber and Paul Brace (eds.), *American State and Local Politics* (New York: Chatham House, 1999), pp. 21–37.

shopping opportunities, flow most directly out of private initiatives but can be influenced by local policies such as regulation. In all these domains, place-based markets for public or private goods within the urban region affect the chances of individual localities to manage growth or to alleviate the difficulties of disadvantaged neighborhoods.

Public school districts in U.S. city regions furnish one of the clearest territorial influences of this sort. The power of local school districts over public education and the dependence of those districts on local taxes imposed incentives in U.S. land use markets with little equivalent in the European settings. In both the Durham and the New Haven urban regions, school districts outside the central city had attracted well-to-do and white families with the promise of better educational opportunities for children than were available in the central city. Outside Durham, the Chapel Hill school district in Orange County, supported through a special district property levy, earned some of the highest rankings in North Carolina from a state rating system based on standardized scores and other data. Within the city, meanwhile, four schools numbered among the thirteen across the state that received the lowest possible rating.[185] Despite a large infusion of state revenues that equalized funding for school districts in and around New Haven, districts in Orange and Woodbridge to the east and Guilford to the west of New Haven had far higher test scores than the city schools.[186] Many of the most privileged enclaves of both city regions clustered around these areas with the best schools. In Madison, the school district encompassed the city along with several suburban towns. Although neighborhood-based allocations of pupils could not remedy the difficulties that students faced in disadvantaged areas like South Madison, the unified system enabled more equalized staffing, curricula and finances. Better schools within the central-city system also removed one of the reasons why residents in greater Durham and greater New Haven fled the urban centers.

With notable exceptions, the school systems of the European settings also discouraged urban flight and segregation. Governed through arrangements at the national or *Land* level, and subject to comparatively little variation in funding, curricula, hiring and parent involvement across a city region, French and German systems offered less apparent criteria for

---

[185] Jonathan Goldstein and Sumathi Reddy, "High Schools Top List," *Raleigh News and Observer*, August 6, 1999, p. A1.

[186] McDermott, "Regionalism Forestalled," p. 47.

territorial sorting. At the same time, institutional distinctions between elite and nonelite tracks performed much of the social selection that the more privileged U.S. families carried out through choices of neighborhoods on the basis of schools. Fewer French and German children proceeded through the college preparatory tracks of the *baccalauréat* or the *Gymnasium* than through the end of the U.S. high school. Ethnic and immigrant minorities fared especially poorly in this process of selection. While foreigners made up nearly 20 percent of the local elementary school population in Bielefeld by the early 1990s, the same group made up only 6 percent of the students in the *Gymnasien* and 38 percent in the lower-status *Hauptschulen*.[187] A parallel disparity had appeared in Freiburg.[188] In France as well, foreigners generally fared much worse academically than natives.[189] Reflecting wider demographic contrasts, elites in comparatively exclusive European downtowns were less likely than privileged Americans in suburban enclaves to have children to send to the neighborhood schools.[190] Unlike their American counterparts, the privileged children who went to school in these neighborhoods did so alongside some of the largest concentrations of minorities in the city region. The segregated concentrations of foreigners in the housing estates of La Paillade in Montpellier or Haut du Lièvre in Nancy furnished the main departures from this pattern. In part because the middle-class and white parents in these areas had secured exceptions to rules requiring neighborhood school attendance, but also because more privileged families avoided these neighborhoods

---

[187] Bielefeld, *Situation der Bielefelderinnen und Bielefelder ausländischer Herkunft*, pp. 43, 45, 50–51.

[188] In 1983–1984 there, foreigners made up 14.6 percent of the students in *Grundschulen* and *Hauptschulen*, but 2.6 percent in *Gymnasien* (C. Beck, "Zur Situation ausländischer Kinder und Jugendlicher in Freiburg im Breisgau," in Amt für Statistik und Einwohnerwesen, *Ausländer in Freiburg im Breisgau* [Freiburg, 1988], p. 119).

[189] Jacqueline Costa-Lascoux, *De l'Immigré au Citoyen* (Paris: La Documentation Française, 1988), Ch. 4.

[190] In nearly all of the downtown European neighborhoods around two-thirds of households had either one or two members. In most, half or more of the total counted only one member. Especially in the German cities, this tendency reflected a more general societal tendency toward more singles and smaller families. At the same time, the European downtowns had created a mix of opportunities for shopping, eating out and night life that attracted unmarried people and those without big families. Just as European families with children gravitated toward less central settings, concentrations of "singles" and childless couples had settled in a few downtown Madison neighborhoods. But even in the central cities of the U.S. settings, the places with the highest concentrations of privilege averaged more than two persons per household.

altogether,[191] proportions of disadvantaged groups and of academic failure ranged far higher here than elsewhere in the metropolitan area. The three elementary schools of La Paillade, for instance, contained 80 percent or more foreigners, and registered from 30 to 66 percent rates of academic failure.[192]

Although shopping was a privately furnished amenity, regulation of it also shaped wider patterns of development. German regulations elaborated at higher levels and written into regional planning employed restrictions on the size of shopping facilities outside urbanized areas to limit inducements to urban sprawl.[193] Even in the western Germany of the 1990s, road maps rarely depicted the locations of malls or shopping centers. At the same time, in the absence of regional governance, U.S. and French localities had taken advantage of *less strict* constraints than placed on their German counterparts to bring additional sprawl and to lock in elite enclaves. In greater New Haven, the flight of central-city retailers and customers to suburban centers like the Connecticut Post Mall and Hamden Plaza had by the late 1990s nearly killed the Chapel Square Mall. Although annexations in Durham kept new shopping centers like New Hope Commons within the city limits, and tax revenues in city coffers, these developments fostered a similar dispersal into the periphery and offered privileged neighborhoods additional advantages. In France, peripheral mayors anxious to fill new commercial and industrial parks often found *hypermarchés* one of the most productive ways to do so. Shopping centers of this sort had spilled out along N. 113 east of Montpellier and south toward the Mediterranean, beyond the central-city limits to the west and south of Nancy, and into the pavillion zones of Aubière and Lempdes to the southeast of Clermont-Ferrand. Only Madison among the U.S. cities and Rennes among the French cities had clearly reined in this expansion of shopping facilities into the periphery. For Madison, confinement of new shopping centers to malls within the city limits and the Beltline highway helped brake pressures to expand development beyond the

---

[191] In France as well, families choose neighborhoods increasingly on the basis of schools and security (Bertrand Bissuel, "Comment un bon lycée fait monter le prix de l'immobilier," *Le Monde*, April 21, 2000, at www.lemonde.fr/article_impression/0,2322,51579,00.html).

[192] *Midi Libre*, December 18 1990, p. X7a.

[193] See Elmar Kulke, "Structural Change and Spatial Response in the Retail Sector in Germany," *Urban Studies* 29(6) (1992): 965–977; Clifford M. Guy, "Controlling New Retail Spaces: The Impress of Planning Policies in Western Europe," *Urban Studies* 35(5–6) (1998): 953–979.

urban growth boundary. Although Rennes could not expand its city boundaries in the same way, local officials there had secured both a ring highway and an armature of major shopping centers close to if not within the city limits. The concentration of development not only contributed to revenues in Rennes, but it enhanced the economic dependence of outlying towns on the central city. Central officials thereby gained added political leverage to sustain the metropolitan policies of the district of Rennes.

Regulatory and other measures to secure environmental amenities in the towns of urban regions followed analogous patterns of variation. In the American and certain French metropolitan areas, natural settings provided part of the inducement for residents to move out from the central city, and one of the defining conditions for some of the most privileged enclaves. In the outlying areas of the U.S. cities, large-lot zoning preserved high levels of natural protection for those who could afford to buy big properties. The pastoral forests of Woodbridge beyond New Haven, the shorelines of Lake Mendota outside Madison and the wooded expanses of Hope Valley or Duke Forest outside Durham offered especially alluring amenities for some of the most privileged local home owners. In the rolling, wooded hills along the Lez north of Montpellier, along the Forest of La Haye to the west of Nancy and at Chamalières near the foot of the volcanic peaks around Clermont-Ferrand, smaller but sizeable numbers of privileged residents also found homes outside the French central cities. Except for a few small concentrations in several Black Forest towns outside Freiburg, the expanded jurisdictions and regional planning of the German cities had prevented a similar process. In doing so, the German cities and their surrounding city regions helped forestall both further sprawl and greater place-based disparities.

Especially to manage spatial expansion, but often for other purposes, local actors have constructed governance outward and upward from central cities. In the absence of such arrangements, the Tiebout model highlights how interlocal markets foster competitive local development policies and how metropolitan variations in educational, shopping and environmental amenities can undermine the pursuit of growth management and territorial equity. Infrastructures imbedded at supralocal levels have furnished authorizations and mandates for metropolitan cooperation, financial inducements to local decision makers and supplies of legal authorities crucial to territorial arrangements of schools, stores and open space. In the German urban regions, less discretionary local finance and more extensive supralocal commands back up an elaborate infrastructure for metropolitan governance. In Rennes and Madison, drawing on less extensive supralocal components, local governing coalitions have secured some of the same advantages from interlocal cooperation as have German central cities.

Conclusion

By the 1990s, in all eleven urban regions, syntheses of policy had emerged around significant initiatives in at least two of the three domains. The variety of urban syntheses and the local political paths that produced them manifest how profoundly global trends still depend on both national and local influences. In each central city, with varying degrees of success, the leaders of local electoral coalitions sought to build governing coalitions around local syntheses. Both as direct influences on policy and as indirect influences on local political and market preferences, supralocal policies framed these efforts. Infrastructures of local government, political parties and interlocal relations established distinctive ranges of possible local policy syntheses. Drawing on these elements from above, local political entrepreneurs and governing coalitions within these urban regions embedded local choices in ordinances, planning strategies, political institutions and development patterns. Across the urban region, interlocal governance often extended the reach of these coalitions. Local choices, and the electoral coalitions and administrative apparatuses that largely made those choices, account for much of the wide variation in local syntheses. Yet crucial aspects of this variation still require further analysis.

The governing syntheses of the late 1980s and early 1990s in the central cities, along with the extensions of policy making into the remainder of the city region, demonstrate the broad range of this variation (Table 4.8). Alongside quantitative indicators like budget totals and staff numbers, the summary assessments of Table 4.8 necessarily rely on qualitative assessment of the diverse initiatives local actors undertook. Beyond policies handed down from above, the leading electoral coalitions during this period in the central cities account for some, but not all, of the difference in local choices. Infrastructures of local government and politics, effects from interlocal markets, even social and spatial conditions also furnish partial, explanations for the anomalies.

In the German cities, local syntheses manifested the least pressure from global economic forces to subordinate equity and environmental quality to development. In a three-dimensional depiction of these ratings that

Table 4.8 *Central City Politics and Urban Policy Syntheses in the Late 1980s and Early 1990s*

	Leading Electoral Coalition	Policy Toward Development	Policy Toward Environmental Quality	Policy Toward Social Equity	Type of Synthesis
Germany					
Bielefeld	(Contested)	X (X)	XX (X)	XXX	Social-Ecological
Freiburg	Center-Left	XX (X)	XXX (X)	XXX	Comprehensive
Göttingen	(Contested)	X (X)	XXX (X)	XX	Social-Ecological
Münster	Right	XX (X)	XXX (X)	XX	Comprehensive
France					
Clermont-Ferrand	Left	XX	X	XXX	Local Fordist
Montpellier	Left	XXX (X)	XX	X	Upscale
Nancy	Center-Right	XX (X)	XX	X (X)	Upscale
Rennes	Left	XXX (X)	XX (X)	XXX (X)	Comprehensive
United States					
Durham	(Contested)	XXX	XX	X	Upscale
Madison	Left	XXX (X)	XX (X)	X	Upscale
New Haven	(Contested)	XX	X	X	Upscale

X = limited or mostly contradictory policies in central city; XX = significant policies in central city; XXX = extensive policies in central city; (X) = policy extended to or applied in surrounding urban region.

takes into account their metropolitan dimensions (Figure 4.15), all four German cities cluster at a similar remove from their French and American counterparts. The colors of dominant political coalitions, and even the existence of a stable dominant coalition, made comparatively little difference for local policy. Even the conservative, business-friendly government of Münster balanced significant efforts to secure social justice and environmental quality with developmental objectives. Overall, local coalitions also evinced comparatively little determination to pursue growth. No central-city government had mobilized around developmental policies as much as Montpellier, Rennes, Durham or Madison, and only Freiburg and Münster had pursued developmental policies consistently and effectively.

Although supralocal policies aimed at environmental protection, social equity and regional planning help to account for the similarities, so do the largely similar infrastructures of politics and government in all four city regions. These infrastructures extend beyond the parallels that party

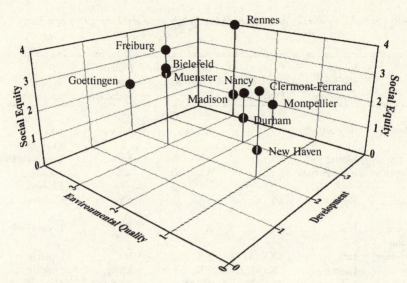

Figure 4.15 Policy Syntheses in Central Cities (with Extensions to Urban Regions), Late 1980s–Mid-1990s

systems, local bureaucracies and local government finance in the central cities helped bring about. Parallel authorities for annexation, interlocal cooperation and metropolitan administration also exerted similar effects on regional market forces. Even somewhat different local institutional infrastructures and different political coalitions could yield largely similar local results. At the same time as a dominant conservative coalition in the Münster City Council elaborated a comprehensive synthesis without a separately elected mayor, SPD mayors Keidel and Böhme in Freiburg relied on strong mayoral authority to lead coalitions around an analogous synthesis. Even under an equalized system of municipal finance, greater prosperity enhanced the funds available to do so.

Ultimately, the similar choices under two different political coalitions also suggest limits to explanations based on either local politics or supralocal and metropolitan policies. If the leading political coalition made such a small difference even for localized choices, then not only external constraints but also similar influences within the urban political economy may be at work. More uniform infrastructures of political parties and administrative bureaucracies and effects from more uniform local finance and interlocal markets surely help to explain the similarity. But so might parallel configuration of interests in local markets and civil society. By the same token, the lack of a dominant political coalition or fewer fruits from prosperity may not fully account for the comparative shortcomings of policy in two of the three domains in Göttingen and Bielefeld.

Despite both federalism and the widest variety in local governmental forms, the variations among the American city regions spanned an even more limited range. More than in either other national context, the urban governing coalitions of these central cities reflected strategies that hierarchical accounts of the global economy predict. The governing coalition under Paul Soglin in Madison exemplified the resulting contradictions. Socially and spatially this urban region resembled those of European cities most closely, and the coalition bore the clearest earmarks of a stable, progressive formation. Yet despite significant contrasts with syntheses in Durham and New Haven, the governing coalition of Madison retained what must be regarded in international perspective as an Upscale emphasis. Already evident in the U.S. literature on bigger cities, this tendency proved even more pronounced in the other U.S. settings. In Durham even the local Progressive coalition came under effective, if temporary challenges from local groups linked to downtown businesses. In New Haven, environmental measures played the most minimal role in local policy making and politics. Recurrent developmental initiatives repeatedly undermined policies that served the interests of disadvantaged neighborhoods and groups. In both urban regions surrounding Durham and New Haven, amenities and other services to privileged or middle-class white residents imposed constant competitive pressures on central-city officials.

As they do in Germany, these patterns follow in part from the policies and political and governmental institutions in which these local governing coalitions nest. In addition to the comparative limitations of supralocal policies, governmental fragmentation, loosely organized parties and frequent voting complicated maintenance of electoral and governing coalitions around social and environmental policy. More than elsewhere, but especially in New Haven, the need to raise taxes locally and the fear of interlocal competition reinforced the preoccupation with developmental policy in the governments of the central cities. In places like New Haven and Durham, greater sprawl and socioethnic division compounded interlocal competition and the effects on localized policy.

At the same time, the significant contrasts between environmental and developmental policy in all three of the U.S. cities suggest forces at work beyond uniform national influences or local social and spatial structures. In the open-structured American context, analysis of electoral coalitions and public administration reveals perhaps the least about the sources of local policy and the reality of its implementation. In the absence of extensive supralocal policies in many areas, the lack of strong political parties, the fragmentation of municipal government and the frequent limits to local policy itself, it is hardly surprising that U.S. analysts of local politics and policy have looked to economic, social and civic organizations and interests. This work has repeatedly underscored the need to look beyond the formal institutions of politics and government to understand local outcomes.

Even under a state that remains comparatively centralized and unitary, the wider variations among the French urban regions confirm the growing importance of governance within urban regions there. The variety of local paths among the French cities demonstrates less the arbitrariness of national policy than the extent that local capacities can affect ultimate choices about policy. Clearly party politics has only partly determined the range of that choice. In Rennes, the coalition under Hervé had built up a comprehensive set of policies in all three domains. In doing so this alliance relied increasingly on extending municipal strategies into the wider urban region. The longer-lived coalition under Quilliot in Clermont-Ferrand supplemented a traditional leftist agenda of service delivery with a modest agenda of development. In Montpellier, a third Socialist-led coalition under Frêche joined powerful developmental impulses with modest efforts toward environmental quality within the central city. Although this coalition also undertook measures for disadvantaged groups and neighborhoods, the contradictions of its synthesis resembled those of the longtime Center-Right coalition in Nancy.

Differences in national policies addressed to these settings helped bring about this variety. So too, in conjunction with the agency of these local actors, did the infrastructure of local government and politics in France. Centralized administrative structures and stable majoritarian coalitions enabled leaders like Hervé, Quilliot and Rossinot to maintain consistent lines of local policy over extended periods. The French system of intergovernmental relations offered influential mayors more opportunities to secure benefits for their cities. Less constraining mandates and a more discretionary system of municipal finance furnished more opportunities than in Germany to fashion local strategies of expenditure and implementation. Despite burgeoning interlocal competition within and among city regions, the system also generated less immediate fiscal pressures on central cities than were imposed in the United States. Authorizations for interlocal cooperation offered choices among a variety of institutional frameworks and left choice among them contingent on local decisions. The fiscal benefits from urban growth brought new opportunities to Rennes and Montpellier, and fewer to Clermont-Ferrand and Nancy.

What neither political parties, nor supralocal infrastructures for government, policy and politics, nor even evolving social and spatial structures imposed in France was the precise direction that local paths would take. In all three countries, local agency grew out of more than simply the political choices and structural condition examined so far. Only further attention to the roots of urban governance in the economy and in civil society can fully illuminate what made local choices more decisive in some settings than in others.

5

The Making of Urban Regimes

Beyond governmental institutions, beyond electoral politics, even beyond interlocal governance, urban governance depends on relations with the economy and society. These relations consist of more than the loose, contingent coalitions that pervaded accounts by pluralists like Dahl. Rather than simply policies backed by stable coalitions among governments, electoral coalitions or other actors, governing coalitions in urban settings from Freiburg to Rennes to Madison regularly take the form of institutionalized arrangements between governments, businesses and other social forces. Increasingly, urban analysts, drawing on a term that traces its origins to the dawn of political science, have characterized the nested arrangements for governance in cities and urban regions as *urban regimes*. As at the national and international levels, the term highlights both the stability and the significance of a governing coalition. An urban regime can either brake or accentuate economic influences from without and can alter or reinforce from below the decisions of national authorities. Business and its organized representatives are critical to these formations, but local social and neighborhood movements have increasingly played a role in urban regimes as well. At nearly every step, as infrastructures embedded at higher levels influence what urban regimes can and cannot do, institutions linked to the nation-state have continued to pervade regime politics.

Even as these emergent forms of urban governance recall the localized arrangements of medieval Europe or ancient Greece, it would be a mistake to identify contemporary regimes completely with the "city-states" of earlier eras. Rather, as analysts of urban governance have recognized, urban regimes continue to nest in the translocal systems of both capitalism and national states. As geographers have often argued, urban regimes also build on social, cultural and spatial conditions of everyday life in an urban region.[1] As a mediating influence on these other elements, a regime can still give a decisive, sustained impetus to urban governance. Although the defining elements of an urban regime have often differed with the author, most accounts agree on several core features:

1. A stable agenda institutionalized in the local policy synthesis.
2. A stable electoral coalition.
3. A stable governing coalition.
4. Participation of private or societal interests, including business and institutional interests from the urban economy, in the governing coalition.

An urban regime is more than just an institutionalized coalition around policy. As a specific type of localized regime, it also consists of elements specific to an urban political economy.[2] The widely adopted regime analysis of Stone, based on the example of postwar Atlanta, portrays businesses or other economic institutions besides government as essential to realize the aims of local officials. Recent urban regimes have also often either integrated social and neighborhood movements into governing coalitions or responded to the challenges of those movements with altered policies.[3]

---

[1] Kevin Cox and A. Mair, "Locality and Community in the Politics of Local Economic Development," *Annals of the Association of American Geographers 78* (1988): 307–325; Kevin Cox and A. Mair, "From Localised Social Structures to Localities as Agents," *Environment and Planning A 23* (1991): 197–213; Kevin Cox, "Questions of Abstraction in Studies in the New Urban Politics," *Journal of Urban Affairs 13*(3) (1991): 267–280.

[2] Other components of the various definitions offered for urban regimes do not strike me as useful or essential. Under my definition, policy objectives may be as important as selective incentives to maintaining a regime; electoral constituencies, through their role in electoral coalitions, may be critical to a regime and the aims of an urban regime can be expected to correspond to the policy synthesis of a city only when a full-fledged urban regime is assembled around those aims. For various recent delineations of regimes, see Clarence N. Stone, "Urban Regimes and the Capacity to Govern," *Journal of Urban Affairs 15*(1) (1993): 1–28; Karen Mossberger and Gerry Stoker, "The Evolution of Urban Regime Theory: The Challenge of Conceptualization," paper presented at Urban Affairs Association Annual Meeting (2000); Alan Di Gaetano and John Klemanski, *Power and City Governance* (St. Paul: University of Minnesota Press, 1999); Keith Dowding, Patrick Dunleavy, Desmond King, Helen Margetts and Yvonne Rydin, "Regime Politics in London Local Government," *Urban Affairs Review 34*(4) (1999): 515–545.

[3] Stone, *Regime Politics: Governing Atlanta* (Lawrence: University of Kansas Press, 1989); Barbara Ferman, *Challenging the Growth Machine* (Lawrence: University of Kansas Press, 1996); Richard DeLeon, *Left Coast City* (Lawrence: University of Kansas Press, 1992).

Urban regimes and efforts to construct and influence them account for differences between the policy syntheses of these cities that the variations so far canvassed cannot. An analysis of these regimes reveals further reasons why the German urban regions attained such firm control over environmental quality and segregation; why the French urban regions diverged so much in their capacities to combine developmental policies with environmental and social ones; and why the American city governments carried out more developmental policies and less ambitious, less effective distributive ones. Comparative analysis of governance in the urban economy and civil society needs to take account of the distinctive national infrastructures of local state-society relations. Under the influence of these infrastructures, urban regimes can assume different forms or even serve divergent purposes. In these different contexts, similar elements of urban regimes can bring about contrasting consequences for policy. Although U.S. analysts have regarded urban regimes of government and business as necessary to effective policy, another infrastructure of local government, politics and state-society relations might enable urban governing coalitions to overcome this need.

The discussion of policy syntheses and leading electoral coalitions in the last chapter has already laid much of the foundation for the analysis of regimes and their consequences. This chapter will focus on local state-society relations in these cities and the corresponding infrastructures of organizations and institutions. First, I consider why business and institutional interests linked to services and high technology in a global economy found it instrumental to pursue local policy syntheses at all. Second, I analyze how infrastructures for relations between businesses, governments and labor in local policy making and the institutions of the local development industry influenced regime-building and its policy consequences. Finally, I compare the local movements that increasingly have appeared in the neighborhoods and communities of these urban regimes, and the role of this activism in regimes and policies.

Local Dependence in the Global Economy

For urban governance to crystallize into an urban regime, businesses and other institutions of the urban economy must ally with officials in the pursuit of local interests. The growth of a global economy might seem to undermine this possibility. In an age of increasingly mobile information, finance, companies and people, businesses and institutions could leave a city either in real or in virtual terms rather than bargain with local electoral leaders. Analyses of the business and financial services tied into networks of international finance often point to such asymmetries of power that local politics appears irrelevant to local outcomes.[4] The businesses and institutions of service and high-tech centers ultimately demonstrate a contrary tendency. Here, the increased mobility and interconnectedness of the global economy have often left even translocal firms more dependent than before on markets and other conditions within urban regions. Mobilizations of businesses and institutions around these locally dependent interests have helped bring about new urban regimes and the expansion of urban policy syntheses. As comparison with centers of traditional manufacturing demonstrates, the roots of this "glocalization" lie in the new high technology and service cores of advanced industrial economies.

General Expectations: High-Tech and Services versus Manufacturing. Before proceeding to an analysis of these interests in the eleven cities of this study, consider the general sources of this new "local dependency" and the consequences for urban politico-economic regimes and policy syntheses. The reasons for local dependency go beyond the investments that businesses and institutions have already made in the facilities and the status of a city.

First, the prospect of growth from localized clusters of advanced technological innovation and its application has mobilized the businesses and institutions as well as the officials of many cities. In the "Fordist" era of mass production, centers of universities and related services often remained comparatively sheltered from the whims of translocal markets. Now not just institutions and firms active in technological innovation and its application, but the entire array of local services that depend on those institutions and firms for business stand to benefit from high-tech growth. Even in the absence of a major high-tech center like the Research Triangle, with its cluster of multinational firms, government agencies and research institutes, the prospects for new growth from knowledge-based development can furnish incentives to these businesses. Even at a more modest scale, the expansion of a hospital community with the latest medical technologies or the growth of a local network of computer graphics firms offer

---

[4] Analyses of global cities often leave this impression (cf. Peter Marcuse and Ronald van Kempen, "Introduction"; Saskia Sassen, *Cities in a World Economy* [Thousand Oaks, CA: Pine Ridge, 1994]).

opportunities for new firms and professional services. Beyond a basic infra-structure of transportation, and links to advanced telecommunications and electronic capacities, centers of this sort thrive on accumulated professional expertise and networks.[5] The high-tech company that consults with local professors, the university that relies increasingly on financing from its hospital, the engineer who repeatedly attempts to commercialize new research all rely on aspects of these local agglomerations. Whether public, nonprofit or private, each of these institutions and professionals shares a stake in the added revenues that expanding local high-tech sectors may bring.

Second, new or accentuated interests in local consumption now compel the businesses and institutions of service centers to pursue localized policies. This source of local economic mobilization lies in the expansion of public, private and nonprofit services for consumers and businesses into an increasingly dominant proportion of urban economies.[6] More and more, local businesses and institutions rely for profitability or survival on services that will bring consumers or clienteles to a place. Mobility among places has both opened up new opportunities to expand this consumption and posed new threats to urban regions that cannot keep local residents or firms. Businesses and research facilities seek to lure translocal networks of professionals to conferences and meetings. Universities rely on attractive local surroundings to draw students and researchers. Entertainment and shopping districts market themselves to customers beyond as well as within a city. Tourist industries look to the local attractions and facilities that will accommodate temporary visitors. One type of consumption interest often leverages others. A university benefits, for instance, from adequate opportunities for students to shop and eat out. Meanwhile even local professionals who are not alumni may attend football games, concerts or lectures that would not take place without the local school. Since the professionals in technologically advanced fields often bring with them ample incomes to spend on local services, and often select residences and jobs on the basis of the quality of life that a locality provides, these interests often mesh with those in high-tech growth. As a group that draws on family resources from disproportionately affluent segments of society, university

---

[5] Susan E. Clarke and Gary Gaile, *The Work of Cities* (Minneapolis: University of Minnesota Press, 1998), pp. 203–207.

[6] A growing recent literature points to the importance of economic interests in consumption as an influence on urban regions. See, e.g., *Urban Studies* 35 (1998) (Special Issue on Consumption); Dennis Judd and Susan Fainstein (eds.), *The Tourist City* (New Haven: Yale University Press, 1999).

students also channel purchasing power from beyond an urban region into consumption of local services. Except where bureaucratic systems of service provision and research constrain local mobilization and shelter local services from losses, these interests feed a positive-sum politics of service expansion among local businesses and institutions.

Compare both of these shifts in interests with the locally dependent interests of a global or national manufacturing business such as Michelin Tire Company in Clermont-Ferrand, the Oetker Company in Bielefeld or the U.S. Repeating Arms Company in New Haven. Among such firms, expansion on a national or international scale offered greater advantages the more local dependency could be reduced. Research facilities in high-tech clusters and local networks like those of the "Third Italy" have elevated innovation to a new, more prominent role in manufacturing production. Yet despite these changes, the plants that hired most of a company's workers continued to depend on a traditional infrastructure and labor skills that were increasingly available in locations throughout the world. As costs of transportation and communication fell, these companies found it increasingly profitable to integrate far-flung networks of production centered in the most profitable locations for each component or product.[7] These corporate calculations of profitability at wider scales supplanted more far-reaching interests in the local economy. Instead of enhancements to the intellectual and professional capital of any given setting, companies like Michelin sought to place production in locales where the investments in plants, infrastructure and training paid off most easily. In contrast with the common interest of service firms and institutions in enhancements to local consumption, global production enterprises retained only a contingent interest in sufficient income and services for local workers.

With such different relations to the global economy, service and high-tech businesses and institutions might be expected to assume different stances from manufacturing firms toward urban regime building as well as to the substantive ends of urban regimes. Even an internationally prominent university like Yale derives direct benefits from policies that foster new high-tech spinoffs or attract students and faculty to the city. Even a local franchise owner for McDonald's will find it profitable to draw new service clienteles with disposable income to the surrounding neighborhood. For both the high-tech and the service clusters that often feed off each other in service centers, mobilization around local developmental

---

[7] Allen J. Scott, *New Industrial Spaces* (Berkeley: University of California Press, 1988).

initiatives makes economic sense. Even if environmental and cultural amenities stand partly in the way of these initiatives, enhancements of this sort to the local quality of life can also draw residents and visitors. At the least, by assuring that speculative expansion did not overly tax resources or physical infrastructure, planning and growth management can aid longer-term prospects for development itself.[8] In provision of social equity, the incentives for high-tech and service industries to pursue local policies appear the weakest. In seeking new managerial and professional workers on the one hand and clienteles with high levels of consumption on the other, both sectors might be expected to favor Upscale emphases in local policy.

Global manufacturing firms, by contrast, have less reason to engage in most kinds of local politico-arrangements. Beyond provision of the basic infrastructure for production, a company like Michelin derived comparatively little benefit for its production facilities from local developmental initiatives. As a multinational company, it needed only to take those benefits into account as part of an overall calculation of transactions costs for production. As Michelin repeatedly cut jobs in Clermont-Ferrand, the company calculated that savings on labor and plant in Brazil and elsewhere more than made up for the costs of leaving the city. Except for its own workers, local engagement in efforts to provide environmental goods also made less sense, U.S. studies suggest, for such a company.[9] With its calculations of profit and loss directed at global product sales rather than at the conditions of the urban region, a national or global manufacturing firm had little to fear from environmental degradation in the city. In the absence of strong worker influence, a similar logic dictates a lack of corporate regard for local housing and social and spatial segregation.

Actual Patterns. The patterns of business interests and governance in the eleven cities furnish the basis for a cross-national test of these hypotheses. In each instance, the city dominated by manufacturing in 1960 retained the largest concentration of employment in manufacturing into the 1990s (Table 5.1). In each country, defections from local coalitions on

---

[8] John R. Logan and Harvey Molotch, *Urban Fortunes* (Berkeley: University of California Press, 1987), p. 49; Glenn Yago, *Decline of Transit* (New York: Cambridge University Press, 1984), p. 86.

[9] Since the 1960s, U.S. analysts have often found deficient environmental policy in manufacturing centers (e.g., Matthew Crenson, *The Unpolitics of Air Pollution* [Baltimore: Johns Hopkins University Press, 1971]; Andrew Hurley, *Environmental Inequalities* [Chapel Hill: University of North Carolina Press, 1995]).

the part of manufacturing enterprises should have detracted from regime formation around local policy syntheses. Service and high-tech concentrations should have produced broad business and institutional coalitions in support of more consensual syntheses. Although the actual patterns bear out this contrast, they also indicate divergences in local paths that the dominant sectors of the urban economies cannot fully explain.

Clearly, service centers with stronger industrial legacies had suffered major disadvantages in their efforts to mobilize around service and high-tech growth. Universities and institutes in Bielefeld, Clermont-Ferrand and New Haven had attracted fewer researchers and students than other service centers in each country.[10] In France and the United States, Clermont-Ferrand and New Haven had hosted fewer and smaller science parks. In all three countries the cities with stronger manufacturing legacies drew fewer visitors from outside to its hotel rooms, luxury hotel rooms or both. In Germany and the United States, the two manufacturing centers had retained smaller retail sectors. In all three countries, but especially in France and the United States, nonprofit and governmental services tied smaller proportions of the manufacturing centers into translocal clienteles and distribution. Financial, legal and other white-collar business services also concentrated more in other service centers than in Bielefeld, Clermont-Ferrand or New Haven.[11]

This lack of success in developmental policy stemmed not only from the lesser attractions of urban centers burdened with abandoned buildings and environmental difficulties but also from the weakness of business mobilization around local agendas. In Clermont-Ferrand and Bielefeld, where prominent manufacturing companies retained a leading position in the local economy, the contingency of their support for local coalition building proved most obvious. In his memoirs, Mayor Quilliot of Clermont-Ferrand stressed how little leverage even a dominant local politician could exercise in the presence of a giant manufacturer like Michelin. Quilliot noted that he had attempted, in repeated meetings with François Michelin in the 1980s and 1990s, to convince the head of the firm to save local jobs. As merely the mayor of the city, however, he found

---

[10] With the University of North Carolina at Chapel Hill included, the total in or around both Durham and Madison rose to higher levels than in greater New Haven.

[11] In Durham and Madison, where the only figures for jobs by workplace were available at the county level, 1990 census statistics by household affirmed that more city residents worked in finance, insurance, real estate and business services than in the city of New Haven.

297

Table 5.1 *Manufacturing, Translocal Services and Central City Governance, by Country*
(Boldface Indicates Strongest Manufacturing Concentrations; Indicators of Lowest Service and High-Tech Concentrations Underscored and Italicized)

	Manufacturing Jobs[a] (%)	Jobs in Business Services and Related Areas[c] (%)	Technology Park Rating (0 [Low] – 5 [High])[b]	University Students / 100 Residents[c]	Hotel Rooms / 1,000 Residents[d]	Rooms in Luxury Hotels / 10,000 Residents[e]	Jobs in Retail[f] (%)	Jobs in Nonprofit and Governmental Services[g] (%)	Local Policy Synthesis, Governing Coalition (1985–1994)
Germany									
Bielefeld	**42**	*15.7*	2	*7.9*	*4.9*	5.0	*9.2*	*7.0*	Social-Ecological, contested
Freiburg	25	18.5	2	16.6	10.2	*3.0*	11.8	13.9	Comprehensive, stable coalition
Göttingen	23	17.3	(Max-Planck-Institutes)	27.4	7.7	10.6	10.2	7.9	Social-Ecological, contested
Münster	19	20.9	2	21.4	12.3	12.4	9.8	16.1	Comprehensive, stable coalition
France									
Clermont-Ferrand	**29.0**	*14.7*	*2*	*14.3*	11.4	*20.4*	7.6	*22.5*	Local Fordist, weak coalition
Montpellier	15.9	19.1	4	20.0	8.9	54.3	8.2	27.9	Upscale, stable coalition
Nancy	17.3	18.1	4	17.3	18.3	38	7.3	28.8	Upscale, stable coalition
Rennes	19.5	19.5	4	17.2	7	30.8	7.6	29.3	Comprehensive, stable coalition

United
States

New Haven	27	*13.3*	*2*	14.6 (private: 8.8)	*9.5*	*0.1*	*11.7*	*24.4*	Upscale, contested
Durham	23	14.0	5	13.5 (metro: 15.5) (private: 6.8)	29.7	9.7	15.5	27.7	Upscale, contested
Madison	17	16.3	4	23.3 (private: 1.2)	25.7	3.7	18.4	36.0	Upscale, stable coalition

[a] Percent of employed adult residents (France, United States) or adults employed in central city workplaces (Germany) in designated activities. *Sources:* (Germany) National, *Land* and city statistical publications, *Arbeitstättenzählung* 1987; (France) INSEE, unpublished data from 1990 census; (United States) U.S. Bureau of the Census, *1990 Census of Population and Housing; Census Tract and State Reports.*

[b] Ratings for all European cities except Göttingen incorporate those from Roger Brunet, *Les Villes "européennes"* (Montpellier: RECLUS, 1989), p. 26; ratings for U.S. cities and Göttingen based on comparison of extent of land and firms in local technology parks.

[c] University students from Deutscher Städtetag, *Statistisches Jahrbuch Deutscher Gemeinden 1993*; European Community, *Directory of Higher Education Institutions in the EC* (Luxembourg, 1993); U.S. Bureau of the Census, *1990 Census of Population and Housing: SMSA Reports.* Population figures from 1990 (France, United States) or 1987 (Germany) census publications.

[d] Hotel room figures from Deutscher Städtetag, *Statistisches Jahrbuch Deutscher Gemeinden 1993*; INSEE, *Communoscope* (1990); U.S. local convention and visitors' bureaus.

[e] European figures include all rooms in local hotels listed as "very comfortable" in *Michelin Guides Rouges 1994* for Germany and France. U.S. figures take all rooms in accommodations rated three stars or better in *Mobil Fodor's Guides* for 1998.

[f] Percent of employed adult residents (France) or adults employed in central city workplaces (Germany, United States) in retail trade. Durham and Madison figures for county. *Sources:* (Germany) National, *Land* and city statistical publications, *Arbeitstättenzählung* 1987; (France) INSEE, unpublished data from 1990 census; (United States) U.S. Bureau of the Census, *1992 Census of Retail Trade: Geographic Area Reports*, and local Chambers of Commerce.

[g] Percent of employed adult residents (France) or adults employed in central city workplaces (Germany, United States) in government and nonprofit services. Durham and Madison figures for county. *Sources:* (Germany) National, *Land* and city statistical publications, *Arbeitstättenzählung* 1987; (France) I.N.S.E.E., unpublished data from 1990 census; (United States) U.S. Bureau of the Census, *1992 Census of Services: Geographic Area Reports*, and local Chambers of Commerce.

himself forced into a simple formula: "Michelin directed its affairs with its personnel; I directed the affairs of Clermont. . . . I had to avoid any decision, any gesture that could supply [the firm] a pretext to retract or disengage [from the city]."[12] As Michelin cut steadily back on local jobs over the 1980s and 1990s, local observers criticized the fragmentation of efforts among businesses and institutions in the city, including the company itself, to mobilize around new local economic opportunities.[13]

In Bielefeld, where more diversified structures of manufacturing had also done little to prevent steady job losses in this sector, mobilizations around new development since the 1960s had relied more heavily than in the other German cities on supralocal programs. Without a more extensive array of local service, tourist and retail businesses to furnish political and market support, developmental policies themselves had remained comparatively limited. Over the late 1980s and early 1990s, efforts at local regime building foundered on confrontations between local manufacturers and other businesses associated with the Right and environmentalists on the local Left.[14] In 1989, with the support of "Citizens for Bielefeld," a voter group led by corporate representatives, the CDU unseated a Red-Green coalition that had increasingly challenged local manufacturing with environmental restrictions. In 1994, the next election, the Left regained a majority and proceeded to alter the agenda of its predecessor.

In New Haven, mayoral coalitions since the 1960s had also relied largely on the funds and incentives in programs from above. Under the guise of Democratic party dominance, contestation and weak coalitions had also marked the period from the DiLieto administration through the Daniels administration to John DiStefano. Since the Lee coalition, however, manufacturing firms like the U.S. Repeating Arms Company had remained conspicuously absent from local coalition building around policy. Like the cigarette industry that once dominated the Durham economy, manufacturing in New Haven had voted more with its feet than through participation in regime building.

For the policy syntheses pursued in these settings, the consequences were decidedly mixed. In all three instances developmental policy suffered

---

[12] Roger Quilliot, *Misères et grandeur des maires de France* (Paris: Albin Michel, 1997), p. 189.

[13] Christophe Beslay, Philippe Bernard and Evelyne Cavet, "Clermont-Ferrand – La difficile transition d'une régulation privée à une régulation institutionnelle" (Université de Toulouse le Mirail, 1994).

[14] Harmùt Hein (ed.), *Ausgerechnet Bielefeld* (Münster: Westfälisches Dampfboot, 1991), pp. 165–182.

from limitations by comparison with other service centers. In each case, stronger supralocal initiatives helped to some degree to make up the difference. In New Haven and Clermont-Ferrand, consistent with other studies of environmental measures in manufacturing centers, local environmental initiatives fell far short of those in other service centers. But in Bielefeld, despite the conflicts with local industry, local policy makers succeeded most clearly in the environmental domain. Not only supralocal policies and metropolitan governance, but the local Greens and consistent local planning administration helped bring about this result. In both Bielefeld and Clermont-Ferrand, though not in New Haven, the longtime Left governments had also helped put in place local policies that into the 1990s preserved comparatively strong emphases on social and spatial equity. Although the leading local manufacturing firms played little direct role in these policies, these firms or their representatives had participated in or at least supported such efforts. In Clermont-Ferrand, Michelin had relied on its own considerable resources to construct large portions of local housing. In both Clermont-Ferrand and Bielefeld, and even in the developmental field in New Haven, other elements overcame shortcomings in the urban politico-economic regime.

Just as the disengagement and conflicting interests of translocal manufacturers hampered local regime building, strong local service and high-tech sectors generally reinforced it. Firms and institutions in these sectors had increasingly mobilized around locally dependent interests in developmental and other policies. In places with some of the strongest such sectors, stable governing coalitions during the late 1980s and early 1990s maintained consistent support among businesses and institutions in these same sectors. In Freiburg and Münster, long-standing networks of association within the local business community came repeatedly to the defense of projects that the local government proposed. In Rennes, Montpellier and to a lesser degree Nancy, local and district officials coordinated associational networks around technology parks and tourist facilities. In Madison, the downtown business association and Chamber of Commerce pursued similar ends in more loosely coupled, ad hoc fashion. Even where urban governance fell short of a full-fledged politico-economic regime, as further analysis will show to be the case in Göttingen and Durham, similar interests rooted in the service and high-tech sectors shaped local agendas. The local universities, as the largest economic institutions in most of these cities, often stood at the center of local economic coalitions of this sort. The value of universities for other firms and institutions often exceeded that of global manufacturers. In addition to the potential benefits from research and innovation, universities furnished new, skilled labor, a plethora of cultural opportunities, heightened consumption and physical development itself.[15]

In most of these mobilizations around service and high-tech interests, developmental ends figured prominently. Up to the 1970s these developmental policies had centered around the expansion of universities and research and improvements to housing, transportation and shopping for new students and researchers. In the 1980s, as the biggest increases in university enrollments tapered off in all three countries, developmental initiatives shifted to research institutes, technology parks, medical centers and facilities like libraries and gymnasiums. In cooperation with local planners, universities carried out their own objectives for expansion. Often, as in the Rotival plan for New Haven or the expansion of Montpellier and Rennes in the 1960s, plans for university expansion dominated local developmental agendas. In other instances, as in the technology parks of the French and United States settings, the Ninth Square project in New Haven or the convention center hotel in downtown Durham, the university contributed to specific projects in concert with local and supralocal officials. Close ties to the university among local political elites often cemented commitments to developmental policies.[16] Only in Germany, where separate institutions like the *Fachhochschulen* took over more of responsibility for activities related to technology transfer and training, did the universities assume less prominent roles in developmental matters.[17]

In all three countries, in accordance with expectations, the cities with strong business and institutional interests in services also evolved more

---

[15] E.g., Yale University, Office of the Secretary, *Economic Impact: Yale and New Haven* (New Haven, 1993); Brian Robson, Neville Topham, Iain Deas and Jim Twomey, *The Economic and Social Impact of Greater Manchester's Universities* (Manchester: Center for Urban Policy Studies, 1995).

[16] The leading council members in Montpellier, Rennes and Nancy came largely from the ranks of local universities and medical centers. Private elite schools like Yale in New Haven and Duke in Durham furnished smaller proportions of local elites than did such large public universities as the University of Wisconsin in Madison and the University of North Carolina at Chapel Hill. Cf. Jefferey M. Sellers, "Grounds of Democracy: Public Authority and the Politics of Metropolitan Land in Three Societies" (Ph.D. diss., Yale University, 1994, pp. 221–233).

[17] For a comparison of the German institutions for job training with the less successful efforts of the French Instituts Universitaires de Technologie (IUTs), see Nicholas Ziegler, "Institutions, Elites and Technological Change in France and Germany," *World Politics* 47 (1995): 27–36.

extensive environmental policies than centers of declining manufacturing (Table 5.1). Support among service businesses and institutions for improved environmental conditions contributed significantly to this result as well. In the German downtowns especially, but also in the French Old Towns and the central areas of Madison, service businesses and institutions often furnished crucial support for the preservationist policies, pedestrian zones and transportation policies that helped constrain sprawl. With forests on the western fringes of Durham and an arboretum in South Madison, Duke University and the University of Wisconsin had also protected open space in areas of urban sprawl. In Freiburg, Göttingen, Münster, Montpellier, Rennes, Madison, New Haven and Chapel Hill, local university faculties in fields like geography and planning furnished expertise, information or training for environmental planners and activists. University personnel or researchers often played critical roles in local environmental movements. However, the primary impetus for land use protections, bicycle paths and parks still usually came from local social and neighborhood movements or from local policy makers rather than from institutions or businesses. Individual service or retail businesses with plans for local expansion also frequently came into conflict with local environmental objectives. In instances like the Wal-Mart development at New Hope Commons in Durham or the numerous *hypermarchés* outside Montpellier these businesses had put together coalitions that overcame opposition among local environmentalists and planners.

As Table 5.1 demonstrates, the coalitions with backing among service and high-tech sectors diverged most systematically in support for social equity. In general, sectoral interests in translocal clienteles enhanced support for local policy syntheses that tolerated high levels of social and spatial inequity. The more that high-tech and service firms and institutions catered to elite visitors like researchers from Silicon Valley, executives from New York or Frankfurt, governmental officials from Paris or tourists with luxury accommodations, the more Upscale the policies.

How these interests figured in local coalitions and policies differed considerably. In the German settings, special economic interests in the attraction of translocal elites had remained comparatively small. Not only had fewer higher-status professionals moved to these cities, as Chapter 2 showed, but technology parks designed to attract high-tech firms remained uniformly small. The universities, though often prestigious in specific domains, served mostly students in the surrounding region. Rooms in luxury hotels also remained fewer than in the French cities. Reinforced through supralocal planning, policies and fiscal arrangements as well as these configurations of local interests, local regime builders in the German cities could pursue policies that addressed social equity and other benefits for local residents.

In both of the French cities with Upscale syntheses as well as in two of their American counterparts, however, local commercial interests in mobile elites had also emerged. In Montpellier and Nancy as well as in Durham and Madison, technology parks housed sizeable local high-tech sectors with connections to networks of researchers and executives beyond the metropolitan area. Both French cities had also acquired concentrations of nationally prominent *grandes écoles* and national research institutes. Not only high overall rates of hotel rooms in these cities, but more numerous luxury rooms attested to stronger efforts to attract elite clienteles. Opportunities inherent in the large preserved Old Towns and other cultural attractions of both cities helped account for these emphases. But local policy making of the 1980s and 1990s had clearly seized on these opportunities. The contrary example of Rennes, with an equivalent concentration of elite educational and research institutions and considerable cultural, historical and aesthetic attractions of its own, highlights the degree of choice in the paths of Montpellier and Nancy. Not only the smaller numbers of luxury hotels in Rennes but also its lower level of local support for higher-status cultural activities like theaters, opera and museums reflected these contrasting emphases.[18] The local and social orientations of the Comprehensive synthesis there had largely thwarted the rise of businesses that might challenge that synthesis in pursuit of tourist and elite clienteles.

All three U.S. urban regions faced supralocal policies, supralocal institutions and local governmental infrastructures that favored Upscale syntheses. In Durham and New Haven, local officials and others confronted an even more difficult problem for regime building in the community. Private, elite institutions for research and education like Yale University in New Haven and Duke University in Durham possessed interests far more at variance with other components of the urban political economy than those of a regional public university. Indeed, universities of this sort

---

[18] Thus Nancy spent $208 per resident on these activities compared to $56 per resident in Rennes and $26 per resident in Clermont-Ferrand. Although on-budget spending in Montpellier came to only $57 per resident, the city also financed and operated its new opera and convention center, the Corum, through a separate parapublic company.

have for decades furnished one of the clearest examples of the mobile cosmopolitan elites that play such a prominent role in recent accounts of global cities. With ties to national and international research networks, a student body from far beyond the city, disproportionate numbers of upper- and upper-middle class social strata, a lack of student interest in permanent residence and funding mostly from out of state, both universities operated nearly as much on translocal scales as did Michelin. Even the University of Wisconsin at Madison, a public university with an international reputation for research, differed from these two schools in most of these respects.[19] Had the Duke or the Yale communities also occupied as much of the city economy and electorate as the University of Wisconsin did in Madison, or as the Massachusetts Institute of Technology and Harvard University did in Cambridge, then regime building might have proven simple. But both Duke and Yale dominated the downtown economies from a small portion of the urban territory, alongside large concentrations of the poor and disadvantaged minorities.

The stark opposition between the interests of these universities and other components in the economies of New Haven and Durham had hampered efforts to build lasting governing coalitions around consistent policy. At the same time that Yale and Duke stood at the centers of more general plans for development, each school focused its efforts as an organization on the parts of the city nearest to university facilities. Even in the period of urban renewal in New Haven, the Rotival plan had explicitly highlighted the expansion of Yale, the enhancement of surrounding opportunities for shopping and other market services and the clearance of nearby neighborhoods as central objectives of local policy there. In Durham, urban redevelopment into the 1970s had removed minority and impoverished neighborhoods close to Duke University and had enhanced highway access to the campus. In the 1980s and 1990s both schools undertook a growing array of initiatives to contribute to local development and

---

[19] Whether public or private, more local schools like Durham Technical College and the University of New Haven have even greater inextricable links to the surrounding urban political economy. Although European universities served a more elite segment of the population than most American state schools did, the institutions of higher education in the French and German cities remained predominantly regional. National and *Land*-level systems of tax-based finance left higher education less dependent than U.S. state schools on student tuition or alumni contributions. Separate systems of research funding under the auspices of the CNRS and often the *grandes écoles* in France and the Max Planck and other institutes in Germany also channeled much of public funding for research into distinct national systems of support.

neighborhood improvements. By and large these efforts continued to focus on the university campus and its surroundings. Although a report by Yale officials enumerated the multiple contributions the university's police and fire services, street maintenance, construction spending and other purchases made to the city,[20] all of these activities centered in this circumscribed geographic area.[21] Even Yale's contributions to such affordable housing projects as Ninth Square served partly to provide accommodations close to the university for students and others. In Durham, the university also continued to shape local agendas in ways tailored to narrower interests. Duke officials had provided much of the impetus for the convention center and luxury hotel built in the downtown in the 1980s. At the same time, the university had little to do with policies toward the poor neighborhoods now clustered on the opposite side of the business district.

In both instances, conflict over development in areas close to or linked with the university had hampered the consolidation of regimes in the 1980s and 1990s. In New Haven, the coalition under John Daniels challenged the aggressive development agendas of the early and mid-1980s under Biagio DiLieto. In Durham, Friends of Durham had challenged the Progressive coalition of African Americans and liberals largely on the need for downtown commercial and hotel developments that Duke officials had advocated. In neither central city did these conflicts forestall mobilization around developmental policies. In both, a Progressive coalition proved unable to sustain as effective a synthesis of developmental policy with social and environmental objectives. In Madison, the university and its students made up a larger, more integrated part of the city and its economy. Drawing partly on university ties, Soglin and other mayors of the 1980s had assembled a full-fledged regime around these objectives. If the resulting policy synthesis could not overcome Upscale tendencies, it had worked more effectively to secure environmental quality.

In all three areas, local businesses and institutions had set their sights increasingly on the translocal processes of the global economy. Many of the same global forces that subordinated local regimes to translocal forces in manufacturing and metropolitan centers fostered localized interests in urban regime building among service businesses and institutions. The more that the governing coalitions in these cities depended on attractions

---

[20] Yale University, *Economic Impact*.

[21] The main exception lay in medical services for poor residents, which federal law had at least partly prescribed.

for mobile elites, the harder local policy makers and service institutions and businesses either worked for Upscale syntheses or sought to undermine alternative syntheses. Even where the stable coalitions that indicated the presence of urban regimes did not emerge over the late 1980s and early 1990s, local policy syntheses clearly had. Contested urban governance yielded Social-Ecological policies in Bielefeld and Göttingen and reinforced Upscale syntheses in Durham and New Haven. The weak, contingent urban coalition in Clermont-Ferrand persisted in Local Fordist policies. A full understanding of these local paths requires analysis of the infrastructures and local institutions for state-society relations in these cities.

Urban Regimes and Their Significance

Even if locally dependent economic interests vary, the growth of localized governance within urban regions could still stem from a "hegemonic project" linked to global business interests.[22] Local influences aside, the most far-reaching constraints on any such single project lie in the institutional arrangements for governance within the domestic political economies of nation-states. To bring these elements into the analysis requires that the institutional infrastructures for urban governance be reconceived to encompass several dimensions of urban economies and state-society relations (Table 5.2). Within every country, urban regimes and their construction nest within the wider systems of organized economic interests and state-society relations that have preoccupied the comparative study of national and international political economies. The rise of urban governance itself reflects a degree of convergence among these systems. At the same time, distinctive national systems of business-government relations have continued to foster different patterns of urban governance. The elements of these infrastructures most visible from above, the systems for the representation of business, labor and other economic interests in public policy, have supplanted as well as reinforced local choices. Localized infrastructures of parapublic firms and public intervention in development markets have rendered the pursuit of urban policy syntheses either more or less reliant on local business support. Although "growth machines" of locally dependent interests in development and real

---

[22] Bob Jessop, "A Neo-Gramscian Approach to the Regulation of Urban Regimes," in Mickey Lauria (ed.), *Reconstructing Urban Regime Theory* (London: Sage, 1997), pp. 51–73.

Table 5.2 *Components of Urban Business-Government Relations*

	Collective Representation	Individual Firms
Policy agendas, policy making, implementation	Organized collective interests (interest intermediation)	Parapublic and private firms, public influences on firms, collective and individual influence of firms on policy
Markets	Formation of interests for collective economic representation	Real estate and development industry (and interests of "growth machines")

estate have formed around local policy syntheses in each country, these formations have reinforced very different sets of local choices. This section examines the consequences from each of these elements of state-society relations in turn.

Organized Business and Labor Interests: Urban Regimes and the Significance of Corporatism. Relations between local governments and the organizations representing business, labor and agriculture in these urban regions reflect well-known contrasts in the capitalist arrangements of advanced industrial countries. Cross-national comparisons of these arrangements demonstrate limits to the important role that U.S. analysts have generally attributed to businesses in urban regimes. In Germany, as urban governance has expanded, traditional arrangements for the hierarchical representation of economic interests have assured little role for organized labor. There and in France, the resulting arrangements might seem to bring organized business interests the same pervasive influence that accounts of U.S. cities have identified as integral to urban regimes. Yet closer examination demonstrates that the German infrastructure of business-government relations, and in some instances its local French analogues, have confined local business to a narrower range of influence than in the U.S. cities.

In all three countries, local relations between local business associations, labor representatives and farm interests nested in distinctive national systems of economic interests. In the national *corporatist* policy making system of Germany, encompassing hierarchical, cooperative, officially recognized organizations represent the interests of both labor and business in wage setting and other matters of policy.[23] In the United States, the *pluralist* system of less encompassing, more fragmented, more competitive organization for both business and labor opposes these arrangements most directly. In France, the degree of organized cooperation between officials and business associations falls between those of Germany and the United States, and labor unions in particular lack a strong corporatist role.[24]

Within the central cities and urban regions, the associations that represented business and other economic interests corresponded only partly to these broad categories. The leading business organizations in the European cities belonged to national networks that dated back to the nineteenth century in Germany and the eighteenth century in France. As public law bodies charged with formal representation of and service to the entire local business community, German and French Chambers of Industry and Commerce as well as their Chambers of Agriculture and Artisans came the closest to local versions of national corporatist interests.[25] Planning procedures that limited participation by other groups and citizens often required that these organizations be informed and allowed to submit comments. In Germany, local union representatives received these same formal participatory rights. In both countries, however, associations with few regulatory tasks and voluntary membership usually assumed the most active role in local policy and in market advocacy and the regimes that pursued it. U.S. metropolitan Chambers of Commerce also lacked the mandatory, comprehensive character, the internal regulatory authority and the formally privileged access of the European chambers. But in the U.S. cities, the most important business organizations often took even more ad hoc and irregular forms.

Studies of the policy consequences from infrastructures for interest intermediation at the national scale point to parallels with local policy syntheses in the German and U.S. cities. Aggregate national data clearly suggest the superiority of corporatist arrangements over pluralist ones as

---

[23] Philippe C. Schmitter, "Still the Century of Corporatism?" in Philippe C. Schmitter and Gerhard Lehmbruch (eds.), *Trends Toward Corporatist Intermediation* (London: Sage, 1978), pp. 7–52; Peter Katzenstein, *Politics and Policy in West Germany: The Growth of a Semisovereign State* (Philadelphia: Temple University Press, 1987).

[24] Lyle Scruggs, "Institutions and Environmental Performance in Seventeen Western Democracies," *British Journal of Political Science 29* (1999): 14–15 n. 32.

[25] On this "local corporatism," see Alan Cawson (ed.), *Organized Interests and the State* (London: Sage, 1985); R. King, "Corporatism and the Local Economy," in W. Grant (ed.), *The Political Economy of Corporatism* (London, Macmillan, 1985), pp. 202–228.

ways to secure social equity[26] and to attain better environmental outputs.[27] Although studies up to the early 1990s also pointed to stronger aggregate economic expansion in corporatist countries, studies since then have stressed the high unemployment and slower growth on the European continent.[28] At neither local nor national scales have previous studies fully illuminated the relation between these wider patterns and urban governance.[29] Hierarchical corporatist arrangements clearly set urban governance in Germany apart from the fragmented, unstructured business representation that American analysts associate with urban regime building. If corporatist arrangements might secure a stronger role for local corporatist representatives in urban interest intermediation and regime building, corporatist hierarchies could also sacrifice local participation for wider organization solidarity.[30] In the latter case, corporatist participation in policy at higher levels would take the place of organized business and labor interests within urban regions.

To compare the influence of business and other organizations in these contexts requires a recognition that this influence might occur at any one of several stages of policy making. Business associations might establish *agendas*, the general goals of policy makers and market actors; shape

[26] David R. Cameron, "Politics, Policy and Distributional Inequality: A Comparative Analysis," in Grant Reeher and Ian Shapiro (eds.), *Democracy and Equality: Essays in Honor of Robert Dahl* (New Haven: Yale University Press, 1989), pp. 219–259.

[27] Detlef Jahn, "Environmental Performance and Policy Regimes: Explaining Variations in 18 OECD Countries," *Policy Sciences 31* (1998): 107–131; Scruggs, "Institutions and Environmental Performance."

[28] Such work as Wolfgang Streeck, "German Capitalism: Does It Exist? Can It Survive?" in Colin Crouch and Wolfgang Streeck (eds.), *Modern Capitalism or Modern Capitalisms?* (Paris: La Découverte, 1995) mark a departure from David R. Cameron, "Social Democracy, Corporatism, Labor Quiescence, and the Representation of Economic Interest in Advanced Capitalist Society," in John Goldthorpe (ed.), *Order and Conflict in Contemporary Capitalism* (Oxford: Oxford University Press, 1984); Geoffrey Garrett and Peter Lange, "Performance in a Hostile World," *World Politics 38* (1986): 517–545.

[29] Only a few single-nation studies of corporatist and pluralist systems of interest intermediation have taken local state-society relations into account, cf. Kathleen Thelen, *A Union of Parts* (Ithaca: Cornell University Press, 1993); Richard Locke, *Remaking the Italian Economy* (Ithaca: Cornell University Press, 1994); Jon Pierre, "Models of Urban Governance: The Institutional Dimension of Urban Politics," *Urban Affairs Review 34*(3): 372–396. Urbanists who look to these systems at all have often neglected to separate out elements at different scales, e.g., H. V. Savitch, *Postindustrial Cities* (Princeton, NJ: Princeton University Press, 1988); Strom, "In Search of the Growth Coalition: American Urban Theories and the Development of Berlin," *Urban Affairs Review 31*(4): 455–462.

[30] Cf. Claus Offe, *Contradictions of the Welfare State* (Cambridge, MA: MIT Press, 1984).

310

policies in pursuit of those objectives; participate in the *implementation* of policies; take part directly in *markets*; or work with parties or other organizations in *electoral* arenas. In the German cities, limits on these occasions for local organizational participation reduced the influence of corporatist and other business interests. In the United States, more unstructured local policy making left urban policy syntheses open to influence from businesses at nearly every stage.

In the German settings, the supralocal policies, local party systems and governmental arrangements limited the local influence of organized business and labor. Corporatist influences at higher levels had undoubtedly contributed to this infrastructure. Yet the growth of environmental and planning issues in urban governance had increasingly supplanted the traditional focus of corporatist governance on workers and conditions within firms. Less corporatist organizations dominated business representation in local governing coalitions and rarely confronted local officials with strong challenges.

For unions the contrast with higher levels was most dramatic. Although comparatively prominent in the national German political economy,[31] labor organizations exercised little visible influence on policy and agendas within these cities. Only in developmental matters did local policy makers report that unions had involved themselves with any regularity. In doing so, the unions usually reinforced pressures from local businesses to retain existing jobs. In Bielefeld, which as a manufacturing center retained the largest local union presence, a planner observed that unions "only participate when it's going badly for an individual firm. Then they do everything possible, but not continually." Unions had cooperated with industry in local initiatives for job training through the *Fachhochschulen* in Bielefeld, Münster and Freiburg. Although blue-collar workers probably had as much interest in environmental issues and neighborhood conditions as other citizens, unions rarely engaged in policy making on issues besides jobs and workplaces. Even when they took up other causes, as in regional planning around Göttingen, planners could easily marginalize them. There, regional unions had added specific suggestions to improve public transportation, waste disposal and traffic systems to their more general concerns about employment. Regional policy makers, citing the

---

[31] Peter Katzenstein, *The Semi-Sovereign State* (Philadelphia: Temple University Press, 1986); Christopher Allen, "Germany," in Mark Kesselman, Joel Krieger and C. S. Allen (eds.), *European Politics in Transition*, 2nd ed. (New York: Prentice-Hall, 1997), pp. 239–334.

specialized technical nature of the issues raised, dismissed all but one of these suggestions as inappropriate to the planning process.[32] At most, effective union influence in the German cities came about through the representation German law assured labor within firms or through labor's connections with the SPD.[33]

Organized business interests in the German cities also usually found themselves in a limited, reactive role. The leading national business associations engaged in bargaining with the unions and national policy makers, the Federation of German Industry and the Federation of German Employers, maintained little if any presence within these cities. Chambers of Industry and Commerce found themselves constrained by legal restrictions and obligations to a voting membership of mostly small and medium businesses. Like the Chambers of Artisans, these chambers confined their activities largely to training and information services. Several sectoral business associations, most notably the Retail Associations, Restaurant and Hotel Associations and the Construction Industry Associations, also asserted interests in matters of local development. Beyond the formal institutional procedures to establish regional or city plans, to approve major projects at the level of the *Regierungsbezirk*, none of these organizations regularly influenced decision making. In and around Freiburg, local elites and activists reported participation by business and professional interests in controversies surrounding only ten of thirty-four contested projects, only three of which had been rated smaller controversies.[34] In only three of all these instances did respondents assign these organized interests more than limited influence. In all four central cities, local planners regarded business concerns to allow adequate businesses space, to impose as few restrictions as possible, and generally to serve "the needs of the economy" as more or less "predictable." Even in negotiations, local officials often held the upper hand. In the early 1980s a court had ordered Freiburg to pay a penalty of one million Deutschmarks to the local Retail Association for the refusal of the city to allow a store to build on a site outside the Old Town pedestrian district. The city held its ground, paid up, and got its

---

[32] Kreisverband Göttingen, *Raumordnungsplan für den Landkreis Göttingen* (Göttingen, 1986), pp. 312–314.

[33] In Freiburg, Bielefeld and Münster, SPD chapters and politicians maintained close connections with union circles. Formal union representation on corporate boards and shopfloors probably limited the exodus of jobs in Bielefeld, and promoted the pursuit of working-class housing by businesses in Münster (Münster, *Wirtschaftsreport 1971*, p. 5).

[34] Sellers, "Grounds of Democracy," p. 194.

way. Despite the extensive efforts of the Chambers of Commerce in areas like job training and advice for smaller firms, the city governments or para-public companies linked to them had maintained ownership of new properties for businesses that might want to settle in a city. The strength of parties rooted in segments of the community besides business posed a further impediment to business influence.[35]

In specific domains, and more under the CDU-led regime in Münster than elsewhere, organized business had mobilized around both developmental and environmental components of urban syntheses. In these initiatives, groups such as the Retail Associations rather than the public law chambers tended to take the lead. In Münster, up to the fall of the CDU-FDP coalition in 1994, the local Chamber of Industry and Commerce and the local Retail Association had probably most closely approached the limits of this influence. Over the preceding twenty years the local government regularly followed the demands of these organizations for new parking areas, new commercial and industrial parks and bigger traffic arteries. In choosing renovation rather than urban renewal, the urban regime in Münster had also left more of other aspects of development to these organizations and their members. In Freiburg, Bielefeld and Göttingen, local business associations negotiated the terms of government-sponsored downtown renewal and restoration. Retail Associations, as representatives of businesses concentrated largely in the downtown, bargained with local planners for more downtown parking, more convenient pedestrian zones and better access for suppliers to stores.[36] In three of the four urban regions, the concentration of outlying development on converted agricultural land also brought a role for the Chambers of Agriculture. Especially in and around Münster and Göttingen, where farmland predominated in the urban periphery, these regional chambers had negotiated the forms and limits of exurban expansion with policy makers.[37]

---

[35] In Göttingen the CDU itself, often a main advocate of local business interests, had helped block expansion of sales space in the downtown. In Münster the CDU had passed a local council resolution in 1978 that expressed opposition "in principle" to any discount super-markets within the city limits (Münster, *Wirtschaftsreport 1983*, p. 33).

[36] In the downtown reconstruction of Freiburg and Münster, for instance, these negotiations had resulted in the addition or enlargement of several parking garages.

[37] Local officials in Münster followed a policy of designating new agricultural land for protection every time new development converted farmland. Planners in the *Landkreis* that included Göttingen had amended the regional plan of 1986 to grant the request of the Chamber of Agriculture for greater protection (Kreis Göttingen, *Raumordnungsplan*, pp. 288, 289).

Even under the corporatist conditions of Germany, this localized coalition building between governments and business or economic interests played a growing role in governance. Most unambiguously in Münster up to 1994, but also by the late 1980s in Freiburg, such a coalition furnished a crucial element of full-fledged urban regimes. Yet neither the labor unions nor the hierarchical business associations most central to German corporatism at higher levels played more than secondary roles in these local processes. Those business representatives that participated found their local opportunities for influence confined to reactive negotiations over established agendas. Even the sole successful electoral initiative based primarily among local business leaders, the voter group Citizens for Bielefeld, had succeeded neither in establishing a new regime nor in greatly altering the local policy synthesis (Table 5.3). Except in specific domains, corporatist organization and intermediation served to limit rather than to accentuate the role of local business associations in urban governance.

In the French cities, neither national systems of economic interests nor the infrastructure for urban government and politics imposed the same limits on local economic associations as in the German cities. Although business organizations and networks played a role in regime building, local political leaders continued to exercise a strong guiding hand over regime agendas and policies.

Reflecting the national weakness of French labor organization, unions played an even less evident role than in Germany. Only through an indirect role in Left coalitions did organized labor affect local policy. Up to the mid-1990s unions had not even stood in the way of the massive export of jobs from Michelin plants in Clermont-Ferrand.[38] In relation to local business associations, local and national officials retained a strong hand in policy and its implementation. In Montpellier, for instance, 52 percent of local elites and activists – more than double the proportion in Freiburg – thought that an individual or a company could make the basic decisions about how to carry out a project after discussions with officials alone.[39] Alongside the strong prerogatives that the French infrastructure of local

---

[38] Patrick Le Galès, *Politique Urbaine et Développement Local* (Paris: L'Harmattan, 1993), pp. 158, 168; Quilliot, *Misères et grandeur*, pp. 28, 53, 188.

[39] Sellers, "Grounds of Democracy," p. 210. This compared to 22 percent in Freiburg and 28 percent in New Haven.

government and politics assure local officials, the low levels of participation in business associations undermined their influence. Even in Montpellier, where local participation in the regional Chamber of Commerce and Industry averaged the highest in France,[40] elites and activists who placed themselves closest to business associations took part in civic associations of any sort at far lower rates than their German or U.S. counterparts.[41] Yet despite this weakness, business associations and the informal networks surrounding them played a significant role in the construction and maintenance of urban regimes in France.

As in Germany, regional public law chambers filled part of this role, but little more. Active like their German counterparts in training, business education and procurement of information for local businesses, these bodies could sometimes enhance their influence through ownership or direct provision of local infrastructure. Chambers ran the airports in Montpellier, Rennes and Clermont-Ferrand; important local industrial zones in all four cities; and in the 1980s and 1990s, new intermodal transportation centers in Nancy and Montpellier. In all four cities, the chambers also stood at the center of more informal networks that encompassed local representatives from national employer associations and much of the downtown business community. Although the chambers possessed extensive legal powers and other resources, "fixed and outmoded statutory norms and requirements" generally inhibited their potential to work for innovations in economic policy.[42] In Montpellier, the chamber had deployed its ownership to assume a comparatively strong role in such development projects as the expansion of the airport and the installation of multimodal transportation facilities.[43] In

---

[40] S. Waters, "Chambers of Commerce and Local Development in France," *Environment and Planning C 16* (1998): 591, 601.

[41] A third of those in the center and 42 percent of those on the Right participated in no associations at all and 43 percent in the center and 47 percent on the Right belonged to only one or two. In Freiburg and New Haven, from 73 percent to 80 percent of those in these same categories cited memberships in at least three associations (Sellers, "Grounds of Democracy," p. 123). Yet in the regional elections for the chamber in Montpellier, participation averaged 35 percent, compared to 24 percent around Clermont-Ferrand, 22 percent around Nancy and 21 percent around Rennes. Waters, "Chambers of Commerce," pp. 591, 601. For an extensive critique of French associative pratices, see Jonah Levy, *Tocqueville's Revenge* (Cambridge: Harvard University Press, 1999).

[42] Waters, "Chambers of Commerce," p. 603.

[43] Usually citing the chamber, respondents pointed to business or professional associations as involved in 20 of 35 controversies (57 percent) and attributed to the associations at least considerable influence in 7 (21 percent).

Table 5.3 *Business Associations and Urban Regimes, 1980s–1990s*

	Regime and Policy Synthesis (Developmental Policies)	Participation (Agendas)	Elective Office	Policies	Implementation, Markets
Germany					
Freiburg	Comprehensive regime (XX)	—	—	Concertation (negotiative influence)	Limited
Münster	Comprehensive regime (XX)	—	—	Concertation (influential)	Limited
Göttingen	Social-Ecological (no regime) (X)	—	—	Concertation (negotiative influence)	Limited
Bielefeld	Social-Ecological (no regime) (X)	—	Bürger gemeinschaft für Bielefeld (1980s–1990s)	Concertation (negotiative influence)	Limited
France					
Rennes	Comprehensive regime (XXX)	CODESPAR (advisory, led by officials)	—	Concertation (limited)	Ownership of facilities

Montpellier	Upscale regime (XXX)	Montpellier LR Technopole (advisory, led by officials)	—	Concertation (limited)	Ownership of facilities, properties for firms
Nancy	Upscale regime (XX)	Smaller groups, incuding Brabois Tehcnopole	—	Concertation (limited)	Ownership of facilities
Clermont-Ferrand	Local Fordist (no regime) (XX)	Several groups	—	Fragmented, uncoordinated efforts at concertation	Ownership of facilities, properties for firms
United States					
Madison	Upscale regime (XXX)	Civic groups	Informal coalitions	Elective office, civic groups	Limited
Durham	Upscale (no regime) (XXX)	Civic groups	Friends of Durham (1980s–1990s), other groups	Elective office, joint ventures, civic groups	Properties for firms
New Haven	Upscale (no regime) (XX)	Downtown Council, other civic groups	—	Civic groups	Limited

Rennes, the chamber had undertaken comparatively little entrepreneurial activity.[44]

The role of the Chamber of Commerce and downtown business associations in local governing coalitions also differed with the political complexion of the dominant local electoral coalition. In Rennes and Montpellier, chambers linked to the Right had actively contested developmental initiatives of the Socialist Hervé and Frêche administrations.[45] From the 1980s, local governments of the Left drew on new organizational means to build politico-economic regimes around aggressive developmental policies. To guide and legitimate local economic development initiatives, local officials brought together local businesses and regional officials and the chambers in formalized associational networks. Like similar organizations in Lille,[46] the CODESPAR in Rennes and the Montpellier Languedoc-Roussillon Technopole in Montpellier helped set priorities in such matters as the initiation and maintenance of technology parks. In maintaining links to the local business communities that leftist governments would have otherwise lacked, these arrangements enabled more dynamic cooperation among businesses and institutions. In each instance local officials retained critical authority to make their own decisions about how developmental and other policies would proceed. In the 1990s in Clermont-Ferrand, as part of a belated effort to mobilize the economy to counter the losses in manufacturing jobs, local officials launched a similar new organization named Auvergne Développement. This local effort came into conflict with uncoordinated, parallel associations linked to Michelin, the right-wing regional government and other sources.

In Nancy, the Center-Right coalition that controlled the local government and sustained political alliances with most of the surrounding towns stood closer to the chamber. At the same time that Rossinot and his administration maintained ties to the local university, they looked to conservative downtown business and residential associations for much of their electoral support. Even in closer political alliance with the chamber, the

---

[44] Cf. Waters, "Chambers of Commerce," pp. 597–598; Le Galès, *Développement Économique*, pp. 198–200.

[45] Le Galès, *Développement Économique*," pp. 198–200; Sellers, "Grounds of Democracy," p. 124.

[46] Peter John and Alistair Cole, "Urban Regimes and Local Governance in Britain and France: Policy Adaption and Coordination in Leeds and Lille," *Urban Affairs Review 33*(3) (1998): 382–405.

regime relied more consistently on the initiatives of ADUAN and smaller associations like the one linked to the technology park at Brabois to promote developmental and other agendas outside the narrow boundaries of the central city. Planners at the agency asserted that the chamber, through reluctance to equip one of its industrial zones with adequate infrastructure, had undermined the efforts of local development advocates to secure a new automobile plant within the urban region for the Swatch-Mercedes car.

The politics of pedestrian zones and urban renewal in the late 1960s through the 1980s demonstrated both the consequences of these domestic variations and the general contrast with German business interests. The German chambers and Retail Associations had generally adopted a favorable stance toward pedestrian zones and a strong commercial center and had exchanged support for such measures as delivery access and parking garages. In France, efforts since the 1970s to build new developments and introduce pedestrian zones into Old Towns had often included little concertation. With varying success, downtown business representatives led opposition to downtown projects of this sort. In Montpellier and Rennes, similar opposition contributed to the downfall of the Delmas and Fréville administrations. Yet administrations of the Left had subsequently employed a combination of negotiation and sheer political will to overcome this opposition. The Frêche administration had extended pedestrian zones and promoted peripheral shopping facilities. The Hervé administration had introduced more limited new pedestrian zones and succeeded in having regional controls on new shopping centers.[47]

In Nancy, the conflicts over proposed new high-rise development in the downtown played out over the 1970s under successive administrations of the Right. The Rossinot administration, responding to downtown demands within the coalition, had extended preservationist restrictions on downtown development but done little to expand pedestrian zones. In Clermont-Ferrand, where the uneasy relation between Michelin and the city government limited local coalition building, downtown developmental initiatives remained fewer and less ambitious.

As in Germany, the strong corporatist mechanisms centered around the Chambers of Agriculture played a distinctive role in urban

---

[47] Decisions about peripheral development reflected a similar bias. Even on the departmental commissions that reserved places for local commercial and business representatives to decide on approvals of shopping centers for a department, the Royer law gave the preponderance of votes to elected officeholders.

governance.[48] Although potentially powerful advocates for preservation of farms and open space, the chambers, in the words of a state official in Clermont-Ferrand, represented "the farmers, not farming." In Montpellier, local officials had negotiated with agricultural representatives and individual farmers to avoid "*mitage*" or piece by piece erosion of the remaining agricultural zones within the city.[49] But farm representatives also had little interest in preventing farmers from selling farmland when encroaching development raised the prices. Except against the background of extensive interlocal cooperation in Rennes, negotiations with the chambers had not prevented the continuous sale of farmland for development.

With the construction of ties to local business and other economic interests, elected officials in both of these French cities had assembled regimes in the local economy as well as among local and supralocal governments. The support these regimes mobilized among businesses helps to account for the intensity as well as the success of developmental policies in these settings after decentralization. In Nancy, less formalized, more traditional networks supported the parallel but less successful efforts of local public officials. Even without the corporatist hierarchies of Germany, business influence within these regimes remained limited (Table 5.3). In Clermont-Ferrand more fragmented relations with business undermined local regime building and detracted from the resulting synthesis.[50]

In the U.S. cities local business mobilization made the most difference for urban governance. As long noted in studies of U.S. political economies, this pervasive role of business stemmed from the organizational capacities these actors furnished for the carrying out of policy. The less extensive supralocal policies, more fragmented local governments, less cohesive electoral organizations, more frequent electoral challenges and greater local fiscal pressures confronted any such organizations at the local level with a less stable or structured environment than either their German or even French counterparts faced. As comparison with corporatist Germany demonstrates, more extensive business influence also depended partly on less extensive business organization.

In the growth coalitions that coalesced around developmental policies in the 1950s to the 1970s, local business associations had often assumed a

[48] John T. S. Keeler, *The Politics of Neocorporatism in France* (New York: Oxford University Press, 1987).

[49] Montpellier, *Révision du Plan d'Occupation des Sols de Montpellier* (1990), p. 72.

[50] On Clermont-Ferrand, see Beslay, Bernard and Cavet, "Clermont-Ferrand."

leading role even in relation to local governments. In New Haven and Durham, as in bigger cities like Atlanta, Boston and San Francisco,[51] organizations representing local businesses and the universities had often emerged as prime movers in urban renewal and related programs. In New Haven, the Downtown Council and other networks connected to Yale and local banks had first sponsored the Rotival plan, then mobilized around renewal programs.[52] Similar mobilizations of business and civic organizations in Durham included business organizations based in the African American community.[53] More in Durham and in Madison than in the machine city of New Haven, organized labor had helped mobilize electoral support for the local governments that supported these alliances.[54] In 1938 the Madison Planning Trust, a civic organization of business leaders and prominent citizens, had commissioned a plan that guided development decisions prior to a new master plan in the 1970s.[55] But the growth coalition that carried out parts of this agenda in the 1960s emerged more from independent initiatives on the part of the university, the state government and local business representatives. Madison's urban renewal also proved more limited than in the other cities; lawsuits and a referendum had defeated an early version of the Monona Terrace convention center.

In the 1980s and 1990s, the more unified initiatives of the 1960s coalitions had dispersed into mobilizations around an array of specific projects or programs. In Durham, the site of the most rapid growth, the Chamber of Commerce developed an unusually comprehensive, aggressive role in recruiting new companies. Chamber officials searched for possible plant sites, coordinated meetings with officials responsible for all the local permits, subsidies and tax breaks, and helped mediate arrangements for worker retraining.[56] The chambers of Madison and New Haven undertook analogous if less extensive efforts. More ad hoc business associations

[51] John H. Mollenkopf, *The Contested City* (Princeton: Princeton University Press, 1983).

[52] William Domhoff, *Who Really Rules? New Haven and Community Power Reexamined* (New Brunswick, NJ: Transaction Books, 1978).

[53] Jean Bradley Anderson, *Durham County* (Durham: Duke University Press, 1990), p. 407.

[54] Robert R. Alford and Harry M. Scoble, *Bureaucracy and Participation: Political Cultures in Four Wisconsin Cities* (Chicago: Rand McNally and Co., 1969), p. 108.

[55] Ladislas Segoe, *Comprehensive Plan of Madison, Wisconsin and Environs* (Madison: Madison Planning Trust, 1938); William F. Thompson, *The History of Wisconsin*.

[56] On a smaller scale, in the "Special Districts" of a number of urban neighborhoods in New Haven, local small businesses also paid a small tax for self-administered collective services. Although these organizations appear to have conducted little advocacy, they did privatize services that would otherwise have been public.

concerned with development in specific neighborhoods now carried out the most significant local initiatives. Prominent business or institutional actors, such as the universities or major development companies, stood behind the most effective such organizations.[57] The Downtown Council of New Haven had continued its activities into the 1990s. Under DiLieto, this association had supported projects like Downtown South/Hill North; under Daniels, then DiStefano, it supported efforts to attract a regional mall. In Durham, Duke University had joined in 1980 with local business leaders in the "Durham Downtown Development Corporation" to shepherd proposals for a hotel and convention center complex through the local governments.[58] In 1989 these efforts culminated in the Downtown Development Revitalization Plan, a series of improvements to be carried out through $110 million in private investment and $37 million in investment by the city government.[59] Despite the existence of a similar organization in Madison, both planners and prominent businesspeople continued to call for greater commitments by local corporate chiefs, the state government and the university to work together.[60] In Madison and in New Haven, businesses in tax increment finance districts in parts of the downtown carried out more localized cooperative arrangements for shared services and improvements.

Although organized labor was now a dwindling presence in local elections, formal and ad hoc business associations had at times mobilized electoral support directly around the agendas of local businesses. In Durham, the ad hoc downtown businesses and professionals organized as "Friends of Durham" constituted the most open, most successful version of a business party. With strong support in the suburban neighborhoods, this group had swept elections in 1979 and again in 1991 with promises to spur

---

[57] Thus in New Haven respondents mentioned the Chamber of Commerce and sometimes other business and professional associations in 12 of 16 (75 percent) of the larger controversies, or a total of 18 of 49 (37 percent) overall (Sellers, "Grounds of Democracy," p. 194). In only 2 controversies (4 percent) did the respondents attribute the chamber with more than "limited" influence.

[58] North Carolina Public Interest Research Group, *Report on the Proposed Convention Center* (Durham, 1982), p. 7.

[59] Durham City-County Planning Department, *Downtown Durham Revitalization Plan* (Durham, 1989), p. 69.

[60] Michelle Cooke et al., *Who Runs Madison? A Sociological Study* (Madison: Madison Public Library, mimeograph, 1980), pp. 13–14; (Madison: Madison Public Library, 1980, mimeograph), p. 14; Madison Department of Planning and Development, *Downtown 2000* (Madison, 1989), p. 63.

development, to reduce local property taxes, to fight crime and to end local cultural and sports subsidies. Even though it soon lost to the Progressive coalition, Friends of Durham succeeded in shifting policy away from environmental and social measures and toward new development. Like the small pro-business voter group that called itself "Citizens for Bielefeld," such a group would have fared worse in the more entrenched party systems of the German cities.[61] In both other U.S. cities, business associations also played more indirect roles in local elections. In Madison during the 1980s, Mayors Skornicka and Sensenbrenner had also relied on business and institutional support in elections. Mayor Soglin integrated elements of this electoral support into his coalition. Both Soglin and his immediate predecessors had however beaten back more radical pro-business challenges of the sort that Friends of Durham had mounted in elections. Even in New Haven, John Daniels would have risked losing electoral support as well as cooperation in governing had he not pursued policies supportive of the downtown business community. Both Mayors DiLieto and DiStefano had secured longer terms partly as a result of stronger business support.

Diverse institutional arenas in the U.S. central cities thus gave locally dependent businesses, institutions and business representatives more pervasive opportunities to influence local agendas than was generally the case in Europe. The same lack of cooperation that hindered organizational regime building enhanced the potential for informal business influence. Only in Madison, however, did consistent local political coalitions combine with this economic representation into a stable urban regime.

Even in the absence of organized business participation, local officials in these cities had ample reason to serve the interests of business. In all three countries, business associations concerned primarily with promotion of developmental policies contributed to the construction and maintenance of urban regimes along local policy syntheses (Table 5.3). In Europe, more structured systems of economic interest intermediation as well as local governmental and political arrangements furnished a stability to urban governance that U.S. practice generally lacked. Even as German urban governance had altered corporatist practices, local business as well as labor still felt the restrictions of corporatist hierarchies on local initiatives. In

---

[61] The Bürgergemeinschaft for Bielefeld had won only 8 percent of the vote. Even in a majority along with the CDU, and after five years in office, the group had succeeded in surprisingly few alterations to the Red-Green synthesis.

France, where national institutions constrained local business-government relations less, activist regimes had built up the developmental components of local syntheses partly through formalized cooperation with organized representatives of businesses. In the United States, the disorganization of business interest intermediation as well as the open-structured infra-structures of local government and politics left the stable governing coalition of an urban regime more difficult to assemble. Precisely this comparative disorganization opened up possibilities for more decisive business influence.

The "Growth Machine" and Instruments for Control of Markets. Especially for the construction of an effective urban governing coalition in pursuit of environmental and social objectives, local institutional capacities for public control over local markets made much of the difference. Whether or not an urban regime had formed, local efforts and supralocal infrastructures for urban governance combined to contribute to these capacities. Under different national systems, these influences ultimately brought about different consequences from the locally dependent interests that Logan and Molotch termed "growth machines." Derived from U.S. cities of the 1960s and 1970s, earlier understandings about these coalitions of real estate and development businesses with other public and private institutions opposed their support of developmental ends to the pursuit of environmental quality and social equity.[62] As local capacities for environmental and other policies have expanded, growth machines have played a part in regimes and governing coalitions that pursued these other ends. Especially in Germany, stronger local instruments for official control of land use markets have altered the political logic of the growth machine itself. Rather than contest or undermine environmental or social aims, local real estate and development interests reinforced the strongest developmental policies in the places with the most effective environmental and social measures.

The institutional tools that local officials mobilized to assert control over local markets within a city often dated back decades or even centuries. How much local officials could take advantage of these tools depended on supralocal authorizations, mandates and other resources as well as on local initiatives. As the European Commission and the International Monetary

---

[62] See David Imbroscio, "Reformulating Urban Regime Theory," *Journal of Urban Affairs* 20(3) (1998): 233–248; Logan and Molotch, *Urban Fortunes*.

Fund (IMF) have stressed, local policy tools of this sort may interfere with the developmental aim of responsiveness to markets.[63] But this same interference can aid the pursuit of policies that qualify or alter the consequences of markets. By and large, parapublic organizations for development, housing, infrastructure and financial companies as well as municipal property ownership strengthened the capacities of political leaders to assemble effective governing coalitions in the pursuit of environmental and social ends. Any developer or other business in negotiation with the city had to contemplate the sanctions as well as the assistance that these instruments made possible. The governing coalitions with the most extensive array of instruments had also usually employed their capacities in the successful pursuit of growth.

Two aspects of public or partial public ownership of crucial firms made the most critical difference for opportunities to exert political control over local markets and informal networks.[64] First, a mayor whose municipality owned companies concerned with development and an array of related areas possessed more effective means to construct and maintain a governing coalition around control of markets. Second, even in the event of parapublic or public ownership, joint ownership with other governments or private shareholders could still impede effective local control. The need to cooperate with other shareholders poses difficulties that unified municipal ownership would not. Within Germany, France and the United States as well as among them, the variations in local policy reflected the resulting differences in capacities (Table 5.4).

Parapublic development companies played one of the most pivotal roles in building these capacities. Although the Development and Redevelopment Authorities of the U.S. cities contracted out an array of renewal activities to private firms, both German and French officials relied on firms owned at least partly by local officials to carry out much of their development in their cities. In France "mixed-economy companies," owned only just over 50 percent by a principal public shareholder, had played an especially extensive role in local policy. Since the 1960s two such companies, the Société d'Équipement de la Région Montpellieraine (SERM) in

---

[63] E.g., Commission of the European Communities, *Third Survey of State Aids in the European Community* (Luxembourg: European Community, 1992).

[64] Functional efficiency and political ideology have generally preoccupied debates over privatization (John Donahue, *The Privatization Decision* [New York: Basic Books, 1989]; Harvey Feigenbaum, Jeffrey Henig and Chris Hamnett, *Shrinking the State* [New York: Cambridge University Press, 1998]).

Table 5.4 *Urban Governance and Instruments for Municipal Control over Local Markets*

	Germany				France				United States		
	Freiburg	Münster	Göttingen	Bielefeld	Rennes	Montpellier	Nancy	Clermont-Ferrand	Madison	Durham	New Haven
Policies	(regime)	(regime)			(regime)	(regime)	(regime)		(regime)		
Developmental	XX	XX	X	X	XXX	XXX	XX	XX	XXX	XXX	XX
Environmental	XXX	XXX	XXX	XX	XX	XX	XX	X	XX	XX	X
Equity	XXX	XX	XX	XXX	XXX	X	X	XXX	X	X	X
Instruments											
Development	L	L	—	—	R	L	R	—	—	—	—
Housing	L	L	L	L	L	L	L	L	L	L	L
Electricity, gas	L	L	L	L	L	—	—	—	—	L	—
Water, sewer	L	L	L	L	L	L	R	L	L	L	R
Waste	L	L	L	L	L	R	R	L	L	L	L
Fire	L	L	L	L	R	R	R	R	L	L	L
Transit	L	L	L	L	L	R	R	R	L	L	L
Airport	L	R	—	—	—	—	R	R	R	R	—
Finance	L	L	L	L	L	L	L	L	—	—	L
Municipally owned land (%)	64	21	38	53	30	10	11	8	10	12	13
	(1969)	(1969)	(1969)	(1969)	(1988)	(1988)	(1988)	(1988)	(1998)	(1999)	(1999)
		15		23							
		(1991)		(1994)							

L = Central city governmental function or company under control of central city government; R = Company or governmental function under control of governments or public authority in urban region.

Sources: *Land* data from Deutscher Städtetag, *Statistisches Jahrbuch Deutscher Gemeinden 1971*, pp. 5–7; INSEE, *Communoscope*; and city statistical offices.

Montpellier and the Société d'Économie Mixte d'Aménagement de la Bretagne (SEMAEB) in Rennes, carried out many of the projects that had brought the fastest rates of metropolitan growth. Although Clermont-Ferrand lacked a similar company, the Société Lorraine d'Économie Mixte (SOLOREM) filled a more modest but similar function in and around Nancy. As intermediaries between the city government and land use markets, these companies purchased land for new construction, cleared it, built the necessary physical infrastructure and then sold the improved land to private developers or others to construct specific buildings. The regime in Montpellier had proven especially adept at using the contractual work of the SERM for other local officials to extend political influence throughout the city region and beyond and to accumulate assets twice as high as any other mixed-economy company in the region.[65]

These parapublic firms undertook much more of local development than similar operations in the German cities. In Freiburg and Münster, the local development firms had confined their activities more to downtown projects on behalf of the city government itself.[66] By comparison with these German counterparts, however, two distinctive features of the institutional infrastructure for French parapublic firms weakened their capacities to weld together a governing coalition opposed to growth and markets. First, because the mixed-economy companies resold partly developed land, local governments that owned them faced the prospect of at least an indirect windfall from aggressive development. As the German development companies not only had undertaken fewer projects but had carried out more of those projects themselves, these firms remained more subject to the control of policy makers. Second, since French law limited ownership on the part of any single government to 51 percent of shares, French city governments could exercise less control over mixed-economy companies. In Rennes and Nancy, moreover, a metropolitan district rather than a single town assumed this ownership role. In German settings like Freiburg and Münster, complete municipal ownership of parapublic firms assured local official total control.

In all the central cities, by contrast, local authorities or city-owned companies ran the core of publicly subsidized housing. In Freiburg, Bielefeld, Rennes and Clermont-Ferrand, larger operations of this sort had helped

---

[65] Jacques Molénat, "Quand les élus jouent aux p.d.g.," *Méridien 13* (April 1990): 30.
[66] *Land*-owned firms of a similar sort carried out major renewal projects in Bielefeld and Göttingen.

carry out the more ambitious policies to advance social and spatial equity through public housing and neighborhood policy. Against the background of much more limited financing and other resources from above, municipal housing authorities in the U.S. cities carried out analogous but less extensive operations.

In an array of infrastructural activities essential to development, local ownership offered further means of control. Germany's city-owned electric companies, gas companies and transit companies could be coordinated more easily around both growth management and social equity. Officials in French cities had to work more with the districts of metropolitan towns that owned basic utilities and with the Chambers of Commerce and Industry that often ran airports and other major transport facilities. Local public control over water and sewer service also presented cities like Madison and Durham, along with other U.S. cities like Ann Arbor, the means to enforce boundaries on new development within the city's jurisdiction.[67]

In Europe, the means of local control extended to financial resources from parapublic local firms. In Germany, local *Sparkassen* (savings and loans) often maintained the most extensive operations of any bank in a city.[68] These institutions and their counterparts at the *Land* level furnished municipalities with loans for projects like the convention center in Freiburg and helped regulate private loans for new development. In France, local *Caisses d'Epargne* helped regularly to finance the investment budgets of municipalities.[69] At the same time, although national public banks like the *Caisse des Dépôts et Consignations* (CDC) no longer monopolized local development finance after 1990, they retained a significant role. The CDC controlled small shares of equity in powerful parapublic development firms like the SERM and acted as a lender to these firms as well as to the cities and districts. Cross-subsidies from other local parapublic companies often enhanced the local financial capacities. In Rennes and Montpellier, the huge sums the local development companies gener-

---

[67] Note that this includes extraterritorial jurisdiction.

[68] In Bielefeld, Freiburg and Göttingen the *Sparkassen* listed the most neighborhood offices in the official city directories of any banks.

[69] In Nancy, for instance, the *Caisse d'Epargne* – described in budget documents as a "public establishment of social character" (Nancy, *Budget Report 1994*, p. 59) – provided the municipality with a loan of 35 million francs in 1994. Montpellier borrowed 40 million francs in 1994 from the *Caisse d'Epargne*. For Clermont-Ferrand, income from "associated banks and establishments" totaled 16.1 million francs in 1995; for Rennes in 1994, 99 million francs (plus 10 million labeled "CDC Caisse d'Epargne").

ated flowed partly into city coffers.[70] The German cities charged "concessions" amounting to tens of millions of marks to the electric companies they owned.[71]

Ownership of land itself proved especially important to control.[72] In maintaining levels of local ownership of at least twice the rate in any U.S. or French city besides Rennes, the German governing coalitions had generally secured greater leverage over land use. Although the rate of ownership in Münster had dropped to a level approaching the French average, Freiburg relied on extensive ownership in city forests to contain development. In Göttingen, for instance, municipal acquisitions of property dating back to 1920 had enabled the city to carry out a program of downtown rehabilitation and social and occupant-owned housing in the 1970s.[73] In France, despite increasing national authority for local preemptive purchase of municipal territory, only Rennes, with 30 percent of local land, had gained direct municipal control over as high a proportion.[74] Its ownership of land had helped enable the regime in Rennes to scatter social housing around the city as well as to maintain parks as the population grew. Despite a renewed shift toward public acquisition of parks and open space in the U.S. cities, local or regional watershed authorities had done more than had central-city governments to impede sprawl through ownership.

In comparing the effects on policy among countries, it would be difficult to sort out these variations in local state-society relations from other aspects of domestic institutions. Within each country, greater capacities

---

[70] Thus in Rennes in 1994, the budget included receipts totaling 164 million francs associated with various local development projects, among them an "advance" of 114 million francs from the SEMAEB for a ZAC at the railroad station. In Montpellier during the same year, the infrastructural investment budget included receipts of 142 million francs, among them a "reimbursement" of 70 million francs from an unspecified body (most likely the SERM) for "acquisitions of property." Other entries in both cities showed that more or less equivalent sums went back into investments in property or other activities of these parapublic enterprises.

[71] In Freiburg the concession to the Stadtwerke Freiburg averaged around 23 million marks between 1993 and 1996, except in 1994, when it reached 44 million marks. In Bielefeld the city granted the same local firm a concession of just over 38 million marks in 1994 and 1995. In Münster the sum came to 31.5 million marks in 1993 and 1994. In Göttingen the concession in 1993 and 1994 stood at 7.5 million marks, and a further concession at 15.6 million marks.

[72] Arnold Heidenheimer, Hugh Heclo and Carolyn Teich Adams, *Comparative Public Policy*, 3rd ed. (New York: St. Martin's Press, 1990), Ch. 6.

[73] Göttingen, *Altstadtsanierung, 1969–1979* (1980), p. 10.

[74] Land acquisitions by the mixed-economy companies in these cities may account for the difference from German ownership.

for local control of local development markets had parallel consequences (Table 5.4). The urban governing coalitions with the most extensive array of instruments for control had in each country carried out the most elaborate policy syntheses. Without full-fledged urban regimes, coalitions generally amassed less extensive instruments for municipal control, and pursued more limited local syntheses. Even in the absence of a regime, however, these instruments helped to shift the local politico-economic balance of power in favor of local officials. In Germany, largely similar tools to those in Freiburg and Münster enabled the coalitions of Göttingen and Bielefeld to carry out Social-Ecological syntheses. In Durham and New Haven, and even to a degree in Madison, more limited tools posed a comparatively weak counterweight to pressures for development.

The real estate and development interests of the "growth machine" depended not only on these mechanisms of market control but on more general features of urban governance and its infrastructure. Logan and Molotch argued that in U.S. cities the incentives of these firms to pursue development also extended to officials, institutions and other businesses.[75] Outside the U.S. as well, private firms in the construction and real estate industries shared analogous profit motives.[76] Even when officials, official networks and supralocal policies wielded greater leverage over markets, governing coalitions and regimes usually formed partly around complementary interests in growth. Yet only in U.S. and French cities did the strongest growth machines drive regimes that pursued development at the expense of environmental or distributive aims. In the German cities the strongest local development industries reinforced precisely the regimes that controlled development most on behalf of other ends.

Comparison between the French and German cities illuminates this seeming anomaly. The largest development industries had emerged in Freiburg and Montpellier, the fastest-growing cities of the 1980s in their respective countries (Table 5.5). But in Freiburg as in Münster, control over development differed comparatively little from policies in and around the other German cities. By comparison with markets, 42 percent of elites and activists I interviewed in and around Freiburg generally held controls to be more important determinants of land use patterns.[77] Despite

---

[75] Logan and Molotch, *Urban Fortunes*.

[76] Especially from a comparative perspective, these industries have received scant scholarly attention. Cf. Susan S. Fainstein, *The City Builders* (Oxford: Blackwell, 1993).

[77] Sellers, "Grounds of Democracy," p. 504.

Table 5.5 *Local Policy Syntheses, by Size of Local Development Industry (Numbers of Firms / 100,000 Residents) (* = Urban Regime)*

(a) Germany

	Freiburg	Münster	Bielefeld	Göttingen
Policy synthesis	Comprehensive*	Comprehensive*	Social-Ecological	Social-Ecological
Builders (*Bauunternehmer, Baugesellschaften*)	39 (3 national firms in city)	23 (3 national firms in city)	8 (3 national firms in city)	16 (no national firms)
Homebuilders (*Fertighäuser, Wohnungsbaugesellschaftten*)	19	7	1	2
Real estate (*Immobilien*)	38	63	38	48
Baugenossenschaften	3	2	2	2
Proportion of employed in construction, 1987 (by workplace) (%)	5.5	5.0	4.2	3.6

(b) France

	Montpellier	Nancy	Clermont-Ferrand	Rennes
Policy synthesis	Upscale*	Upscale*	Local Fordist	Comprehensive*
Developers (*promoteurs-constructeurs*)	53 (10 national groups in city)	14 (4 national groups in city)	4 (all local)	24 (6 national groups in city)
Homebuilders (*maisons individuelles*)	21	30	31	23
Establishments in real estate, 1996 (*unité urbaine*)	322 (310)	245 (113)	151 (120)	178 (73)
Proportion of resident workers in construction, 1990 (%)	6.3	5.2	5.8	4.8

(c) United States

	Durham	Madison	New Haven
Policy synthesis	Upscale	Upscale*	Upscale
Real estate developers	8	17	4
General and building contractors	56	44	51
Homebuilders	7	9	2
Real estate	59	39	38
Proportion employed residents in construction, 1990 (metro area) (%)	4.9 (5.6)	2.8 (4.3)	3.9 (3.4)

Sources: United States and France: phone listings collected 1992–1996 (in France, for city; in United States, for metropolitan area). Germany: official city handbooks, 1995–1996. Employment data from census statistics. French data on real estate firms from Sirène series. "National" firms include those known to have operations outside the larger region where the metropolitan area was located.

331

occasional grumbling, developers in Freiburg proved remarkably sanguine about the local policy toward construction. In fact, the intervention of the regime had also opened up opportunities for development that cities with Red-Green syntheses like Bielefeld and Göttingen lacked. Development firms themselves had a comparatively limited hand in this intervention. As the limited presence of national development firms suggests, external speculative investment and the accompanying pressures for development had not arrived in Freiburg. Alongside more constrained interlocal markets for place and the political and corporatist components of urban governance, legacies from the strong nonprofit housing sector in Germany contributed to the limited influence of for-profit development.[78]

In France, fast-growing Montpellier and Rennes had attracted distinctive local development industries. The different influences of the development industry accounts to a significant degree for the contrasting syntheses of these settings. In Montpellier, a faster-growing city than Rennes, national and regional developers swarmed to plant stakes in a local regime built around aggressive development. Alongside the economic clout and political power that the SERM brought to this pursuit, the national development "groups" (Bouygues, Cogedim, and Copra) that often dominated development markets in France concentrated offices in the city.[79] In contrast to Freiburg, only 26 percent of the elites and activists here identified regulation as more important than markets.[80] Oriented primarily toward prosperous new residents, the groups furnished a powerful set of interests in the Upscale orientation of the regime. In Rennes, the sole French city region where the regime had pursued effective growth management, local development activity remained subdued by compari-

---

[78] Nonprofit housing firms with longtime roots in the cities had also built much of the social housing. In addition to Neue Heimat, the scandal-plagued firm linked to the labor unions, local "construction cooperatives" (*Baugenossenschaften*) of this sort typically maintained close connections to the local SPD or to other parties. Once the Kohl government removed this nonprofit status in the 1980s, however, many of these firms shifted their new construction to more upscale markets (Manfred Konkiewitz, "Taming the Housing Market," in Jan-Erik Lane (ed.), *State and Market* [London: Sage, 1985], pp. 181–198).

[79] Werner Heinz (ed.), *Public-Private Partnership – ein neuer Weg zur Stadtentwicklung?* (Stuttgart: W. Kohlhammer, 1993). According to Eurostat statistics on companies with 20 or more workers (Hauptverband der Deutschen Bauindustrie, "Konzentration in der Bauwirtschaft," *Informationen für die Bauindustrie 5* [1990]: 1), the share of employees and earnings in German construction companies with over 500 workers was lower than in France but higher than in Italy. But in both Great Britain and Italy the larger firms held more of the market than they did in France.

[80] Sellers, "Grounds of Democracy," p. 504.

son. Despite a rate of growth much higher than those of the other French cities besides Montpellier, and several regional offices for national developers, the local construction industry remained remarkably small. Even fewer resident workers in Rennes were employed in this field than those living in either Nancy or Clermont-Ferrand. Especially in the outlying towns of the urban region, where growth management had been in place for decades, real estate establishments remained few. Pressures like those from development interests in Montpellier would have made it difficult for the regime in Rennes to maintain a Comprehensive policy synthesis.

Both Durham and Madison, as faster-growing city regions, had accumulated generally larger local real estate and development industries than had New Haven (Table 5.5c). The same elements that fostered the more pervasive role for business in general assured development firms more prominent roles in local policies on growth. The fragmentation of local government and politics, the demands of interlocal competition, even the weakness of organized representation for business generally left developers with considerable latitude to shape their projects. In and around New Haven, 55 percent of elites and activists – nearly twice the proportion in either Freiburg or Montpellier – pointed to the private developer as the one among several local professionals with the most "freedom of action." With a growing trend toward integration in the construction market,[81] large national developers like Trammell-Crow or the Rouse Company frequently operated as the prime movers behind larger mall or housing projects. In most towns of an urban region, a national firm could dominate the city administration in the development process.[82] Much of effective policy toward development evolved more through bargains that developers worked out individually with local governments, infrastructure firms and neighborhood groups than through more encompassing policy decisions.[83]

---

[81] Barry James Sullivan, *Industrialization in the Building Industry* (New York: Van Nostrand Reinhold Co., 1980).

[82] In the 1990s Trammell-Crow had built a 1,500-unit housing complex in Hamden, north of New Haven, and was also involved in major projects around Durham. Rouse had renovated and for a time owned the Chapel Square Mall in downtown New Haven. For an extensive account of Rouse Company operations, see Bernard Frieden and Lynn Sagalyn, *Downtown, Inc.* (Cambridge, MA: MIT Press, 1991).

[83] Cf. Kevin Cox, "Governance, Urban Regime Analysis, and the Politics of Local Economic Development," in Mickey Lauria (ed.), *Reconstructing Urban Regime Theory* (Thousand Oaks, CA: Sage, 1997), pp. 99–121.

Even in the United States, growth management in Madison and Durham had begun to apply brakes to the growth machine. As in Rennes, the smaller development interests within Madison reflect a constricted outlook for growth there. In all three U.S. downtowns, nonprofit community development corporations also qualified the emphasis of private developers on more upscale projects. In the disadvantaged neighborhoods that for-profit development had mostly bypassed, these firms pursued social services and affordable housing as well as business interests.[84] Partly dependent on governmental and private foundation grants, these organizations remained too small to counter wider market forces. Nonprofits could alleviate neighborhood decline, but rarely reversed it.[85]

Reinforced by the locally dependent interests of service and high-tech businesses, and centered in the arena of developmental matters, urban politico-economic regimes assembled around the most extensive policy syntheses in each country. Even when full-fledged formations of this sort had failed to emerge, individual businesses and business associations could decisively influence local choices. In Germany, where corporatism and stronger official capacities for market control supplemented an infrastructure of more extensive supralocal policies and political organization, local business influence made less difference for local choices. In the absence of politico-economic regimes that embraced development alongside other objectives, as in Freiburg and Münster, urban governance revolved around the environmental and social policies of the Social-Ecological synthesis. As a result, real estate and development firms asserted the strongest interests in new development in cities with extensive environmental and social policies. In France, considerable local political powers and instruments for control over development markets failed to overcome the need for regimes based on alliances with elements of the local business community. If the regime in Rennes had prevented real estate and development interests

---

[84] The Hill Development Corporation in New Haven had secured jobs and business opportunities linked to the Downtown South/Hill North project; the Hayti Development Corporation in Durham, two shopping centers and 170 housing units (Durham City-County Planning Department 1995); and Transitional Housing Inc., in Madison, had purchased and repaired scattered-site housing for homeless people. Cf. Gordana Rabrenovic, *Community Builders* (Albany: State University of New York Press, 1996).

[85] Alex Schwartz Rachel G. Bratt, Avis C. Vidal, and Langley C. Keyes, "Nonprofit Housing Organizations and Institutional Support: The Management Challenge," *Journal of Urban Affairs 18*(4) (1996): 389–407; Edward Goetz, *Shelter Burden* (Philadelphia: Temple University Press, 1993).

from imposing Upscale agendas, its counterpart in Montpellier had not. In the United States, the fragmentation of business representation as well as local politics and government had aggravated the difficulties that diverse business and institutional interests already posed for the formation of politico-economic regimes. This same fragmentation usually enhanced the central position in urban governance of local businesses and institutions in general, and real estate and development businesses in particular. This critical role for business kept developmental policies at the forefront.

Movement Politics and Urban Governance

The grassroots politics of local activism has also fostered the growth of urban governance. Throughout the advanced industrial world, social movements rooted in the cultural patterns of everyday life, and politically active beyond the sphere of conventional electoral politics, have grown into a familiar, increasingly institutionalized element of state-society relations.[86] Since the debates over community power in the United States of the 1950s, analysts of urban governance have debated whether movements of this sort can alter the agendas of economic and political elites. For present purposes the issue amounts to whether an urban regime or some other governing coalition *incorporated* movements through institutionalized participation and chances for influence; and regardless of whether incorporation took place, what effect the movements had. Increasingly, infrastructures at higher levels underwrite opportunities for movements with statutory requirements like local notice, public hearings and environmental impact statements. Movements draw not only on these opportunities but also on increasingly transnational networks of organization, information and support, on local concerns and on the "social capital" of civic traditions.[87] By the 1990s, the coalitions in most of these cities had at least partly incorporated local social and neighborhood movements. Even where incorporation remained ambiguous, local movements had usually influenced local policy syntheses. Both the strength and objectives of the movements and the stance of local governing coalitions affected these variations in these results.

[86] Ronald Inglehart, *Culture Shift in Advanced Industrial Society* (Princeton: Princeton University Press, 1990); Hanspeter Kriesi Ruud Koopmans, and Jan Willem Duyvendack, *New Social Movements in Western Europe* (St. Paul: University of Minnesota Press, 1995).

[87] On this use of the term "social capital," see Robert Putnam, *Making Democracy Work* (Princeton: Princeton University Press, 1993).

Not only the willingness of other political and economic interests to accommodate those movements but the interests the movements assert can vary widely. On the one hand, civic activism within communities might seem to furnish the best chance for advocacy on behalf of cosmopolitan concerns about global environmental conditions and resources, the quality of life in cities and social justice.[88] On the other hand, neighborhood politics may defend the protective "enclave consciousness" of well-to-do neighborhoods or the self-regarding consumption interests of "a gigantic Club Méditerranée."[89] Protection of private ownership rights remains one of the main objects of movement activism. Both the orientation and the strength of the movements depend on who participates, which in turn depends on the wider social and spatial structures of an urban region. Citizens with higher education and bigger incomes generally take part more.[90] Disadvantaged ethnic and immigrant minorities, as a result of lesser participation, face compounded disadvantages.[91] Internationally, universities have repeatedly furnished activists for movements around cosmopolitan concerns, points of access in the diffusion of cosmopolitan knowledge and organizations and other "mobilizing structures" for movement activity.[92] As part of a sociocultural professional sector generally supportive of traditional left concerns, university staff and students also contribute added

[88] Kenneth A. Gould, Adam S. Weinberg and Allan Schnaiberg, *Local Environmental Struggles* (New York: Cambridge University Press, 1996); cf. Sarah M. Evans and Harry C. Boyte, *Free Spaces: The Sources of Democratic Change in America* (New York: Harper and Row, 1986); Jane Jacobs, *The Death and Life of Great American Cities* (New York: Random House, 1961); Larry Bennett, *Neighborhood Politics* (Garland, 1997); Donald Rosdil, "The Context of Radical Populism in U.S. Cities," *Journal of Urban Affairs 13*(1) (1992): 77–96.

[89] Elliot J. Feldman and Jerome Milch, *Technocracy versus Democracy: The Comparative Politics of International Airports* (Boston: Auburn House Publishing Co., 1982); Logan and Molotch, *Urban Fortunes*; Sidney Plotkin, "Enclave Consciousness and Neighborhood Activism," in Joseph M. Kling and Prudence S. Posner (eds.), *Dilemmas of Activism* (Philadelphia: Temple University Press, 1991), pp. 218–239; Rolf Böhme, *Je mehr wir haben, desto mehr wir wollen* (Bonn: Verlag J. H. Dietz Nachfolger, 1994), p. 36.

[90] Norman H. Nie, Jane Junn and Kenneth Stehlik-Barry, *Education and Democratic Citizenship in America* (Chicago: University of Chicago Press, 1996); Jefferey M. Berry, Kent E. Portney and Ken Thomson, *The Rebirth of Urban Democracy* (Washington: Brookings Institution, 1993), pp. 81–84; Sidney Verba, Norman Nie and Jae-on Kim, *Participation and Political Equality* (New York: Cambridge University Press, 1978).

[91] Sidney Verba, Kay Schlozman and Henry Brady, *Voice and Equality* (Cambridge: Harvard University Press, 1995), pp. 232–233.

[92] Sidney Tarrow, *Power in Movement* (New York: Cambridge University Press, 1993), pp. 135–150.

constituencies for concerns about equity.[93] Centralized, integrated urban settlement fosters interests among residents in collective goods like parks, pedestrian zones and mass transit and can facilitate associational activity. Dispersed, segregated settlement enables well-to-do residents in particular to secure more amenities for themselves through private ownership or policies like large-lot zoning and can depress mobilization.[94]

In U.S. and European cities, the incorporation of urban movements into governing coalitions often represents a shift from the occasionally violent confrontations with movements in the 1960s and 1970s.[95] Especially in centers of service and high-tech businesses, convergent interests laid the groundwork for incorporation. At the same time that local political leaders drew on the electoral constituencies and political activism of movements, service and high-tech businesses and institutions capitalized on the efforts of social or environmental movements to improve the quality of life. Yet infrastructures of urban governance and the choices of local political and economic elites have continued to furnish divergent opportunities for movements to participate in local decision making. Over the longer term, these influences have shaped the strength and orientation of those movements. My account will analyze these influences first in the French and German central cities, then in their U.S. counterparts and finally in the urban regions beyond the central-city limits.

Movements and Governance in the German and French Central Cities.
In the cities of France and Germany, movement politics took the form of neighborhood groups on the one hand (usually *associations de défense* in France and *Bürgerinitiativen* in Germany), and Green parties along with environmental and preservationist groups on the other. In both countries, urban governing coalitions responded irregularly to these movements. In the German cities, stronger movements contributed in different ways

---

[93] Hanspeter Kriesi, "The Transformation of Cleavage Politics," *European Journal of Political Research 33*(2) (1998): 165–195; Herbert Kitschelt, *The Transformation of European Social Democracy* (New York: Cambridge University Press, 1994), p. 12.

[94] I have analyzed the logic of these influences in nine of these cities in Sellers, "Public Goods and the Politics of Segregation," *Journal of Urban Affairs 21*(2) (1999): 237–262.

[95] Cf. Susan S. Fainstein and Clifford Hirst, "Urban Social Movements," in David Judge, Gerry Stoker and Harold Wolman (eds.), *Theories of Urban Politics* (London: Sage, 1995), pp. 181–204, see p. 182; Peter Franz and Donald I. Warren, "Neighborhood Action as a Social Movement," *Comparative Political Studies 20*(2) (1987): 229–246.

to regimes around the Comprehensive policy syntheses of Freiburg and Münster. In the French cities, where participation in movements generally fell below German levels, more intensive local movements fostered Upscale regimes. Consider first the strength and then the incorporation and ultimate consequences of these movements.

a. Mobilization in Movements. Aggregate data on participation in civic and political activities furnish useful comparative indicators of the strength of local engagement in movements. In general, the more citizens engage in associational and political activity, the more indispensable movements should be to governing coalitions and the stronger the contribution movements should make to local policy.[96] The local performance of the Green parties that have taken up environmental and social causes on behalf of local movements furnishes one indicator of this engagement (Table 5.6).[97] Wider patterns of "social capital" or civic engagement,[98] evident in the overall propensities of associational membership and newspaper readership, reinforce the constituencies and activism of these movements. The strength of the German indicators in comparison with the French reflects a comparative civic engagement also apparent in national surveys.[99] Any such national cultural propensities grow partly out of the different social and spatial conditions in cities like these.

In the German cities all of these activities took place more often. In every setting except Bielefeld, as in German university towns more generally, the Greens had averaged higher totals in local elections than the French ecological parties.[100] This participation corresponded to greater average mobilization in social movements as well as to generally higher civic involvement. Especially by comparison with the rates in the French *unités urbaines*, which corresponded more closely than the central cities to the scale of the German city limits, associations per resident also averaged

[96] Cf. Berry et al., *Rebirth of Urban Democracy*; Robert Putnam, *Making Democracy Work* (Princeton: Princeton University Press, 1993).

[97] Cf. Herbert Kitschelt, *The Logics of Party Formation* (Ithaca, NY: Cornell University Press, 1989); Jefferey M. Sellers, "Litigation as a Local Political Resource," *Law and Society Review 29*(3) (1995): 494.

[98] Cf. Richard Locke, *Remaking the Italian Economy* (Ithaca, NY: Cornell University Press, 1995).

[99] In the World Values Survey of 1990–1993, for instance, 35 percent of Germans but fully 61 percent of the French said they belonged to no group. Everett C. Ladd, *The Ladd Report* (New York: Free Press, 1999), p. 133.

[100] Jefferey M. Sellers, "Place, Post-industrial Change, and the New Left," *European Journal of Political Research 33* (1998): 198.

Table 5.6 *Local Policies, Green Performance and Social Structure by Rates of Civic Participation, 1980s–1990s*

	Local Policy Synthesis (* = Urban Regime)	Green Performance (%)	Civic Participation		Local Newspaper Sales[a] / 100 Residents	Social Structure	University Students / 100 City Residents
			Associations / 1,000 Residents			Proportion Higher Status Groups in City (%)	
Germany		(Results of local council elections, 1985–1995)	(City)			(Degree from *Hochschule* or *Fachhochschule*)	
Freiburg	Comprehensive*	21	13		40	18	17
Münster	Comprehensive*	14	13		40	18	21
Göttingen	Red-Green	14	6[b]		37	19	27
Bielefeld	Red-Green	11	6		24	9	8
France		(First-round local council results in 1989, 1995)	(City)	(Unité urbaine)		(*Cadres, professions intellectuelles supérieures*)	
Nancy	Upscale*	8	11	6	37	22	17
Montpellier	Upscale*	7	11	10	22	20	20
Clermont-Ferrand	Local Fordist	6	9	7	31	13	14
Rennes	Comprehensive*	11	8	8	13	17	17

[a] Circulation of leading local daily newspaper within each central city.

[b] Includes *Landkreis* and central city.

Sources: French associations taken from unpublished INSEE Sirène data, 1996; German *Vereine* from *Amtsgericht* for the corresponding *Stadt-* or *Landkreis*, 1996; newspaper sales figures from local newspapers; population data from 1990 (France) and 1987 (Germany) censuses.

higher. In all but one of the German cities, residents bought local news-papers at higher rates than in all but one of the French cities. Parallel survey data from the German and French cities with two of the highest rates of association, Freiburg and Montpellier, suggest that even these aggregate numbers fail to capture the stronger movement presence of the German cities. On both the Left and the Right, German elites and activists concerned with land use reported much more intensive personal civic participation. German respondents also reported that environmental and neighborhood associations had played roles in a wider range of land use disputes.[101] Since the French and German cities contained a similar range of higher-status workers as well as university students, social structural conditions can hardly account for this consistent cross-national contrast.

In the two German cities where the last chapter found more Comprehensive syntheses of local policies, civic associations and newspaper readership averaged the highest among all the European cities. In Freiburg one of the strongest local Green parties in Germany had by the late 1980s also won a role in the dominant electoral coalition. In Münster, a parallel synthesis had emerged even as the Greens remained in the opposition. The strength of civic engagement in these cities helps account not only for somewhat higher environmental scores than elsewhere but for the success of the local regime in combining other aims with development. In both cities, associational networks based largely among students and other younger residents had proliferated since the 1970s. In Freiburg, the national mobilization of environmental groups in opposition to a proposed nuclear power plant at nearby Wyhl had spurred this growth. A guide to the "Alternative Scene" there in 1985 listed some one thousand local peace groups, women's associations, unemployment centers, pro-immigrant initiatives, artistic groups and health collectives as well as recycling cooperatives and other environmentalist associations.[102] In Münster too, nearly half of the 296 "institutions, associations, free groups and initiatives" in a local "Culture Address Book" from 1985 had first emerged over the previous fifteen years.[103] These activities also mirrored older associational traditions that extended to the business community and the local Right. As

---

[101] Sellers, "Grounds of Democracy," pp. 123, 301.

[102] Netzwerk Dreyeckland E. V., Politische Buchhandlung Jos Fritz, and Stadtzeitung für Freiburg, *Stattbuch Freiburg Dreyeckland* (Freiburg: Walter Marx, 1985).

[103] Karl Teppe, "Politisches System, gesellschaftliche Strukturen und kulturelles Leben seit dem Zweiten Weltkrieg," in Franz-Josef Jakobi (ed.), *Geschichte der Stadt Münster*, vol. 2, (Münster: Aschendorff, 1993), pp. 1–82, see p. 73.

medieval market towns with strong guilds and Catholic bishophorics, both cities retained extensive networks of traditional associations linked to such traditions as Carnival and the Singing and Shooting Associations of the nineteenth century. In major controversies like the one surrounding Congress and the Convention Center in Freiburg, these networks mobilized much of the local business and professional community on behalf of projects even as leftist and preservationist associations mobilized others in opposition. As in that case, countermovements in favor of development often enabled even disputed projects to proceed.[104] This simultaneous mobilization around conflicts in different segments of the community thus helps to account for the successful, simultaneous pursuit of developmental as well as other objectives.

In the other two German cities, policies from higher levels and practices of localized governance maintained largely similar environmental and social policies to those in Freiburg and Münster. In each city mobilization through networks of students and leftist groups had kept Green vote totals at least as high as in any of the French cities.[105] But in Bielefeld, where manufacturing continued to dominate the local economy, both newspaper sales and associations point to lower levels of civic engagement in the community. Bielefeld's smaller university and elite populations mobilized less numerous, less powerful components of the city. In Göttingen, by contrast, the university community of students and highly educated professionals dominated the local electorate. Local businesses and professionals lacked the power as well as the extensive associational legacies of more important earlier market towns. Since the 1970s, a comparative consensus around limited downtown development had emerged from a decade of conflict. By the end of the 1980s a local scholar writing on policy in this area found "practically nothing critical to be heard from citizen initiatives and the rest of the public."[106]

In the French cities, associations not only participated less than they did in the German cities, but they mobilized narrower, more elite

[104] Böhme, *Je mehr*, pp. 115–116.

[105] Hein, *Ausgerechnet Bielefeld*, pp. 165–181; Andrea Gabler, *Strum im Elfenbeinturm* (Göttingen: Verlag Die Werkstatt, 1993).

[106] Hans-Dieter von Frieling, "Erneuerung oder 'Kahlschlagsanierung'? Der Umbau der Göttinger Innenstadt seit 1960," in Kornelia Duwe, Carola Gottschalk and Marianne Koerner (eds.), *Göttingen ohne Gänseliesel* (Gudensberg-Gleichen: Wartberg Verlag, 1989), p. 136. After 1990, with the fall of the east German border, an expanding population and market opportunities led to new demands for development.

segments of society. In standardized responses, two-thirds of local elites and activists in Montpellier, compared to only 45 percent in Freiburg, held that a degree of cultural sophistication was necessary for citizens "to understand and participate effectively" in the system of local land use regulation.[107] Although the leading activists I interviewed in Freiburg included not only students and recent graduates but also a local sales clerk and an unemployed person, most respondents in Montpellier were either established professionals or retirees. Concentrated more among higher social and economic strata rather than among students and others, movements and other civic activity varied largely according to the proportion of professionals in the local employment structure. In Montpellier and Nancy, moreover, the highest levels of civic engagement among the French cities helped reinforce Upscale regimes. Although Green parties in both cities remained weaker than their counterpart in Rennes, neighborhood, preservationist and environmental associations exercised significant influence on the course of local politics. In neither city did the most disadvantaged neighborhoods or their interests figure prominently in these movements. Instead, associations sought preservation and environmental improvements that reinforced local tendencies toward gentrification and segregation. Within the central city of Rennes, lower levels of civic association had accompanied the more Comprehensive synthesis that included stronger environmental measures. Despite the larger Green vote that a national leader of the French Greens, Yves Cochet, had helped mobilize, the density of enviromentalist associations also remained lower than elsewhere.[108] Still, associations based in university neighborhoods of housing estates like Villejean had maintained a critical voice on behalf of ecological and social concerns.[109] In the industrial center of Clermont-Ferrand, not only Green voting but associational participation remained low. Comparatively high newspaper readership made this contrast with the other French cities less uniform than in the case of Bielefeld.

---

[107] Sellers, "Grounds of Democracy," p. 337; cf. S. Body-Gendrot, "Plant Closures in Socialist France," in Michael P. Smith and Joe R. Reagin (eds.), *The Capitalist City* (Oxford: Basil Blackwell, 1987), pp. 237–251.

[108] In 1999 the list of organizations authorized by the Environment Ministry to participate in concertation illustrated this contrast. In Rennes, only six organizations within the entire metropolitan area qualified. In Montpellier a total of 19 did so, including 11 in the central city. In the metropolitan areas of Nancy and Clermont-Ferrand, only 11 did so.

[109] Le Galès, *Développement Économique* pp. 208–209.

b. Incorporation and Consequences of Local Movements. The course and consequences of environmental and neighborhood activism can only ultimately be understood in terms of their relation to wider patterns of urban governance. Within the bounds of different infrastructures for local state-society relations as well as government and politics, urban governing coalitions in France and Germany incorporated local movements to varying degrees. Local policy making not only accorded these movements distinctive sets of opportunities for influence but had itself contributed to the rise of local movements with divergent objectives.

With the elaboration of local policy making as well as the proliferation of local movements, the opportunities for neighborhood and environmental activists to affect outcomes had expanded. That the German cities had incorporated the participation of these groups more fully is suggested by both the policies that resulted and the processes that produced them. German "neighbor law," with roots in medieval practices, had long mandated that the viewpoints of neighboring property owners be taken into account in decisions about permits.[110] More recently, as planners in all four German cities acknowledged in interviews, local movements had contributed to a broad shift toward environmental, preservationist and neighborhood "values" in planning.

In Freiburg and Münster local movements reinforced the strongest local environmental policies of the eleven cities and fostered accommodation of developmental policies with ecological and social measures. Even as Mayor Böhme played off against each other antidevelopment and prodevelopment activists, the regime partly accommodated both. At the same time that Green appointments in the bureaucracy secured the movement's administrative representation, the local government moved forward with scaled-down development projects, including, in the face of movement opposition, the Freiburg Congress Center. Elites and even some activists there generally agreed that those directly affected by a project could play effective roles in formal decision making.[111] In Münster, a more ambiguous incorporation into the regime won for local movements largely analogous results. Although the Left remained excluded from the governing council majority up to 1994, environmental and social policies of the regime had

---

[110] Ulrich Battis, *Öffentliches Baurecht und Raumordnungsrecht*, 2nd ed. (Stuttgart: W. Kohlhammer, 1987), pp. 278–289; Bernd Bender and Rolf Dohle, *Nachbarschutz im Zivil- und Verwaltungsrecht* (Munich: C. H. Beck'sche Verlagsbuchhandlung, 1972).
[111] Sellers, "Grounds of Democracy," pp. 319, 323.

carried out much of the ecological and even a portion of the social agenda of Left movements. Even as Left and Right contested control over the local council through the 1980s and early 1990s in Bielefeld and Göttingen, local movements in those cities also maintained a degree of incorporation into the shifting governing coalitions. Budgets for all four city governments continued to list an array of subsidies for the neighborhood, environmental and cultural associations that helped sustain local movements.[112]

In the French cities the local governing coalitions confronted local movements with stronger conservative tendencies, and incorporated those movements to varying degrees. In Nancy, the urban regime of the 1980s and 1990s under the Center-Right had brought the preservationist neighborhood associations that fought downtown development since the 1970s into local governance. Rossinot had enlisted these groups directly in the processes of formulating a new comprehensive plan and had carried out a program of improvements and cleaning for the facades of buildings in the Old Town. If these measures had failed to suppress a local challenge from ecologists, Left governments in similar cities accommodated downtown interests more ambivalently. Like its rightist counterpart in Nancy, the Frêche administration in Montpellier had also sought to enlist a network of neighborhood associations to reward political loyalists and contain opposition. At the same time, in appeals to the environmentalist Left, it appointed an adjoint from the Socialist ecological party Génération Écologie, established a "house of the environment" for associations and conducted occasional negotiations with those associations over projects. Despite such gestures, the elites and activists in Montpellier, unlike their counterparts in Freiburg, believed that neighborhoods and activists generally lacked the opportunity to influence decisions.[113] The Quilliot coalition in Clermont-Ferrand displayed a similar ambivalence. Although the Socialists had allied with ecologists in the second round of the hard-fought

---

[112] In Freiburg, over one million marks for subsidies went to three dozen environmental, neighborhood and social organizations in cultural and miscellaneous administrative categories. In Münster, neighborhood associations helped administer over five hundred thousand marks in finances for neighborhood recreational centers and planning procedures. In Göttingen, the city gave over three hundred thousand marks for traditional activities linked to neighborhood and shooting associations and sixty thousand marks for an environmental center. In Bielefeld, where the financial constraints as well as the Right coalition of the early 1990s had limited subsidies for the same activities, the city spent thirty-six thousand marks for the environmental center and two hundred thousand marks for other cultural activities.

[113] Sellers, "Grounds of Democracy," p. 319.

1995 elections, the environmentalists had attacked the municipality in the first round for its neglect of neighborhood associations. Only in Rennes did the local Left regime incorporate neighborhood associations that raised an effective critical voice against local developmental measures.[114] Even before the Socialist electoral coalition there reached out to an ecological party in 1995, financial support analogous to that of the German city governments helped sustain critical voices of this sort. In Rennes, in contrast to the other French cities, the city budget listed subsidies for a variety of neighborhood associations as well as for scores of other social and cultural organizations.[115]

Local governing coalitions thus responded in a variety of ways in each country to the rising challenge of movements and the supralocal reforms that encouraged it. Along with other influences that made local administration and policy more or less responsive, much of the difference lay in the greater political opportunities for German Green parties in elections and on local councils. Proportional representation, stronger party organization and different trajectories of party competition at supralocal as well as local levels all help to account for the greater strength of the German Greens.[116] French ecological parties, usually lacking 15 percent of the vote in the first of the two French electoral rounds for local councils, faced potential marginalization in the second round. So long as no party won a first-round majority, the Socialists could draw the voters for an independent ecological slate by incorporating a competing ecological party into their coalition. Beyond contrasts in local politics, or the distinctive national cultural propensities among higher-status groups, the differences among local movements had a spatial dimension. By the 1980s, as movements based in the German downtowns struggled for more Comprehensive syntheses, those based in the French downtowns supported more Upscale ones. In influencing these orientations of movements in the Old Towns, urban governance had set movement politics on divergent paths.

Differences in patterns of party support in the old cities of Germany and France manifest this underlying contrast in urban grassroots

---

[114] Le Galès, *Développement Économique*, pp. 208–209.
[115] A detailed list of local budget subsidies for 1994 included 4,124,802 francs for various social and cultural associations, several million francs for neighborhood cultural centers and related associations, 109,182 francs for neighborhood associations, 593,491 francs for the "maison verte" and 93,929 in subsidies for the Breton Society for the Protection of Nature and twelve other outdoor and nature associations. Rennes, *Municipal Budget*, 1994.
[116] Sellers, "Litigation," pp. 192–193.

mobilization. In Bielefeld, Freiburg and Göttingen, the downtowns had emerged as centers of Green voting and activism (Table 5.7). In all three, percentages for the party averaged nine to thirteen points higher than the city average. Although these percentages varied widely between the center and other areas,[117] higher-status residents had only concentrated by two to five percentage points more in the center. Much of the Green support in these neighborhoods stemmed instead from the large numbers of students and other younger voters in the downtowns. In these same areas, an "alternative" culture of specialty shops, health food stores, self-help organizations, bicycle repair centers, restaurants and cafés had grown up. In these neighborhoods supporters of the local environmental and social movements found opportunities for consumption attuned to alternative political values, chances to get involved in local political activities and often employment in nonprofit or other businesses. In Münster, a more limited but similar alternative concentration had formed in the neighborhoods just south of the Old Town.

In the absence of such enclaves, the French downtowns of the 1980s and 1990s had remained bastions of both elite residence and the traditional French Right (Table 5.8). In all of these cities, but especially Nancy and Rennes, the highest status occupational groups concentrated their residences more in the Old Towns. Unlike in every German city except Münster, residents of these neighborhoods voted for Right parties besides the National Front at rates higher than the city average. Voting for the local ecological parties varied much less widely than it did in the German cities. Standard deviations remained less than two; totals in the Old Towns had not exceeded city averages by more than 3.5 percent.

This divergence between Old Towns was the product of localized policy and market decisions. In the German cities, the more extensive policies that had emerged by the 1960s had not only framed the objects of mobilization but also furnished the policy making capacities to carry out more ambitious environmental and social aims. Officials and the university in these settings had either placed the new buildings of the expanded university and its medical center within the vicinity of the reconstructed Old Town, or (in Bielefeld) made the new university campus easily accessible by bus. Everywhere but in Münster, plans for urban renewal in the 1960s and early 1970s had depressed prices for housing in older areas of the downtown. Students, foreigners and lower-income service workers

---

[117] Standard deviations of 5.5 to 8.3 indicate the extent of this variation.

Table 5.7. *Territorial Concentrations of Local Council Voting in German Cities, 1980s–1990s*

	Greens (%)	(s.d.)	CDU (%)	(s.d.)	SPD (%)	(s.d.)
BIELEFELD						
Average percentage, 1989, 1994	*11.3*	5.5	35.4	3.1	40	5.8
Old city	*24.5*		33.2		30.5	
(Degree from *Hochschule* or *Fachhochschule*, 1987) (percentage above average)	(14.6) (+5.3)					
FREIBURG						
Average percentage, 1989, 1994	*21.2*	6.1	24.9	5.2	24.3	5.6
Old city	*30.3*		23.2		17.1	
(Degree from *Hochschule* or *Fachhochschule*, 1987) (percentage above average)	(19.9) (+2.2)					
GÖTTINGEN						
Average percentage, 1986, 1991	*14.3*	8.3	34.6	6.8	39.4	8.2
Old city	24.7		28.5		37.7	
(Degree from *Hochschule* or *Fachhochschule*, 1987) (percentage above average)	(23.2) (+4.3)					
MÜNSTER						
Average percentage, 1989, 1994	*14.3*	4.7	44.1	5.3	33.8	4.3
Old city	*16.7*		47.2		28.3	
(Degree from *Hochschule* or *Fachhochschule*, 1987) (percentage above average)	(21.6) (+3.8)					
Adjacent Green strongholds	*23*		35.1		35.2	
(Degree from *Hochschule* or *Fachhochschule*, 1987) (percentage above average)	(20.6) (+2.8)					

Sources: Electoral and census data from city statistical offices (see Table 2.4 for explication of educational figures).

Table 5.8. *Territorial Concentrations of First-Round Votes in Local Council Elections in French Cities, 1989–1995*

	Ecologists		Traditional Right		Socialist Slates	
Clermont-Ferrand		(s.d.)		(s.d.)		(s.d.)
Average percentage, 1989, 1995	6.2	1.7	*34.3*	7.1	49.7	7.6
Old city	9.7		42.2		37.4	
(*Cadres, professions intellectuelles supérieures*, 1990) (percentage above average)	(31.5) (+18.9)					
Montpellier						
Average percentage, 1989, 1995	6.6	2.9 (1989), 1.7 (1995)	*30.2*	5.9 (1989), 7.3 (1995)	48.5	6.3 (1989), 6.9 (1995)
Old city	7.6		*38.9*		39.1	
(*Cadres, professions intellectuelles supérieures*, 1990) (percentage above average)	(26.6) (+6.6)					
Nancy						
Average percentage, 1989, 1995	7.6	1.3	*47.8*	3.6	23.7	3.5
Old city	7.1		*49.5*		21.3	
(*Cadres, professions intellectuelles supérieures*, 1990) (percentage above average)	(38.2) (+16.2)					
Rennes						
Average percentage, 1989	14	2.6	*27*	8.2	49.9	9.9
Old city	14		*40*		33.4	
(*Cadres, professions intellectuelles supérieures*, 1990) (percentage above average)	(31.3) (+13.9)					

Sources: Electoral data from local newspaper of record: *L'Est Républicain* (Nancy), *Midi Libre* (Montpellier), *La Montagne* (Clermont-Ferrand), *L'Ouest France* (Rennes). Occupational data from Institut National de la Statistique et des Études Économiques (see Table 2.4).

took advantage of lower rents or abandonment. When the governing coalitions undertook to clear the neighborhoods for purposes of gentrification, resistance among these groups garnered support from higher-status residents and segments of downtown business. In each of these three downtowns, local movements among these groups helped spearhead the wave of squatting, demonstrations and sometimes violent protest that swept across western Germany and the Netherlands in the 1970s and 1980s.[118] Although local officials had usually enlisted the police to suppress the most radical initiatives with violence, local policy makers had ultimately accommodated and even furnished support for movement organizations.[119] Policies of renewal in the downtown, or in Münster in the Hafen area, furnished rallying points for movements. The compactness of these same neighborhoods probably helped perpetuate networks of support for movements in local cafés, shops, residences and meeting places. Local Green parties in each city grew largely out of these movement circles.

In the French cities, as occurred to a limited degree in Münster, different policies set the Old Towns on the path of gentrification. Here local policies had diverted new construction to the urban outskirts and brought intensified gentrification rather than students and poor residents to the Old Town. In all four French cities, local or supralocal policy makers expanded university facilities primarily on multiple new campuses at a distance from the Old Town. Peripheral housing estates further removed poorer residents and students from the center. Within the medieval centers, local residents and businesses won strict protections under the Malraux law that reinforced earlier preservationist restrictions on aggressive new development. In the comparative absence of efforts to plan or reconstruct the Old Towns of provincial French cities,[120]

---

[118] Volkart Schönberg, "Bewegung in bestzten Häusern, 1975–1980, 1. Teil," in Netzwek Dreyeckland, *Stattbuch Freiburg*, pp. 70–75; Von Frieling, "Erneuerung oder 'Kahlschlagsanierung'?" pp. 126–137; Roland Epper, "Eindrücke vom Häuserkampf," in Kornelia Duwe, Carola Gottschalk and Marianne Koerner (eds.), *Göttingen ohne Gänseliesesl* (Gudensberg-Gleichen: Wartberg Verlag, 1989), pp. 138–143; Christian Presch, "'. . . Denn sie wissen nicht'. Stadtplanung a la Bielefeld," in Hein, *Ausgerechnet Bielefeld*, p. 162.

[119] Cf. Margit Mayer, "Restructuring and Popular Opposition in West German Cities," in Smith and Feagin, *The Capitalist City*, pp. 343–363.

[120] The large downtown developments, like Polygone and Antigone in Montpellier or Colombier in Rennes, usually located either on the outskirts of the downtown or on abandoned military land. See also Jacques Joly, *Formes urbaines et pouvoir local* (Roulouse: Presses Universitaires du Mirail, 1996), pp. 157–158.

gentrification built on entrenched concentrations of privileged, conservative residents. In Nancy, the resulting bastion of the Right furnished a mainstay of support for the regime. In the other three French cities, the Old Town harbored some of the strongest opposition to the governing coalition. In Rennes, partly as a result of local policies that integrated local housing, local movements linked to the Left also arose in university neighborhoods.

The local governing coalitions of cities in Germany and France incorporated local movements to some degree into their policy making. Regardless of whether or how far a regime incorporated them, the stronger movements exercised greater influence. If incorporation facilitated influence, even ambivalent incorporation like that of Münster or Montpellier could yield consequences for policy. In the German cities the strongest movements had contributed not just to environmental and social policies but to a reconciliation of these with developmental aims. Local governance there, in assuring more socially integrated housing in the Old Towns, had fostered downtown movements on behalf of equity as well as the environment. In the French cities the strongest downtown movements reinforced the disproportionate attention that Upscale regimes paid to the privileged. There local and national policies, in promoting downtown gentrification and preservation, had helped give rise to movements around more exclusive aims.

Environmental and Neighborhood Activism in the United States Cities. In the U.S. cities in this study, local activism, if not uniformly more intense than in Germany or France, was more essential to urban governance. In the face of fragmented supralocal infrastructures, unstructured local politics and pervasive influences from markets and businesses, environmental and neighborhood movements furnished much of the impetus on behalf of either ecological improvements or social equity. Local participation drew on one of the strongest national propensities toward civic participation in the advanced industrial world,[121] enhanced with larger numbers of the managers and professionals who in each country participated more. Yet even the more active movements had usually failed to bring about environmental or social policies to rival those of most of the German cities. The constraints on local policy making limited the possibilities for urban

---

[121] Of all countries in the World Values Survey, "only the Netherlands rivaled the United States in frequency of group memberships." Ladd, *Report*, p. 132.

movements to affect policy. Divided, dispersed communities and externally oriented economies also restricted movements and their objectives to more Upscale ends.

Except for newspaper subscriptions, no yardstick existed to compare overall levels of movement activity in the U.S. cities with levels in their European counterparts. But rates of participation across a range of parallel national civic organizations with local activities provide an overview of the aggregate tendencies (Table 5.9). Along with per capita memberships in two environmentalist organizations, the Sierra Club and the National Audubon Society, the League of Women Voters measured activism directed at other questions of policy. Similar to the indicator for the European cities, rates of subscriptions to local newspapers measured how many people followed the news of the city. Because these activities recruited primarily privileged or middle-class white residents, the civic indicators include at least one in which local minorities and poor people were more likely to take part. Inner-city African American youth comprised the main participants in the Boys and Girls Clubs of each city. Since blood donation required no dues payments, poor as well as rich people could also give blood. Put together, these multiple indicators revealed both patterns of local participation that extended beyond any single organization and variations among groups within each city.

All but two of these figures reflect the stronger mobilization around civic associations in Madison. Wisconsin had maintained one of the highest levels of civic participation of any U.S. state.[122] Since the Progressive era, the capital city had stood at the center of environmental and social movements.[123] Even in the early 1960s Alford and his colleagues found not only more civic groups of most kinds in Madison than in three other Wisconsin cities but among Madisonians significantly higher rates of participation in political parties and other organizations.[124] Starting with the activities of the Madison Park and Pleasure Drive Association around the turn of the last century,[125] associations had often driven the environmental policies that set the city apart from the other U.S. service centers. A coalition formed of state government bodies and civic associations that included the League of Women Voters and Zero Population Growth

[122] Robert Putnam, *Bowling Alone* (New York: Simon and Schuster, 2000), p. 292.
[123] Mollenhoff, *Madison*, pp. 408–411.
[124] Alford and Scoble, *Bureaucracy and Participation*.
[125] David V. Mollenhoff, *Madison: A History of the Formative Years* (Dubuque, IA: Kendall/Hunt Publishing Co., 1982), pp. 324–341.

Table 5.9. *Policies and Social Structures in U.S. Cities by Rates of Civic Participation, 1990s*

	Madison	Durham	New Haven
Policy synthesis, regime	Upscale regime	Upscale, no regime	Upscale, no regime
(Environmental policy	XX (X),	XX,X	X,X
Equity)	X		
Civic participation			
Sierra Club members / 10,000 residents	178	74	157
National Audubon Society members / 10,000 residents	225	3	43
League of Women Voters members / 10,000 residents	13	7	6
Boys and Girls Club members (African American or mixed race) / 100 African American youth	6	10	8
Annual blood donations / 100 residents	8	11	7
Newspaper subscriptions / 100 residents	27	17	14
Ranking for types of participation			
First	4	2	0
Second	1	2	3
Third	1	2	3
Social structures			
Managers and professionals / employed residents	35	34	30
College and university students / 100 residents	23	13	15

contributed to a report that laid much of the groundwork for the city and county planning of the 1970s.[126] Audubon Society and Sierra Club memberships of the 1990s manifested the strength of local participation in environmental associations. A dense network of neighborhood associations also worked for environmental and other improvements on a smaller scale. A 1994 municipal guide listed nearly eighty such organizations located

[126] Capital Community Citizens, "More Is Less: The Case Study of a City that May Be Growing Too Big for Its Citizens' Good," report (Madison, 1973).

throughout the city. In the Isthmus area and around the University of Wisconsin, preservationist groups had pressed for the protections of design districts. Since the 1960s, these neighborhoods had also emerged as centers of leftist groups like the coalition that issued an "Agenda for People" in 1970 and made subsequent efforts to introduce rent control and a local income tax.[127] Only among the small local minority community and the poor did local civic activity remain comparatively limited. In the 1990s, only blood donations and Boys and Girls Club memberships, the two types of civic participation that measured involvement among disadvantaged groups, ranged lower in Madison than in the other two U.S. service centers.

In Durham, the comparative strength of civic participation varied more among different sectors of the population. From the late 1960s, local environmentalist groups and neighborhood associations had worked to defeat new development and secure new parks and zoning in the western and northern areas of the city.[128] In the 1980s and 1990s neighborhood associations throughout the city assumed leading roles in neighborhood planning. In elections, civic groups like the Durham Voters' Alliance and the Sierra Club had essentially taken the place of parties as the central participants in the Progressive coalition. At the same time, the comparatively low overall participation in environmentalist and other organizations reflected the low levels of civic association that typified North Carolina as a state.[129] The local African American community furnished the main exception to this pattern. Under Jim Crow the local black community had developed a separate business and institutional establishment that included insurance and financial enterprises and the North Carolina Central University.[130] From as early as 1922 through the turmoil of civil rights protests in the 1950s and 1960s,[131] successive generations of local black leaders mobilized the local community. From initiatives to build public housing in the 1940s to the activities of the Hayti Development Corporation in the 1980s and 1990s, organizations linked to the black community had worked to improve the conditions of disadvantaged neighborhoods.

[127] "Agenda for People," Special Edition of University of Wisconsin *Daily Cardinal*, 1970.
[128] Anderson, *Durham County*; Durham City-County Planning Department, *Downtown Revitalization Plan*, p. 3.
[129] Putnam, *Bowling Alone*, ibid.
[130] Anderson, *Durham County*, p. 276.
[131] Ibid., p. 306; William Keech, *The Impact of Negro Voting* (Westport, CT: Greenwood Publishing, 1968).

Although these efforts had only had limited effects on local outputs, the strong local participation in Boys and Girls Clubs, and perhaps the high rate of blood donations in the city, suggested somewhat higher levels of civic involvement among African Americans and lower-status groups in Durham than in Madison.

In New Haven, the indicators of civic involvement averaged lower than in either other city. In the Progressive era activist local elites had provided much of the impetus behind efforts to establish the sizeable park system and the social services of the city.[132] Even in the 1990s, reflecting the higher levels of civic activity in Connecticut more generally, the surrounding suburbs maintained comparatively high rates of newspaper subscriptions and League of Women Voters membership. Within the central city, local participation in the Sierra Club and the National Audubon Society stood at comparatively high levels in relation to Durham. But in the politics of New Haven itself, only the local Preservation Trust and local neighborhood representatives had asserted environmentalist or preservationist concerns consistently. Participation in the League of Women Voters, in Red Cross blood drives and in newspaper readership ranged lower than in either Durham or Madison. The Community Development Corporations in the Hill and Newhallville neighborhoods, sustained through locally administered federal programs and private grants, often represented the interests of the poorest neighborhoods in policy making. But how low rates of participation in Boys and Girls Clubs in the 1990s suggest how low civic activity in these neighborhoods remained.

Incorporated to varying degrees into urban governance, movements often gave the main initial impetus even for environmental policies that served the interests of local businesses in attracting clienteles. Formal participatory procedures and informal norms among officials generally fostered a comparative openness to neighborhood groups. In the absence of strong party organizations, even local electoral coalitions often revolved around neighborhood and movement organizations. Yet the local challenges these groups mounted to projects backed by business frequently fell short.[133] Even more systematically than it did in Europe, segregation

---

[132] Judith A. Schiff, "The Social History of New Haven," in F. Shumway and R. Hegel (eds.), *New Haven: An Illustrated History* (Woodland Hills, CA: Windsor Publications, 1987), pp. 94–113.

[133] Sellers, "Grounds of Democracy," pp. 316–324; Sellers, "Litigation."

also left the consequences of movement mobilization contingent on who participated where. Distressed neighborhoods often faced the compounded disadvantage of weaker movements mobilized around their interests.

In Madison, movement activists had enjoyed the most extensive incorporation and influence. Paul Soglin had relied on downtown movements based in the university community in his early campaigns, and in the 1990s he built upon the incorporation of associations into neighborhood planning under the earlier mayoral administration of Joel Skornicka. In citywide controversies surrounding the new civic center on State Street and ultimately the Monona Terrace project, antidevelopment forces had forestalled these major projects through a series of referenda and lawsuits over four decades. Despite his initial opposition to versions of each project, Soglin had ushered both through to completion.

In both other cities local incorporation proved to be either more contested or more ambiguous. In Durham, conflict between pro-business coalitions and the Progressive coalition that incorporated neighborhood and environmentalist movements undermined movement influence. Especially with the mayoral terms in the 1980s of Wib Gulley, a former Public Interest Research Group activist, the Progressive coalition emphasized growth management and neighborhood planning. A term of control by Citizens for Durham put a temporary halt to these efforts. Even in the 1990s, under Sylvia Kerchoff, divisions between environmentalist and liberal groups and the African American neighborhoods represented by the Durham Committee and other organizations continued to threaten the Progressive coalition. Alliances between black neighborhood groups and local conservatives linked to the white business community had on occasion overcome environmentalist and neighborhood objections to approval for new commercial projects like the Wal-Mart at New Hope Commons. In New Haven, poor and minority neighborhoods predominated over much of the city, and citywide movements played only a small role in politics and policy. The neighborhood politics of political wards and the Community Development Corporations (CDCs) dominated grassroots participation. Only the mobilization of minority neighborhoods on behalf of John Daniels in 1989 had challenged this pattern. Development interests seldom encroached on the wealthiest neighborhoods such as those north of Yale. But neighborhood associations elsewhere rarely stood in the way of projects that raised a prospect of new prosperity and jobs. In the early 1990s elites and activists rated restrictions on development in the central city of New Haven the most lenient in the entire urban region.[134]

In all three U.S. cities, governing coalitions supported CDCs and other nonprofit social services that aimed to bring prosperity to the cities at large as well as to improve conditions in the most disadvantaged neighborhoods. Even with this support, local activism had at best only stabilized these neighborhoods. With the smallest pocket of poor neighborhoods, and the highest levels of activism overall, Madison might seem the setting where this activism would be most likely to make a difference. By the early 1990s the city devoted over $2 million to community services carried out under contract by over fifty civic associations. But the low Boys and Girls Club participation among African American youth in the city reflected generally lower levels of activism among the poor and minorities (Table 5.9). Even as the Isthmus neighborhoods with more active neighborhood groups had sustained continuing federal programs and ultimately more investments, South Madison had languished. Successive mayoral task forces, consisting more of city elites and business people than neighborhood activists, had taken over responsibility for improvements in this area.[135] In Durham, the black community, based in neighborhoods like South Central, had gained more local investment and a voice in the Progressive coalition. But the 1991 sweep by Citizens for Durham with suburban support had undercut the growth of neighborhood planning and housing programs and made clear the limits on policies for minority neighborhoods. In New Haven, the efforts of the Daniels administration to bring African American constituencies more securely into local governing and electoral coalitions had foundered largely on the weakness of mobilization in poor and minority neighborhoods. Here, not only the weakness of activism in the community but also the exit of local businesses and the limits to local revenues imposed the strictest constraints on what neighborhood organizations could accomplish.

Despite these disparities, social and spatial attributes that made Madison more like the European cities had helped to foster more active local movements as well as more consistent incorporation. First, a bigger university community than either Duke or Yale, with stronger regional and local ties, the University of Wisconsin could furnish more students and

---

[134] Sellers, "Grounds of Democracy," p. 504.   [135] See sources listed *supra*, p. 247n. 137.

recent graduates to participate in the local movements. Students at Duke and Yale had less to do with the city either before or after their time at the school and while attending school generally participated less in the civic life of the community beyond the university campus.[136] Second, more centralized settlement in Madison had given rise to a downtown center of leftist activism much like those that distinguished the German Old Towns from their French counterparts. Populated by a mixture of students, young professionals and some minorities as well as by businesses, the Isthmus neighborhoods sustained the most active neighborhood associations of the city, a persistent leftist faction on the local council and an alternative weekly newspaper. Both as consumers and as political supporters, neighborhood residents had contributed to such measures as the State Street Mall, downtown preservation, expanded parks and public bus service. Finally, neighborhood and social movements in Madison, like their counterparts in France and Germany, faced less far-reaching divisions along racial lines than they did in Durham and New Haven. Minorities in each case comprised so small a proportion of the local population that communitywide movements could mobilize effectively based solely among the white majority. In Durham and New Haven, by contrast, Progressive coalitions had to overcome racial division to attain an electoral majority. In the mid-1980s, a "New Haven Green" party had faltered in an initial challenge to the DiLieto administration out of a failure to mobilize the local African American community.[137]

These conditions help to explain why stronger movements persisted in Madison and had helped to consolidate a stable urban regime and to secure effective urban environmental policies. Yet in Madison, too, infrastructures of government, politics and business-government relations limited the forms and consequences of movement politics. Even when local movements mobilized more intensively than the German citizen initiatives, local participation brought about less effective environmental policy than in Germany. In efforts to redress the social disparities that poor neighborhoods faced, neighborhood activism brought still less success.

---

[136] Even the relatively high rates of membership the Yale community appear to have brought to the Sierra Club in New Haven made little difference for environmental policy in the city itself.

[137] Mary Summers and Philip Klinkner, "The Election of John Daniels as Mayor of New Haven," *PS: Political Science and Politics* 13(2) (1990): 142–145.

Local Movements and Growth Management outside the Central Cities.
Accounts of suburban politics outside the biggest U.S. cities have often
pointed to local antidevelopment movements as a source of both growth
control and social exclusion.[138] Even in midsize urban regions with little
metropolitan governance, like greater New Haven, movement politics had
both of these effects. Elsewhere in the United States, and most systematically in Germany, patterns of metropolitan governance had limited the
direct effects from exurban movements.

Outside the German central cities, for instance, local movements
against development had sprung up in towns like Schallstadt, west of
Freiburg; Telgte, east of Münster; Herford, northeast of Bielefeld; and
Bovenden, north of Göttingen. As in the central cities, local Green parties
often stood at the core of these movements. The higher-status civil servants and professionals of the central cities commuted in growing numbers
from these settings and furnished part of the base for these movements.
Statistical analysis of the relations between these activities and the new
housing index from Chapter 3 measures how much these movements had
affected overall patterns of growth across the city regions (Table 5.10).
Alongside variables for Green performance in local elections in the 1980s
and the proportion of local adults with higher educational status,[139]
this analysis also considered how protection varied among towns with
indicators for objects of protection like forestland and distance beyond
the downtown. Where these ends predicted control over development
better than higher levels of activism or higher-status social composition,
then rules have superseded movements in importance. To indicate whether
local business communities might have mobilized in favor of development,
I took the total number of workers in local workplaces for each town.
Bivariate correlations and multivariate regressions compared the effects
of these variables on new housing in 1969–1978, 1979–1987, and between
the two periods. In 1969–1978, planning had already taken place
under *Land* auspices around Bielefeld and Münster and at the metropolitan level around Göttingen and Freiburg. In 1979–1987, the restrictions
of the Natural Protection Law and other legislation imposed new

---

[138] E.g., Mike Davis, *City of Quartz* (Boston: Verso, 1992), Ch. 3; Mark Silver and Martin
Melkonian, *Contested Terrain* (Westport, CT: Greenwood Press, 1995).

[139] Data on educational status and land use from the beginning of both periods would have
facilitated this analysis. But educational figures were unavailable at the communal level
for these metropolitan areas before the 1987 census, and the government began national
collection of land use data only in the middle 1970s.

mandates on all four city regions. In this last period the Greens had also emerged.

If these figures verify significant effects from community-based movements on patterns of new housing, the movements clearly made only a small portion of the difference. In the 1970s, markets for development and rules to control those markets dominated as influences on local outcomes. In all four settings, new housing already correlated with proximity to rather than distance from the central city. Around Bielefeld this effect proved significant in regressions and accounted partly for a similarly negative correlation with the amount of forest in cities. Rather than reduce development, sites where higher-status residents would concentrate in three of the four city regions attracted new housing into the periphery. In Göttingen and Münster new housing also followed the general trend out of the places with the biggest business communities.

Although the Greens and local movements emerged to influence subsequent development in at least one of the city regions, this effect remained limited. Around Freiburg, the city with the highest Green performance, local parties in peripheral towns managed to significantly shift elsewhere housing production that had formerly centered in their towns. Outside Münster, the Green concentrations depressed overall rates of new housing at a rate just short of .05 percent significance. In Göttingen, despite little evidence of a Green role, movements or declining demand on the part of higher-status residents had reduced levels of new housing significantly. But in Bielefeld and Freiburg, larger forests now emerged as the most reliable predictor of constraints on current new housing development. In both places development continued to cluster toward the central city. In Münster, exurban Green movements against development had only slightly altered the exodus beyond the central city of those with a higher education.

Into the mid-1990s, local Green parties and concentrations of managers and professionals retained too slight a presence in too few towns of any German metropolitan area to constrict urban expansion.[140] Since exurban concentrations of elite or educated workers rarely if ever approached even the levels in the Old Towns, the constraints that exurban movements had imposed brought few exclusionary consequences.

---

[140] Green parties had not yet formed and run in 7 of 39 towns around Bielefeld, 63 of 75 around Freiburg, 15 of the 29 around Göttingen, and 16 of 49 around Münster.

Table 5.10. *Correlation and Multivariate Analysis of the Effects from Green Strength on Exurban Growth (Pearson Correlations with New Housing Index by Town, and Regression Results)*

	New Housing Index, 1969–1978			Change in Index, 1970s–1980s			New Housing Index, 1979–1987		
	r	Coeff.	t	r	Coeff.	t	r	Coeff.	t
Bielefeld (n = 39)									
Higher education[a]	–.019	–.281	–1.54	(no significant relations)			–.078	–.230	–1.04
Total Employed[b]	.061	–.077	–.489				.053	–.045	–.28
Forest[c]	–.360*	–.075	–.439				–.415**	–.180	–2.62**
Km to center	–.480**	–.615	–3.11**				–.434**	–.527	–1.01
Green strength[d]	—	—	—				–.050	–.103	–.54
R²		.243						.222	
Freiburg (n = 75)									
Higher education[a]	.433**	.395	2.67**	–.315**	–.237	–1.57	.313**	.220	1.43
Total Employed[b]	–.061	–.147	1.36	.017	.150	1.35	–.118	–.182	–1.61
Forest[c]	–.152	–.134	–1.25	.063	–.037	–.33	–.238*	–.228	–2.01**
Km to center	–.349**	–.084	–.55	.226	.000	–.06	–.328**	–.201	–1.30
Green strength[d]	—	—	—	–.399**	–.382	–3.28**	.069	–.085	–.72
R²		.186			.172			.207	

Göttingen (n = 29)									
Higher education[a]	.520**	1.002	3.27**	-.437*	-1.03	-2.19**	(no significant relations)		
Total Employed[b]	-.014	-.618	-3.12**	-.088	.349	1.02			
Forest[c]	.156	-.147	-.15	-.195	.095	.42			
Km to center[d]	-.436*	.051	.21	.206	-.391	-1.22			
Green strength[d]	—	—	—	-.282	.069	.14			
R^2	.399			.151					
Münster (n = 49)									
Higher education[a]	.268	.482	2.57**	-.211	-.261	-1.13	.126	.388	2.00**
Total Employed[b]	-.356*	-.646	-4.78***	.119	.323	1.97**	-.409**	-.588	-4.27**
Forest[c]	.129	.055	.46	-.200	-.126	-.87	-.087	-.103	-.85
Km to center[d]	-.288*	-.14	-.84	.152	-.007	-.04	-.246	-.240	-1.43
Green strength[d]	—	—	—	-.229	-.197	-1.24	-.215	-.250	-1.87*
R^2	.353			.066			.343		

[a] Proportion of nonstudent population aged 15 to 64 with degrees from *Hochschule* or *Fachhochschule*, 1987 census.

[b] Total number of workers employed in local workplaces, 1970 census.

[c] Proportion of local land in forest, 1978 or 1979.

[d] Green performance in local council elections in 1984 (Bielfeld, Freiburg, Münster) or in 1981 and 1986 (Göttingen).

Sources: Publications and computerized data from *Land* statistical offices.

Although statistics on occupational categories in French metropolitan areas remained sketchier,[141] largely the same conclusions apply for France. Small numbers of outlying towns like Chamalières west of Clermont-Ferrand, St. Clément north of Montpellier, Laxou west of Nancy and Cesson east of Rennes had attracted proportions of higher-status workers that usually approached and sometimes exceeded those in the Old Towns of the central city. Subsequently, before densities in these settings approached the level in the central city, the towns clamped down on new development. Around Rennes, planning within the district continued to direct new development slightly more to higher-status concentrations. But overall, regulation and markets had fostered shifts to higher-status places in 1968 to 1975, and shifts away from them in 1975 to 1982. A similar but less dramatic pattern marked the urban region of Clermont-Ferrand.[142] Around Montpellier and Nancy, where the regimes based in the central cities had engaged in more aggressive strategies to bring higher-status workers, reductions in the 1980s followed an initial surge of development.[143] Interviews in the urban region around Montpellier in the early 1990s found occasional antidevelopment restrictions. But local Green representatives had attained council seats even more rarely in this area than in outlying German towns, and the local governments had usually absorbed any movement activities. In St. Clément just north of Montpellier, for instance, the mayor himself had imposed restrictions on new housing following a spurt of development.[144]

[141] In contrast with German and U.S. census data, French statistics about the occupational status of residents are only available outside the central cities for cantons, a bigger jurisdictional unit than communes.

[142] Around Rennes, increases in the new housing index between 1962 and 1968 and 1968 and 1975 correlated at .30 with concentrations of cadres and professionals in 1982 ($n = 70$); reductions in the index between 1968 and 1975 and 1975 and 1982 correlated at −.27 with the same figure. Within the narrower district, the correlations remained slightly positive for both periods (.20, .14, $n = 27$). Around Clermont-Ferrand, the correlations for the same two periods stood at .27 and .19 ($n = 77$).

[143] Although higher scores on the new housing index in and around Montpellier continued to be correlated with higher-status residents between 1975 and 1982 and 1982 and 1990 at .16 ($n = 60$), changes between the two periods correlated at −.19 with concentrations of *cadres* and professionals. In and around Nancy changes in the index had correlated at .22 between 1968 and 1975 and at −.27 between 1975 and 1982 and 1982 and 1990 ($n = 76$).

[144] Although the new tools offered by decentralization may have played a role in the reductions in this metropolitan area, the reductions in the other places occurred too early for this to be the case. There as in Madison, the attempts at supralocal planning during the 1970s may have offered local elites of the more privileged communities opportunities to seize control over local development.

In the outlying areas of the U.S. city regions, home owners faced added incentives to take part in local movement politics. At the same time that the system of property taxation imposed a greater burden on home owners to finance local government than in Europe, home owners could also affect local finance more directly through local participation. Infrastructures of local politics and government often left local movements as the only alternative to domination by business. Much of the U.S. literature on local growth control underscores how even strong movements of this sort have often proven unable to impose effective constraints on development.[145]

The antidevelopment movements of greater New Haven during the 1970s and 1980s manifest this problem. The overall shift of development back toward the center in the late 1980s came about through simultaneous local political shifts in several distinct types of communities. The exclusive white suburbs of Guilford, Madison, Orange and Woodbridge, with 39 to 50 percent proportions of working residents in professional or managerial jobs in 1990, generally succeeded in imposing limits on new development without broad-based home owner movements. With a few exceptions, such as the defeat of a proposed regional mall in Orange in the 1980s, zoning restrictions enacted as early as the 1930s to protect farmland still reflected a local consensus enforced by elected commissions. Housing permits granted during the boom years of the 1980s fell below levels in the boom years of the 1970s, and house prices declined in relation to elsewhere.[146]

In the more mixed suburbs that made up over half of the metropolitan housing market, however, "revolts" against development had checked only the most intensive speculative outbursts of the boom. In North Haven, Branford and later Hamden, movements based in professional and middle-class neighborhoods challenged local coalitions between politicians, developers and the local business community. Neighborhood-based movements like the Branford Hills Association in Branford and townwide anti-mall groups in North Haven and Hamden mobilized large numbers of residents in these challenges, and ultimately swept new local administrations into elective office. Unlike in the wealthiest suburbs, however, the rate of permitting and the proportion of metropolitan development in these mixed suburbs averaged higher in the 1980s than in the 1970s. Suburbs with fewer managerial and professional workers also pursued new development

---

[145] John R. Logan, Rachel Bridges Whaley and Kyle Crowder, "The Character and Consequences of Growth Regimes," *Urban Affairs Review* 32(5) (1997): 603–630.
[146] Sellers, "Grounds of Democracy," p. 677.

aggressively. As a result, larger proportions of higher-status workers corresponded the most of any city region with reductions in development, at correlations of $-.20$ in the early 1980s and $-.53$ over the course of the 1980s.

Although regional planning and regulation in the other U.S. settings had emerged partly in response to local movements, regimes of metropolitan governance also limited the direct effect of neighborhood movements on patterns of development. Outside Madison, where growth management at the county level had been in place since the 1970s, local movements against development were rare. More typical of the European urban regions than of most U.S. counterparts, only four of fifty-nine metropolitan towns had attracted proportions of managerial and professional workers higher than the central city. The small exclusive towns within the city limits, like Maple Bluff and Shorewood Hills along Lake Mendota, accounted for little if any of the control over growth.

In greater Durham, zoning and planning at the county level also qualified the effects of neighborhood movements as well as development markets. Outside the city of Durham itself, only movements in the university town of Chapel Hill had mounted persistent challenges to projects. There a historic district and urban design restrictions as well as zoning helped secure protection for the exclusive neighborhoods surrounding the University of North Carolina campus in Chapel Hill similar to the restrictions in Woodbridge, Connecticut. Although zoning did not penetrate large portions of the county until the 1970s, Chapel Hill representatives in the Orange County government also succeeded by the end of the 1980s in extending protections on development even to the rural areas. County policies included a "green belt" of large-lot zoning negotiated with the city of Chapel Hill. In Durham County too, the growth boundary that joint city and county planning administered after 1988 directed more of new development toward infill projects in areas where higher-status residences already concentrated. As a result, new housing in the two counties over the course of the 1980s shifted slightly back ($r = +.09$) toward the townships with more managers and professionals.

Whatever the other influences on exurban development,[147] regimes of planning and regulation for the entire city region, or large portions of it,

---

[147] A full analysis of the local influences on development outside the central cities would have to take account of such additional components of exurban economies as the political economy of farmers (Thomas Rudel, *The Politics of American Land Use Policy* [Cambridge: Cambridge University Press, 1989]).

far outweighed local movements among residents as sources of effective growth management. Especially in the absence of this regional governance, movements could serve the interests of privileged residents in Upscale forms of environmentalism. Much less than French urban regions with even greater governmental fragmentation, U.S. urban regions like New Haven paid for openness to influence from local exurban movements with both greater social exclusion and less environmental control.

Social and neighborhood movements still generally lack the central position of local government, conventional political organization and business in urban coalitions. Even the urban regimes that have incorporated these movements into electoral coalitions and decision-making processes have rarely done so without an element of ambiguity. Yet decentralized policies and participatory opportunities have given these movements new chances to shape local policy. Local movements have mobilized most intensively where expanding service and high-tech businesses have attracted larger numbers of professionals and students, and the resulting development has posed new threats to the local quality of life. In the United States and Germany, where urban movements of the 1980s and 1990s have generally proven most active, the strongest movements have contributed to the most extensive environmental policies. In Madison and Freiburg, incorporation of these movements into urban regimes has accommodated their influence with that of local businesses and institutions. In Münster, more ambiguous incorporation has had much the same result. The less mobilized movements of the French cities have generally influenced policy somewhat less. There, as well as in the U.S. urban regions, movement politics has had the most severe consequences for social equity.

Not only the consequences of movement politics but also its intensity and orientation have depended heavily on the supralocal structures, governing coalitions and local policies that formed its context. In Germany, supralocal infrastructures, local governments, corporatist representation and local party systems confined what movements could do to affect local syntheses (Table 5.11). Outside the central cities, influences from metropolitan and higher levels left local movements of limited relevance for policy. Inside, despite differences in the strength of local movements, Green parties and local bureaucratic procedures insured parallel means of incorporation and helped bring about largely parallel urban syntheses. In Freiburg and Münster, more pronounced traditions of civic engagement gave rise to both stronger movements around environmentalist aims and

Table 5.11. *Consequences, Characteristics and Sources of Social and Neighborhood Movements by Degree of Mobilization, 1980s–1990s*

	Developmental, Environmental Policies and Urban Regimes	Degree of Mobilization in Central City (Compared within Countries)	Incorporation of Movements (Means of Incorporation and Challenge in Central City)	Main Effect of Movements on Policies Toward Social Equity in Central City	Influential Local Social and Spatial Conditions	Direct Influence of Movements on Growth Management Outside Central City	Exclusionary Consequences of Movements for Growth Control
Germany							
Freiburg	XX (X) XXX (X) (urban regime)	High	Moderate (Green party in dominant electoral coalition, challenges to projects, governmental funding)	Positive	University in central area, renewal of old town	Limited	Limited
Münster	XX (X) XXX (X) (urban regime)	High	Ambivalent (Green party in minority electoral coalition [to 1994], challenges to projects, governmental funding)	Positive	University in central area, renewal of Hafen area	Limited	Little
Göttingen	X (X) XXX (X)	Moderately high	Contested (Green party in Left electoral coalition, challenges to projects, governmental funding)	Positive	University in central area, renewal of Old Town	Little	Limited
Bielefeld	X (X) XXX (X)	Low (higher in university community)	Contested (Green party in Left electoral coalition, challenges to projects, governmental funding)	Positive	University outside central area, renewal of Old Town, fewer higher-status workers	Little	Little
France							
Nancy	XX (X) XX (urban regime)	High	Moderate (Ecologist minority, local majority, challenges to projects, neighborhood planning)	Negative	University campus outside city, preserved Old Town	Little	Limited
Montpellier	XXX (X) XX (urban regime)	Moderately high	Ambivalent (Ecologist minority, party in local majority, challenges to projects, neighborhood hearings)	Negative	University campus outside central area, preserved Old Town	Little	Limited

Clermont-Ferrand	XX X	Moderately low	Ambivalent (Ecologist minority, part of majority coalition after 1995)	(Limited)	University campus outside city, preserved Old Town, fewer higher-status workers	Little	Little
Rennes	XXX (X) XX (X) (urban regime)	Low	Moderate (Ecologist minority, party in local majority, challenges to projects, governmental funding)	Positive	University campus outside central area, preserved Old Town	Little	Little
United States							
Madison	XXX XX (X) (urban regime)	High	Strong (Dominant electoral coalition, citywide groups, challenges to projects, neighborhood planning)	Negative / positive	University in central area, intact urban center and suburbs, more higher-status workers	Little	Limited
Durham	XXX XX	Low (but higher than elsewhere among African Americans)	Contested (Mostly dominant electoral coalition, some citywide groups, community development corporations, challenges to projects, neighborhood planning)	Negative	Elite university community, dispersed urban structure, large segregated minority, more higher-status workers	Limited	Moderate
New Haven	XX X	Low	Ambivalent (party machine, community development corporations, one citywide group, governmental funding, challenges to projects, neighborhood negotiations)	Negative / positive	Elite university community, dispersed urban structure, large segregated minorities, more higher-status workers	Moderate	Systematic

stronger mobilization around developmental ones. The resulting regimes synthesized efforts in both areas. In three of the four cities, urban reconstruction had fostered and helped provoke movements more supportive of social equity alongside environmental ends.

In France, more limited mobilization and more ambivalent incorporation generally brought movements fewer results. Local leaders, fortified through central-local entrepreneurship, a centralized structure of local government and politics and coalitions in the local economy, could more easily marginalize urban movements. In the wake of downtown preservation, all four French downtowns had persisted as conservative bastions rather than as strongholds of ecological parties. Where civic mobilization was strongest, as in Montpellier and Nancy, movements worked more for environmental and other policies that favored privileged groups. In Rennes, the sole Comprehensive regime incorporated elements of a comparatively weak movement sector.

In the United States, the governmental and political infrastructures as well as the business-government relations left movement politics with more of the burden for carrying out urban govenance. Here movements based among neighborhoods of white home owners outside the downtowns generally dominated downtown movements based in poor and minority neighborhoods. In the more dispersed, more segregated neighborhoods of Durham and New Haven, elite, externally oriented university communities further fragmented the interests of neighborhood movements. The resulting tensions aggravated the difficulties of stable coalition building. Even in the central city of Madison, where a regionally oriented university and an intact urban center fostered movements more attentive to social equity as well as environmental concerns, exurban movements reinforced the Upscale policy synthesis.

Conclusion

Contemporary urban governance seldom stops at the ill-defined border between local state and local society. Even local leaders with the official powers of Mayor Hervé in Rennes or Mayor Böhme in Freiburg have relied on formal or informal cooperation with businesses and institutions and their representatives, on organizational tools for local political control over markets and on attention to the growing voice of social and neighborhood movements. The divergent policy syntheses of Left coalitions in Montpellier and Rennes, and the similarly Comprehensive syntheses under the Left in Freiburg and the Right in Münster trace largely to these arrangements. Electoral coalitions and supralocal infrastructures offer no competing explanations for these trajectories. Even beyond these specific differences, analysis of the local economy and civil society reveals additional causes for the wide range of domestic and national variations in policy.

In all three countries, the urban governing coalitions that succeeded in maintaining urban regimes built upon locally dependent interests in services and related high-tech activities. If Bielefeld, Clermont-Ferrand and New Haven had also enjoyed stable regimes in prior periods, by the mid-1980s departures and defections among manufacturers as well as internal divisions in the communities had undermined coalitions in these cities (Table 5.12). In Montpellier, Durham and New Haven, local service and high-tech sectors oriented toward translocal service clienteles also posed a constant risk to local coalition building around policy. Where this translocal orientation did not thwart the construction of urban regimes altogether, it shifted the terms of coalition building in favor of Upscale syntheses.

Both national infrastructures and local choices dictated the course and consequences of local coalition building and regime formation around these interests. Within the corporatist infrastructure of Germany, coalitions under Mayor Böhme in Freiburg and the CDU-led majority in Münster had each integrated local businesses in limited ways into local decision-making processes. To varying degrees, each had employed considerable local instruments for control over development markets. More ambivalently in the CDU-governed city, but to some degree in both, urban governance had incorporated neighborhood and social movements. In France, the diverse local governing coalitions of Rennes, Montpellier and Nancy had also supplemented stable electoral coalitions with localized regimes of business-government relations and tools for control of markets. Though partly incorporated into each of these regimes, local movements played more limited roles in these local syntheses. In the United States, where the urban regime as a concept originated, the infrastructure of government and politics as well as the structure of business representation made urban regimes themselves the most difficult to maintain. Only in Madison had Paul Soglin incorporated local business and institutional interests alongside strong neighborhood movements into a stable coalition.

Even in the absence of a full-fledged urban regime, urban governing coalitions usually built on cooperative relations with local businesses,

Table 5.12. *Urban Regime Formation in Central Cities, 1980s–early 1990s*

	Policy Synthesis	Stable Coalition, Agenda	Economic Dependence	Direct Influence of Organized Business	Development Interests	Strength of Movements	Incorporation of Movements	Regime
Germany								
Freiburg	Comprehensive	Yes (under mayor)	Local services	Supralocal and local concertation	Moderate	Strong	Yes	Yes
Münster	Comprehensive	Yes (to 1994)	Local services	Supralocal and local concertation (strong)	Moderate	Strong	Ambiguous	Yes
Göttingen	Social-Ecological	Contested	Local, some translocal services	Supralocal and local concertation	Weak	Moderate	Contested	Contested
Bielefeld	Social-Ecological	Contested	Translocal manufacturing, local services	Supralocal and local concertation, elective office	Weak	Moderate	Contested	Contested
France								
Rennes	Comprehensive	Yes	Local services	Agendas, concertation, markets	Moderate	Weak	Ambiguous	Yes
Montpellier	Upscale	Yes	Local, some translocal services	Agendas, concertation, markets	Strong	Moderate	No	Yes
Nancy	Upscale	Yes	Local services	Agendas, concertation	Moderate	Moderate	Yes	Yes
Clermont-Ferrand	Local Fordist	(Limited agenda)	Translocal manufacturing	Agendas, concertation, markets	Weak	Weak	Ambiguous	No
United States								
Madison	Upscale	Yes	Local, some translocal services	Agendas, electoral coalitions, policies, markets	Moderate	Strong	Yes	Yes
Durham	Upscale	Contested	Translocal services	Agendas, electoral office, markets	Strong	Moderate	Contested	Contested
New Haven	Upscale	Contested	Translocal services	Agendas, policies, markets	Moderate	Weak	Ambiguous	Contested

institutions or social movements. Local arrangements of this sort, and with them infrastructures like those for local government and politics, could profoundly influence the policy synthesis of a city (Table 5.13). The consequences of domestic variations, as well as of the international variations, manifest this influence in numerous domains. Among the German cities, and to a more limited degree among their French and U.S. counterparts, bigger clienteles for services and related high-tech activities corresponded to more extensive local environmental policies. In France and the United States, externally oriented service firms and institutions linked to high-tech activities and tourism had fostered more Upscale orientations. In the German cities, more locally dependent service interests had generated fewer such pressures.

As in much of the literature on urban governance, the variations among the U.S. and to some degree the French cities demonstrate an opposition between business participation and environmental and social objectives. Along with the other features of the German infrastructure for local policy, more structured systems of businesses-government relations enabled governing coalitions there to transcend this opposition. Hierarchical representation for business and labor helped reduce the direct role of organized business in urban regimes. Local officials, wielding exclusive control over the most systematic array of instruments in markets for development, housing and physical infrastructure, could more easily set the terms of urban governing coalitions. As a result, the German coalitions that had pursued stronger growth had attained more ambitious environmental and social ends at the same time. The most powerful local growth machines assembled around these regimes as well. In France too, the Left regimes in Rennes and Montpellier had built up a strong organized presence in urban and regional development markets as well as formalized concertation with businesses and institutions in the surrounding region. Although these arrangements contributed to developmental policies in both settings, other features of the two regimes maintained divergent paths in environmental and social policies. In Montpellier, interests in a more externally oriented local service economy and the most powerful "growth machine" among the European cities compelled Upscale emphases. In Rennes, the urban regime had minimized both types of pressures. Even among the U.S. cities, the regime in Madison demonstrated the potential compatibility of development with environmental policy and municipal control in markets. But individual businesses in the U.S. cities gained greater freedom from organized representation and municipal control.

Table 5.13. *Components of Urban Regime-building and General Consequences for Policy, Overall and within Countries*

Components of Regime	Consequences for Local Syntheses	German Cities	French Cities	U.S. Cities
Relations with Translocal Markets				
Service / high-tech clienteles	Environmental policy (+)	Yes	Limited	Limited
	Social equity (−)	No	Yes (where external orientation)	Yes (where external orientation)
Relations between Local Officials and Local Business				
Organized business	Growth (+)	Limited	Limited	Yes
	Environmental policy (−)	(Contrary relation)	Limited	Limited
	Social equity (−)	(Contrary relation)	No	Yes
Instruments of municipal control	Growth (−)	(Contrary relation)	(Contrary relation)	Limited
	Environmental policy (+)	Yes	Limited	Yes
	Social equity (+)	Yes	Limited	No
Size of development industry	Growth (+)	Yes	Yes	Yes
	Environmental policy (−)	(Contrary relation)	No	Limited
	Social equity (−)	Limited	Limited	No
Social and Neighborhood Movements				
Stronger movements	Environmental policy (+)	Limited	Limited	Yes
	Social equity (−)	(Contrary relation)	Yes	Yes

The Making of Urban Regimes

Beyond their role in local electoral coalitions, social and neighborhood movements usually exercised more limited influence. In all three countries, albeit to various degrees, local movements had contributed to stronger environmental measures. Only in the German cities did the social and neighborhood movements linked to the Greens pursue social equity effectively alongside other aims. In French cities like Montpellier and Nancy, conservative downtown elites reinforced Upscale choices. In the United States, despite the efforts of neighborhood development corporations and others in poor neighborhoods, home owners in dispersed, segregated neighborhoods dominated movement politics and decisively shaped its consequences. Only in Madison did movements among students and others in the downtown mount a challenge to governance similar to those in the downtowns of the German cities.

In many of these respects urban state-society relations thus nested in wider systems of translocal governments, markets and interests as well as the social and spatial structures of urban regions. As localized governance both carried out and altered influences from above, it shaped and reshaped the structures of everyday life, and the roots of policy.

6

Urban Governance and the Global Economy

So, what's new?

Looking from below at the transformations under way in cities through-out Europe and the United States opens up an altered perspective on the processes identified with globalization. Many of these processes extend far beyond global cities. Parallel trends within the urban region of different countries have often proven more crucial to these changes than activities that cross national boundaries. The rise of developmental, environmental and social policy within urban regions; the mobilization of urban economies around this shift; the expansion of mobile clienteles for services and residences; and the spread and institutionalization of neighborhood and social movements all constitute developments as local as they are global. In the age of the internet, as opportunities for connections with other localities around the globe expand, this decentered but global change will continue to alter the conditions of governance. The urban governance that they have fostered remains a limited but crucial enterprise. The experiences of these eleven cities offer a glimpse into the difficulties that efforts to reconcile developmental, social and environmental aims are likely to confront.

The most general lessons that follow from the foregoing analysis concern the nature of the transformations linked to globalization. Accounts of global forces and their effects within and upon cities have too often taken the firms and other actors in transnational or translocal markets as the prime movers and presumed that those effects have come about through direct assertions of economic power. Even analysts who have acknowledged that legislators at higher levels of national states contribute to the growth of urban governance have continued to point to dominant economic forces at wider scales as the ultimate

374

cause.[1] To emphasize this source of global convergence exclusively, however, neglects the breadth and the power of the forces that have both propagated urban governance and limited its potential.

Ultimately, this globalization is also a matter of transformed cognitions and norms. In policies as well as markets, changing opportunities for governance are only as powerful as the recognition that they are there. Among policy makers and other elites as well as among activists and ordinary people throughout the advanced industrial world, shifting local orientations have been as much a part of this process as pressures from without. The expansion in local environmental initiatives, the growing orientation toward translocal markets and the accumulating neglect of distributive equity have emerged from the bottom up as well as been ordained from the top down. Beyond the intervention of hierarchical firms or governments, information flows and networks among local elites and social movements have enabled such shifts. Since the fieldwork for this study was completed, interlocal associations like the International Coalition for Local Environmental Initiatives and the European Cities and Towns Campaign have accelerated the growth of these lateral connections. The internet promises to do so at an exponential rate.

Logics inherent in policy and the organization of states help compel this localization. Along with the politics of credit claiming and blame avoidance at higher levels of states, expanded policy making at national and supranational levels has laid growing institutional foundations for urban governance. In pursuing developmental, environmental and social objectives from above, supralocal legislators and interests have generated tensions that must be alleviated from below. The more precisely these policy makers seek to calibrate these pursuits to the markets and politics of specific localities, and the more local interests mobilize around those efforts, the more likely the resulting supralocal initiatives will include localized elements. Expanding policy making has thus fostered greater reliance on urban governance even when formal or informal devolution has not. This localization may even have added credence to perceptions of globalization. From the vantage point of an observer seated in a sunken sitting area, the surrounding room can easily seem wider as well as taller than it otherwise would. Translocal forces too are likely to

---

[1] For example, see Bob Jessop, "A Neo-Gramscian Approach to the Regulation of Urban Regimes," in Mickey Lauria (ed.), *Reconstructing Urban Regime Theory* (London: Sage, 1997), pp. 51–73.

appear all the more global and more powerful when confronted from below.

Even part of the economic impetus behind the globalization of urban governance stems not from the pressures that globalizing firms have placed on national states, but from mobilizations of economic interests within cities. The expansion of mobile clienteles like students, researchers, professionals and tourists has given local businesses and institutions that have invested in provision of services to these groups ever more interest in bringing and retaining local consumption. Increasingly, the bulk of firms and institutions in urban regions depend for their livelihood on services of this sort. In urban economies like Durham and its surroundings, where high-tech activities have succeeded the most dramatically in luring new growth, developers and service businesses and institutions have led much of the mobilization around growth. Heavily invested in the opportunities and assets of a specific locality, these diverse service sectors depend on the clienteles and consumption that high-tech employers bring. As the dominant source of employment even in high-tech centers, service businesses and institutions typically make up far more of the local economic beneficiaries from high-tech clusters than do the high-tech firms themselves. At the same time, the amenities and other services these sectors provide help to attract and keep the professionals of high-tech clusters.

Beyond the transnational elites and firms that dominate models of global urban dualization, globalization itself is also taking place from below. Both this transformation and the rise of policy making that defies the traditional organizational hierarchies of nation-states require new multilevel approaches to understanding governance. Comparative analysis must not only consider causes at international, national, regional and local levels but also take into account how causes at multiple levels combine. Analysis of this sort will ultimately yield revised accounts of the differences that national political economies make for urban governance and a new understanding of the difference that urban governance makes in the global economy itself.

The Possibilities of Urban Governance

In earlier worlds under the domination of city-states, like the Greece of Aristotle and the Italy of Machiavelli, the governance of cities stood at the center of politics. In both the advanced industrial countries and the developing countries of the contemporary world, governance within urban regions has also emerged with a crucial role in policy and markets.[2] The more that policy, its politics and related economic interests concern themselves with the outputs and actual effects of state activity, the more this importance is likely to grow. Yet unlike its historical precedents, this newly localized governance inhabits a world of nation-states, multilevel policies, transnational information flows, global firms and international regimes. At the same time that the local trajectories in these urban regions demonstrate the significance of urban governance for local outcomes, they manifest the difficulties that this emerging form of governance confronts.

At the root of this transformation stands an increasingly de-centered state. Distinct domains of policy have followed divergent logics of decentralization. In the domain of developmental policy, localization has emerged through the efforts of actors at multiple levels to respond to markets. At the same time, both supralocal administrators and local businesses have mobilized arround the formation of localized clusters of research, development and innovation. In the environmental domain, where the quality of life often plays an essential role, land use and other measures that rely on the attributes of specific places have proliferated since the 1960s. In this domain elites and activists within localities have often provided the decisive impetus for the expansion of local elements. In social matters, and others linked in various ways to social equity, decentralization has most frequently come about through the efforts of elites at higher levels to scale policies back. The need to reconcile the policies in all of these diverse domains within urban regions has compounded demands for localized governance.

As examples of this governance, the urban regions analyzed in this study represent neither the biggest nor the smallest, nor the richest nor the poorest in advanced industrial societies. Instead, these settings present a range of variations in a distinctive but increasingly important type of post-industrial place. Much of the growth in advanced industrial societies has taken place in similar centers of services and high-tech facilities. Large proportions of urban residents now live in or regularly visit such settings. With the elaboration of policy in environmental and developmental as well as distributive domains, localized governance in these settings exemplifies how the straightforward opposition that earlier analyses of urban politics

---

[2] World Bank, *Urban Policy and Economic Development* (Washington: World Bank, 1991); Goran Hyden, "Civil Society, Social Capital and Development," *Studies in Comparative International Development* 32(1) (1997): 3–31.

posed between economic development and other ends has given way to more complex choices. By the early 1990s, local syntheses of policy embraced various combinations among the three types of objectives. Governing and electoral coalitions coalesced around these syntheses, and often contested them. Especially because these urban regions often decisively shaped outcomes in the surrounding regions, patterns at the wider regional scale remain insufficient to account for the local contrasts.

An overwhelming conclusion has emerged from analysis of governance in these settings. Even among a set of cities that on the whole occupied comparatively privileged positions in the global economy, local coalitions of the late 1980s and early 1990s only occasionally sustained the pursuit of policy in all three domains. Where urban governance accomplished this feat – Freiburg, Rennes, to a lesser degree Münster – success built over time on the institutionalized coalitions, organizations and policy agendas of urban regimes. Each such regime also capitalized on the "place luck" of favorable market positions and local environmental conditions. Even among service centers, such a conjunction between willing governing coalitions and favorable conditions has remained rare. In comparison with the Upscale biases and environmental difficulties that regularly dominate the biggest urban regions, this relative success stands out even more. For the exploding megacities of the developing world, Comprehensive policy syntheses remain distant ideals.

Success for the regimes of these service centers grew partly out of favorable economic and fiscal contexts. Both the two German cities and Rennes had taken advantage of the benefits that local or regional prosperity brought to local public coffers. As a result of both local and supralocal institutional arrangements, each faced minimal disadvantages in fiscal competition with other localities. Each had maintained sufficient attractions for firms, residents and developers to allow local officials to impose social and environmental measures without undermining demand for local development. Although each regime pursued growth, none attracted the overwhelming numbers of managers, professionals and other elites who might have undermined Comprehensive syntheses. In none did influxes of new residents burden local capacities to ensure environmental quality and sufficient physical infrastructure. For each, growth itself remained only one among several objectives of coalition building and governance.

Comparison with the other settings highlights these advantages. In each country, the cities that had declined or had failed to sustain expansion suffered comparative disadvantages in most other policy domains. On the one hand, governing coalitions in these cities confronted constraints on tax revenues available to support any local initiatives. On the other, local policy makers had to struggle to maintain businesses and residents in the city. Faced with such unfavorable conditions in Bielefeld, Göttingen, Clermont-Ferrand and New Haven, urban governing coalitions had failed to build the full-fledged urban regimes that reinforced Comprehensive syntheses. Even those that had still carried out extensive policies, like the two German cities in environmental domains, generally fell short of counterparts in their own country.

If a favorable position in the global economy enabled cities to escape this fate, it in no way guaranteed either Comprehensive syntheses or stable regimes. In Durham, Madison and Montpellier, coalitions built around Upscale syntheses often undermined their own successes. In all three urban regions, aggressive development drew growing numbers of highly educated managers and professionals with ambivalent attitudes toward social and often environmental priorities. Like the Comprehensive regimes, the urban coalitions in these cities benefitted fiscally from enhanced public revenues. Both new development itself and strong demand in markets for place contributed to this local advantage. In Madison and Montpellier, urban politico-economic regimes drew on these resources to pursue some environmental amenities as well as development. In Durham a more contested synthesis embraced analogous aims. In all of these settings the local syntheses served privileged groups at the expense of social equity.

Comparative analysis throws the sources of these divergent local paths into sharp relief. The political economy of leading economic sectors, the infrastructure of national political and economic institutions and the social and spatial makeup of urban regions have sometimes constrained, sometimes enabled local choices. Urban governance has shaped these influences even as it has constantly responded to them.

The Political Economy of Economic Sectors. Whatever the national political economy, centers of manufacturing followed different paths from the other centers of services and high-tech. In Bielefeld, Clermont-Ferrand and New Haven, the governing coalitions of the late 1980s and early 1990s proved unwilling or unable to sustain an urban regime. Partly as a result, developmental and environmental initiatives fell short of those in older centers of services within the corresponding country. Much of the difficulty can be traced to the translocal forces of the global economy. As

379

economies based on services and high-tech clusters mobilized more and more around local policies, manufacturing companies looked increasingly beyond local economies. These patterns had implications for the largest metropolitan political economies as well (Table 6.1).

The growing orientation of mass manufacturing companies toward global markets and production networks has for years attracted the attention of urban political economists.[3] Michelin in Clermont-Ferrand differs little in this respect from General Motors in Detroit or German machine tool makers. Even industrial districts of smaller craft producers, like northern Italy, probably present only a partial exception to this trend.[4] Beyond physical infrastructure and proximity to suppliers and subcontractors, firms of this sort have traditionally made limited demands on developmental policies. To compete in increasingly global product markets, these firms seek to reduce the costs of labor and other factors of production. Either automated forms of production or shifts to places with lower labor costs can further this purpose. Faced with the alternative of relocation to the developing world or in low-wage developed countries, these manufacturing firms have often found exit more advantageous than local engagement. At the same time, even in an era of greater environmental consciousness, traditional manufacturing owners in search of plant locations still pay little attention to environmental, cultural and leisure amenities.[5] The ease of shifting production has also undermined the local social measures that workers and their representatives often secured in manufacturing centers. As worker organizations have lost power, firms like Michelin have often disengaged from even these initiatives.

In service centers, by contrast, the global economy has generated locally dependent business and institutional interests in these same policies. Even when a leading service institution like the local university did not itself pursue these interests, supralocal elites, local policy makers or even local social movements usually did. In part, service centers like Durham,

---

[3] E.g., Bryan Jones and Ann Bachelor, *The Guiding Hand* (Lawrence: University of Kansas Press, 1986); Edmond Preteceille, "Political Paradoxes of Urban Restructuring," in John Logan and Todd Swanstrom (eds.), *Beyond the City Limits: Urban Policy and Economic Restructuring in Comparative Perspective* (Philadelphia: Temple University Press, 1990), pp. 27–59.

[4] See Richard Locke, *Remaking the Italian Economy* (Ithaca, N.Y.: Cornell University Press, 1994).

[5] Netherlands Economic Institute, *New Location Factors for Mobile Investment in Europe* (Brussels: Commission of the European Communities, 1993), p. 108.

Table 6.1. *Consequences of Core Economic Sectors for Local Business and Institutional Interests in Developmental, Environmental and Distributive Policies*

	Traditional Manufacturing Center	Center of Research and Technological Innovation	Specialized Service Center	Metropole (Regional, National or Global)
Core economic activity	Production for external markets	Research, innovative production for external markets	Services to clienteles (researchers, other professionals, students, tourists)	Administration of finance, production, markets (plus others)
Interests in developmental policies	Infrastructure for production, aggregation economies, replacement of departing industrial activity	Infrastructure for production, aggregation economies, access to research networks, attraction of researchers and highly skilled workers	Extension of services, new clienteles, infrastructure for access to services; less pronounced if clienteles secure	Offices, access to world markets and networks, infrastructure for offices (plus others)
Interests in environmental policies	Limited to worker quiescence, or to develop substitutes for industry	Attraction of researchers and highly skilled workers	Attraction of clienteles	Consumption interests of business and financial elites (plus others)
Interests in selective benefits	For owners of production	For researchers and highly skilled workers	For clienteles (broad or selective), especially higher-status workers	For business and financial elites (plus others)

Madison, Rennes, Montpellier and Freiburg relied for local prosperity on their place in institutionalized national and international systems for research, development and applied innovation. Public universities, private universities, university hospitals, research institutes or related facilities often occupied more of employment in these urban political economies than did any private firms. High-tech companies like IBM brought production facilities to technology parks like the Research Triangle in Durham and the Millénaire in Montpellier. All of these activities required not only a local economy but also local living conditions sufficiently attractive to draw and keep highly skilled professional workers. At the same time, many of these same institutions depended on provision of services to clienteles from outside the central city if not outside the urban region altogether. Education required students; health care, patients; tourism, tourists; retail stores, customers; social services, clients. Diverse businesses and institutions shared a common, localized dependence on consumption of their services. In centers of high-tech activities, this dependence encompassed the managers and professionals that activities surrounding technological innovation brought to the city. Many of these service activities also provided pools of potential activists for social movements focused on the local quality of life.

In all three countries, political constituencies, economic organizations and social movements linked to high-tech and service economies mobilized alongside supralocal elites around local policy syntheses. In Freiburg, Münster, Montpellier, Nancy, Rennes and Madison these mobilizations usually encompassed parts of an engaged, incorporated social movement sector that furnished much of the basis for stable urban regimes. The strongest mobilizations among local businesses and institutions in these sectors coalesced around local developmental policies. Although stronger environmental measures usually traced to initiatives of local officials or social movements, these locally dependent economic interests found environmental amenities useful to attract higher-status workers and clienteles. Governing coalitions in these service centers diverged most on questions of social equity. Amid increasingly polarized structures of employment and unemployment, the U.S. coalitions and the regimes in Nancy and Montpellier pursued Upscale syntheses. Policies in Rennes and the German service centers emphasized measures for disadvantaged groups at the same time as environmental and, often, developmental ends. The more that local universities and other services looked to elite, external clienteles, the more local policy making privileged the interests of these clienteles over social equity.

Even in the absence of the corporate headquarters or the starker income polarization that have absorbed the attention of students of urban dualization in the biggest cities, Upscale syntheses with the backing of local businesses and institutions often emerged. Since international business elites have played such a minor role in the political economy of these urban centers, these cases provide ample reason to question the role attributed to those elites in the largest centers. Beyond clusters of selective amenities, luxury services and office towers for corporate clienteles, New York, Paris and Hamburg also thrive as centers of research and innovation, higher education, retail trade and tourism. In these places, many of the same locally dependent service businesses and institutions as in samller places propel the Upscale thrust of local policy.[6]

As the contrast with manufacturing centers suggests, the growing predominance of services and high-tech activities has everywhere fostered local mobilizations around urban governance. In all three countries, the business interests and local constituencies of manufacturing centers brought about more limited mobilizations and less effective local policies. Local services, oriented increasingly toward translocal market and political opportunities, generally promoted Upscale objectives. Yet local agency and the institutions that framed it could sometimes alter this choice.

Translocal Governmental and Political Influences. Nation-states continue to matter for urban governance. How they do depends increasingly less on policies handed down directly from the heights of states, and more on how supralocal enactments and organizations combine with localized governance within urban regions. In Europe as well as the United Sates, civic activity as well as market initiatives figure prominently in this governance. To characterize national institutional infrastructures for these activities requires alterations to typologies based on national variations in local government. The resulting patterns account for more of the differences and similarities among urban policy syntheses in these settings than either vertical integration of the state at higher levels or patterns of economic organization and representation.

Beyond the structures of local government and relations between local and higher level governments, infrastructures of urban governance extend to the other sectors of state-society relations where local elites and activists have engaged in constructing urban regimes (Table 6.2). First, as analyses linked to fiscal federalism have pointed out, the institutions of local government need to be understood in terms of effects like those that the Tiebout model posits in markets among places. But the consequences from infrastructures of urban governance stretch well beyond this. These structures also impose legal and other conditions for the growing lateral relations among localities within and beyond urban regions. They define parameters for the organizational, regulatory, financial and other instruments of control over local and interlocal markets. Through national systems for intermediation of business and other economic interests, they

---

[6] See, e.g., John H. Mollenkopf, *A Phoenix in the Ashes* (Princeton: Princeton University Press, 1992), p. 52.

Table 6.2. *National Infrastructures of Urban Governance: Features and Effects on Performance*

	Organized	Government-Centered	Market-Centered	Common Trends
Features				
State-local relations				
Supralocal policy	Centralized	Centralized	Decentralized	Increasing authorities and mandates
Administration	Decentralized	Centralized	Decentralized	More decentralized
Intergovernmental entrepreneurship	Limited	Strong	Moderate	(Diverse)
Local government				
Local finance	Standardized	Largely standardized	Highly variable	Declining resources
Vertical integration of local government	Varied but generally high	High	Varied but generally low	(Diverse)
Party and electoral systems	Strong parties	Moderately strong party coalitions	Weak or nonexistent parties	(Diverse)
Interlocal cooperation	Standardized, enforced	Contingent	Contingent	More cooperation
Local market control	Strong	Contingent but strong	Limited	Less control
Organized business interests	Strong, national	Contingent, local	Contingent but strong, local	More local participation
Local civic incorporation	Organized, somewhat important	Contingent but less important	Contingent but more important	More incorporation
Performance				
Growth	Limited, but more even	Uneven	Strong, but uneven	Increasing efforts
Environmental control	Generally effective	Depends	Depends	Increasing efforts
Equity	Generally effective	Depends	Ineffective	Decreasing efforts

384

have set much of the terms for local relations between business and government. They structure the procedural opportunities, substantive policies and organizational capacities that shape the mobilization, aims and influence of neighborhood and social movements. Finally, the incentives that supralocal tax systems, property rights, shopping regulation and other policies give to individual citizens and firms have also influenced trajectories of urban governance. Mapping infrastructures for urban governance within the three contries points to three distinctive patterns in these institutional matrices.[7] Throughout each infrastructure, state-society relations as well as governmental policy making follow distinctive logics. As an influence on the performance of urban governance, each infrastructure has demonstrated different weaknesses and strengths.

In Germany, the infrastructure resembled those found in other northern European democracies like Sweden and the Netherlands.[8] Rather than differ with the dynamics of markets or the choices of local governments, the local economy and civil society as well as politics and administration followed an underlying logic of formally *organized* markets, policy making and interest intermediation. Limits on local intergovernmental entrepreneurship and on localized fiscal advantages discouraged competition among towns and helped bolster urban fiscal resources. Provisions for interlocal cooperation enabled urban governance to extend into metropolitan regions. Within cities, highly coherent political parties and systems of corporatist interest intermediation channeled and constrained the representation of local interests. A national system of local, bureaucratized policy fostered similar policies and implementation in analogous locales across the country. The infrastructure of local state-market relations endowed local officials with comparatively extensive capacities for control over markets. Other features like parties, bureaucracies and procedures set the terms for incorporation of local social movements in ways that limited their influence.

As the detailed analyses of the last three chapters have shown, numerous aspects of this infrastructure contributed to the more consistent, more effective local pursuit of environmental control and territorial equity. More organized political, social and civic interests and stronger, more consistent local bureaucracies helped mobilize local elites more consistently

---

[7] For somewhat analogous types, styled as "models" rather than as institutional patterns, see Jon Pierre, "Models of Urban Governance," *Urban Affairs Review 34*(2) (1999): 372–397.

[8] Ibid.

around these collective ends. Limits on local political entrepreneurship and civic incorporation and the means for local political control over markets ensured local officials greater capacities to assert control over local political economies. Interlocal cooperation and standardized local finance constrained how much markets among localities could encourage shirking in the pursuit of these goals. Even as postindustrial cities in France and the United States suffered severe declines, this infrastructure helped redirect public resources to aid postindustrial economic reequilibration in Bielefeld. In limiting how far markets and individual entrepreneurship could alter environmental and social policies, however, this infrastructure also offered less robust incentives for urban coalitions to pursue local growth. Only when urban regimes mobilized strongly in support of new development, as in Freiburg and Münster, did developmental objectives emerge as a leading component of local syntheses.

In contrast to the extensively structured local state-society relations of Germany, the *government-centered* infrastructure in France fostered a central role for governmental institutions and elite governance. Not only in local government but in state-society relations, this pattern resembled those elsewhere in southern and eastern Europe and in Latin America.[9] The decentralization that culminated in the reforms of the 1980s has only partly modified the underlying logic of this infrastructure. The centralized authorities of the prefectoral system retain substantial power, and political entrepreneurship from below remains crucial to state-local relations. Fortified with new legal and fiscal capacities, and nested in a less standardized system of local finance than in Germany, urban mayors could also take advantage of centralized local administration and strong, stable electoral coalitions. Through cooperative arrangements among communes, ample legal and organizational instruments of market control and locally organized business and institutional interests, coalitions within the central city extended their dominance of local government into the local economy and the urban periphery. These and other elements enabled local elites to marginalize neighborhood and social movements or incorporate them ambiguously. Infrastructures of local taxation, interlocal cooperation, market control and corporatist representation shifted much of the burden for building local capacities for urban governance to these same elites.

[9] Ibid. More extensive comparative research remains necessary to establish how closely the state-society relations of other societies, with similar local government systems, correspond to those found in France.

386

In comparison with German and U.S. counterparts, this infrastructure facilitated the construction and maintenance of relatively stable urban governing coalitions. In all but the one French city where global manufacturing interests dominated, local leaders built and maintained full-fledged urban regimes. But where the German infrastructure fostered consistent policy even in the absence of urban regimes, the French enabled interlocal variety. In Rennes the Progressive regime under Hervé had developed environmental strategies that compared favorably to those in German settings, limited the emergence of ghetto-like concentrations among the disadvantaged and consistently sought opportunities for new development. In both Montpellier under the Left and Nancy under the Right, the pursuit of developmental objectives and the provision of environmental and other amenities for privileged groups had aggravated rather than alleviated social and economic disparities. In both Nancy and Clermont-Ferrand, local coalitions had mobilized less effectively than their counterparts in Bielefeld on behalf of new development. In France, more than in Germany, and more in the domain of social equity than in the United States, local outcomes depended on urban governance.

An analysis that takes account of the infrastructure for governance beyond the formal institutions of local government also furnishes a clearer view of the logic that distinguishes urban governance in the United States. Under the influence of this *market-centered* infrastructure, governance has depended more systematically than in either European context on markets and civic activity. Decentralized, fragmented governmental organization, weak or nonexistent political parties and constricted local powers constrain the capacities of urban coalitions. Officials lack strong legal and organizational means to assert control over markets for development. Much more than in either type of European infrastructure, municipal finances depend on the capacities of individual municipalities to raise their own funds. Even as specific firms and institutions have built growing translocalities, political and economic interests generally remain decentralized. In these circumstances, effective urban governance depends heavily on local political entrepreneurship, on incorporated civic activity and on interlocal cooperation in a city region. Such an infrastructure requires that urban governance rely, as U.S. analysts of urban regimes have often found that it does, on the civic and organizational capacities that businesses provide.

The most striking consequence from this dependence on markets and local civic activity lies in the consistent weakness of politics addressed to social and spatial equity. In all three U.S. urban regions, efforts to attract

387

or appeal to well-to-do professionals and the firms that hired them usually overrode other local policies. Even the urban coalitions that incorporated the most disadvantaged groups, like the Daniels coalition in New Haven, failed to redress the wide, often growing local disparities in the quality of housing, the levels of environmental amenities and the economic and social status of urban neighborhoods. Especially in the central cities, mobilization around growth offered local governments a way to overcome local fiscal limitations and enlist the support of business and institutional leaders. Yet even for governing coalitions that embraced this aim, building and maintaining an urban regime usually proved more difficult than in the more structured European settings. In Madison, the sole U.S. urban regime of the late 1980s and early 1990s had formed around pursuit of environmental as well as developmental aims. In addition to interlocal cooperation, supralocal finance, civic mobilization and tools to exert control over markets, this regime capitalized on the favorable financial and market position of the city. In Durham under highly favorable economic conditions and in New Haven under much less favorable ones, local governing coalitions had been unable to overcome the obstacles to regime building.

More established typologies for analysis of national differences account for less of the international variation. As Chapter 3 showed, the vertical integration embodied in such practices as federalism and separation of powers at higher levels of the state would have led to contrary expectations about both the French and German results. In France, the most centralized, unitary state should have been able to decree the most consistent policy from above. Instead, divergent local regimes had produced more varied outcomes than in the two federal countries. Vertical integration at higher levels may even have enabled the more powerful urban regimes in Rennes and Montpellier to compound their advantages with benefits secured from the top. In Germany, contrary to what the fragmentation of a federal system might imply, stricter national policies and more uniform local practices had brought about the most consistent local outcomes. Only in the United States did fragmentation at higher levels of the state reinforce the institutional patterns in infrastructures of urban governance and the consequences from those infrastructures.

The systems of economic interest intermediation at the core of national capitalist differences could also account for little of the variation. Although corporatist elements played a limited part in the urban environmental and distributive successes of Germany, organized labor, and with occasional exceptions organized business interests, participated little outside of a few developmental issues. Other elements of the German infrastructure of urban governance proved more crucial to the successes there.[10] In the United States and France, where corporatist elements weighed less in policy making at higher levels, local businesses and business associations often exercised more influence. In the loosely coupled coalitions of U. S. cities, associations of businesses with low degrees of organization could sometimes attain greater influence. In the French urban regions, local officials employed local corporatist practices in support of regimes centered around official elites.

With the growth of urban governance, the previous chapters have also documented a degree of convergence among these infrastructures (Table 6.2). New authorities, mandates and organizations have ushered in policies with centralized components in Germany; established a growing array of institutional resources for localized governance in France; and added at the level of American states to the decentralized, limited authorities of U.S. urban governance. As administration has generally remained at lower levels or shifted there, supralocal financial resources for local governments have generally declined. Especially in Europe, where new supranational authorities, financial resources and transborder relations have multiplied, local political entrepreneurship and business mobilization have increased. In both France and Germany, European pressures for the privatization of utilities and for an end to governmental participation in local transit and savings banks are introducing new elements of markets into urban political economies. Everywhere, urban governance has built upon growing metropolitan cooperation, relied increasingly on markets and firms and incorporated new local activism. Locally as well as at higher levels, efforts to capitalize on opportunities for new development and to extend control over the urban environment have proliferated. At most, coalitions in pursuit of these ends have relegated social equality to one among several objectives of urban governance.[11]

---

[10] It would require more extensive analysis to specify precisely how much interest intermediation and other specific components of infrastructures for urban governance contributed to the overall patterns.

[11] Perhaps indicative of these wider trends, at the end of the 1990s in all four German cities, the Right had wrested back control of either the local council or the executive from Red-Green coalitions. On these convergent trends, see Robert J. Bennett, "Local Government in Europe: Common Directions of Change," in Robert J. Bennett (ed.), *Local Government in the New Europe* (London: Belhaven Press, 1993), pp. 28–50; Hellmutt Wollmann, "Local Government Systems: From Historic Divergence Towards Convergence?" *Environment and Planning C: Government and Policy 18* (2000): 33–55.

Despite these common trends, the infrastructures that had fostered the most uniform results in Germany and the most varied in France have persisted. In all three countries, despite the different conditions these infrastructures have imposed, local choices continue to influence local outcomes.

Social and Spatial Structures. Socioeconomic and spatial structures within city regions also accounted for part of the variation in urban governance and outputs. Especially in the U.S. cities, pervasive ethnic and racial divisions had helped undermine effective urban governance. In France as well as in the United States, dispersed, segregated settlement had reinforced local interests in Upscale policy syntheses. Neither these effects nor even "place luck" could entirely explain the divergences in results.

Although it would be difficult to underestimate the role of ethnic and racial difference in the U.S. urban regions, governing coalitions pursued similar syntheses even in its absence. In Durham and New Haven, divisions between whites and large populations of disadvantaged minorities aggravated the obstacles to urban regime building. White flight had largely driven the economic decline of New Haven and the economic difficulties that Durham faced into the 1970s. In the suburbs of New Haven, and within the central city in Durham, whites had repeatedly rebuffed efforts to redirect benefits to poor neighborhoods or even furnish collective environmental goods. In Madison, however, these minorities had remained too small to play a major role in local electoral coalitions. Yet the urban regime that persisted there maintained the same Upscale emphases as in New Haven and Durham. Historically, local decisions also lay at the origins of the small minority communities. Madison voters of the postwar era, anxious to keep the disadvantaged out, had banned new public housing under federal programs. In Europe, the much smaller variations in local populations of disadvantaged minorities made even less substantial differences for the divergences in policy.[12]

Although spatial patterns profoundly influenced electoral and market governance, these patterns also remained susceptible to influence from

---

[12] White reactions to the somewhat larger numbers of North Africans in Montpellier may help to account for the Upscale syntheses of the Left regime in Montpellier. But longtime, traditional Social Democratic administrations in both Clermont-Ferrand and Bielefeld had incorporated nearly the same proportions of foreigners into local housing markets with low levels of segregation.

urban governance. Among businesses as well as among residents, dispersed exurban settlement gave rise to interests in opposition to extensive environmental governance.[13] Centralized urban settlement fostered more supportive interests. Among the U.S. cities, dispersion compounded the difficulties faced by progressive urban coalitions in Durham and New Haven. By comparison, their counterpart in Madison benefitted from the stronger environmentalist preferences and movements that more centralized settlement had fostered. In Europe as well, the outlying universities and other new developments of the French cities furnished less robust bases for new environmental and social movements than the inner-city universities and development of the German cities. By a similar logic, residential segregation from disadvantaged and other groups in Nancy, Montpellier and the U.S. cities had limited support among privileged groups for either public goods like environmental measures or distributive policies to redress social disadvantages. Segregation thus fostered political interests that reinforced itself. Both of these spatial influences seldom operated independently of urban governance. Local decision makers had imposed a growth boundary that limited dispersion around Madison; local and national officials had chosen to build the new housing estates that later led to stronger segregation in Montpellier rather than in Rennes.

Local choices had also played an essential role in the benefits from such natural environmental advantages as the Black Forest around Freiburg, the Mediterranean outside Montpellier and the lakes in Madison. At the same time these attributes had helped attract new development, they gave rise to local support for environmental measures. Political action furnished preconditions for the realization of these advantages. Without local efforts to capitalize on it, the prime tourist site of Puy de Dôme long provided little benefit to the economy of Clermont-Ferrand. Without local protections, the Black Forest would long ago have vanished, and the Madison shoreline would have disappeared beneath asphalt and concrete. Locational advantages from the placement of physical infrastructure, universities, or the French regional governments depended on similar local contingencies.

Urban governance operates alongside influences from economic sectors, national infrastructures and social and spatial structures.

---

[13] Based on analysis in nine of these cities, I have outlined these influences in Jefferey M. Sellers, "Public Goods and the Politics of Segregation," *Journal of Urban Affairs* 21(2): 237–262.

Whatever the translocal and local structures it mediates, it brings to them the essential element of local agency. Episodic decisions to build a project or to protect a tract of land rarely go very far toward governance of this sort. To make a significant difference requires the consistent, sustained pursuit of a local policy synthesis over time. The difference between trajectories of governance under Left and Right parties furnishes perhaps the most obvious instance of this influence. Where the Left regime of Rennes had pursued Comprehensive syntheses, its analogue on the Right in Nancy followed an Upscale agenda. Where the Progressive coalitions of Durham and Madison sought stronger environmental policies, the Rodenhizer coalition of Durham aimed to substitute more development. But local divergences as a result of urban governance extended well beyond the influence of political parties. Under pressure from local economic interests, a Left regime in Montpellier had carried out Upscale agendas closer in many ways to those of Nancy than to those of Rennes. In all three countries, governing coalitions that failed to establish lasting urban regimes had succeeded to a more limited degree in local policy making. Even resemblances among local trajectories often owed as much to governance within urban regions as to translocal influences. Not just the more uniform German infrastructure but the rise of parallel local movements and the analogous choices of local officials produced the similar policy syntheses of Freiburg under the Left and Münster under the Right. In the U.S. urban regions, the choices in local markets and politics most pervaded urban governance. Yet even a wide variety of local arrangements in that country had all led to Upscale results.

In developing countries, where corruption or other dysfunctions have often left the central state weak, localized governance of the sort evident in these cities acquires even more crucial importance.[14] The difficulties urban governance has confronted in even these comparatively privileged urban regions demonstrate how hard a task it ultimately is. Only institutionalized regimes of local policies, institutions, economic bases and local spatial arrangements have mustered the support to carry out Comprehensive policy syntheses. Without favorable market positions and supportive policies at higher levels, leaders in Rennes, Freiburg and Münster would have found such a synthesis impossible.

[14] See World Bank, *Urban Policy and Economic Development*; Hyden, "Civil Society, Social Capital, and Development."

Urban Governance and the Decentered State

Throughout the developed world, the spread of this nested governance is reordering arenas for critical choices about policy. In a political economy at once increasingly international and more and more decentered, urban governance has assumed the burden of significant portions of national policy.[15] As decentralization grows to dominate policy making in the developing world as well,[16] the forms and consequences of this governance furnish an ever more powerful lens on the character and consequences of national political economies.

In Germany, consistent social and environmental successes in urban governance contributed to the most distinctive achievements of the national political economy. Greater spatial equity within urban regions complemented and reinforced the greater social equity that corporatist institutions and the strong welfare state helped assure.[17] Effective environmental management within cities laid much of the foundation for the international leadership that Germany has increasingly assumed in environmental policy. German environmental successes that top-down analyses have sometimes attributed to corporatism probably stem largely from these patterns of urban governance.[18] At the same time, urban governance has reflected and probably reinforced the weaknesses that beset the German economy from the early 1990s. With the exception of Freiburg, and the partial exception of Münster, urban governance and the accompanying institutional infrastructures generally did less than in the service centers of the other countries to foster urban growth. In the 1990s, an IMF study criticized German fiscal equalization and related arrangements for failure to preserve either fiscal accountability on the part of state and local governments or the "efficiency" that interlocal markets might

---

[15] For a reintepretation of political economy centered around urban regions, see William Barnes and Larry Lebedeur, *The New Regional Economies* (Thousand Oaks, CA: Sage, 1998).

[16] Daniel Treisman, "Decentralization and Inflation: Commitment, Collective Action or Continuity?," *American Political Science Review 94*(4) (2001): 837–858.

[17] Wolfgang Streeck, "German Capitalism: Does It Exist? Can It Survive?" in Colin Crouch and Wolfgang Streeck (eds.), *Modern Capitalism or Modern Capitalisms?* (Paris: La Découverte, 1995); David R. Cameron, "Politics, Public Policy, and Distributional Equality: A Comparative Analysis," in Grant Reeher and Ian Shapiro (eds.), *Essays in Honor of Robert Dahl* (New Haven: Yale University Press, 1989).

[18] E.g., Lyle Scruggs, "Institutions and Environmental Performance in Seventeen Western Democracies," *British Journal of Political Science 29*(1999): 11–31.

assure.[19] With time, the policy changes to address such economic critiques could undermine a crucial basis of German environmental and social successes. Pushed by European decisions as well as domestic groups, privatization in such areas as electricity, gas, transit and banking is already likely to remove or alter significant parts of the existing infrastructure for urban governance. "Market-preserving" critiques[20] could also extend to the static planning frameworks, local market interventions and constraints on interlocal competition that play crucial roles in this infrastructure. Restructuring of this sort, however, if pursued to its logical conclusion, would undermine the institutional bases for some of the most successful regimes of urban governance in the world.

In France the analysis has shown decentralization to amount to more than the superficial shift that many commentators expected and to have brought measurable improvements to urban governance as well as new difficulties.[21] In particular city regions and selected policy areas, local regimes have seized on the opportunities of the 1980s and 1990s to carry out effective policies far beyond what the central state had been able to muster. Burgeoning interlocal competition has helped spur mobilization around policy with city regions and boosted mobility among places. By the end of the 1990s, local and regional mobilization of this sort had helped build France into one of the most dynamic large economies in Europe. But as late as the middle 1990s, local policy making capacities remained unevenly distributed. The very success of urban regimes in places like Rennes and Montpellier helped draw residents, businesses and municipal financial resources from places like Clermont-Ferrand and Nancy. As local coalitions across the country mobilized around efforts to attract the most desirable service and high-tech workers, economic and spatial polarization came to faster-growing as well as declining city regions. The difficulties of environmental policy in France trace in large measure to problems of urban governance. Only local arrangements that have succeeded in other

---

[19] Paul Bernd Spahn and Wolfgang Föttinger, "Germany," in Teresa Ter-Minassian, *Fiscal Federalism in Theory and Practice* (Washington: International Monetary Fund, 1997), pp. 226–248.

[20] Cf. Barry R. Weingast, "The Economic Role of Political Institutions: Market-Preserving Federalism and Economic Development," *Journal of Law, Economics and Organization 11*(1) (1995): 1–31.

[21] These results bear out only partly the more skeptical assessments of decentralization (e.g., Jacques Rondin, *Le Sacre des notables* [Paris, 1985]; Jonah Levy, *Tocqueville's Revenge* [Cambridge, MA: Harvard University Press, 1999]).

types of policy making have carried out extensive, effective local environmental programs.

A country with landscapes and a population as diverse as the United States could hardly import the organized model of urban governance from northern and middle Europe. Market-centered urban governance has also fostered localized and regionalized economic development policies that have undoubtedly contributed to the recent dynamism of the U.S. economy.[22] In a mirror image of the organized infrastructure, however, the limited, sporadically effective environmental policies and the reinforcements to social and spatial polarization in U.S. urban regions have undermined national policies in both domains. Even without the national legislation that anchors German planning at the federal level, reductions in tax supports for sprawl, in financing for highways, in disparities among schools, in urban crime and in subsidies for wasteful forms of energy could address the environmental and social difficulties of American cities more effectively. The systematic policies needed to do so fully would require major alterations to the market-centered pattern.[23]

In the developing world, much of the poverty and environmental degradation of the twenty-first century will center in urban regions.[24] For these settings, results from the advanced industrial world are all the more telling. In a context of weak policy-making institutions at higher levels, more extreme local polarization than in the United States and urban concentrations unprecedented in size, the difficulties of urban governance will be all the more daunting. Yet even more than in advanced industrial settings, the solutions will have to come from the bottom up as well as the top down.

---

[22] See Barnes and Lebedeur, *The New Regional Economies*; Alberta Sbragia, *Debt Wish: Entrepreneurial Cities, U.S. Federalism, and Economic Development* (Pittsburgh: University of Pittsburgh Press, 1996).

[23] For a balanced discussion see Pietro S. Nivola, *Laws of the Landscape* (Washington: Brookings Institution, 1999).

[24] See United Nations Conference on Human Settlements, *Report of the United Nations Conference on Human Settlements (Habitat II): Istanbul 3–14 June 1996* (New York: United Nations, 1997).

Index

Index

Index

European Union, 108–9, 122–6, 122–6, 138–9
Expert Group on the environment, 138–9

Fachhochschulen, 302
farmers and farmland, 54, 55–6, 58, 62, 144, 152, 159, 320
FDP, 190–1, 202–2n37, 209–10
federalism, 19, 101, 96, 98–9, 101–3, 114, 116, 138
Federation of German Employers, 312
Federation of German Industry, 312
Festge, Otto, 241
financial equalization, 102–3, 268
Fonds Nationale de l'Emploi, 121
forest, 53, 54, 55, 58, 59, 62, 144, 146, 194
Forest and Natural Protection Laws, 144
fragmentation, governmental, 101
France: corporatism in, 314–15, 318–20; environmental policies in, 148–56; movement politics in, 441–2, 344–5, 346, 348, 362; planning and regulatory authorizations in, 105–7; role of intermediate-level governments in, 100–1, 103–4; school systems in, 280–1; spatial segregation in, 166–9; supralocal policies in, 133–5, 137, 174, 175, 176; urban governance in, 186–7, 214–15, 288. *See also individual cities*
Frêche, Georges, 124n69, 215, 222, 224, 226, 270, 288, 319, 344
Freiburg: Betzenhausen, 197; bureaucracy in, 192n23; city planning in, 193–7; Congress and Convention Center, 196, 341, 343; civic participation in, 343, 365, 366; corporatism in, 312–14; density gradient, 60, 62; described, 3–4; development industries in, 330, 332; economy of, 32, 33, 88, 298;

environmental amenities of, 55; growth rate, 42, 43, 44; housing in, 147, 165–6, 196–7, 359; income levels, 46, 49, 50; and interlocal competition, 269–70; jobs in, 50, 65, 68; land use planning in, 142, 146, 150, 196–7; landownership in, 329; Landwasser, 197; parapublic firms in, 327; political parties in, 191, 194, 197, 340–1; Rieselfeld project, 196–7; social polarization in, 72; Seepark, 194; spatial segregation in, 75, 78, 83, 84, 165; unions in, 311; urban renewal in, 136
Fréville, Henri, 134, 217, 219, 319
Friends of Durham, 255, 256, 306, 322

Génération Écologie, 344
Germany: corporatism in, 308–14; 319–20; environmental policies in, 140–8; movement politics in, 337–41, 343–4, 346–7, 358–61; planning and regulatory authorizations in, 105–6, 108; role of intermediate-level governments in, 101–3; school systems in, 280–1; spatial segregation in, 164–6; supralocal policies in, 135–6, 174–5, 176; urban governance in, 185–6, 190–3, 308–14. *See also individual cities*
Gewerbesteuer, 268n171
Giscard d'Estaing, Valéry, 120n56, 135, 233
global cities, 7, 41–4, 45–7, 52–3, 67–73, 77–82, 381–3
global economy, 1–3, 7–8, 294–6, 306–7, 379–83
global urban dualism, 7, 10–11, 21, 27, 29, 70, 74, 284–6, 378
globalization, 1–3, 374–6
Göttingen: bureaucracy in, 192n23; city planning in, 208–14; civic participation in, 341, 344, 366;

Index